THE COMPLETE GUIDE TO LITERARY CONTESTS 2001

THE COMPLETE GUIDE TO LITERARY CONTESTS 2001

COMPILED BY
William F. Fabio,
James M. Plagianos
AND
Jerome Madramootoo

Prometheus Books
59 John Glenn Drive
Amherst, NY 14228-2197

Published 2001 by Prometheus Books

Inquiries should be addressed to
Prometheus Books
59 John Glenn Drive
Amherst, New York 14228-2197
VOICE: 716-691-0133, ext. 207
FAX: 716-564-2711
WWW.PROMETHEUSBOOKS.COM

04 03 02 01 00 5 4 3 2 1

ISBN 978-1-57392-850-2

Acknowledgments

We give special thanks to our parents, family, friends, Steven L. Mitchell and Christine Kramer of Prometheus Books, Pamela Filipski of Writing & Editorial Services, Katharine Smith of White Rabbit Design Studio, and all the organizations holding writing contests for their support.

We thank Thomas Lavin of Murphy and Lavin for his thoughtful, excellent and honest guidance. Tom is a strong friend and a dedicated, hard working professional.

In particular, we thank and give recognition to the Association of Authors' Representatives, Inc. for permitting us to print their material in our publication.

We regret all of the organizations holding writing contests could not be included in this book due to lack of information, the wrong information, or an unsigned permission form. We hope to add these competitions in future editions.

INTRODUCTION

We have created *The Complete Guide to Literary Contests* in the hope of giving writers in diverse areas the opportunity to receive recognition for their efforts. Besides major writing awards such as the Pulitzer Prize and the Caldecott Award, and better-known sponsors such as the Kennedy Center, there are over 200 lesser known prizes and sponsors. These may include writing contests for those who like horses, bowling, or tennis; have a specific interest in women's studies; or are just beginning their published careers as poets or playwrights.

This guide also contains practical information which any writer will find useful, including a listing of arts councils, instructions on how to obtain and complete copyright forms, basic copyright information every writer should know, and Form TX guidelines. Also included, courtesy of the Association of Authors' Representatives, Inc., is information regarding specific questions writers may want to ask literary agents.

Contest sponsors are contacted each year for updates to their contests to ensure that each entry has the most current information possible. Last-minute changes are sometimes inevitable; therefore we suggest you contact the sponsoring organization before making your submission.

HOW TO USE THIS BOOK

We suggest you take a moment to look through the Table of Contents to gain a feel for the guide's layout. Organizations and foundations are listed alphabetically, along with the prizes and awards they sponsor. The categories of fiction, poetry, drama, non-fiction, etc., are indicated wherever possible, as well as the categories open to unpublished and/or published writing. (This refers to the specific work that would be entered in the contest, not to whether or not the author has been published in the past.)

In a special section following the Table of Contents, prizes and awards are cross-referenced by category, so poets can locate the poetry contests at a glance, fiction writers the fiction contests, and so forth.

We have provided names, addresses, phone and fax numbers when given permission to do so, along with e-mail and web site addresses when available. You may want to request information regarding past winners, or order a sample issue of a magazine, book or other publication by that organization. It is in your best interest to discover who is publishing work similar to your own and to explore new market niches so that this and subsequent editions of this guide can serve your writing needs.

For your convenience, all deadlines are given at the beginning of each entry in bold typeface. Many organizations (as noted) accept the postmark as the deadline date. When this is not indicated in the text, entries should be in the hands of the sponsoring organization *on* or *before* that date. When two dates appear, entries must be submitted between those dates; i.e., arrive (or be postmarked) after the submission date and before the deadline date.

When submitting contest entries, be sure to note that submission addresses may differ from that of the sponsor. Both addresses are included when needed.

Be sure all guidelines, formats, rules and regulations are met before submitting your work. We encourage you to contact an organization when clarity is at issue *before* you submit. Do not send the only copy of your work. Some organizations require a nominal reading fee to be included with your submission. Do not mail cash. Keep all cancelled checks or money orders as part of your own record file. In the memo section of your check(s) write the contest name (if different from the name of the organization sponsoring the contest).

A sponsoring organization may give permission for the return of a manuscript in a self-addressed, stamped envelope, but if your manuscript is heavy you should check with your local post office about current postal regulations. Recent changes in postal regulations indicate that packages that weigh more than one pound must be posted at a mail facility. This means that heavier manuscripts cannot be returned in self-addressed, stamped envelopes (unless provided with a metered postal strip without the date). Make sure that return postage is correct.

Use the copyright information supplied in the Appendix to familiarize yourself with basic copyright knowledge and procedures. Call the copyright office with any questions. A copyright is for your protection and a responsibility that demonstrates confidence. A secured copyright becomes the intellectual property of the person/writer who registers their work. Take time to read more about copyright law in libraries and bookstores or call a copyright lawyer with any questions you may have.

Take your time, have patience, make contact with organizations, and use the resources of the writing and publishing industries to your advantage. We hope our efforts satisfy your needs so that your literary interests may grow in education, involvement, encouragement and entertainment.

William F. Fabio and James M. Plagianos

TO ALL CONTEST HOSTS, ORGANIZATIONS,
EMPLOYEES AND AFFILIATES

Our goal is to open as many doors as possible for aspiring writers, and we are thankful for your encouragement, patience, and participation in helping to bring this book to light. We believe it is not only the remarkable feeling of recognition a writer attains by being the recipient of a professional status award, but the act of writing for one that is in itself, excellent.

We ask all organizations that offer writing contests (and especially those that have not yet been included in our book) to send, with permission to use, (1) updated rules, (2) regulations, (3) submission formats/guidelines, and (4) entry forms for 2001 to:

William F. Fabio, 242-33 89 Avenue, Bellerose, NY 11426

TO OUR READERS

Drop us a line at the above address and let us know how you feel about the book we have compiled for you and how we may do better on next year's project.

Record of Entries

This form will help you keep a record of where you have submitted work.
Photocopy this page for each entry.

Organization Name ______________________________

Exact Contest Name ______________________________
(if different from organization name)

Date Sent ______________________________

Date Notified of Receipt ______________________________
(if applicable)

Date of Announcement of Winner ______________________________

Title of Work ______________________________

Page Count ______________________________

Title of Work ______________________________

Page Count ______________________________

Title of Work ______________________________

Page Count ______________________________

Title of Work ______________________________

Page Count ______________________________

List of Awards ______________________________

____

____

Good Luck!

TABLE OF CONTENTS

Contents

FICTION

FICTION, continued

FICTION, continued

FICTION, continued

FICTION, continued

NON-FICTION

NON-FICTION, continued

NON-FICTION, continued

PLAYS (see also Drama)

PLAYS, continued

POETRY

POETRY, continued

POETRY, continued

POETRY, continued

POETRY, continued

POETRY, continued

DRAMA (see also Plays)

CONTESTS FOR CHILDREN

GRANTS AND FELLOWSHIPS

MISCELLANEOUS

MISCELLANEOUS, continued

THE AKRON POETRY PRIZE 2000

The University of Akron Press
374B Bierce Library
Akron, OH 44325-1703

Deadline: May 15, 2001 – June 30, 2001 postmark

Prize: $1,000 and publication of his or her book

Guidelines

For all poets writing in English, who speak in original and compelling voice. Manuscripts must be typed, preferable double-spaced, and consecutively numbered, for a total length between 60 and 100 pages. Clear photocopies are acceptable. Do not send manuscripts bound or closed in covers. Manuscripts must include a cover page (with author's name, address, phone number, and manuscript title), a title page (with no biographical information), and an acknowledgments page listing poems previously published in periodicals. Simultaneous submissions are permitted, but The University of Akron Press must be notified immediately if the manuscript is accepted elsewhere.

An entry fee of $20 is required for each manuscript submission. Make check or money order payable to The University of Akron Press. The cancelled check will serve as notification of receipt. Include with each submission a self-addressed, stamped envelope for notification of contest results in September. No manuscript can be returned.

Manuscripts should be sent to the above address.

AMELIA

329 "E" Street
Bakersfield, CA 93304-2031
Phone (805) 323-4064

Annual Contest Information, Deadlines, and Guidelines

All of our competitions are annual. They may be entered at any time with the understanding that decisions are made eight – ten weeks following deadline date. All deadline dates are postmarks. Any number may be entered. Include a self-addressed, stamped envelope with all entries (one for each category entered) if return is desired. If no self-addressed, stamped envelope is included, non-winning entries will be destroyed following the announcement of winners. Neither *Amelia* nor its staff can be responsible for materials lost in the mails. Except for the quarterly Encore Awards, first North American serial rights are required of all winners, otherwise the entry will be disqualified. Be sure that name, address, and social security number appear on each entry. Telephone numbers also may be helpful.

Deadline: January 1, 2001

THE ANNA B. JANZEN ROMANTIC POETRY AWARD
Best romantic poem, any type to 100 lines, $100 award. Entry fee is $4 each.

THE BERNICE JENNINGS POETRY AWARD
Best poem, any type to 100 lines, $100 award. Entry fee is $4 each.

THE LESTER R. CASH SHORT POEM AWARD
Best short poems, any form to 14 lines. Six awards: $50, $30, and $20; plus three honorable mentions of $5 each are offered. Entry fee is $4 each.

THE MARGUERETTE CUMMINS QUARTERLY BROADSIDE AWARD
Best poem, any type to 500 lines, $50 award or 100 copies. Winner will be distributed free to all *Amelia* subscribers. Entry fee is $5 each.

THE CHARLES KATZMAN AWARD
Best poem with social issues as theme, to 50 lines, $50 award. Entry fee is $4 each.

Deadline: February 1, 2001

THE AMELIA MYSTERY/HORROR FICTION AWARD
Best mystery or horror fiction to 3,000 words, $100 award. Entry fee is $5 each.

THE KATE SMITH AWARD
Best poem, any form to 50 lines, on a patriotic or American theme; $50 award. Entry fee is $4 each.

THE AMELIA ONE-LINER AWARD
Best one-liners, including haiku. Six awards: $35, $15, and $10; plus three $3 honorable mentions are offered. Entry fee is $2 each.

NEW & UNPUBLISHED WRITER'S AWARD
Best poem to 200 lines or best short story to 3,500 words by a writer who has not yet been published in a magazine with a circulation larger than 1,000. A writer's library valued at $250 approximately is offered. Entry fee is $10 each.

Deadline: February 15, 2001

THE PATRIK T. BRADSHAW FICTION AWARD
Best short story or novella, any genre to 25,000 words, $200 award. Any number may be entered. Entry fee is $10 each.

THE DARK RAMBO GAY/LESBIAN POETRY AWARD
Best poem, any form to 100 lines, $50 award. Entry fee is $5 each.

Deadline: March 1, 2001

THE GEORGE STARBUCK GALBRAITH
LIGHT/HUMOROUS VERSE AWARD
Best light or humorous verse, any form to 39 lines. Six awards: $100, $50, and $25; plus three honorable mentions of $5 each are offered. Entry fee is $4 each.

THE ARDIS WALKER HAIKU AWARD
Best haiku sequence, $50 award. Entry fee is $4 each.

THE AMELIA ENCORE AWARD
Best poem, any form to 50 lines, for which second rights are available (include acknowledgment), $50 award. Entry fee is $5 each.

THE AMELIA NATIVE AMERICAN POETRY AWARD
Best Native American poem or poem with Native American theme, including Chicano(a), length to 100 lines. Award is beautiful Native American artwork. Entry fee is $5 each.

Deadline: April 1, 2001

THE WILLIE LEE MARTIN SHORT STORY AWARD
Best short story, any type to 4,500 words, $200 award. Entry fee is $7.50 each.

THE LUCILLE SANBERG HAIKU AWARD
Best haiku, traditional or experimental. Sequences are eligible only if each haiku is entered separately; however, should any one haiku in the

sequence win, the entire sequence will be published. Six awards: $50, $30, and $20; plus three $5 honorable mentions are offered. Entry fee is $3 each.

THE CHARLES WILLIAM DUKE LONG POEM AWARD
Best long poem, unlimited length, will be published in most appropriate format (usually in chapbook form). Award is $150 or 100 copies. Entry fee is $10 each.

THE MARGUERETTE CUMMINS QUARTERLY BROADSIDE AWARD
Best poem, any type to 500 lines, $50 award or 100 copies. Will be published in broadside format (flat or folded as appropriate) and distributed free to all *Amelia* subscribers. Entry fee is $5 each.

Deadline: May 1, 2001

THE AMELIA EROTIC POETRY AWARD
Best erotic poem, any form to 100 lines, $100 award. Entry fee is $5 each.

THE GRACE HINES NARRATIVE POETRY PRIZE
Best narrative poem, any form to 100 lines, $100 award. Entry fee is $4 each.

THE AMELIA SHORT-SHORT FICTION AWARD
Best short-short fiction, any type to 500 words, $50 award. Entry fee is $4 each.

THE AL STANLEY LYRIC POETRY AWARD
Best lyric poem to 50 lines, $50 award. Entry fee is $3 each.

Deadline: May 15, 2001

THE FRANK MCCLURE ONE-ACT PLAY AWARD
Best one-act play to 45 minutes running time, $150 award. Winner will be published in *Amelia* and the playwright will receive 10 free copies. Play may have been produced (include acknowledgments) but not published. Entry fee is $15 each. (Include $9.95 if copy of issue with winning play is desired when published.)

Deadline: June 1, 2001

THE CASSIE WADE SHORT FICTION AWARD
Best short story, any type to 5,000 words, $200 award. Entry fee is $7.50 each.

THE JOE LOGAN SHORT HUMOR AWARD
Best short humor, poem or prose, to 500 words. Six awards: $30, $20, and $15; plus three $3 honorable mentions. Entry fee is $4 each.

THE AMELIA NEW FORM/AVANT GARDE POETRY PRIZE
Best new form or avant garde, any form to 100 lines, $50 award. Now is your chance to create your own new forms. Avant garde poems may relate to such matters as alternative life-styles, etc. Entry fee is $4 each.

THE AMELIA ENCORE AWARD
Best poem, any form to 50 lines, for which second rights are available (include acknowledgment), $50 award. Entry fee is $5 each.

THE CICADA AWARD
Best sequence, renga, tanka, haibun, etc. Award is a beautiful crystal valued at approximately $100. Winner will be featured in *Cicada*. Entry fee is $5 each.

Deadline: July 1, 2001

THE AMELIA CHAPBOOK AWARD
Best chapbook to 48 pages, no more than 35 lines per page (include acknowledgment). Winner will be published in chapbook form. Award is $250 plus 10 copies. Any number of manuscripts may be entered. Entry fee is $15. (Include $9.95 if copy of winning chapbook is desired when published.)

THE JOHANNA B. BOURGOYNE POETRY PRIZE
Best poem, any form to 50 lines. Six awards: $100, $50, and $25; plus three $5 honorable mentions. Entry fee is $4 each.

THE AMELIA EROTIC FICTION AWARD
Best poem, any type to 500 lines. Award is $50 or 100 copies. Winner will be published in broadside format (flat or folded as appropriate) and distributed to all *Amelia* subscribers. Entry fee is $5 each.

Deadline: August 1, 2001

THE EARL STINE SHORT FICTION AWARD
Best story, any type to 1,500 words, $100 award. Entry fee is $5 each.

THE NOVA TREMBLEY ASHLEY SHORT POEM PRIZE
Best short poems, any form to 10 lines. Six awards: $50, $30, and $20; plus three $5 honorable mentions. Entry fee is $4 each.

THE DOUGLAS MANNING SMITH EPIC/HEROIC POETRY PRIZE
Best epic/heroic poem, traditional or experimental, to 200 lines; $100 award. Entry fee is $5 each.

THE BERNARD ASHTON RABORG ESSAY AWARD
Best essay, including opinion and criticism, to 2,500 words. Award is a handsome engraved plaque. Entry fee is $7.50 each.

THE RICHARD HUGO POETRY AWARD
Best poem, any type to 100 lines, $100 award. (It is always helpful to read a few of Richard Hugo's poems, which are available in any library.) Entry fee is $4 each.

Deadline: August 15, 2001

THE STELLA WADE CHILDREN'S STORY AWARD
Best story to 1,500 words, $125 award. Illustrations may be included, but they will be considered only after announcement of winner. Entries from children under age 17 must be signed by a parent, teacher, or guardian verifying originality. Entry fee is $7.50 each.

THE ANNIE LOUIS RABORG POETRY AWARD
Best poem dealing with handicaps and other traumatic conditions such as AIDS, MS, MD, etc., any form to 50 lines, $50 award. Entry fee is $3 each.

Deadline: September 1, 2001

THE REED SMITH PRIZE FOR FICTION
Best short story to 3,000 words, any type, $200 award. Entry fee is $7.50 each.

THE HILDEGARDE JANZEN PRIZES FOR ORIENTAL POETRY
Best Asian poetry including Indian and South Pacific (indicate form attempted on manuscript). Six awards: $50, $30, and $20; plus three $5 honorable mentions. Entry fee is $4 each.

THE FLORENCE BALSOM POETRY AWARD
Best poem, any form to 50 lines, $50 award. Entry fee is $3 each.

THE JAYE GIAMMARINO POETRY AWARD
Best poem, any form to 20 lines, $50 award. Entry fee is $3 each.

THE AMELIA ENCORE AWARD
Best poem, any type to 50 lines, for which second rights are available (include acknowledgment), $50 award. Entry fee is $5 each.

THE CICADA AWARD
Best sequence, renga, tanka, haibun, etc. Award is a beautiful crystal valued at approximately $100. Winner will be featured in *Cicada*. Entry fee is $5 each.

Deadline: October 1, 2001

THE CHARLIE HENNING FICTION AWARD
Best story, any type to 1,500 words, $100 award. Entry fee is $5 each.

THE EUGENE SMITH SONNET PRIZES
Best sonnets, traditional or experimental. Sequences are eligible only if each sonnet is entered separately; however, if any sonnet from the sequence wins, the entire sequence will be published. Six awards: $100, $50, and $25; plus three $5 honorable mentions. Entry fee is $4 each.

THE ALICE MACKENZIE SWAIM POETRY AWARD
Best poem, any form to 50 lines, $50 award. Entry fee is $3 each.

THE MARCUS SMITH POETRY AWARD
Best poem, any form to 50 lines, $50 award. Entry fee is $4 each.

THE A & C LIMERICK CONTEST
Best limericks. Six awards: $50, $30, and $20; plus three $5 honorable mentions. Entry fee is $4 each.

THE MARGUERETTE CUMMINS QUARTERLY BROADSIDE AWARD
Best poem, any type to 500 lines. Winner will be published in broadside format (flat or folded) and distributed free to all *Amelia* subscribers. Award is $50 or 100 copies. Entry fee is $5 each.

Deadline: November 1, 2001

THE RUBY DOYLE RICE SHORT-SHORT FICTION AWARD
Best short-short fiction, any type to 1,500 words, $100 award. Entry fee is $5 each.

THE LESLIE EDWARD RABORG POETRY AWARD
Best poem, any form to 50 lines, $50 award. Entry fee is $3 each.

THE MME. EVA LEFEVRE AWARD
Best French-form poem (villanelle, sestina, etc.), traditional or experimental, $100 award. Entry fee is $4 each.

THE RICHARD ARMOUR HUMOROUS VERSE AWARD
Best humorous poem, any form to 10 lines, $50 award. Entry fee is $3 each.

THE MONTEGUE WADE POETRY AWARD
Best poem, any type to 100 lines, $100 award. Entry fee is $4 each.

Deadline: December 1, 2001

THE AMELIA AWARD
Best poems, any form to 100 lines. Six awards: $200, $100, and $50; plus three $10 honorable mentions. First prize winner also receives a plaque. Entry fee is $10 each.

THE ERIN PATRIC RABORG CHILDREN'S POETRY AWARD
Best poem, any form to 50 lines with children as its theme, $50 award. Entry fee is $3 each.

THE CICADA AWARD
Best sequence, renga, tanka, haibun, etc. Award is a beautiful crystal valued at approximately $100. Winner will be featured in *Cicada.* Entry fee is $5 each.

THE CICADA CHAPBOOK AWARD
Best haiku chapbook, to 16 pages (include acknowledgments). Award is publication plus 50 copies. Any number of scripts may be entered. Entry fee is $10 each

THE AMELIA ENCORE AWARD
Best poem, any type to 50 lines, for which second rights are available (include acknowledgment), $50 award. Entry fee is $5 each.

Deadline: December 15, 2001

THE AMELIA SCIENCE FICTION/FANTASY AWARD
Best science fiction or fantasy to 3,000 words, $100 award. Entry fee is $5 each.

THE ARDIS WALKER POETRY AWARD
Best poem, any type to 50 lines, $100 award. Entry fee is $4 each.

THE WILLIAM WALKER COVER AWARD
Best photo, cartoon, or illustration (color or black-and-white); $100 award. Winner will be published on *Amelia* cover. Entry fee is $10 for one to five entries.

THE AMELIA STUDENT AWARD

329 "E" Street, Bakersfield, CA 93304-2031
Phone (805) 323-4064

Deadline: May 15, 2001

THE AMELIA STUDENT AWARD
Best poem to 100 lines or short story to 1,500 lines written by a high school student, $200 award. One entry per student, each entry must be signed by a parent, teacher, or guardian verifying originality. No entries will be returned. There is no entry fee. For guidelines and sample send a self-addressed stamped envelope and $3 handling to: Amelia Student Award, 329 "E" Street, Bakersfield, CA 93304-2031.

AMERICAN LIBRARY ASSOCIATION

Association For Library Service To Children
50 East Huron Street
Chicago, IL 60611-2795
Phone (312) 280-2163; Fax (312) 280-3257
Toll Free (800) 545-2433, ext. 2163

CALDECOTT AWARD

Terms

1. The Medal shall be awarded annually to the artist of the most distinguished American picture book for children published in the United States during the preceding year. There are no limitations as to the character of the picture book except that the illustrations be original work. Honor Books may be named. These shall be books that are also truly distinguished.

2. The Award is restricted to artists who are citizens or residents of the United States.

3. The committee in its deliberations is to consider only the books eligible for the Award, as specified in the terms.

Definitions

1. A "picture book for children" as distinguished from the other books with illustration, is one that essentially provides the child with a visual experience. A picture book has a collective unity of story-line, theme, or concept, developed through the series of pictures of which the book is comprised.

2. A "picture book for children" is one for which children are a potential audience. The book displays respect for children's understanding, abilities, and appreciation. Children are defined as persons of ages up to and including fourteen and picture books for this entire age range are to be considered.

3. "Distinguished" is defined as: marked by eminence and distinction; noted for significant achievement; marked by excellence in quality; marked by conspicuous excellence or eminence; individually distinct.

4. The "artist" is the illustrator or co-illustrators. The artist may be awarded the Medal posthumously.

5. "Original work" means that illustrations reprinted or compiled from other sources are not eligible.

6. "American picture book published in the United States" specifies that books originally published in other countries are not eligible.

7 "Published...during the preceding year" means that the book has a publication date in that year, was available for purchase in that year, and has a copyright date no later than that year. A book might have a copyright date prior to the year under consideration but, for various reasons, was not published until the year under consideration. If a book is published prior to its year of copyright as stated in the book, it shall be considered in its year of copyright as stated in the book. The intent of the definition is that every book be eligible for consideration, but that no book be considered in more that one year.

8. "Resident" specifies that the artist has established and maintained residence in the United States as distinct from being a casual or occasional visitor.

9. The term, "only the books eligible for the Award," specifies the committee is not to consider the entire body of the work of an artist or whether the artist has previously won the award. The committee's decision is to be made following deliberations about the books of the specified calendar year.

Criteria

1. In identifying a distinguished picture book for children committee members need to consider: excellence of execution on the artistic technique employed; excellence of pictorial interpretation of story, theme, or concept; appropriateness of style of illustration to the story, theme or concept; delineation of plot, theme, characters, setting, mood, or information through the pictures.

   Committee members must consider excellence of presentation in recognition of a child audience.

2. The only limitation to graphic form is that the form must be one which may be used in a picture on the illustrations, but other components of a book are to be considered especially when they make a book less effective as a children's picture book. Such other components might include the written text, the overall design of the book, etc.

The award is for distinguished illustrations in a picture book and for excellence of pictorial presentation for children. The award is not for didactic intent, or for popularity.

NEWBERRY AWARD

Terms

1. The Medal shall be awarded annually to the author of the most distinguished contribution to American literature for children published in the United States during the preceding year. There are no limitations as to the character of the book considered except that it be original work. Honor books may be named. These shall be books that are also truly distinguished.

2. The Award is restricted to artists who are citizens of the United States.

3. The committee in its deliberations is to consider only the books eligible for the Award, as specified in the terms.

Definitions

1. "Contribution to American literature" indicates the text of a book. It also implies that the committee shall consider all forms of writing – fiction, non-fiction, and poetry. Reprints and compilations are not eligible.

2. A "contribution to American literature for children" shall be a book for which children are a potential audience. The book displays respect for children's understanding, abilities, and appreciations. Children are defined as persons of ages up to and including fourteen, and books for this entire age range are to be considered.

3. "Distinguished" is defined as: marked by eminence and distinction; noted for significant achievement; marked by excellence in quality; marked by conspicuous excellence or eminence; individually distinct.

4. "Author" may include co-authors. The author may be awarded the medal posthumously.

5. In defining the term, "original work," the committee will consider books that are traditional in origin, if the book is the result of original research and the retelling and interpretation are the writer's own.

6. "American literature published in the United States" means that books originally published in other countries are not eligible.

7. "Published...in the preceding year" means that the book has a publication date in that year, was available for purchase in that year, and

has a copyright date no later than that year. A book might have a copyright date prior to the year under consideration but, for various reasons, was not published until the year under consideration. If a book is published prior to its year of copyright as stated in the book, it shall be considered in its year of copyright as stated in the book. The intent of the definition is that every book be eligible for consideration, but that no book be considered in more than one year.

8. "Resident" specifies that author has established and maintained residence in the United States as distinct from being a casual or occasional visitor.

9. The term, "only the books eligible for the Award," specifies that the committee is not to consider the entire body of the work by an author or whether the author has previously won the award. The committee's decision is to be made following deliberation about the books of the specified calendar year.

Criteria

1. In identifying distinguished writing in a book for children committee members need to consider: interpretation of the theme or concept; presentation of information including accuracy, clarity and organization; development of plot; delineation of characters; delineation of setting; appropriateness of style.

   Because the literacy qualities to be considered will vary depending on content, the committee need not expect to find excellence in each of the named elements. The book should, however, have distinguished qualities in all of the elements pertinent to it.

   Committee members must consider excellence of presentation for a child audience.

2. Each book is to be considered as a contribution to literature. The committee is to make its decision primarily on the text. Other aspects of a book are to be considered only if they distract from the text. Such other aspects might include illustrations, overall design of the book, etc.

3. The book must be a self-contained entity, not dependent on other media (i.e., sound or film equipment) for its enjoyment.

The committee will keep in mind that the award is for literary quality and quality of presentation children. The award is not for didactic intent or for popularity.

ELI M. OBOLER MEMORIAL AWARD INTELLECTUAL FREEDOM ROUNDTABLE

American Library Association

Deadline: December 1, 2001 postmark

This award is to be granted to what the selection committee judges determine to be the best published work in the area of intellectual freedom to appear in the two-year period ending in the December prior to the Annual Conference at which the award is granted. To be considered, the work must meet the following criteria:

1. It must be an article (including a review article), a series of thematically connected articles, a book, or a manual published on the local, state, or national level, in English or in English translation. It need not have appeared in the "library press."

2. It must have as its central concern one or more issues, events questions, or controversies in the area of intellectual freedom, including matters of ethical, political, or social concern related to intellectual freedom.

3. It must also be demonstrably relevant to the concerns and needs of members of the library community, including the worlds of publication (print and nonprint) and communication.

4. It must, in the opinion of the judges (which is final), meet high standards of literary quality, accuracy, and responsibility. The principal focus of evaluation will, of course, be the writing, but other considerations may, in the opinion of the judges, be relevant. These may range from the use of particularly effective illustrations, to recognition for the difficult nature of the background research or the subject itself, or for special courage or persistence displayed in writing and publishing the work.

Write for years under consideration.

Eli M. Oboler Memorial Award Nomination Form

AUTHOR(S): ______________________________

____

____

TITLE OF WORK: ______________________________

____

FULL CITATION (Name of Publisher, Date and Place of Publication, Periodical Title if appropriate, Volume/Issue Numbers if appropriate, Pagination): ______________________________

____

____

____

TYPE OF WORK (Article, Book, etc.): ______________________________

ADDRESS/PHONE NUMBER OF AUTHOR(S): ______________________________

____

____

ADDRESS OF PUBLISHER: ______________________________

____

____

NAME/ADDRESS OF NOMINATOR (If different from Author or Publisher): ______________________________

____

____

Postmark deadline for nominations: December 1, 2001
Please use a separate sheet to explain any special circumstances surrounding the publication. Send three (3) copies of the entry to: Office for Intellectual Freedom, IFRT Staff Liaison, 50 East Huron Street, Chicago, IL 60611.

AMERICAN LITERARY REVIEW

P.O. Box 311307
Denton, TX 76203
Website http://www.engl.unt.edu/alr

Deadline: October 2, 2001 postmark

AMERICAN LITERARY REVIEW 2001 FICTION CONTEST
Prize: $500 and publication in Fall 2002 issue

The author's name should not appear on the manuscript but on a separate cover sheet with story title, address, and phone number.

Please include a $10 reading fee per story. Include a self-addressed, stamped envelope for a list of finalists.

Send submissions to: American Literary Review, Fiction Contest, English Department, University of North Texas, Denton, TX 76203-1307

AMERICAN MORGAN HORSE ASSOCIATION

P.O. Box 960
Shelburne, VT 05482-0960
Phone (802) 985-4944; Fax (802) 985-8897

Deadline: October 1, 2001

AMERICAN MORGAN HORSE ASSOCIATION LITERARY CONTEST "Morgans - A Link to the Past, A Bridge to the Future." Tell us in your own words what this means to you! Write either an essay, 1,000 words or less, or a poem and send it with the entry form to the American Morgan Horse Association (AMHA) by October 1, 2001. (The entry form must be attached to your work in order to be considered in the contest.) There is no entry fee. Cash awards of $25 will be presented to the winner in both essay and poetry categories. Ribbons will be awarded to the first through fifth place winners in each category.

The contest is open to juvenile authors. Participants must NOT have reached their 22nd birthday as of October 1, 2001.

Essays and poetry will be judged on general style, originality, grammar, spelling, and punctuation. The judge's decision will be final.

Entries will NOT be returned. Work submitted may be used for promotional purposes by AMHA. You may see your poem or essay in *The Morgan Horse* magazine or on the youth pages in the AMHA News and Morgan Sales Network.

American Morgan Horse Literary Contest Entry Form

"Morgans - A Link to the Past, A Bridge to the Future."

Deadline: October 1, 2001

Name: ______________________________

Street: ______________________________

City, State, Zip: ______________________________

____

Telephone Number: ______________________________

Date of Birth: ______________________________

I fully understand that this work becomes the property of the American Morgan Horse Association, Inc. and that it may be used for promotional purposes; furthermore, I understand that this work will not be returned to me. I give unqualified consent to the above.

Signature:______________________________

(If under 18, signature of parent or guardian required.)

Mail this form with your essay or poem by October 1, 2001 to:
AMHAY Literary Contest, The American Morgan Horse Association,
P.O. Box 960, Shelburne, VT 05482-0960
Phone (802) 985-4944; Fax (802) 985-8897

AMERICAN SOCIETY OF CHURCH HISTORY

P.O. Box 8517
Red Bank, NJ 07701

Deadline: November 1, 2001

THE AMERICAN SOCIETY OF CHURCH HISTORY (ASCH) AWARDS
The American Society of Church History (ASCH) awards the following prizes:

THE FRANK S. AND ELIZABETH D. BREWER PRIZE
A subvention fund of $1,000 is offered annually to assist a press in publishing a book-length manuscript in church history. The Brewer Prize is limited to first books. Works already accepted for publication may be submitted for this award, but the winning manuscript must have printed, preferably on its title page: "The Frank S. and Elizabeth D. Brewer Prize Essay of the American Society of Church History." The monetary grant, within a maximum time period of two years, will be made upon receipt of a commitment in writing from a publisher accepting the manuscript. Entries in their final form must be received by November 1st at the ASCH office (address above). Manuscripts may not be submitted in more than one ASCH competition. The award will be presented at the Society's annual Spring meeting.

Deadline: March 1, 2002 (accepted in even numbered years)

THE ALBERT C. OUTLER PRIZE
The prize, in the amount of $1,000, is awarded to the author of the best book published in the two previous calendar years in ecumenical church history. "Ecumenical" is to be construed as concerned chiefly with problems of Christian unity and disunity (doctrinal, cultural, institutional) or with interactions between Christianity and other religious movements in any historical period. Authors of eligible books or any member of the Society may nominate titles for consideration; authors should submit a copy of the book. Titles may not be submitted in more than one ASCH competition. Nominations must be received by March 1st in even-numbered years at the ASCH office (address above). The award will be presented at the Society's annual Winter meeting.

Deadline: March 1, 2003 (accepted in odd numbered years)

THE PHILIP SCHAFF PRIZE
The award, in the amount of $1,000, is presented to the author of the best book published in the two previous calendar years, originating in the North American scholarly community which presents original research on any period in the history of Christianity. Authors of eligible

books or any member of the Society may nominate titles for consideration; authors should submit a copy of the book. Titles may not be submitted in more than one ASCH competition. Nominations must be received by March 1st in odd-numbered years at the ASCH office (address above). The award will be presented at the Society's annual Winter meeting.

Deadline: August 1, 2001

THE JANE DEMPSEY DOUGLASS PRIZE
An annual award in the amount of $250 is presented to the author of the best essay published during the previous calendar year on any aspect of the role of women in the history of Christianity. Authors of eligible articles and any member of the Society may nominate titles for consideration. Nominations, accompanied if possible by a copy of the article, must be received by August 1st at the ASCH office (address above). The award will be presented at the Society's annual Winter meeting.

Deadline: July 1, 2001

THE SIDNEY E. MEAD PRIZE
Offered annually, the prize is awarded in the amount of $250 for the author of the best unpublished essay in any field of church history written by a doctoral candidate or recent graduate whose manuscript stems directly from doctoral research. The manuscript will be published in *Church History*. Entries of no more than 25 double spaced pages, including double spaced endnotes, must be submitted by July 1st to the ASCH office (address above). The award will be presented at the Society's annual Winter meeting.

ASCAP-DEEMS TAYLOR AWARDS COMPETITION

ASCAP-Deems Taylor Awards
American Society of Composers, Authors & Publishers
One Lincoln Plaza
New York, NY 10023

Deadline: April 30, 2001

ASCAP-DEEMS TAYLOR AWARDS COMPETITION
FOR BOOKS AND ARTICLES ON MUSIC
The ASCAP-Deems Taylor Award program is an important series of annual awards presented to American authors and journalists whose books and articles on the subject of music are selected for their excellence. The Awards were established in 1967 to honor the memory of composer/critic/commentator Deems Taylor who died in 1966 after a distinguished career that included six years as President of ASCAP.

Awards: $500 for best book. $250 for best newspaper, journal or magazine article (includes program and liner notes). Plaques are also presented to the authors and journalists as well as to their respective publishers.

Guidelines
There is no official entry form or fee, however, all submissions must include a cover letter containing the following information:
(a) the title of book, article, program or liner notes.
(b) copyright date of book or date of publication for the article (or issue date for recording liner notes).
(c) name, address, and daytime phone number of all authors of the book or article.
(d) contact name, address, and daytime phone number of the publisher or publication in which the article appeared.

Materials To Be Submitted
Four copies of each entry are required.

Books and articles submitted will not be returned.

For articles, submissions are limited to three entries per author; those articles that were published as a series of articles on a single, specific subject may be considered as one entry.

When submitting one or more articles, be sure four copies are collated and put into four file folders (these folders will be distributed to the judges).

Liner notes should be limited to 4,500 words and include four copies of each recording.

Eligibility
Written works must be published in the United States, in English, during the calendar year 2000.

The subject matter may be biographical or critical, reportorial or historical — any form of nonfiction prose about music and/or its creators — not an instructional textbook, how-to-guide, or a work of fiction.

Paperbacks that were originally published in hardcover are not eligible.

Reprints or translations of works that were previously published outside the United States that are now being published in the United States for the first time are eligible.

Program notes and recording liner notes are also eligible.

For additional information, contact: Esther SanSaurus (212) 621-6323

AMERICA'S INTERCULTURAL MAGAZINE

P.O. Box 1174
Maywood, IL 60153
Phone (773) 874-6184

Deadline: August 15, 2001

Once a year America's Intercultural Magazine (Aim) sponsors a short fiction award of $100 for a previously unpublished story that embodies our goals of purging racism and furthering the brotherhood of man through the written word.

The contest is open particularly to new writers. We're looking for compelling, well-written stories with lasting social significance, proving that people from different racial/ethnic backgrounds are more alike than they are different. The story should not moralize. Maximum length is 4,000 words.

The winning story is published every year in the Fall issue.

Send typewritten entry to: Aim, P.O. Box 1174, Maywood, IL 60153.

AMHERST WRITERS AND ARTISTS PRESS

P.O. Box 1076
Amherst, MA 01004
Phone and Fax (413) 253-7764
E-mail awapress@javanet.com

Deadline April 1, 2001 postmark

SIXTH ANNUAL PEREGRINE PRIZE
Awards: First place in Fiction, $500, publication in *Peregrine,* and two copies. First place in Poetry: $500, publication in *Peregrine,* and two copies. Best of the Nest: $100, publication in *Peregrine,* and two copies. Honorable Mention: name listed in *Peregrine,* and one copy

Guidelines and Rules
Manuscripts must be original, typed, and not previously published.

Each prose manuscript, double spaced, is limited to 4,200 words.

Each poetry manuscript (one-three poems), is limited to 70 lines (and spaces) per poem.

Name and other identifying information must not appear on manuscript.

Cover sheet to include: name, social security number, address, day and evening phone numbers, titles of poem(s) and line count(s), title of short story and word count, 40 word (max) biography.

$10 reading fee per manuscript. Submit as many manuscripts as you choose, but send all in one envelope, accompanied by one check for total. Check or money order made payable to AWA press.

All submissions will be considered for regular publication.

Enclose a self-addressed, stamped envelope for notification of winners. Announcement of winners will take place after June 1.

No manuscript will be returned.

For acknowledgment of manuscript receipt, include a self-addressed, stamped postcard. NO phone calls.

Send submissions to The Peregrine Prize at above address.

ANAMNESIS PRESS

P.O. Box 51115
Palo Alto, CA 94303
Phone (415) 255-8366; Fax (415) 255-3190

Deadline: March 15, 2001 postmark

POETRY CHAPBOOK AWARD
Prize: $1,000 and 20 copies of the winning chapbook

Anamnesis Press is sponsoring its 6th annual poetry chapbook award competition. They are looking for poetry with intellectual and emotional depth that avoids cliches and has an ear for sound and music, although formal structure is not necessary. Genre poetry (science fiction/fantasy/horror) is fine, but they are looking for a high level of sophistication and imagination. Pet peeves: trite, mawkish or "inspirational" poetry. Previously published material is OK, as long as the author owns the rights to the work and provides acknowledgments.

The winner will receive a cash prize of $1,000 an award certificate suitable for framing, and 20 copies of the winning chapbook.

They encourage poets to submit 20-30 pages of their best poems. Manuscripts must be typed or laser printed, single-spaced with no more than one poem per page, and must include a table of contents (showing page numbers) and two title pages. Include your name address on only one of the title pages. No manuscripts will be returned.

The winner will be announced in June.

The reading fee is US $15 per manuscript. Please make check or money order payable to Anamnesis Press in US dollars drawn on a US bank.

Note: All contestants will receive a copy of the winning chapbook.

Include a self-addressed, stamped envelope for notification.

Send submissions to Poetry Chapbook Award at above address.

ANHINGA PRESS

P.O. Box 10595
Tallahassee, FL 32302
Website http://www.anhinga.org

Deadline: January 1, 2001 – March 31, 2001

THE ANHINGA PRIZE FOR POETRY
The award has been offered annually since 1983 for a manuscript of original poetry in English. The competition is open to writers from all regions. The winner will receive $2000 and the winning manuscript will be published by Anhinga press. Contests manuscripts are screened by qualified readers appointed by the press. The final selection is made by a poet of distinguished achievement, who remains anonymous until the winner is announced in mid-October.

Submission Guidelines
The award is open to poets trying to publish a first or second book of poetry. Previous publication of self-published books and chapbooks do not make a poet ineligible.

Entries must be original poetry in English; however, a few translations in a manuscript are acceptable.

Poems previously published in journals and anthologies should be accompanied by an acknowledgments page. Authors may submit multiple manuscripts if each one is accompanied by a reading fee.

Previously submitted manuscripts and manuscripts under consideration by other publishers are also eligible. Should your manuscript be accepted by another press, please notify us as soon as possible.

Once we receive a manuscript, we cannot accept alterations or additions to it. Please check your manuscript carefully before you mail it.

Rules
$20 reading fee. Make checks payable to Anhinga Press.

Do not put your name on your manuscript. Make two title pages – one with the manuscript title, your name, address and phone number, and a second title page with only the manuscript's title.

Manuscripts must be 60-84 pages, excluding front matter. They may be single or double-spaced, and all pages must be numbered. Please do not staple or bind your manuscript.

Include a self-addressed, stamped envelope for results.

Manuscripts will not be returned.

Mail manuscripts to Anhinga Press, P.O. Box 10595, Tallahassee, FL 32302.

ANOTHER CHICAGO MAGAZINE

Another Chicago Magazine
3709 N. Kenmore
Chicago, IL 60613-2509

Deadline: December 10, 2001

Award: $1,000 and publication in ACM for the winning story. $1,000 and publication in ACM to the winning poem. Entry fees: $10/ story, 6,500 words maximum; $10/ set of three poems, 300 lines per entry; $5/ each additional poem up to 100 lines.

Guidelines

Checks payable to Left Field Press.

No names on manuscript; include cover page with name, address, titles, word count (fiction)/ line count (poetry).

Manuscripts will not be returned; include self-addressed, stamped envelope for notification of winners; self-addressed, stamped postcard for acknowledgment of entry.

No previously published work eligible; if work is under consideration elsewhere, ACM must be notified and work withdrawn upon other acceptance.

Send work to Left Field Press-Awards at above name and address.

Notification: By April 2002

ANTIETAM REVIEW

A Journal of Creative Writing and Photography
Published by the Washington County Arts Council
41 South Potomac Street
Hagerstown, MD 21740
Phone (301) 791-3132

Deadline: July 1, 2001 – September 1, 2001

Antietam Review literary magazine announces its Literary Award for short fiction and poetry. First prize for fiction is $100, publication in the year 2002 issue of AR, and two copies of the magazine. First prize for poetry is $50, publication in the magazine, plus two copies. ALL entries are considered for publication. Please enclose a $10 reading fee per short story, $3 per poem. Submit up to five (5) entries at a time. Fiction should be less than 5,000 words, poetry less than 30 lines. Include a self-addressed stamped envelope for notification, no manuscripts are returned. Guidelines for *Antietam Review* are available upon receipt of a self-addressed stamped envelope. The contest is open to natives or residents of Maryland, Pennsylvania, Virginia, West Virginia, Delaware, and Washington, D.C. Send entries to the above address.

ASHLAND POETRY PRESS

Ashland University
Ashland, OH 44805

Deadline: May 15, 2001

THE RICHARD SNYDER PUBLICATION AWARD
Award $500 and publication in a paperback edition of 1,000 copies

Guidelines

1. Book-length poetry manuscripts

2. Original collection of poems of 50 to 80 pages, no more than one poem per page

3. Single spaced

4. Letter quality printer: no dot matrix

5. Bound by a single clip: no folders, notebooks

6. Two title pages: one with name, address, phone number, and one with title only

7. $15.00 reading fee made payable to The Ashland Poetry Press. For notification, enclose only a letter-size self-addressed, stamped envelope. All manuscripts other than the winning one will be recycled.

Mail to: Richard Snyder Poetry Award at above address.

THE ISAAC ASIMOV AWARD

University of South Florida
School of Mass Communications
4202 E. Fowler
Tampa, FL 33620
Rick Wilber, Awards Administrator (813) 974-6792

Deadline: December 15, 2001

The Isaac Asimov Award for undergraduate excellence in Science Fiction and Fantasy Writing has been established by Asimov's science fiction magazine and the International Association for the Fantastic in the Arts with the support of the School of Mass Communications at the University of South Florida. The award honors the legacy of one of science fiction's most distinguished authors through an award aimed at undergraduate writers.

The $500 award will go to the best unpublished and unsold science fiction or fantasy short story submitted by a full-time undergraduate college student. The winner will be invited to the IAFA Annual Conference on the Fantastic in mid-March in Fort Lauderdale, Florida, and the winning story will be considered for publication in Asimov's science fiction magazine.

In general, the winner of the Asimov Award will be the story that best meets the expectations of Asimov's editors. Those stories typically are character oriented; i.e., the characters rather than the science provide the main focus for the reader's interest. Serious, thoughtful, yet accessible fiction will have the best chance of success. The editors do enjoy humorous stories, but pun endings have little chance of success, and the editors are not interested in sword and sorcery, elves, trolls, or dragons; nor are they interested in explicit sex or violence.

Generally, bear in mind that all fiction is written to examine or illuminate some aspect of human existence, but that in science fiction the backdrop against which events occur is the size of the universe.

The contest is open to all full-time undergraduates at accredited colleges and universities. The award is not limited to unpublished authors, but all submissions must be previously unpublished and unsold, and they should be from 1,000 to 10,000 words long. Writers may submit an unlimited number of stories, but each manuscript must include the writer's name, address, phone number, and the name of the university the writer attends.

There is a $10 entry fee per entrant. An entrant may submit from one to three stories. Checks should be made out to the Asimov Award.

Manuscripts should be neatly typed, double spaced on one side of the sheet of paper, with adequate margins. Mail it flat in a 9 x 12 inch envelope. Computer print-outs should have the pages separated.

Make sure the cover sheet of the manuscript includes your name, address, phone number, and the university you attend. Your name should not be on the manuscript itself.

The editors reserve the right to double-check your university status. For this year's contest, you must have been a full-time undergraduate during the Fall 2000, Spring 2001, Summer 2001, or Fall 2001 semesters (or quarters) of your university.

Story submissions should have been written during your time as a student. However, if you attended college full-time during a qualifying semester and then graduated, went to part-time status, or quit entirely for a time, you are still eligible.

Stories by previous Asimov Award winners are available at the Asimov's Science Fiction homepage at: www.asimovs.com

Manuscripts cannot be returned, so make sure you keep a copy of the story for your files.

The winner will be determined by the editors of Asimov's magazine and the award administrator. Submissions should be sent to: Asimov Award, School of Mass Communications, 4202 E. Fowler, Tampa, Fla 33620.

If you have any questions, call Awards Administrator Rick Wilber at (813) 974-6792.

ASSOCIATION OF JEWISH LIBRARIES

15 East 26th Street, Suite 1034
New York, NY 10010-1579

Deadline: January 15, 2001

THE SYDNEY TAYLOR MANUSCRIPT COMPETITION
The Association of Jewish Libraries (AJL) is pleased to coordinate the Sydney Taylor Manuscript Competition. The writer must have no previously published books. The contest is intended as an incentive for beginning authors. Your entry must be postmarked by January 15, 2001. Do not submit elsewhere until after May 15, 2001 when our winner will be determined and notified.

Guidelines for Submission

1. Material should be a work of fiction in English, with universal appeal of Jewish content for readers aged eight to eleven years. It should serve to deepen the understanding of Judaism for all children, Jewish and non-Jewish, and should reveal positive aspects of Jewish life. Short stories or collections of short stories are not eligible.

2. The manuscript should be submitted typewritten in duplicate (two copies) and should be a minimum of 64 pages and a maximum of 200 pages long, double spaced.

3. Each entrant may submit ONE manuscript.

4. To assure impartiality, the author's name must appear on the cover sheet ONLY. This rule must be adhered to for the manuscript to be considered. Type the TITLE on the top of each page of manuscript.

5. AJL offers no publication guarantees.

6. The prize will be $1,000. If a prizeworthy manuscript is not found, a prize will not be given.

7. No manuscripts will be returned. Upon choice of a winner, all other manuscripts will be promptly destroyed.

8. If you wish to be notified on receipt of manuscript, please enclose a stamped, self-addressed postcard.

9. An entry form with the author's name, address, and telephone number should accompany each manuscript.

10. No manuscript will be read unless a release form is signed and submitted along with it.

    All manuscripts will be circulated within a limited and carefully chosen group of judges. Nevertheless, this form must be signed and submitted with your manuscript. No manuscript will be read unless you have signed this release.

    Please note that the Release from Liability is in no way intended to infringe on your rights as an author. In order for a non-profit, professional group to undertake such a far-reaching project, it is necessary to consider all of its ramifications. We have been advised, therefore, to require a signed release from litigation before accepting submissions.

11. Submit manuscripts, entry form, and release form to: Paula Sandfelder, 1327 Wyntercreek Lane, Dunwoody, GA 30338 Phone (770) 394-2060; Fax (770) 671-8380

Association of Jewish Libraries
Sidney Taylor Manuscript Competition
Entry Form

15 East 26th Street, Suite 1034, New York, NY 10010-1579

Author: ______________________________

Address: ______________________________

Phone: (H) ______________________________

Phone: (W) ______________________________

Title of Manuscript ______________________________

____

Previous Publications: ______________________________

____

____

____

Send manuscript to:
Paula Sandfelder, 1327 Wyntercreek Lane, Dunwoody, GA 30338
Phone (770) 394-2060; Fax (770) 671-8380

Association of Jewish Libraries Sidney Taylor Manuscript Competition Release From Liability

Association of Jewish Libraries
Sydney Taylor Manuscript Competition

I, ______________________________

freely and voluntarily submit my Manuscript ______________________________

____

____

____

(from now on referred to as the "ms") to the Association of Jewish Libraries (AJL). My signature below shows that I understand and agree to the following terms and conditions which are prerequisite to the AJL's acceptance of this manuscript.

1. AJL accepts no responsibility for any unauthorized publication of this ms, whole or part, in any form of media at any time by any person or group for whatever reason.

2. I, the author, agree that at no time nor for any reason will any type of action be brought against AJL or it agents, officers, or judges.

3. I, the author, agree to waive any right I may ever have against AJL that in any way relates to the original ideas or likenesses contained in this ms. I recognize that ideas are not unique nor are they able to be copyrighted and should any materials containing similar ideas or likenesses be published or produced at any time in any form by any company, I release AJL from any liability therefor.

Signed:______________________________ Dated:__________

(Sign both copies; retain one for your files.)

ASTRAEA, NATIONAL LESBIAN ACTION FOUNDATION

The Astraea Foundation
116 East 16th Street, 7th Floor
New York, NY 10003
Phone (212) 529-8021; Fax (212) 982-3321

Deadline: March 8, 2001 postmark

EMERGING LESBIAN WRITERS AWARDS
You are eligible for an award from the Lesbian Writers Fund if:

1. You are a lesbian writer of either fiction or poetry.
2. You reside in the United States.
3. Your work includes some lesbian content.
4. You have published at least one piece of your writing (in any genre) in a newspaper, magazine, journal, or anthology, and not more than one book. (Published work may be in any discipline. Self-published books are not included in the one book maximum.)

SAPPHO AWARD OF DISTINCTION
There is no application process for this award. One established lesbian writer is selected by the Board of Directors of Astraea for her outstanding literary contributions.

Submission Guidelines and Requirements
In order to be considered for an award from the Lesbian Writers Fund, you must submit the following:

1. A completed cover sheet.
2. A one paragraph biographical statement.
3. A $5.00 check or money order for processing, payable to The Astraea Foundation.
4. Three (3) copies of a selection of your writing (please see "Writing Sample" below).

Each application form has an identification number stamped in the upper right-hand corner. You may call the office for your identification number before submitting your entry. Please type or print clearly the same number on every page of your submission, including biographical statement and manuscripts.

You may only submit in one category (fiction or poetry) per year.

Winners from previous years are not eligible to apply. Board and staff members of the Astraea Foundation are not eligible to apply.

Incomplete applications will not be considered.

Writing Sample
Applicants must submit a sample of poetry or fiction as described. Please do not put your name on any pages of the writing sample.

Fiction: Select up to 30 pages from a novel or a collection of short stories that you wish the panel to read. In addition, you may submit a project outline of up to two (2) pages that describes your selection in the context of the larger work. (Project outline, submitted in triplicate, must also include your entry number.) Manuscripts must be double spaced.

Poetry: Select at least 10 and no more than 15 pages of poetry that you wish the panel to read. Include at least two poems. Poetry submissions must be collated.

Instructions for Manuscripts (please read carefully)
Three (3) copies of the manuscript are required. Each copy must be paper clipped together (NO BINDERS OR STAPLING). Each copy of your submission must be complete. Please do not send uncollated material. If you are including a project outline, one copy must accompany each submission. Manuscripts must be typed on 8-1/2 x 11 inch paper. Fiction manuscripts must be typed double spaced using a 12-point font and have one-inch margins. All pages must be chronologically numbered at the bottom of each page. In addition, the identification number appearing on the top, right-hand corner of the cover sheet must be copied onto the top, right-hand corner of every page of your submission. Only clear, readable copies are acceptable; otherwise manuscripts will not be read. Books, magazines, and photocopies will not be accepted. Do not attach or bind the cover sheet and biographical statement to the manuscript. Your name must NOT appear on any of the pages of your manuscript, including any title page. Manuscripts will not be returned.

Selection Process
All applications will be reviewed by a panel of lesbian writers who will remain anonymous until after the process has been completed. The names of applicants will not be known to the panelists.

Announcement of Awards
The selection process will be completed by June 30, 2001. All applicants will be notified of the results by mail. Please do not call the office.

Submission
Submit your entry to: Lesbian Writers Fund, Astraea National Lesbian Action Foundation, 116 E. 16th Street, 7th Floor, New York, NY 10003. Call the office for your identification number.

Lesbian Writer's Fund Cover Sheet

Please type or print clearly

Name ______________________________

Address ______________________________

City ______________________________

State ______________________________ Zip ______________

Phone (day) ______________ Phone (eve) ______________

E-mail ______________________________

Indicate the category in which you are applying:

Poetry ______________ Fiction ______________

$5.00 check or money order enclosed ______________

List publications, including date, in which your work has appeared: (If you have published a book, include title, date published, and publisher.)

____

____

____

List title(s) and number of pages of the writing sample that you are submitting with this application:

____

____

____

____

THE ATHENAEUM OF PHILADELPHIA

219 South Sixth Street
Philadelphia, PA 19106-3794
Phone (215) 925-2688

December 31, 2001

THE ATHENAEUM OF PHILADELPHIA LITERARY AWARDS
Nominations of candidate books for this annual prize shall be made in writing to the Literary Award Committee of The Athenaeum of Philadelphia by the author, the publisher, or a member of The Athenaeum and shall be accompanied by a copy of the book or books in question.

The presentation of the medals and citations shall be made at a meeting held in The Athenaeum in the spring of the year. The award will be granted to those books chosen by the judges from among the publications of the preceding calendar year.

Eligibility
Any volume of general literature (fiction, history, biography, drama, belles letters) written by a Philadelphian. (Technical, scientific, exclusively educational, and juvenile books are not included.) The term "Philadelphian" shall mean one who was a bona fide resident of Pennsylvania within a radius of 30 miles of City Hall, Philadelphia, at the time his or her book in question was written or was published. In the case of dual authorship, residence as herein stipulated of any of the authors shall qualify the book. An award may be given to both a fiction and a non-fiction title in any year, at the discretion of the judges.

Rules and Guidelines
Consideration of nominations is to be on the basis of their significance and importance to the general public as well as on literary excellence. The decision of the judges shall be final and all books submitted shall become the property of The Athenaeum of Philadelphia. The judges may reject any or all nominations. The Literary Award Committee of The Athenaeum of Philadelphia shall appoint a board of judges which shall make the award.

The Award, given annually since its first presentation in February 1950 (for a book published in the calendar year 1949), consists of a bronze medal bearing the name of the award, the seal of The Athenaeum of Philadelphia, the title of the book, the name of the author, and the year in which it was conferred.

ATLANTA REVIEW

P.O. Box 8396
Atlanta, GA 31106

Deadline: postmarked by May 1, 2001

USA/INTERNATIONAL POETRY COMPETITION 2001
Prizes: Gold- $2,000 Silver- $500 Bronze $250 plus 50 International Merit Awards. All entries will be considered for worldwide publication in *Atlanta Review.*

Guidelines

1. Entry fee: $5 for the first poem, $2 for each additional poem.
2. Poems must be previously unpublished.
3. No entry form or special format required.
4. Please include a self-addressed, stamped envelope. (IRC outside the US.)
5. Make checks payable to *Atlanta Review.*

Mail to above address

Contest issue $4 or free with a $10 subscription to *Atlanta Review.*

AUTHORS IN THE PARK

P.O. Box 85
Winter Park, FL 32790-0085
Phone (407) 658-4520; E-mail foley@magicnet.net

Deadline: March 31, 2001 postmark

AUTHORS IN THE PARK (AIP) SHORT-STORY CONTEST
AIP offers annual awards for best short story. Prizes include $500 for first place, $250 for second place, and $125 for third place. Top stories of 2001 will be published in '01 *Fine Print*.

Rules and Guidelines

1. Stories must be original and no more than 5,000 words.

2. Stories must be typed, double spaced, on 8-1/2 x 11 inch white paper, minimum one-inch left and right margins. Paperclip entries – no staples please.

3. Title must appear at the top of every page of the story.

4. Author's name must NOT appear anywhere on the manuscript.

5. Title, author's name, address, home and work phone numbers must be typed on a 3 x 5 card.

6. Two copies of each entry must be submitted. Entries will not be returned.

Please enclose a reading fee of $8 per story – checks only, payable to Authors In The Park. The fee includes a 2000 edition of *Fine Print* released in September.

Entries must be postmarked by March 31, 2001.

Mail entries to: AIP/Short Story Contest, P.O. Box 85, Winter Park, FL 32790-0085.

BAKER'S PLAYS

100 Chauncy Street
Boston, MA 02111-1783
Phone (617) 482-1280; Fax (617) 482-7613

Deadline: January 31, 2001 postmark

BAKER'S PLAYS HIGH SCHOOL PLAYWRITING CONTEST
Open to any high school student, plays should be about the "high school experience," but also may be about any subject and of any length as long as the play can be reasonably produced on the high school stage.

The first place award is $500.00 and the play will be published by Baker's Plays. Second place is $250.00 and an honorable mention. Third place is $100.00 and an honorable mention. Winners will be notified by the end of May 2001.

Guidelines
Plays must be accompanied by the signature of a sponsoring high school Drama or English teacher, and it is recommended that the play receive a production or a public reading prior to the submission. Multiple submissions and co-authored scripts are welcome. Teachers may not submit a student's work.

The manuscript must be typed and firmly bound. Include a self-addressed, stamped envelope with enough postage to cover the return of the manuscript. Plays that do not come with a self-addressed, stamped envelope will not be returned. Do not send originals; copies only. All plays must be postmarked by January 31, 2001. Plays postmarked after this date will not be considered. Playwrights will be notified during the month of May 2001. Awards are based on merit and if no submission warrants an award, no prizes will be given.

Send all plays and correspondence to the address above.

BANTAM DOUBLEDAY DELL BOOKS FOR YOUNG READERS

Marquerite de Angeli Contest
Bantam Doubleday Dell Books For Young Readers
1540 Broadway
New York, NY 10036

Deadline: April 1, 2001 – June 30, 2001 postmark

MARGUERITE de ANGELI CONTEST
The 9th annual Marguerite de Angeli Contest prize of a book contract (on the Publisher's standard form) for a hard-cover and a paperback edition, including an advance and royalties, will be awarded annually to encourage the writing of contemporary or historical fiction set in North America for readers age seven – ten. The award consists of $1,500 in cash and a $3,500 advance against royalties. Winners will be announced no later than October 31, 2001.

Eligibility

1. The contest is open to U.S. and Canadian writers who have not previously published a novel for middle-grade readers.

2. Foreign-language manuscripts and translations are not eligible.

3. Manuscripts sent to Bantam Doubleday Dell may not be submitted to other publishers while under consideration for the prize.

4. Authors may not submit more than two manuscripts to the Marguerite de Angeli Contest; each must meet all eligibility requirements.

Submission Guidelines

1. Do not submit art with your manuscript unless you have illustrated the work yourself. The publisher will be responsible for selecting and compensating the illustrator. If you do submit artwork, do not send originals; photocopies, slides, or prints will suffice. If you submit a dummy, please also submit the text separately as detailed in Step 4, below.

2. Manuscripts should be no shorter than 40 typewritten pages and no longer than 144 typewritten pages. Include a brief plot summary with your covering letter.

3. Each manuscript should have a cover page listing the title of the work and the author's name, address, and telephone number. The title should also appear on each manuscript page.
4. Manuscripts should be typed double spaced on 8-1/2 by 11 inch

good quality white paper, and pages should be numbered consecutively. The type should be easy to read, preferably 12 point.

5. Photocopies are acceptable if readily legible and printed on good quality white (not gray) paper.

6. Do not submit manuscripts in boxes. A padded envelope will do.

7. Please note that postal regulations have recently changed. All domestic mail weighing 16 ounces or more that bears stamps, and all international and military APO/FPO mail weighing 16 ounces or more, MUST be presented to a retail clerk at a post office. This means that the Bantam Doubleday Dell mailroom CANNOT return your manuscript in your own stamped self-addressed envelope. Please consider sending a manuscript that does not need to be returned. Send a manuscript copy that can be discarded at the end of judging, and a business-size, stamped, self-addressed envelope for notification.

   If you would like to have your manuscript returned, you must send an envelope or book mailer large enough to accommodate the manuscript, with a METERED POSTAL STRIP that can be used for return postage; otherwise, the manuscript cannot be returned. Please do not enclose checks for postage.

8. Send manuscripts to: Marquerite de Angeli Contest, Bantam Doubleday Del Books For Young Readers, 1540 Broadway, New York, NY 10036.

   The publisher cannot guarantee the return of any manuscript, and is not responsible for late, lost, misdelivered, or misplaced submissions.

Judging

1. The judges are the editors of Bantam Doubleday Dell Books for Young Readers.

2 The judges reserve the right not to award a prize.

3. The judges' decision will be final.

4. The editors of Bantam Doubleday Dell Books for Young Readers will not be able to offer critiques of manuscripts or enter into correspondence about the manuscripts other than with the winning author.

ALSO SEE Delacorte Press, a division of Bantam Doubleday Dell, for a contest for a first book for young adults.

THE BEAR DELUXE MAGAZINE

P.O. Box 10342
Portland OR 97296
E-mail bear@teleport.com

Deadline: September 7, 2001

EDWARD ABBEY FICTION AWARD
Prize: $500 and possible publication to honorable mention finalist

Guidelines
Short fiction that uniquely explores a theme reminiscent of the well-known Western writer, Edward "Cactus Ed" Abbey. Interested in creative, original approaches to Abbey's themes of: wilderness, desert, solitude, the commercialization of natural spaces, rabble rousing, etc.

Submit original, unpublished works of fiction to "Abbey Award," at above address. Double-spaced and type-written manuscripts only. Include name, address and phone number on first page only.

Make a $5 reading fee check or money order, per entry, payable to *The Bear Deluxe.* Include a self-addressed, stamped envelope for announcement.

Manuscripts will not be returned.

Announcements will be mailed to each contestant in their self-addressed, stamped envelope by December 1, 2001.

E-mail submissions are accepted if the entry fee is received prior to the deadline.

Send all submissions to above address. Use above e-mail address for e-mail submissions.

BEAR STAR PRESS

185 Hollow Oak Drive
Cohasset, CA 95973

Deadline: November 30, 2001 postmark
Prize: 1,000 and 25 author copies. Submissions read September-November for a book of poems by a writer living in the Western States; (within Mountain or Pacific time zones, plus Alaska and Hawaii).

Guidelines

1. All work must be original. Any form or subject is acceptable. Use a plain 10-12 font (no Mistral).

2. Manuscripts should not exceed 65 pages. There is a $16 reading fee made payable to Bear Star Press. Unpublished writers are welcome to submit.

3. Simultaneous submissions acceptable so long as BSP is apprised of changes in manuscript status. Rights revert back to the author upon publication. Winner notified on or before February 1, 2001.

4. Publication by Fall 2002.

5. Name, address, and phone number should appear on a separate cover sheet only. No manuscripts will be returned. Please do not send your only copy!

6. You must enclose a letter-sized self-addressed, stamped envelope for contest results.

Bear Star Press is a member of the Council of Literary Magazines and Presses.

Send submissions to above address.

THE BELLETRIST REVIEW

Marmarc Publications
P.O. Box 596
Plainville, CT 06062-0596

Deadline: October 1, 2000 – July 15, 2001 postmark

THE BELLETRIST REVIEW FICTION CONTEST
The winning story will receive a $200 award for best fiction, and an interview with the writer will appear in the September 2001 issue of the *Belletrist Review*. The winning story also will be eligible for year 2002 Pushcart nomination.

Rules and Guidelines
The story may deal with any subject matter. Preferred story length is 2,500-5,000 words. Manuscripts must be typed and double spaced. No stories previously published are eligible. There are no simultaneous submissions.

Contest entries may be submitted starting October 1, 2000 but must be postmarked on or before July 15, 2001. A $5 entry fee is required per submission, the check or money order should be made out to: Marmarc Publications.

Enclose a self-addressed, stamped envelope for a personal response; enclose adequate postage if you desire return of your manuscript as well.

Send submission and entry fee to: Marmarc Publications, Fiction Contest, P.O. Box 596, Plainville, CT 06062-0596.

BELLINGHAM REVIEW

Bellingham Review
Mail Stop 9053
Western Washington University
Bellingham, WA 98225

Deadline: January 4, 2001 – March 4, 2001 postmark

FIFTH ANNUAL TOBIAS WOLFF AWARD FOR FICTION
Awards: First Prize, $1,000; Second Prize, $250; and Third Prize, $100. The winning story or novel excerpt will be published in *The Bellingham Review*. Runners-up will be considered for publication.

Guidelines
The story or novel excerpt may be in any style and on any subject.

Any number of stories or chapters may be submitted.

The maximum length is 10, 000 words per story or chapter.

Manuscripts should be typed.

The entry fee is $10 for the first entry, $5 per story/chapter thereafter. Please make checks payable to The Western Foundation/Bellingham Review. Anyone entering the competition will receive a complimentary two-issue subscription to *The Bellingham Review* beginning with the Winter 2002 issue.

No previously published works, or works accepted for publication, are eligible. Stories/chapters may be under consideration elsewhere, but they should be withdrawn from the competition if they are accepted.

The author's name must not appear anywhere on the manuscript. Enclose with your story/chapter one 3 x 5 inch index card with the titles of stories/chapters submitted; a word count for each story/chapter; the author's name and address; and the phone number, fax number, e-mail address, if any.

Manuscripts will not be returned. Include a self-addressed, stamped envelope for announcement of winners. If you want to be notified of the receipt of your manuscript, also enclose a self-addressed, stamped postcard.

Winners will be announced in July of 2001.

Deadline: January 4, 2001 – March 4, 2001 postmark

FIFTH ANNUAL ANNIE DILLARD AWARD IN NONFICTION
Awards: First Prize, $1,000; Second Prize, $250; and Third Prize, $100. The winning essay will be published in *The Bellingham Review*. Runners-up will be considered for publication.

Guidelines
The essay may be in any style and on any subject.

Any number of essays may be submitted.

The maximum length is 10,000 words per essay.

Manuscripts should be typed.

The entry fee is $10 for the first entry, $5 per essay thereafter. Please make checks payable to The Western Foundation/Bellingham Review. Anyone entering the competition will receive a complimentary two-issue subscription to *The Bellingham Review* beginning with the Winter 2002 issue.

No previously published works, or works accepted for publication, are eligible. Essays may be under consideration elsewhere, but they should be withdrawn from the competition if they are accepted for publication.

The author's name must not appear anywhere on the manuscript. Enclose with your essay(s) one 3 x 5 inch index card with the titles of poem(s) submitted; the first line of poem(s); the author's name and address; and the phone number, fax number, e-mail address, if any.

Manuscripts will not be returned. Include a self-addressed, stamped envelope for announcement of winners. If you want to be notified of the receipt of your manuscript, also enclose a self-addressed, stamped postcard.

The winners will be announced in July of 2001.

Deadline: October 1, 2001 – December 1, 2001 postmark

SIXTEENTH ANNUAL 49TH PARALLEL POETRY AWARD
Awards: First Prize, $1,000; Second Prize, $250; and Third Prize, $100. The winning poem will be published in *The Bellingham Review*. Runners-up will be considered for publication.

Guidelines
Poems may be in any style and on any subject.

Any number of poems may be submitted.

No maximum line length, though poems within a series of poems will each be treated as a separate entry.

Manuscripts should be typed.

The entry fee is $5 per poem. Please make checks payable to The Western Foundation/Bellingham Review. Anyone submitting two or more poems will receive a complimentary two-issue subscription to *The Bellingham Review* beginning with the Summer 2002 issue.

No previously published works, or works accepted for publication, are eligible. Poems may be under consideration elsewhere, but they should be withdrawn from the competition if they are accepted for publication.

The author's name must not appear on the manuscript. Enclose with each submission a 3 x 5 inch index card with the titles of poem(s) submitted; the first line of poem(s); the author's name and address; and the phone number, fax number, e-mail address, if any.

Manuscripts will not be returned. Author should submit one copy of the manuscript for judging. Include a self-addressed, stamped envelope for announcement of winners. If you want to be notified of the receipt of your manuscript, also enclose a self-addressed, stamped postcard.

The winners will be announced in April of 2002.

THE BELOIT POETRY JOURNAL

24 Berry Cove Road
Lamoine, ME 04605

Deadline: Ongoing submissions

CHAD WALSH POETRY AWARD
Award : $4000 in 1997

The Chad Walsh Poetry Award is selected by the editors from all the poems published in the BPS in that calendar year. No application needed.

Send poetry for publication to the above address.

BEREA COLLEGE

Chair, Weatherford Award Committee
Appalachian Center
CPO 2336, Berea College
Berea, KY 40404-2336
Phone (606) 986-9341 ext. 5140; Fax (606) 986-4506

Deadline: By December 31 of the year the work is published

WEATHERFORD AWARD
Prize: $500 to the author of a work published anywhere in the United States which, in the opinion of the judges, best describes and analyzes the challenges, personalities, and qualities of the Appalachian South.

The winning work must be a book length, or shorter, and it may be fact, fiction or poetry. It must be published during the year for which the award is made. The work may be nominated by its publisher, by a member of the award committee, or by any reader. Persons making nominations are asked to arrange that seven copies of the nominated work be sent to the chair of the award committee.

The winning work and the award will be presented during the spring of the following year.

Judging: A committee of independent persons from various parts of the Appalachian South.

Send submissions to above address.

THE BEVERLY HILLS THEATRE GUILD

2815 N. Beachwood Drive
Los Angeles, CA 90068-1923
Phone (213) 465-2703

Deadline: August 1, 2001 – November 1, 2001 postmark

JULIE HARRIS PLAYWRIGHT AWARD COMPETITION
The Beverly Hills Theatre Guild (BHTG) annually sponsors the Julie Harris Playwright Award Competition to discover new dramatists and to encourage established and aspiring playwrights to develop quality plays for the theatre. First place award is $5,000 (The June Moray Award); second place award is $2,000 (The Janet and Maxwell Salter Award); and third place award is $1,000 (The Dr. Henry and Lilian Nesburn Award).

Rules and Guidelines

1. Entries must be original, full length plays (minimum of 90 minutes playing time), unpublished, unproduced, and not currently under any option. "Unproduced" means no previous production of any kind (Equity or Non-Equity) for which actors or authors were paid or admission was charged, or both.

2. Authors must be U.S. citizens. Co-authorships are permissible.

3. An author may submit only one entry, whether under his or her name, a pseudonym, or as a co-author.

4. The following entries are not eligible: musicals, short one-act plays (less that 90 minutes), groups of short one-act plays (related or unrelated), adaptations, translations, plays for children, a play that has won any other competition, or a play that was a winner in any prior years of the Beverly Hills Theatre Guild Playwright Award Competition.

5. Entries must be submitted with completed application and received by the BHTG with a postmark no later than November 1st. Entries will only be accepted from August 1st through competition deadline. Results will be announced the following June.

6. Submissions in non-compliance of these rules, and the submission procedures (following), will be ineligible for entry in the competition. Ineligible submissions will not be returned. Include a self-addressed stamped envelope for our response.

7. The BHTG has the right to accept or reject any entry without explanation and will not correspond with or discuss with any person the results of the competition or the acceptance or rejection of any entry.

8. Judges' decisions are final in all respects.

9. As a sponsor of the competition, the BHTG has the following rights, which it may exercise at its sole discretion:
   - To declare any entry ineligible if prior to the announcement of the winner at the competition's close (June 1), the entry is in violation of Rule 1. Authors must notify the BHTG of any change in status.
   - To reproduce as many copies of an entry as are necessary for distribution among the judges or to request an author to supply a specified number of copies. The author must comply with that request.
   - To use the author's name and title of any award winning entry for publicity about this Playwright Award and the results of the competition.
   - To present a script-in-hand, rehearsed reading of an award winning entry to an invited, non-paying audience. No royalty payment will be due to the entry's author for that reading.

10. Each award winner shall, at all times, in connection with publication, production, publicity, programs, posters and advertisements about an award winning entry, designate that the play is an "Award Winner of The Beverly Hills Theatre Guild/Julie Harris Playwright Award Competition."

11. Each entry shall be free from copyright restriction relating to this Award, and the author shall hold The BHTG, its officers, and director free and harmless from all copyright claims.

Submission Procedures

1. You must submit your entry with a completed application form. You may obtain additional forms by sending a self-addressed, business-size stamped envelope to: Playwright Award Competition, 2815 N. Beachwood Dr., Los Angeles, CA 90068-1923.

2. You must personally sign the application. A proxy or agent signature is not acceptable.

3. Bind your entry securely, and include the following: cast list, time and place, number of acts and scenes.

4. Do not show your name, address, or any identifying information on any page or on the cover of your entry. Attach with a removable paper clip a sheet containing the title of your entry, your name, address, phone number, and any other information. You may enter the copyright or registration date and number on the title page of the bound script.

5. To preserve anonymity, all entries will be identified by numbers for judging; all identifying marks will be removed.

6. Your submission will not be returned. Enclose a stamped, self-addressed envelope for our response.

7. The following are optional enclosures: a self-addressed stamped postcard for acknowledgment of receipt of your entry; and a stamped, self-addressed, business-size envelope for an announcement of the competition winners in June.

8. The BHTG is not responsible for loss or damage to entries. Address all inquiries the address above.

Application for Entry
Julie Harris Playwright Award Competition

2815 N. Beachwood Drive
Los Angeles, CA 90068-1923

(Please print or type)

Playwright's Name ______________________________

Street Address ______________________________

Phone ______________________________

City ______________ State ______ Zip Code ______

Co-Author's Name(s) ______________________________

(Please use reverse side for names, address, phone numbers of co-authors.)

Title of Entry: ______________________________

____

____

I have read the Competition Guidelines and Submission Procedures of The Beverly Hills Theatre Guild – Julie Harris Playwright Award Competition and I agree to abide by them. I have retained a copy of the rules.

I certify that this entry is an original play and is not subject to any copyright restrictions or violations.
(The word, I, includes Co-authors.)

____
Date Signature of Playwright

____
Date Signature of Co-Author

THE BEVERLY HILLS THEATRE GUILD PLAY COMPETITION FOR CHILDREN'S THEATRE

2815 N. Beachwood Drive
Los Angeles, CA 90068-1923
Phone (213) 465-2703

Deadline: January 15, 2001 – February 28, 2001 postmark

THE MARILYN HALL AWARD
The Beverly Hills Theatre Guild annually sponsors a competition for plays written for children's theatre to encourage the creation of dramatic works of excellence for youth audiences: plays that not only entertain but also foster an appreciation of and an interest in live theatre. The award is a prize of $1,000 which is divided $750 to the winner and $250 to the first runner-up. Winners will be announced in June.

Rules and Guidelines

1. Entries must be unpublished, unproduced, dramatic work suitable for youth audiences 7 through 14 years of age. Play length must be from 40 to 50 minutes playing time. "Unproduced" means no prior production of any kind (Equity or Non-Equity) for which actors or authors were paid or admission was charged, or both.

2. Authors must be U.S. citizens. Co-authorships are permissible.

3. An author may submit only one entry, whether under his or her name, a pseudonym, or as a co-author.

4. Entries may be original, or adaptations and/or translations. Authors of adaptations and/or translations of works under copyright must have permission from the copyright holder(s) to so use such works.

5. Plays with less than 40 minutes playing time and plays entered in a previous BHTG competition for children's theatre are not eligible for entry.

6. Submissions received with postmarks before January 15th or after the last day of February will not be accepted for entry. Authors will be notified of ineligible submissions and the reason why.

7. Submission in non-compliance of these rules and the Submission Procedures (following) will be ineligible for entry in the competition. Ineligible submissions will not be returned. Include a self-addressed, stamped, business-size envelope for our response.

8. The BHTG has the right to accept or reject any entry without explanation and will not correspond with or discuss with any person the results of the competition or the acceptance or rejection of any entry.

9. Judges' decisions are final in all respects.

10. As a sponsor of the competition, the BHTG has the following rights, which it may exercise at its sole discretion:
    - To declare any entry ineligible if, prior to the announcement of the winner at the competition's close (June 1), the entry is in violation of Rule 1. Authors must notify the BHTG of any change in status.
    - To reproduce as many copies of an entry as are necessary for distribution among the judges or to request an author to supply a specified number of copies. The author must comply with that request.
    - To use the author's name and title of any award winning entry for publicity about this Playwright Award and the results of the competition.
    - To present a script-in-hand, rehearsed reading of an award winning entry to an invited, non-paying audience. No royalty payment will be due to the entry's author for that reading.

11. Each award winner shall, at all times, in connection with publication, production, publicity, programs, posters and advertisements about an award winning entry, designate that the play is an "Award Winner of The Beverly Hills Theatre Guild/Children's Theatre Competition."

12. Each entry shall be free from copyright restriction relating to this Award, and the author shall hold the BHTG, its officers and directors free and harmless from all copyright claims.

Submission Procedures

1. Bind your entry securely and include a title sheet with the name of the play and, if desired, copyright or registration number and date (instead of your name, please use "by the author").

2. On the second page list all characters, time, place, and other pertinent information such as whether the work is an adaptation or translation, musical, or makes use of special effects, e.g., puppetry.

3. Do not show your name, address, or any personal information on any page of your entry. Include a separate, unbound sheet (attached to the front with a paperclip) with the name of the play,

your name, address, and phone number.

4. To preserve anonymity, all entries will be identified by numbers for judging; all personal identifying marks or information will be removed.

5. Entries as well as ineligible submissions will not be returned. Enclose with your submission a stamped, self-addressed, business-size envelope for our response.

6. The following are optional enclosures: a self-addressed, stamped postcard for acknowledgment of receipt of your entry; and a stamped, self-addressed, business-size envelope for an announcement of the competition winners in June.

7. The BHTG is not responsible for loss or damage to entries. Address your entry and all inquiries to: Play Competition for Children's Theatre, 2815 N. Beachwood Drive, Los Angeles, CA 90068-1923.

BOSTON AUTHORS CLUB

Adrienne Richard
45 Chiltern Road
Weston, MA 02493

Deadline: January 1, 2001

The Boston Authors Club takes pleasure in announcing its year 2001 award for a book published in 2000. Fiction, nonfiction, poetry, children's books and memoirs will be considered.

The author must live or have lived within one hundred miles of Boston. Self-published work will not be considered.

There will be two awards in the amount of $500 each. One prize will go to the outstanding children's/young adult book. The other will go to the outstanding work directed toward adults. The prizes will be awarded at the club's annual meeting on May 6, 2001, to be held at The College Club in Boston.

Books cannot be returned.

Send submissions to the above address.

THE BOSTON GLOBE-HORN BOOK, INC.

The Horn Book, Inc.
11 Beacon Street, Suite 1000
Boston, MA 02108
Phone (617) 227-1555; Fax (617) 523-0299

Deadline: May 15, 2001

THE BOSTON GLOBE-HORN BOOK AWARDS
The Boston Globe and The Horn Book, Inc. have annually co-sponsored the Boston Globe-Horn Book Awards for excellence in literature for children and young adults since 1967. This award program has grown to become one of the most prestigious in the nation. Award recipients receive $500 and an engraved silver bowl. Honor recipients receive an engraved silver plate. In the case of dual winners, prize money will be divided.

Submission Guidelines

1. Books to be considered are submitted by publishers. Publishers may submit up to ten books from each juvenile imprint divided into any three categories. The categories for every submission must be designated to each judge on a list of all books submitted. Categories are Fiction, Non-fiction, and Picture Book. Two honor books in each category may be designated by the judges. The quality of the entire book will be considered for the award. Text and illustrative material will be evaluated as they work together.

2 Books must have been published in the United States between June 1, 2000 and May 31, 2001. Reissued editions are not eligible, though new editions of previously issued books are eligible. No manuscripts please.

3. Any juvenile book is eligible, though no textbooks will be considered. The judges reserve the right to give the award to any children's book published in the U.S. during the designated period.

4. The deadline for mailing books is May 15, 2001. Books should be sent to the judges as soon as possible.

5. A copy of each book entered should be mailed directly to each of the three judges. Judges are announced in January of each year. Publishers who have requested a copy of these submission rules will be sent a January update which includes a list with judges' names and addresses.

6. For control purposes, please send one copy of each entry to: Stephanie Loer, Boston Globe Children's Book Editor, 298 North Street, Medfield, MA 02052.

7. Winning authors and illustrators are encouraged to attend the award ceremonies to be held at the 2001 Fall Conference of the New England Library Association.

These rules are also published in the Hunt Breakfast section of the March/April issue of the *Horn Book Magazine*. Publishers who have requested these rules will be sent an update in January 2000, which will include the judges' addresses. For more information contact: The Horn Book, Inc., 11 Beacon Street, Suite 1000, Boston, MA 02108; (617) 227-4709.

BOULEVARD EMERGING WRITERS

Boulevard Emerging Writers Contests
PMB 332
4579 Laclede Avenue
St. Louis, MO 63108

Deadline: December 15, 2001
Award: $1,200 and publication in *Boulevard.*

For a writer who has not yet published a book of fiction, poetry, or creative non-fiction with a nationally distributed press.

Rules and Guidelines
Simultaneous submissions are allowed, but previous accepted or published work is ineligible. Entries will be judged by the editors of *Boulevard* magazine. No manuscripts will be returned. Send typed, double-spaced manuscript(s) and self-addressed, stamped postcard for acknowledgment of receipt, and an optional self-addressed, stamped envelope for receipt of the contest results to above address.

Each individual story requires a $15 entry fee; entries are limited to two stories per author. Entry fee includes a one-year subscription to *Boulevard.* Make checks payable to *Boulevard.*

Maximum length is 7,500 words. Author's name, address, and telephone number, in addition to the story's title and "Boulevard Emerging Writers Contest" should appear on page one. Cover sheets are not necessary.

The winning story will be published in Spring or Fall 2002 issue of *Boulevard.*

BOWLING MAGAZINE

5301 South 76th Street
Greendale, WI 53129-1127
Phone (414) 421-6400; Fax (414) 421-1194

Deadline: December 15, 2001

BOWLING MAGAZINE WRITING COMPETITION
Editorial, Feature, and News stories published during December 2000 and January through November 2001 in newspapers or magazines, or presented by broadcast media may be entered. Materials which appeared in *BOWLING* Magazine are ineligible.

Entry guidelines for the three categories are:

EDITORIAL – Any opinion expressed in the media concerning a tenpin bowling related subject.

FEATURE – A non-fiction story concerning any individual, facility, equipment, or organization related to tenpin bowling involvement.

NEWS – A tenpin bowling related story written under deadline with proof of following day publication.

Entries are limited to three per author in each division.

First place in each division will carry a $300 award. In addition to first place awards, other awards will be: News and Editorial – $225, $200, $175, $150, $75, and $50; Feature – $225, $200, $175, $150, $125, $100, $75, $50 and $50. There also will be five honorable mention certificates awarded in each category.

Send entries to: *BOWLING* Magazine Writing Competition, Public Relations Dept., 5301 S. 76th St., Greendale, WI 53129.

BOX TURTLE PRESS, INC.

184 Franklin Street
New York, NY 10013
Phone (212) 219-9278

Deadline: April 30, 2001

FIFTH ANNUAL *MUDFISH* POETRY PRIZE
Judge: an internationally renowned poet to be announced.
Prizes: $1,000 plus publication *Mudfish 16*. Publication for honorable mentions. Every poem entered is considered for publication.

Guidelines

1. Unpublished poetry.

2. Include a self-addressed, stamped envelope for notification of results. Manuscripts will not be returned. Include a cover page with name, address and title of poems. Do not allow name to appear on poem pages.

3. Enclose $15 for three poems and $2 for each additional poem.

4. Make checks payable to Box Turtle Press.

Submit to *Mudfish* Poetry Prize, at above address.

BPNICHOL

316 Dupont Street
Toronto, Ontario CANADA M5R 1V9

Deadline: March 30, 2001

THE bpNICHOL CHAPBOOK AWARD
A prize of $1,000 is offered for the best poetry chapbook in English published in Canada in 2000.

The chapbook should be between 10 and 48 pages long.

The poet or publisher should submit three (3) copies (not returnable) and a brief *curriculum vitae.*

BREAD LOAF WRITER'S CONFERENCE

Ian Pounds
The Bakeless Contest
c/o Bread Loaf Writer's Conference
Middlebury College
Middlebury, VT 05753
Phone (802) 443-2018
E-mail bakeless@middlebury.edu
Website http://www/middlebury.edu/~blwc

Deadline: January 1, 2001 – March 1, 2001

The Bread Loaf Writer's Conference of Middlebury College sponsors the Bakeless Literary Publication Prizes, an annual book series competition for new authors of literary works in poetry, fiction, and creative nonfiction. The Bakeless Prizes, named for Middlebury College supporter Katharine Bakeless Nason, were established in order to support emerging writers.

Awards: Winners of the Bakeless Prizes will have their book-length manuscripts published by Middlebury College/University Press of New England, a consortium of university presses which includes Wesleyan, Dartmouth, Brown, Tufts, New Hampshire, Rhode Island, Vermont, and Brandeis. In addition to the publication prize each winner will be awarded a fellowship to attend the Bread Loaf Writer's Conference. Manuscripts received with postmarks after March 1, 2001 cannot be considered. Winners announced in August 2001.

Guidelines

The competition welcomes manuscripts from all authors, including non-US citizens, writing in English who have not yet published a book in their entry's genre. Scholarly, critical, and historical works will not be considered in the creative nonfiction category. Manuscripts may contain stories, poems, chapters, and essays that have already been published individually in magazines, anthologies, and periodicals, but the manuscript itself cannot have been published previously as a whole, commercially or privately.

Multiple submissions of manuscripts are allowed but contestants are asked to notify the Bread Loaf Writer's Conference if a manuscript has been accepted for publication elsewhere.

Typed and double-spaced on letter-size, 8 x 11 inch paper.

Poetry manuscripts may be single-spaced.

Printed manuscripts are acceptable. (Dot-matrix printed manuscripts will not be considered.)

Include a cover page containing the author's name, address, phone number, manuscript title, and genre.

The author's name must not appear on any page of the manuscript.

Do not include an author's note or biographical information.

Do not include a publication acknowledgments page.

Revisions and additions will not be accepted once manuscripts have been received.

The above guidelines will help to insure efficient handling of the manuscripts as well as the process of judging them anonymously. In the case of a manuscript not conforming with the above guidelines, the manuscript becomes ineligible for consideration and the entry fee will be returned.

Requirements for Submission
Send one copy of each submission.

Include a $10 processing fee for each submission, payable to Middlebury College; a self-addressed, stamped postcard for confirmation of manuscript receipt; a self-addressed, stamped envelope for receiving announcement of the judges' decisions.

Manuscripts, even if accompanied by a self-addressed, stamped envelope, cannot be returned.

Rules of Eligibility
The Bakeless Prizes require that poetry manuscripts contain 45-60 pages of text. Fiction, which includes novels and short-fiction collections, 150-450; creative nonfiction, 150-300.

Judges for the 2001 prizes have not been determined yet. Write for details, or visit our web page.

CALIFORNIA WRITERS' ROUNDTABLE

c/o Women's National Book Association, Los Angeles Chapter
P.O. Box 7034
Beverly Hills, CA 90212-0034

Deadline: September 30, 2001 postmark

CALIFORNIA WRITERS' ROUNDTABLE WRITING CONTESTS
Under the auspices of the Los Angeles Chapter of the Women's National Book Association, The California Writers' Roundtable is proud to announce its annual writing contests.

The Opinion Essay Contest offers a First Prize of $50; Second Prize of $25; and Third Prize of $10. The Poetry Contest offers a First Prize of $50; Second Prize of $25; and Third Prize of $10. Short Story Contest First Prize is $150; Second Prize is $75; and Third Prize is $25.

There are no entry fees for WNBA members. WNBA members should send a photocopy of proof of membership in lieu of entry fee(s).

Rules and Guidelines

OPINION ESSAY CONTEST
Entries should be 1,000 to 1,500 words. All entries should be typed, double spaced on one side of 8-1/2 x 11 inch bond paper. Submit three (3) copies. Word count must be in the upper right-hand corner. The author's name should NOT appear on the entry. A 3x5 card should be included, with the author's name, address, and phone number, along with the title of the essay, enclosed in a small, sealed envelope with the essay title only on the outside. Non-member's entry fee is $3.00.

POETRY CONTEST
Authors are limited to a total of three (3) submissions, no more than 42 lines each. Themes may be general, humorous, haiku, etc., but all poetry will be judged together, not in individual categories. All entries must be typed (please, no Script or Gothic fonts!) on standard 8-1/2 x 11 inch paper. The title of the poem must appear on each page. Send three (3) copies of each poem submitted. Include, in a small envelope, a 3 x 5 card with the author's name, address, and phone number, along with the title(s) of the poem(s) submitted. Seal the outside. Do not put the author's name on the poems or on the outside of the sealed envelope. If these rules are not followed, submissions may be disqualified. Non-member's entry fee is $3.00 per poem.

SHORT STORY CONTEST

One entry may be submitted per author, with a 3,000 word limit. Manuscripts must be typed, double spaced on standard paper, 8-1/2 x 11 inches with a 1 inch margin on all sides. The title of the short story must appear on each page; and all pages should be numbered.

Send three (3) copies of the short story. Include a small envelope with a 3x5 card containing the author's name, address, and phone number. The title of the short story only should appear on the outside of the envelope. Do not put the author's name on the manuscript. Nonmember's entry fee is $5.00.

General Rules

All submissions must be unpublished as of the contest deadline date.

Please: No plastic covers, cardboard backs, file folders, plastic clips, staples or binder clips!

If an entry is submitted more than 90 days prior to the deadline, please post-date check(s) to the deadline date. All checks must be payable to California Writers' Roundtable.

If Judges do not deem entries to be of professional quality in any contest, no prize will be awarded.

Six entries will constitute a contest. If less than six entries are received in a contest, that contest will be canceled and the entry fees and entries will be returned to authors. Otherwise, if you wish your entry to be returned, please include a self-addressed envelope with adequate postage for one manuscript. No manuscripts will be returned without sufficient postage! Envelopes will be seen only by the Contest Chairperson, not the Judges. Judges do not know the authors' names until after winning entries are announced.

Decisions of the Judges will be final.

Results of all contests will be announced at the November meeting of the Women's National Book Association, Los Angeles Chapter. For a winners' list, please include a self-addressed, stamped envelope with entry.

FAILURE TO ADHERE TO GUIDELINES WILL RESULT IN DISQUALIFICATION OF ENTRY WITH NO REFUND OF ENTRY FEE!

Mail entry to: Women's National Book Association, P.O. Box 7034, Beverly Hills, CA 90212-0034.

Entry Form
2001 California Writers' Roundtable Contests

Name ____________________

WNBA Member? ____________________

Address ____________________

Phone ____________________

City ____________________ State ____________________

Zip ____________________

CATEGORY: ( ) Short Story ( ) Poetry ( ) Opinion Essay

( ) I enclose $__________
payable to California Writers' Roundtable for my entry.

( ) I enclose my proof of membership in WNBA in lieu of entry fee.

CANADIAN AUTHORS ASSOCIATION LITERARY AWARDS

Canadian Authors Association
National Office
Box 419, 320 South Shores Road
Campbellford, Ontario K0L 1L0 Canada
Phone (705) 653-0323; Fax (705) 653-0593
E-mail canauth@redden.on.ca
Website www.CanAuthors.org/national.html

In its long tradition of "writers helping writers", the CAA has been proud to honour fellow writers who have achieved success in their chosen genres. In co-operation with the donors of the following prizes, the CAA administers the award process, culminating in the winners reading from their work during the annual CAA conference, and the presentation of the awards at the Annual Awards Dinner. We have been delighted to hear from many of our winners that the prizes they received have made a difference in their careers, allowing them greater access to continued success.

Deadline: December 15, 2001

LELA COMMON AWARD FOR CANADIAN HISTORY
Winners receive $2,500 and a silver medal. The CAA Lela Common Award for Canadian History was established in 1997. It is made possible by a generous bequest from the estate of Lela Florence Common, a long-time member of the Hamilton branch of the Canadian Authors Association. Mrs. Common had a life-long interest in history, and was active in research and writing on historical topics. Past award winners: 1997, Phil Jenkins, *An Acre of Time*; 1998, Dorothy Harley, *Eber Images of Justice*; and 1999, Rod McQueen, *The Eatons*.

All entries must be historical non-fiction on Canadian topics by Canadian authors. The books must be English-language literature for adults (not "young adults"). Translations are not eligible, nor are books published at the author's expense.

Deadline: December 15, 2001

CANADIAN AUTHORS ASSOCIATION AWARD FOR FICTION
Winners receive $2,500 and a silver medal. In 1975 the CAA reinstated its awards for literary achievement, a programme originally begun in 1937 with the creation of the Governor-General's medals for literature. The objective of reinstatement of the awards was to honour writing that achieves literary excellence without sacrificing popular appeal. The

CAA award for Fiction was funded by Harlequin Enterprises of Toronto, from 1975 through 1997. For 1998, it was funded by Chapters.

Throughout their existence, these CAA Literary Awards have been designed as objective rewards for excellence. Judging is carried out by panels selected in confidence. No short lists are published. The Journal (CBC) has referred to them as "The major awards given annually by authors to authors." Past Fiction Awards winners: 1997, Ann-Marie MacDonald, *Fall on Your Knees*; 1998, Rita Donovan, *Landed*; and 1999, Wayne Johnston, *The Colony of Unrequited Dreams*.

Entries must be full-length English-language literature for adults by Canadian authors. Reprints are not eligible, nor is self-published work or work which has been published at the author's expense.

Deadline: December 15, 2001

BIRKS FAMILY FOUNDATION AWARD FOR CANADIAN BIOGRAPHY
Winners receive $2,500 and a silver medal. This new award is made possible through the generosity of the Birks Family Foundation. It is for a biographical work about a Canadian written by a Canadian. Past award winners: 1998, Charlotte Gray, *Mrs.King: the Life and Times of Isobel Mackenzie King*; and 1999, Leslie Yeo, *A Thousand and One First Nights.*

Entries must be full-length English-language literature for adults by Canadian authors. Reprints are not eligible nor is self-published work or work which has been published at the author's expense.

Deadline: December 15, 2001

JUBILEE AWARD FOR SHORT STORIES
Winners receive $2,500 and a silver medal. The CAA Jubilee Award for short stories was established in 1997 by a generous anonymous donor. It allows recognition of Canada's outstanding writers of short stories who have not been eligible for the CAA Award for Fiction. Past award winners: 1997, Alice Munro, *Selected Stories*; 1998, Joanne Gerber, *In the Misleading Absence of Light*; and 1999, Dennis Bock, *Olympia.*

All entries must be collections of short stories by a Canadian author. The stories must be English-language literature for adults (not "young adults").

Translations are not eligible nor are books published at the author's expense.

Deadline: March 31, 2001

AIR CANADA AWARD
This award, provided by Air Canada and administered by the Canadian Authors Association since 1979, honours a Canadian writer under the age of thirty deemed to show the most promise for the future in the field of literary creation. The CAA Air Canada Award to promising young authors is but one of several contributions made by the airline to cultural activities in Canada. Air Canada recognizes and encourages artistic achievement in many fields as part of its wide-ranging program of involvement in community affairs. Past award winners: 1997, Richard Van Camp (Fort Smith, NWT); 1998, Lynn Coady (Vancouver, BC); and 1999, Rob McLennan (Ottawa, ON).

Nominations for this prestigious prize are made through CAA branches (there are currently 15 across Canada), other writing organizations or publishers. Self-nominations are not accepted. Membership in CAA is not required.

There are no restrictions as to the type of writing done by the nominee. It may be in the field of fiction, non-fiction, poetry or playwriting for any medium.

Deadline: December 15, 2001

CANADIAN AUTHORS ASSOCIATION AWARDS FOR POETRY AND DRAMA
Winners receive $2,500 and a silver medal. In 1975 the CAA reinstated its awards for literary achievement, a program originally begun in 1937 with the creation of the Governor General's medals for literature. The objective of reinstatement of the awards was to honour writing that achieves literary excellence without sacrificing popular appeal. The CAA Awards for Poetry and Drama (for any medium) were funded by Harlequin Enterprises of Toronto from 1975 to 1997. In 1998, they are funded by a member of the CAA who chooses to remain anonymous.

Throughout their existence, these CAA Literary Awards have been designed as objective rewards for excellence. Judging is carried out by panels selected in confidence. No short lists are published. The Journal (CBC) has referred to them as "The major awards given annually by authors to authors." Past Poetry Award winners: 1997, E.D. Blodget, *Apostrophes: Woman at a Piano*; 1998, Anne Szumigalski, *On Glassy Wings;* and 1999, Janice Kulyk Keefer, *Marrying the Sea.* Past Drama Award winners: 1997, Jason Sherman, *The League of Nathans*; 1998, Judith Thompson *Sled*; and 1999, David Young, *Inexpressible Island.*

Entries must be full-length English-language literature for adults, by Canadian authors. Reprints are not eligible, nor is self-published work or work which has been published at the author's expense.

Deadline: December 31, 2001

VICKY METCALF AWARDS
The Vicky Metcalf Awards were created in 1963 by the Toronto librarian whose name they bear. There are now three separate awards: $10,000 cash prize for a body of work, whether fiction, non-fiction, poetry or picture books; $3,000 cash prize for a short story published in an English language periodical or anthology; and $1,000 cash prize to the editor responsible for publishing the prize-winning short story, if published in a Canadian periodical or anthology. "The prizes are given solely to stimulate writing for children by Canadian writers," said Mrs. Metcalf when she established the awards. "We must encourage the writing of material for Canadian children without setting any restricting formulas."

Past Body of Work Award winners: 1997, Tim Wynne-Jones; 1998, Kit Pearson; and 1999, Joan Clark. Past Short Story Award winners: 1996, Bernice Friensen; 1998, W.D. Valgardson; and 1999, Anne Carter. Past Short Story Editor Award winners: 1996, Susan Musgrave; 1998, Shelley Tanaka; and 1999, Linda Holeman.

Nominations may be made by an individual person, publisher, or association.

A Body of Work or Short Story Award may be won by a writer only once.

In the case of the Body of Work Award, the nomination should be in letter form listing the published works of the nominee along with the biography of the author.

In the short story category, four tearsheets, or photocopies of the published work must be submitted along with a biography of the writer, and the name of the editor.

ALLAN SANGSTER AWARD
Annually since 1968 the CAA has honoured one of its members for long and meritorious service. This award is in memory of Allan S. Sangster, a CBC producer, especially in the realm of classical music, who had a particular interest in the field of Canadian writing. He was urged to accept the National Presidency but felt he could not spare the time this

office deserved and remained Vice-President for Ontario until his untimely death in 1967. Originally the award consisted of a stylized owl motif cast in black iron by a Winnipeg sculptor discovered by then National President, Vinnia Hoogstraten. In 1973, her husband Neil was invited to submit a variation on this theme for the Association's re-instituted silver medal (1975). In time, it became the logo of the national organization. Past award winners: 1997, Eleanor McEachern; 1998, Anna Marie Kowalski; and 1999, Bert Reynolds.

The most recent winner of the Allan Sangster Award is responsible for arranging a secret vote by all former recipients to choose the next winner and making the presentation at the conclusion of the annual Awards Dinner.

It may be won only once by any individual.

THE CANADIAN CHILDREN'S BOOK CENTRE

Hadley Dyer, Coordinator
The Canadian Children's Book Centre
35 Spadina Road
Toronto, Ontario M5R 2S9 Canada
Phone (416) 975-0010; Fax (416) 975-1839
E-mail ccbc@sympatico.ca

THE GEOFFREY BILSON AWARD FOR HISTORICAL FICTION
$1,000 prize. The purpose of the award is to reward excellence in the writing of an outstanding work of historical fiction for young people by a Canadian author, published in the previous calendar year.

The selection jury of the Award shall be drawn from the following categories: writer, bookseller, children's book specialist (book reviewer, teacher at a post-secondary institution, etc.), historian, and librarian. A member of the Our Choice Committee of The Canadian Children's Book Centre will act as chairperson, and the jury will be approved by the Board of Director's of the Centre. The voting process shall be by majority. Voting records shall be maintained by the Centre for each title submitted. Committee deliberations will remain confidential, except at the written request of the author, illustrator or publisher concerned. Selections of the jury will remain confidential until a written announcement is mailed simultaneously to participating publishers and sufficient grace has been allowed for delivery.

Guidelines
All books written by Canadians and selected for inclusion in Our Choice will be eligible for consideration.

A Canadian shall, for the purposes of the Committee, be deemed a citizen of Canada or a permanent resident who has lived in Canada for at least two (2) years.

Historical fiction is fiction in which history informs the work in a significant way and is historically authentic. A historical setting alone does not constitute a work of historical fiction.

Contact: Hadley Dyer, Coordinator

THE NORMA FLECK AWARD FOR A CANADIAN CHILDREN'S NON-FICTION BOOK

$10,000 prize. The creation of this award will serve to enhance recognition of authors of this burgeoning genre. "Until now, there has been little distinct recognition in Canada for Canadian children's non-fiction books, although this country is acknowledged internationally as a leader in the publishing of high caliber books of this genre," says Don Mills, President of the Canadian Children's Book Centre. "Therefore, it is extremely gratifying that the new award will recognize this category of books and the talented people who create them."

Text must be of exceptional quality and present the subject matter in a way that both informs and excites interest. Visuals, also of an exceptional quality, should clarify, extend and complement the text.

Only those books written and illustrated by Canadian citizens or landed immigrants will be considered.

The winning entry will be based on an original subject or will explore a familiar subject in a new and interesting way.

Research must be sound and the information contained in the book must be correct and current. Treatment of the material must be respectful of the subject and of the reader.

All nominated books must have good production values, with a visual design that presents the material in a clear and engaging manner.

Publishers may nominate trade books published between May 1, 1999 and April 30, 2000. Non-fiction books in the following categories are eligible: cultural/the arts, concept, science, biography, history, geography, reference, sports, and activities and pastimes.

There will be five short-listed books resulting in one winner and four honour books.

The award is for the book. The award will go to the author unless 40 percent or more of the text area is composed of original illustrations, in which case the award will be divided equally between the author and the artist.

CANADIAN HISTORICAL ASSOCIATION

Canadian Historical Association
395 Wellington
Ottawa, Ontario K1A ON3 Canada
Phone (613) 233-7885; Fax (613) 567-3110

Deadline: November 1, 2004

FRANCOIS-XAVIER GARNEAU MEDAL
The Canadian Historical Association is pleased to announce the seventh competition for its most prestigious prize, the Francois-Xavier Garneau Medal. The prize consists of a specially-minted medal bearing the name of the recipient, and a cash award of $2000. The prize will be presented at the annual meeting of the CHA in June 2005.

The Garneau Prize, established by the CHA to commemorate Canada's first serious historian, Francois-Xavier Garneau (1809-1866), shall be awarded to a Canadian citizen, or landed immigrant living in Canada, who has published an outstanding scholarly book in the field of history during the five-year period 1993-1997. The award of the prize shall be based on a published work in either of the two official languages of Canada.

The four previous winners of the Garneau Medal have established a high standard of excellence: Louise Dechene (1980) for *Habitants et marchands de Montreal au XVIIe siecles* (Librairie Plon), Michael Bliss (1984) for *A Canadian Millionaire: The Life and Business Times of Sir Joseph Flavelle* (Macmillan of Canada), John M. Beattie (1989) for *Crime and the Courts in England 1660-1800* (Princeton University Press), and Joy Parr (1994) for *The Gender of Breadwinners: Women, Men and Change in two Industrial Towns, 1880-1950* (University of Toronto Press).

Those wishing to submit works with an imprint for the years 1993-1997 inclusive should send one copy directly to each judge, clearly marked The Francois-Xavier Garneau Medal.

Deadline for entries is November 1, 2004.

Deadline: December 1, 2001

SIR JOHN A. MACDONALD PRIZE
The CHA is pleased to announce its twenty-fourth Sir John A. Macdonald Prize competition. The prize in the amount of $1,000 will be awarded by the CHA at its Annual Meeting in May 2002, for the non-fic-

tion work of Canadian history "judged to have made the most significant contribution to an understanding of the Canadian past".

Publishers wishing to submit works with a 2001 imprint should forward one copy of each entry to each of the jury members on or before December 1, 2001, clearly marking each The Sir John A. Macdonald Prize.

Authors of eligible books are encouraged to check with their publishers to ensure their work has been submitted.

Diaries, textbooks, edited collections of essays, translations, or books of documents are not eligible for consideration.

Deadline: February 1, 2002

THE ALBERT B. COREY PRIZE
The Albert B. Corey Prize in Canadian-American Relations, jointly sponsored by the Canadian Historical Association and the American Historical Association, will be awarded in May 2002 at the annual meeting of the CHA. The prize, which carries an award of $1,000 (Canadian), will be awarded to the best book dealing with the history of Canadian-American relations or the history of both countries.

Books bearing an imprint of 2000-2001 are eligible for the 2002 prize. One copy of each entry should be sent to each judge.

The deadline for entries is February 1, 2002.

All entries should be clearly marked "Corey Prize".

Deadline: December 1, 2001

WALLACE K. FERGUSON PRIZE
The CHA is pleased to announce its Ferguson Prize competition. The prize in the amount of $1,000 will be awarded to a Canadian citizen or Canadian landed immigrant who has published the outstanding scholarly book in a field of history OTHER THAN CANADIAN HISTORY during the past year. The award will be given in May 2002 at the annual meeting of the CHA.

Publishers wishing to submit works with a 2000 imprint should send one copy of each entry to each judge on or before December 1, 2001, clearly marked, Wallace K. Ferguson Prize.

Authors of eligible books are encouraged to check with their publishers to ensure their work has been submitted.

Diaries, textbooks, edited collections of essays, translations, or books of documents are not eligible for consideration.

Deadline: November 30, 2001

JOHN BULLEN PRIZE

The CHA is pleased to announce the John Bullen Prize competition. The prize in the amount of $500 will be awarded in 2002 for the Outstanding historical dissertation written by a Canadian Citizen or landed immigrant living in Canada accepted for the doctoral degree at a Canadian University between October 1, 1999 and September 30, 2000. The award will be given in May 2002 at the annual meeting of the CHA.

Departments should send a complete submission to each judge on or before November 30, 2001.

Each complete submission must include a copy of the dissertation; a copy of a letter from the university's faculty of graduate studies attesting that the dissertation was accepted for the doctoral degree between the period October 1, 1999 and September 30, 2000; and a copy of a letter of presentation from the department head, chair, or graduate chair.

Where the department submits more than a single dissertation, the letter should address the qualities of the various submissions.

Clearly mark John Bullen Prize and send to above address.

Deadline: December 31, 2001

THE CLIO AWARDS

The Regional History Committee of the Canadian Historical Association wishes to announce that it is soliciting nominations for its Clio Awards. These annual awards are given for meritorious publications, or for exceptional contributions by individuals or organizations to regional history.

A copy of the nominations and supportive documentation for candidates who have made contributions to regional history should be submitted before December 31, 2001 to the appropriate regional representative and two other copies to the CHA.

Books must bear a 2000 copyright imprint, or, if not previously submitted, a 1999 imprint.

Clearly mark The Clio Awards and send to above address.

Deadline: February 1, 2001

THE HILDA NEATBY PRIZE IN WOMEN'S HISTORY
The purpose of the Hilda Neatby Prize in Women's History, awarded since 1983 by the Canadian Committee on Women's History at the annual meeting of the Canadian Historical Association, is to encourage the publication of scholarly articles in women's history and gender's history as it relates to women, in Canadian journals and books. Two prizes are awarded, one for best article in English and the other one for best article in French.

Any academic article published in Canada during 2000 and deemed to make an original and scholarly contribution to the field of women's history is eligible for nomination for the 2001 Neatby Prize.

Send nominations and three copies of the nominated article to the CHA, c/o the Hilda Neatby Prize Committee by February 1, 2001.

CAROLINA QUARTERLY

CB# 3520 Greenlaw Hall
University of North Carolina
Chapel Hill, NC 27599-3520

Deadline: Ongoing

ANNUAL CHARLES B. WOOD AWARD
Prize: $500. Writers without major publication credits are eligible for the annual Charles B. Wood Award for distinguished writing. The award goes to the best poem or short story by an unestablished writer published in each volume.

No separate application is required. Everything published in *The Carolina Quarterly* is considered.

Submit work to the appropriate editor. Editor: Robert M. West, Fiction editor: Brian Carpenter, Poetry editors: Al Benthall and Christopher Windolph.

CASE WESTERN RESERVE UNIVERSITY

Department of Theater Arts
10900 Euclid Avenue
Cleveland, OH 44106-7077

Deadline: May 15, 2001 postmark

THE MARC A. KLEIN PLAYWRITING AWARD
The Marc A. Klein Playwriting Award is an annual playwriting award designed to encourage and stimulate artistic growth among student playwrights currently enrolled at an American college or university. In addition to rewarding creativity, the award also was established to provide CWRU students with the experience of participating in the production of a previously unproduced play.

The award carries a cash prize of $1,000 and the play will receive a full mainstage production by CWRU's Department of Theater Arts, which is solely responsible for the selection of the award-winning script.

The winning entry will be announced by August 1, 2001.

Rules and Guidelines

1. The author of the award-winning manuscript will receive a total of $1,000: $500 upon the announcement of the award and an additional $500 during the rehearsal period in order to defray travel cost and living expenses while he or she is in residence for the world premiere production of his or her play.

2. Playwrights must be currently enrolled at an American college or university.

3. Manuscripts must be endorsed by a faculty member of a university theater or drama department.

4. Only plays which have not been professionally produced or received tradebook publication are eligible. Scripts given staged readings or nonproduction oriented workshops may be entered.

5. Submission is restricted to an original full-length play or an evening of related short plays. Musicals and children's plays will not be accepted.

6. A playwright may submit as many scripts as he or she wishes, each accompanied by an endorsed application form.

7. The director of the Klein Award play reserves the right to work with the playwright on script revisions in advance of production.

8 All scripts must be accompanied by a stamped, self-addressed (manuscript-size) return envelope and by an official Marc A. Klein Playwriting Award application form. Entries must be postmarked no later than May 15, 2001.

Mail entries to: The Marc A. Klein Playwriting Award, Department of Theater Arts, Case Western Reserve University, 10900 Euclid Ave., Cleveland, OH 44106-7077.

The Marc A. Klein Playwriting Award Application

Please type or print clearly.

Name ____

Current Address ____

City State Zip Code ____

Permanent address, if different than above. ____

____

____

University/college ____

Title of Play ____

Manuscript endorsed by:

____

Name ____

City/State/Zip ____

Signature ____

I certify that the manuscript I have submitted is an original script and has never been produced or published in any tradebooks. I understand and accept the criteria and conditions that govern The Marc A. Klein Playwriting Award and will abide by the final decision of the judges.

Signature ____

Date ____

CENTER PRESS

Gabriella Stone, Publisher
Box 16452
Encino, CA 91416
Website http://www.concentric.net/–medianet/index.html

Deadlines: March 15, June 15, September 15, & December 15, 2001

THE MASTERS LITERARY AWARDS
The Masters Literary Awards, sponsored by Center Press since 1981, include: Fiction, Non-fiction, and Poetry. Quarterly nominations are made for honorable mention, from which are chosen a yearly Grand Prize of $1,000. Center Press retains the option to publish winners in our Internet Journal. Copyrights remain with the authors. Published and unpublished manuscripts are eligible. Three literary professionals judge the awards. Winning names are circulated through public media, libraries, schools, subscriber membership, and over the Internet.

Guidelines
FICTION: Submit one short story, vignette, or novel, stage, or screenplay excerpt of no more than 20 pages, up to a maximum of 5,000 words. Current material is preferred. Any style or genre is acceptable, with an emphasis placed on literary merit.

NON-FICTION: Submit one essay or editorial manuscript, no more than 20 pages, with a 5,000 word maximum, illustrating social consciousness. Humor and satire are welcome.

POETRY: Submit a maximum of five poems or song lyric pages (no tapes) totaling no more than 150 lines. Any poetic style or genre is acceptable, but a clear and fresh voice, discipline, natural rhythm, and a certain individuality should be evident.

Submissions are accepted throughout the year. Nominations will be made March 15th, June 15th, September 15th, and December 15th. Submissions received prior to each date are eligible for the subsequent award. No award will be granted if a manuscript of sufficient merit is not received by the deadline. No originals please! Manuscripts are not returned! There are no restrictions on gender, ethnicity, or age but manuscripts must be in English language. A #10 self-addressed, stamped envelope is required. A *vitae* or brief letter of introduction must accompany all entries. The suggested reading fee is $15.00 per entry. Make checks payable to the Masters Literary Award and mail your submission to:

Gabriella Stone, Publisher
Center Press/ Box 16452, Encino, CA 91416.

CENTER THEATRE ENSEMBLE

Play Contest Coordinator
1346 West Devon Avenue
Chicago, IL 60660
Office Phone (773) 508-0200; Fax (773) 508-9584
Box Office Phone (773) 508-5422

Deadline: August 15, 2001 postmark

CENTER THEATRE ENSEMBLE INTERNATIONAL PLAYWRITING CONTEST

The Center Theatre Ensemble (CTE) International Playwriting Contest offers a Grand Prize of $300 and production option along with honorable mention of finalists. Winners will be published in a mailing sent to TCG theatres, which will include a description and synopsis of each play.

Rules and Guidelines

1. Full-length scripts only, cast size of eight or less. Doubling is possible. We recommend casting be available for age range 20-50's to fit the needs of our acting ensemble. Minimal technical or set requirements.
2. All styles and subject matter accepted.
3. Plays must be standard script form, plus a one-page synopsis and character breakdown.
4. Name, address, and phone number must appear on the title page or your entry is invalid.
5. You may enter more than one play. Each must be unpublished, unproduced, and not under option.
6. Each entry must be accompanied by an official entry form or facsimile, and a check or money order made payable to "Center Theatre Ensemble" for the required $15 entry fee.
7. Entries must be stapled or clipped. Scripts will not be returned so submit good quality photocopies. Keep the original.
8. Every qualified entry will be read by the judges and their decisions will be final. Prize money will be awarded to the top three finalists if no grand prize is found.
9. Entries must be postmarked by midnight August 15, 2000. We cannot acknowledge receipt of play scripts. Play award is in lieu of production royalties. Winners may be given a workshop or full production under contracted agreement.

Center Theatre Ensemble International Playwriting Contest Entry Form

Name ______________________________

Address ______________________________

____

____

Entry Fee $15 ______________________________

Phone ______________________________

Title of Play ______________________________

____

Cast Size ______________________________

Theme ______________________________

____

____

Please mail entries to:
Center Theater Ensemble, Play Contest Coordinator, 1346 West Devon Ave., Chicago, IL 60660
Office (773) 508-0200; Box Office (773) 508-5422; Fax (773) 508-9584

CENTRAL OHIO FICTION WRITERS

4700 Glendon Road
Columbus, OH 43229
Contest Coordinators: Beverly Shippey, (614) 888-7037
Jodelle Brohard, (614) 891-9680

Deadline: August 31, 2001 postmark

CENTRAL OHIO FICTION WRITERS IGNITE THE FLAME CONTEST
The Central Ohio Fiction Writers (COFW) announce their 7th annual Ignite the Flame Contest for unpublished writers. The categories are Contemporary and Historical, but futuristic entries will be accepted and judged by Contemporary judges, and Time Travel will fall under the Historical category. Entry fee is $20. Score sheets and critiques will be given to each entry. Total scores will be averaged to determine winners.

Rules and Guidelines
Entrants must be Romance Writers of America (RWA) members unpublished in book-length fiction. (You may contact the contest coordinators for membership information.) Submit three (3) copies of hero and heroine's first meeting, up to 15 pages, plus a one-page setup. Include a self-addressed Priority Envelope ($3.00 postage) for return of manuscripts and score sheets. Entrants may enter both categories or submit more than one entry for each category, but a separate fee of $20 must accompany each entry as well as a separate self-addressed, stamped envelope for return of manuscripts.

Entries must be postmarked by August 31, 2001. Contest is limited to the first 100 entries. Winners will be notified by October 15, 2001.

Manuscripts should be typed (photocopies are acceptable), double spaced with one inch margins, and bound by a large paper clip/clasp. Include a one-page setup describing necessary background information about the scene you are submitting. Please start the entry as page one, even if it is extricated from an existing manuscript. Header on every page should contain only the title in the upper left-hand corner and page number in the upper right-hand corner. The author's name must not appear anywhere on the manuscript.

Each submission will be evaluated by two qualified writers, at least one being a published author. If a 20 point variance occurs, a third judging will take place (the two closest scores will be averaged to determine winners).

Total scores will be averaged to determine winners. The top three finalists in each category will be reviewed by editors in the Romance Publishing Industry. First, second, and third place winners in each category will also receive certificates of merit. Fourth and fifth place winners will receive honorable mention certificates.

Each entry must be accompanied by:

1.___ $20 entry fee for each category entered.

2.___ Completed Entry Form/Signed Contestant's Agreement.

3.___ Self-addressed Priority Envelope w/$3.00 Postage for return of entries.

4.___ Three (3) copies of first meeting scene (15 pages maximum) plus one-page setup.

5.___ NOTE: Author's name must not appear anywhere on the manuscript.

For more information contact:
Beverly Shippey, phone (614) 888-7037 or
Jodelle Brohard, phone (614) 891-9680
4700 Glendon Road, Columbus, OH 43229

Contest Entry Form
2001 COFW-RWA Ignite the Flame Contest

PLEASE COMPLETE THIS FORM (PHOTOCOPIES ARE ACCEPTABLE) AND ENCLOSE IT WITH THREE (3) COPIES OF YOUR CONTEST ENTRY. REMEMBER TO INCLUDE YOUR $20 ENTRY FEE AND SELF-ADDRESSED, STAMPED ENVELOPE WITH SUFFICIENT POSTAGE FOR RETURN OF YOUR ENTRY. THOSE WITH INSUFFICIENT POSTAGE MAY BE HELD OR DESTROYED COORDINATOR'S DISCRETION.

Send to: Beverly D. Shippey, 4700 Glendon Rd., Columbus, OH 43229
Deadline: August 31, 2000
Questions: Call Bev at (614) 888-7037

NAME (Please Print): ______________________________

ADDRESS: ______________________________

____

TELEPHONE WITH AREA CODE: ______________________________

R.W.A.# ______________________________

TITLE OF ENTRY: ______________________________

____

CATEGORY: (Check one) ____ Contemporary ____ Historical

CONTESTANT'S AGREEMENT

I have read, I understand, and I agree to abide by the official rules of the COFW-RWA Ignite the Flame Contest. I further understand and agree that any questions regarding the interpretation of the official rules and any matters relating to the Ignite the Flame Contest which are not specifically covered by the official rules will be decided by the contest officials in any such matters. I also realize and accept that manuscript judging is subjective by nature. Accordingly, I will accept and abide by the decisions of any judges and/or contest officials regarding finalists or winners for the contest. I understand and accept as reasonable the statements above. I am signing this Contestant's Agreement in exchange for the acceptance and processing of my entry in COFW-RWA's Ignite the Flame Contest. I realize that COFW-RWA, the contest officials, and the contest judges are relying on the truth and sincerity of my statements. I further realize that my contest entry would not be accepted if I did not show acceptance of this Contestant's Agreement by signing my name below.

Name: ______________________________ Date: __________

THE CHELSEA AWARDS

Chelsea Award Competition
P.O. Box 1040
York Beach, ME 03910

Chelsea, a nonprofit literary magazine founded in 1958 and appearing twice a year, awards two annual prizes of $1000, for the best work of short fiction and for the best group of poems selected by the editors in anonymous competitions. Winning entries are published in *Chelsea*, and all work entered is considered for publication. The magazine has been funded in part by the National Endowment for the Arts and the New York State Council of the Arts as well as private foundations.

Deadline: December 15, 2001 postmark
Poetry Competition: Submit four to six poems. The entire entry should not exceed 500 lines. The editors look for overall excellence; it is not necessary that the poems be related thematically. Annual deadline: postmarked by December 15.

Deadline: June 15, 2001 postmark
Fiction Competition: Send only one work of fiction. The manuscripts should not exceed 30 typed pages or about 7500 words. The editors welcome both traditional and experimental fiction. Annual deadline: postmarked by June 15.

Guidelines
All manuscripts must be typed. Fiction must be double-spaced with standard margins; poetry may be single-spaced. The writer's name should not appear on the manuscript itself. Instead, include a single, separate cover sheet with title(s), name, address, and telephone number. Only previously unpublished work is eligible, and the manuscript should not be under consideration elsewhere or scheduled for book publication within eight months of the competition deadline. Manuscripts cannot be returned.

An entry fee of $10 is required, for which entrants will receive a subscription to *Chelsea*. Please make checks payable to Chelsea Associates, Inc. (Be sure to notify the editors promptly of any changes of address since the post office will not automatically forward copies of the magazine).

Winners will be announced about two months after each deadline. Include an self-addressed, stamped envelope for notification of competition results.

General submissions and other matters of business should be directed to the Editor, Box 773, Cooper Station, New York, NY 10276-0773

ChLA RESEARCH FELLOWSHIP AND SCHOLARSHIPS

Scholarship Committee
Children's Literature Association
P.O. Box 138
Battle Creek, MI 49016-0138
Phone (616) 965-3568
E-Mail chla@mlc.lib.mi.us

Deadline: February 1, 2001 postmark

ChLA Research Fellowships and Scholarships have a combined maximum fund of $1,000 per year, and individual awards may range from $250 to $1,000, based on the number and needs of the winning applicants. The fellowships are awarded for proposals dealing with criticism or original scholarship with the expectation that the undertaking will lead to publication and make a significant contribution to the field of children's literature in the area of scholarship or criticism. In honor of the achievement and dedication of Dr. Margaret P. Esmonde, proposals that deal with critical or original work in the areas of fantasy or science fiction for children or adolescents will be awarded the Margaret P. Esmonde Memorial Scholarship.

Funds are not intended for work leading to the completion of a professional degree. The awards may be used only for research-related expenses, such as travel to special collections or materials and supplies. The awards may not be used for obtaining advanced degrees, for researching or writing a thesis or dissertation, for textbook writing, or for pedagogical projects. Winners must either be members of the Children's Literature Association or join the association before they can receive any funds. Winners should acknowledge ChLA in any publication resulting from the award.

Guidelines

Applications and supporting materials should be written in or translated into English.

Winners will be notified shortly before the annual ChLA conference and the awards will be announced at the conference. Winners are urged to attend the conference if at all possible and will be notified in sufficient time to make plans to collect travel funding from their institution.

All proposals are read and judged by the ChLA Scholarship Committee.

Members of the Executive Board of ChLA and of the Scholarship Committee are not eligible to apply. Recipients of a Research Fellowship or Scholarship are not eligible to reapply until the third year from the date of the first award. (In the event the ChLA Board institutes another time interval – whether longer or shorter — the vote of the Board shall supercede the three-year interval rule).

If there are no proposals for any of the grants that the Scholarship Committee deems of quality to support ChLA's aims, no grants will be given.

Grant recipients should be prepared to submit either a progress report or a summary of the completed project to the Scholarship Committee the February of the year following the award. Copies of all publications resulting from the research fellowships and scholarships should also be forwarded to the Committee.

Application should include the following information:

1. Name, telephone number, mailing address and e-mail address if available.

2. Academic institution and academic status (professor, librarian, student, etc.), or institution applicant is affiliated with (library, publisher, etc.)

3. A detailed description (not exceeding three single-spaced pages) of the research proposal, indicating the nature of the project, where it will be carried out, the expected date of completion, and the projected costs of such main budget items as transportation, mailings, subsistence funds, and supplies.

4. A *vitae* which includes a bibliography of major publications and scholarly achievements (degrees, honors, etc.).

5. Three letters of reference attesting specifically to the significance of the project and to the applicant's capacity to carry it out. These letters can accompany the application or may be mailed directly to the Scholarship Committee.

Deadline(s): send five (5) copies of the application postmarked by February 1, 2001.

CHIRON REVIEW PRESS

Jane Hathaway, Poetry Contest Coordinator
522 E. South Avenue
St. John, KS 67576-2212

Michael Hathaway, Editor
Chiron Review Chapbook Contest
702 N. Prairie
St. John, KS 67576-1516

Deadline: July 20, 2001

CHIRON REVIEW POETRY CONTEST
The *Chiron Review* Poetry Contest awards seven prizes for poetry. First Prize is $100 and a full-page feature in the Winter 2001 issue of *Chiron Review*. Second Prize is $50 and full-page feature in the Winter 2001 issue of *Chiron Review*. Third Prize (five awarded) is a one-year subscription to *Chiron Review*; a poetry book from CR Press; and the winning poem published in Winter 2001 issue of *Chiron Review*.

Guidelines

1. Any subject, style, or length is acceptable. There are no taboos.

2. Previously published, simultaneous submissions, and clean photocopies are acceptable for the contest.

3. The poet's name and address should appear on each page, preferably on the back.

4. The contest opens January 1, 2001 and entries must be received by July 20, 2001. Winners will be notified by September 1, 2000.

5. Enclose a self-addressed, stamped envelope (optional) for return of manuscript. Also enclose a separate, large, self-addressed, stamped manila envelope for a copy of the issue with winning poetry, or a regular self-addressed, stamped envelope for winner's list only. Please specify what envelopes are for.

6. Entry fee is $5 for six poems. There is no limit on entries. Cash preferred. Checks must be made out to Chiron Review, U.S. funds only.

7. Send to: Chiron Review Poetry Contest, Jane Hathaway, Contest Coordinator, 522 E. South Ave., St. John, KS 67576-2212.

Deadline: September 1, 2001

CHIRON REVIEW PRESS CHAPBOOK CONTEST

The *Chiron Review* Press Chapbook Contest is open to all poets. CR Press books are perfectbound and professionally typeset. The winning chapbook will be copyrighted in author's name. The winner will receive 50% of the press run of 100-200 copies.

Guidelines

1. Send complete manuscript, no queries.

2. Previously published, simultaneous submissions, and clean photocopies are acceptable.

3. Any subject or style admissible. There are no taboos.

4. Include your name and address on a separate sheet as the last page of manuscript, along with magazine acknowledgments, if any.

5. Send a large self-addressed, stamped envelope (optional) for return of your manuscript and the title of the winning manuscript and author's name; or a small self-addressed, stamped envelope for the winner's name only.

6. Manuscripts must be between 32 and 48 pages.

7. The entry fee is $10 per manuscript. There is no limit on the number of entries.

8. Deadline is September 1, 2001.

9. For a sample CR Press book include an additional $7 with your entry.

10. Send entries to: *Chiron Review* Chapbook Contest, Michael Hathaway, Editor, 702 N. Prairie, St. John, KS 67576-1516.

CINCINNATI PLAYHOUSE IN THE PARK

Box 6537
Cincinnati, OH 45206-0537
Phone (513) 345-2242; Fax (513) 345-2254
Ticket Office (513) 421-3888

Deadline: July 1, 2001 – December 31, 2001

THE LOIS AND RICHARD ROSENTHAL NEW PLAY PRIZE
Deadline: Open to submission from July 1 to December 31, 2001

The Rosenthal Prize was established in 1987 to encourage the development of new plays that are original, theatrical, strong in character and dialogue, and make a significant contribution to American Dramatic Literature.

The winning play receives a full production at Cincinnati Playhouse in the Park as part of the theatre's annual season and is given regional and national promotion. The playwright receives a $10,000 award plus travel and residency expenses for the Cincinnati rehearsal period.

Plays must be full length in any style: comedy, drama, musical and so-forth. However translations, adaptations, one-acts and any play previously submitted for the Rosenthal Prize are not eligible. Plays must be unpublished prior to submission and may not have received a fullscale, professional production. Plays that have had a workshop, reading, or non-professional production are still eligible.

Submit a two-page abstract including title, character breakdown, story synopsis and playwright biography or resume, along with five pages of sample dialogue. If submitting a musical, include a tape of selections from the score. After abstracts and dialogue samples are read, selected manuscripts will be solicited. Do not send a manuscript with or instead of the abstract and dialogue sample. Abstracts and dialogue samples are to be submitted together and then your play may be solicited after the abstract and dialogue sample are properly and carefully evaluated. All unsolicited manuscripts will be returned unread.

Submitted materials, including tapes, will be returned only if a self-addressed, stamped envelope with adequate postage is included. Only one submission per playwright each year.

CLEVELAND STATE UNIVERSITY

Rita M. Grabowski, Poetry Center Coordinator
1983 East 24th Street, Rt 1841
Cleveland, Ohio 44115-2440
Department of English
Rhodes Tower, Room 1815
Phone (216) 687-3986; Fax (216) 687-6943
E-mail poetrycenter@popmail.csuohio.edu

Deadline: February 1, 2001
Prize: $1,000 and publication in the CSU Poetry Series
The Poetry Center expects to publish one or more of the runners-up for the prize competition in its CSU Poetry Series.

Guidelines
The deadline is November 1, 2000 until postmark February 1, 2001. Late entries will not be read.

The award is offered for the best full-length volume of original poetry.

Typed or printed (no dot matrix), clear photocopies acceptable, on 8-1/2 x 11 inch standard letter-sized paper. Typed only on one side of the page with only one poem per page. Include cover sheet with manuscript title, poet's name, address, home and work phone numbers, and e-mail address. Paginated consecutively, with a table of contents, and acknowledgments. Manuscript should contain material for a book of 50-100 pages bound with a spring clip or enclosed in a plain manila folder. Do not use Duo-tangs, spiral, or any other type of binding.

Do not include art work or illustrations that need to be returned.

Include a self-addressed, stamped postcard for notification of manuscript receipt. Include a business-sized, self-addressed, stamped envelope for faster notification of results. Once submitted, manuscripts cannot be altered.

Poets whose manuscripts are selected will be given the opportunity to make changes before publication. Simultaneous submissions are acceptable as long as we are informed if the manuscript is accepted elsewhere. Please retain a copy of your manuscript because they will not be returned. Winners will be notified in June.

Each entry must be accompanied by the appropriate reading fee.

We prefer that multiple submissions be sent together, however, if multiple submissions are sent under separate cover, reference the title(s) of the other manuscript(s) on each manuscript's cover sheet.

Eligibility and Reading Fees
Manuscripts containing poems that have been previously published individually must be listed, with publisher, on an acknowledgments page. Manuscripts that have been previously published in their entirety, including self-published, are not eligible. Translations are not eligible.

There is a $20 reading fee for a full-length manuscript and a $15 reading fee for a chapbook. Make check or money order payable to Cleveland State University, payable in US currency. Do not send cash.

Chapbooks are considered during the same reading period. Minimum of 20, but fewer than 50 manuscript pages. Chapbooks are not eligible for the $1,000 prize. Indicate "chapbook" on your cover sheet, and on the memo line of your check or money order. All full-length manuscripts are considered for publication as a chapbook, so it is not necessary to send a full-length manuscript as well as a chapbook containing the same poems.

CLEVELAND POETS SERIES

For Ohio Poets:
The CSU Poetry Center also publishes a Cleveland Poets Series, open only to poets who reside in the state at the time the manuscript is submitted. There is no reading fee for this series, but these submissions are not eligible for the Poetry Center Prize.

Ohio poets may submit either chapbook-length or full-length manuscripts to this series without a reading fee. Ohio poets need to submit a $20 reading fee only if they wish to have a full-length manuscript considered for the Poetry Center Prize. Full-length manuscripts by Ohio poets that are submitted for the Poetry Center Prize will be considered automatically for the Cleveland Poets Series if they are not selected for the CSU Poetry Series.

Send all submissions to above address.

CNW/FLORIDA FREELANCE WRITERS' ASSOCIATION

CNW/FFWA
P.O. Box A
North Stratford, NH 03590
Fax (603) 922-8339; E-mail danakcnw@moose.ncia.net

Deadline: March 15, 2001 postmark

FLORIDA FREELANCE WRITERS' ASSOCIATION (FFWA)
FLORIDA STATE WRITING COMPETITION
The CNW/FFWA 18th annual Florida State Writing Competition is open to all writers. You do not have to be a member of Florida Freelance Writers' Association or a resident of Florida. However, members of CNW [FFWA members and *Freelance Writers' Report* (FWR) subscribers] do save 50% on entry fees. If you need membership information, contact CNW/FFWA at the address above. Winners will be notified by mail no later than May 31, 2001.

There are three Divisions with a total of nine Categories. Entrants may compete for both Category and Division Awards with each entry.

Non-fiction Division: Previously Published Article, Open/Feature Article, Essay/Column

Fiction Division: Literary Short Story, Genre Short Story, Short-Short, Novel Chapter.

Children's Literature Division: Short Story, Non-fiction Article/Nonfiction Book Chapter.

Best in Division is a $50 Bonus Award plus certificate. First Place in each Category is $75 plus a certificate. Second Place in each Category is a six-month membership in FFWA ($48 value) for Florida residents or a one year subscription to *Freelance Writers' Report* ($39 value) for non-residents, and a certificate. Third Place in each Category is a book or gift, and a certificate. Honorable mention certificates will be awarded in each category as warranted.

Rules and Guidelines
Entries must be unpublished (except for the adult Previously Published Article category). Previously Published Article category entries may be submitted in double spaced manuscript format or published articles may be cut out and pasted on 8-1/2 x 11 inch paper, with all publication artwork cut away.

Any length is acceptable for Fiction and Non-fiction except Short-Short Fiction which must be under 1,000 words.
Enter as many manuscripts in as many categories as you wish. Entry fee and a separate Official Entry Form must accompany each entry; photocopies of the entry form are acceptable.

An entry fee of $5 (members) or $10 (non-members) must accompany each entry under 3,000 words; an entry fee of $10 (members) or $20 (non-members) must accompany each entry of 3,000 words or longer. Reduced member fees refer to active CNW members (FFWA members and FWR subscribers).

Entries not conforming to contest rules will be disqualified; entry fees will not be returned.

Judges reserve the right not to award prizes where not enough entries meet winning criteria.

Do not staple manuscript pages, entry forms, or checks. Use paper clips only.

Acknowledgment of receipt of manuscripts cannot be made and manuscripts CANNOT be returned; therefore, legible photocopies or computer printouts are suggested for submission.

For the list of winners, send a self-addressed, stamped #10 envelope (4 x 9-1/2 inch) marked "winners" on the outside. The winners list will be mailed by May 31, 2001.

Neither entries nor winners will be published in an anthology or other publication; authors retain all rights to their works.

Specific Division/Category Guidelines
The author's name must NOT appear on the manuscript, nor on any published article entry. Indicate the Division and Category to which the entry is being submitted on the upper right corner of the first page of the manuscript.

NON-FICTION DIVISION
- Open/Feature Category is for unpublished research articles.
- Essay/Column can be opinion, personal experience, nostalgia think-piece, or humor.

FICTION DIVISION
- Literary Short Story emphasizes character; Genre Short Story emphasizes plot. If a Genre Short Story is entered, indicate genre

(mystery, romance, science fiction, horror, western, action adventure) on the first page.

FICTION DIVISION, CONTINUED

- Indicate the book title on Fiction/Novel Chapter entry; chapter title is optional.

CHILDREN'S LITERATURE DIVISION

- Indicate the age group for which the material was written on the first page of the entry.
- On a Non-fiction entry, indicate whether it is a magazine article or a non-fiction book chapter.

Judging criteria includes presentation (format, follows rules, neatness, spelling, punctuation, grammar, print quality); suitability (correct category, correct age group, and appropriate length if children's division); as well as tightness, clarity, structure, strength of lead/beginning, transitions, impact, and satisfactory close.

Non-fiction is also judged on logic; use of quotes, statistics, and anecdotes; order; provocative ideas; and lead and satisfactory close.

Fiction is also judged on characterization, conflict, dialogue, plotting, beginning, ending, and figures of speech.

Official Entry Form
CNW/FFWA Florida State Writing Competition

A separate form must accompany each entry (photocopy before completing for multiple entries).

1. Author's LAST name ______________________

   FIRST name ______________________

2. Author's mailing address ______________________

   ____

3. Author's daytime phone number (   ) ______________________

   evening phone (   ) ______________________

4. TITLE of entry ______________________

   ____

5. FIRST LINE of entry ______________________

   ____

   ____

6. Circle Division/Category of this entry:

   A: Non-fiction/Previously Published
   B: Non-fiction/Open Feature Article
   C: Non-fiction/Essay, Column
   D. Fiction/Literary Short Story
   E: Fiction/Genre Short Story
   F: Fiction/Short-Short
   G: Fiction/Novel Chapter
   H: Children's/Short Story
   I: Children's/Non-fiction Article/ Non-fiction Book Chapter

7. ENTRY FEE (check one and enclose):

   ___ $5, I am a current CNW member and entry is under 3,000 words.

   ___ $5, I am not a member, enclosed are my CNW membership application and dues, and entry under 3,000 words.

   ___ $10, I am not a member and am not joining at this time, and entry is under 3,000 words.

   ___ $10, I am a current CNW member (or membership is enclosed), and entry is 3,000 words or longer.

   ___ $20, I am not a member, and entry is 3,000 words or longer.

$ ________ Total entry fee and ________ total entries in this package (necessary only on one form per package).

Make entry fee check or money order payable to: CNW/FFWA. One check may be written to cover multiple entries if all are mailed in same package (but enclose separate entry forms for each entry). (US $ only.)

If submitting five (5) or more entries at one time, you can charge entry fees to: VISA, MasterCard, Amex Card.

______________________ exp. date ________

Credit card signature ______________________

8. Send entry form(s), with fee(s) attached, to: CNW/FFWA, PO Box A, North Stratford, NH 03590.

Official Entry Form

THE COALITION FOR THE ADVANCEMENT OF JEWISH EDUCATION

261 West 35th Street, Floor 12A
New York, NY 10001
Phone (212) 268-4210; Fax (212) 268-4214
E-mail 500-8447@mcimail.com

Deadline: December 31, 2001

THE DAVID DORNSTEIN MEMORIAL CREATIVE WRITING CONTEST FOR YOUNG ADULT WRITERS

Young writers between the ages of 18 and 35 may submit an original short story of no more than 5,000 words on a Jewish theme or topic. Up to $1,000 will be awarded to up to three winners. In the event that only one story is selected as a winner, the author will receive $1,000. If two stories are chosen, the first place winner will receive $750 and the second place winner will receive $250. If three stories are chosen, the first place winner will receive $700, the second place winner will receive $200, and the third place winner will receive $100. All winning submissions will be published in consecutive issues of CAJE Jewish Education News.

Submission Guidelines

1. The authors must be between the ages of 18 and 35 on December 31, 2001.

2. All submissions must be typed, doubled spaced. Manuscripts will not be returned to the writers.

3. All stories must be accompanied by a cover sheet listing the author's name, address, phone number, and the title of the story. Only the title should appear on the story. Do not put your name, address, and/or phone number on the story.

4. The story submitted must never have received an award or have been published.

5. To verify submission requirements, include a copy of your driver's license or other document to prove age and a signed statement verifying that your story has not been published.

6. Entrants may submit only one story in any calendar year.

7. CAJE Board, staff, contest committee members, judges and their relatives may not enter the contest.

8. CAJE will have the right to publish prize-winning submissions and to disseminate them to the CAJE membership at any time. Credit will be given to the author.

9. The deadline for the contest is December 31, 2001. Judging will take place from January 1st to May 31st. Winner(s) will be notified by June 30, 2001.

Submit entries to: CAJE, 261 West 35th Street, Floor 12A, New York, NY 10001.

COLONIAL PLAYERS, INC.

108 East Street
Annapolis, MD 21401
Phone (410) 263-0533; Box Office (410) 268-7373
Renard Court Annex Phone (410) 224-2065

Deadline: September 1, 2001 – December 31, 2001 postmark

2001 PROMISING PLAYWRIGHTS CONTEST
Prize: $750 and a main stage production of the play.

Competition is open to any aspiring playwright residing in any of the states descendant from the original 13 colonies (Connecticut, Delaware, Georgia, Maryland, Massachusetts, New Hampshire, New Jersey, New York, North Carolina, Pennsylvania, Rhode Island, South Carolina, and Virginia), West Virginia, or Washington, D.C.

The deadline is between September 1, 2001 and December 31, 2001. Plays received with postmarks before or after this time period will not be considered. Final decision of the judges will be announced no later than June 30, 2001.

Only full-length plays, suitable for arena production, with up to two settings, and running not less than 1-1/2 hours and not more than two hours, excluding intermission, will be considered. Cast sizes are limited to ten actors or fewer. Musicals and adaptations in copyright will not be considered. In addition, plays that have been previously produced professionally will not be considered. In the event no entry is deemed suitable, no prize or production will be awarded. The decision of the judges will be final.

Colonial Players, Inc., reserves the right to produce the play on a royalty-free basis within two years after the award is announced. Subsequent productions of the play (at other theaters) must give credit to Colonial Players, Inc., for premiering the play. The award-winning playwright must agree to attend rehearsals of their play, with a schedule to be arranged with the director of the play. The purpose of the playwright's attendance at rehearsals is to allow for rewrites and other changes deemed necessary by the director and the playwright.

Scripts must be typewritten and firmly bound in a cover; no brads, please. The first sheet must include only the title of the play. The second sheet must contain a description of the setting(s), characters, and the time of the action. The author's name and address should not appear on the manuscript, but be attached to the manuscript in a sealed envelope. Scripts will be numbered for judging. Plays submitted that do not adhere to these requirements will not be considered. Plays submitted must be free of royalty and copyright restrictions that would prevent Colonial Players from producing the play. Collaborations of two or more authors are acceptable. If the play has been produced non-professionally, or had a staged reading or workshop production prior to submission, please list all of the places and dates. This information should be included in the sealed envelope with your name, address, phone number, etc. Only plays which receive Honorable Mention from previous Colonial Players' contests, and meet all of the other criteria stated herein, may be resubmitted for consideration.

No responsibility can be assumed by Colonial Players for lost manuscripts. All reasonable care will be taken to avoid loss. Scripts will not be returned unless accompanied by a manuscript size, self-addressed, stamped envelope. If you wish to have a written acknowledgment that we have received your play, please include a self-addressed, stamped postcard.

Send submissions to: Frances Marchand, Colonial Players Inc., Promising Playwright Contest, P.O. Box 2167, Annapolis, MD 21401.

THE COMMONWEALTH CLUB OF CALIFORNIA

595 Market Street
San Francisco, CA 94105
Phone (415) 597-6700
E-mail bookawards@aol.com
Website www.commonwealthclub.org

Deadline: January 31, 2001 postmark

CALIFORNIA BOOK AWARDS
Deadline: Postmarked no later than midnight January 31, 2001. Earlier entries are appreciated.

Awards will consist of not more than two gold medals and eight silver medals: One Gold Medal for fiction, one gold medal for nonfiction, two silver medals for outstanding entries, regardless of classification, one silver medal for an author's first published work of fiction, one silver medal for poetry, one silver medal for fiction or nonfiction for children ages up to ten, one silver medal for fiction or nonfiction for children ages 11-16, one silver medal for fiction or nonfiction relating to California, one silver medal for a notable contribution to publishing (outstanding book production). Awards are presented to books exhibiting exceptional literary merit.

A Brief History: The Commonwealth Club of California is the nation's oldest and largest public affairs forum, founded in 1903. Based in San Francisco and San Jose, The Club hosts speeches, debates and discussions on topics of regional, national, and international interest.

The California Book Awards were established in 1931 to provide recognition and encouragement to California authors who, Club members felt, were unfairly receiving less attention than East Coast authors. Over the years, the California Book Awards have recognized many unknown writers who later became famous, such as John Steinbeck and Ray Bradbury.

Submission Guidelines
Each entry must be made on an official form, or a facsimile thereof. Entries are restricted to books bearing a 1999 original publication date. The author(s) must have been a legal resident of California at the time the manuscript was accepted for publication. To be eligible for an award in notable contribution to publishing, the publisher must be headquartered in California. Copies of entries cannot be returned.

There is no entry fee. Entries may be made by either authors or publishers. At least three copies of each book entered must be provided with the following entry form, or a facsimile, to the Book Awards Jury at the Commonwealth Club of California, 595 Market Street, San Francisco, CA 94105

The California Book Awards
Entry Form

Name of book: ______________________________

Author(s): ______________________________

Date of publication: ______________________________

Suggested Classification:

_____ Fiction - Californiana
_____ Non-fiction
_____ Poetry
_____ Juvenile (ages 11-16)
_____ Juvenile (ages up to 10)

Publisher

Address: ______________________________

City: ______________ State: ______ Zip: ______

Name of Contact: ______________________________

Contact's Title: ______________________________

Phone: ______________ Fax: ______________

Author

Present Residence: ______________________________

City: ______________ State: ______ Zip: ______

Phone: ______________________________

Was the author a legal resident of California when the manuscript was delivered to the publisher? _____ Yes or _____ No

For further information we should contact: _____ Publisher or
_____ Author

Signed: ______________________________

First Work of Fiction Notable Contribution to Publishing

____

Date: ______________________________

COMMUNITY CHILDREN'S THEATRE OF KANSAS CITY, INC.

Mrs. Blanche Sellens
8021 East 129th Terrace
Grandview, MI 64030
Phone (816) 761-5775

Deadline: January 31, 2001

THE MARGARET BARTLE ANNUAL PLAYWRIGHTING AWARD

Plays must be written for an elementary school age audience. Original ideas, legends, folklore, historical incidents, biographies, and adaptations of children's classics are subjects that usually provide good plays. An award of $500 will be given to the best script submitted. In the event that two or more scripts are judged worthy of the award, the prize money will be apportioned at the discretion of the Reading Committee. If no script is judged suitable, the Committee reserves the right to withhold the cash award. The winner or winners will be announced in April or May. The prize winning script(s) will be kept for production.

Rules and Guidelines

1. Plays should have eight or fewer characters.

2. All characters are performed by adults with women in the primary roles; male roles should not be overly virile.

3. The location is different for each presentation; therefore technical requirements should take this into account.

4. Plays should be less than 60 minutes in length.

5. Manuscripts should be typed, double spaced, and securely bound. Author's name and full address must appear on the fly page.

6. If you wish your manuscript returned, please enclose a self-addressed, stamped envelope.

7. Published plays are not acceptable.

8. Please do not submit seasonal plays. Our productions are trouped throughout the school year.

9. Violence, mature love stories, slang or cursing are not acceptable.

Community Children's Theatre reserves the right for one of its units to produce any prize-winning play royalty free for one or two consecutive years. The play may or may not be produced the year it receives the award. The author will be advised of production dates.

Mail entries to: Mrs. Blanche Sellens, 8021 East 129th Terrace, Grandview, MI 64030.

THE INA COOLBRITH CIRCLE

Judy Hardin Cheung, Contest Chair
704 Brigham Avenue
Santa Rosa, CA 95404

Deadline: August 10, 2001 postmark

THE INA COOLBRITH CIRCLE POETRY CONTEST
The Ina Coolbrith Circle 82nd annual Poetry Contest is open to all Circle members (including those out-of-state); and nonmember California residents.

Rules and Guidelines
Rules must be followed exactly or entries will be disqualified!

1. Three (3) poems may be entered per contestant, but no more than one (1) poem in any one category.

2. Line limit is 42 lines or fewer in each poem. (See categories below for special limits.)

3. Categories are:
   A. Serious Poetry, any traditional form (identify the form used: sonnet, ballad, etc.).
   B. Long free verse
   C. Short free verse – 16 line limit.
   D. Light or humorous verse, any form.
   E. Short poems, 12 lines or fewer, any form.
   F. Poems on California, any form.
   G. Poems about journeys, any kind, any form.
   H. Poems about nature, any form.

4. There is no fee to Circle members whose 1999-2000 dues are paid by August 10th; and a $2 fee per poem (three poem limit) for nonmember California residents.

5. To be submitted each poem must:
   A. Have a title.
   B. Be original, unpublished, and in English.
   C. Not be submitted to an editor nor entered in another competition during the contest period (Ina Coolbrith Circle Anthology submissions are eligible).
   D. Not have been an award winner in any previous contest (honorable mentions are acceptable).
   E. Be submitted in duplicate, i.e., two (2) clear typewritten copies of each poem on standard size 8-1/2 x 11 inch typing paper

(clear photocopies acceptable).

F. Include the category of each poem typed in the upper right corner of both copies.

G. Include ON ONE COPY ONLY in upper left corner the typed name, address, phone number, and status (member or nonmember) of the poet.

H. Be mailed in one single envelope with sufficient postage.

Make all checks payable to Ina Coolbrith Circle. Keep copies of your poem(s) as none will be returned to you. Authors retain all rights. Decisions of judges are final.

Current and new members should fill out and return the Entry Form on the next page and enclose contest entries, and dues (if applicable).

Mail entries to: Judy Hardin Cheung, Contest Chair, 704 Brigham Avenue, Santa Rosa, CA 95404

The Ina Coolbrith Circle Annual Poetry Contest

__I am applying for membership in The Ina Coolbrith Circle in the category checked below.

__I am also including poems for entry in the 80th annual Poetry Contest.

__I have also included a donation of $____ to support the Contest.

__Active ($15/Year), __Sustaining ($20/Year), or
__Junior, under 18 ($6/Year)

I am a writer of ___ poetry, ___ fiction, ___ non-fiction, and/or ___ I am interested in the literature and history of California as an appreciator.

(Please list any literary accomplishments.)

____

____

Name _________________________ Phone (   ) _____________

Address ____

City _________________________ State _________ Zip _________

Make all checks payable to The Ina Coolbrith Circle.
Write or call for prize information.

CREATIVE WITH WORDS PUBLICATIONS

Brigitta Geltrich, Editor-in-Chief/Publisher
P.O. Box 223226
Carmel, CA 93922
Fax (408) 655-8627; E-mail cwwpub@usa.net

See what's new at Creative With Words Publications (CWW). CWW furthers folkloristic matter, creative writing in children (poetry, prose, language and computer art), and creative writing by all ages. CCW also fosters creative writing in special interest groups, senior citizens (state age), the disabled (state why), and shut-ins of any kind (state why).

Guidelines should be followed. Include a self-addressed, stamped envelope with all entries. If at all possible, use standard a submittal form. There are three divisions for CWW publications:

ADULTS ONLY (20 and up)
Deadline: February 27, 2001
The Eclectics, Volume 2a.
Deadline: August 31, 2001
The Eclectics, Volume 2b. (Gives annual accumulative list of adult authors in alphabetical order.)

Thereafter, there will be a volume a. and b. each year.

CHILDREN ONLY (19 and under)
Please state age of child (up to age 19) and verify authenticity of writing.
Deadline: May 31, 2001
We are Writers, Too! (Annual salute to sponsors of creative writing in children is included.)
Deadline: November 30, 2001
We are Writers, Too! Volume 2b. (Gives annual accumulative list of children authors in alphabetical order.)

Thereafter, there will be a volume a. and b. each year.

WRITERS OF ALL AGES
Once a year, the CWW editors and readers evaluate the previous year's program. During the last twelve months, CWW has treated a variety of themes. Some were favorably received by poets and writers, some were not. It became evident that we had to give adult writers equal time with children writers. The themes most favorably received by poets and writers will now be offered on a regular basis. These are:

Deadline: January 31, 2001 for February 15, 2001. The subject is Matters of the Heart (Love)

Deadline: February 27, 2001 for March 15, 2001. *The Eclectics* Volume a. The subject is Animals.

Deadline: March 31, 2001 for April 15, 2001. The subject is School and School Subjects.

Deadline: April 30, 2001 for May 15, 2001. The subject is Folklore of any kind.

Deadline: May 31, 2001 for June 15, 2001. *We are Writers, Too!,* Volume a.

Deadline: June 30, 2001 for July 15, 2001. The subject is Travel, Vacation.

Deadline: July 31, 2001 for August 15, 2001. The subject is Nature.

Deadline: August 31, 2001 for September 15, 2001 *The Eclectics,* Volume b. Open for special theme.

Deadline: September 30, 2001 for October 15, 2001. The subject is Seasons, Weather.

Deadline: October 31, 2001 for November 15, 2001. The subject is Holidays, Celebration.

Deadline: November 30, 2001 for December 15, 2001. *We are Writers, Too!,* Volume b.

Deadline: December 31, 2001 for January 15, 2002. The subject is Humor.

You may submit year round to these themes. (It might take a few months for CWW to get into this cycle. So, please be patient along with us.)

Guidelines

1. Manuscripts should be in English only, but CCW will accept translations by a native English speaker from another language. All manuscripts will be edited by the CWW project editor.

2. Manuscripts should be typed or legibly written double spaced (prose), one poem per page, 1-1/2 inch margins on all sides; name, home address, and age (if child, up to 19) on the top left on every page; all pages should be numbered. Do not fax manuscripts.

3. Poetry should be 20 lines or less, no more than 45 characters across any line. Prose should be a maximum of 1,500 words, excluding title. Note: Shorter poems/prose have a better chance, if of quality. Our staff readers do count the words.

4. For poems (except haikus), authors should not indent each line dif-

ferently, or put a single word on a separate line, unless it is a language-art piece and the poem is a graphic depiction. Title prose, use a standard font, and double space.

5. Poetry may be any type, unless otherwise stated by CWW on the theme list. Folkloristic tales and such may be any type. For folkloristic research use the latest *MLA Handbook for Writers of Research Papers, Theses, and Dissertations.* Prose should be quality writing. Do not include brand names, names of companies, movies, television shows, etc., in stories and poems. CWW is not their sponsor.

6. CWW publishes according to set themes. Poetry or prose containing violence of any nature, over-preoccupation with death, racial slurs or preferences, pornographic material, or current sensationalisms will not be accepted.

7. Manuscripts must be accompanied by cover letter or CWW submittal form, stating the name of the project submitted. Name of author, home address, child's age (up to 19), senior/disabled/shut-ins status, must be given on each page and officially verified by a responsible adult.

8. Multiple submissions are not accepted.

9. Previously published manuscripts are not accepted. If of folkloristic nature, entries will only be accepted if permission of reprint is enclosed.

10. A self-addressed, stamped envelope with sufficient postage plus two oz. postage for CWW material must accompany all manuscripts and correspondence. If no self-addressed, stamped envelope is enclosed, you will receive a very delayed or no response. Manuscripts and correspondence submitted without a self-addressed, stamped envelope are generally destroyed at the end of the month submitted. Note: A self-addressed envelope without postage is not acceptable.

11. Query is preferred. CWW does not publish self-contained books. CWW publishes anthologies according to themes set twice a year and according to specific length.

12. Copyright is CWW Publications. After publication, rights revert back to the author for submission elsewhere. CWW requests a credit line

be given to CWW for having published the item first. Content and graphics submitted must be copyright-free or a copyright clearance statement must be included.

13. Manuscripts are read and evaluated by CWW staff or guest readers. Folkloristic items are read by guest scholars of folklore. CWW editors take the reader's and scholar's suggestions into consideration when further evaluating manuscripts. All manuscripts are subject to be edited to reflect the standards of CWW. CWW offers suggestions how to improve the story/poem.

14. Reading time is one to two months after deadline of theme. Tentative deadlines are set twice a year. Therefore, first notice might come one year after submitting to a specific theme. It is the writer's responsibility to notify CWW of any changes.

15. Writers published by CWW receive a 20% discount on every copy purchased of the issue containing the writing; on orders of ten copies or more, there is an additional 10% discount. Note: A poet or writer does not have to order a copy to get published. There are no tearsheets or free copies. Byline (name of writer/poet, age of child/senior), city, and state is given with poem/prose. Best of the Month writer receives one free copy of *The Eclectics* general anthologies or US $10.

16. Manuscripts and graphics accepted are not returned.

17. No contract is issued. A statement of publishing intent is forwarded with acceptance notification, at which time a writer/poet may withdraw the manuscript within a given time.

18. There are eleven to twelve publications per annum written by all ages; two anthologies containing the writing and language/computer artwork by children only (must be written by children up to 19 years of age, not by well-meaning adults); and two *The Eclectics* for adults only.

19. Market/readership includes family, schools, libraries, universities, editors, physicians, political and religious leaders, and shut-ins. CWW publications are evaluated at trade fairs and trade conferences and are presented at book fairs.

20. Editors/advisors are Editor-in-Chief/Publisher, Brigitta Geltrich; Visiting Editor, Bert Hower; and Advisor, D.G. Spencer Ludgate.

Address correspondence to Editorial Office: P.O. Box 22326, Carmel, CA 93922; Fax (408) 655-8627; E-mail cwwpub@usa.net.

21. Cost of single issues is US $9 – $12 ($9 for 50–60 pages; $11.50 for 61–80 pages; $12 for 81 pages and up). Special issues are US $15–$20; Back issues are US $6 (CWW determines when an issues becomes a back issue). Subscriptions are 12 issues for US $60; 6 issues for US $36; 3 issues for US $21 (inform whether to include the two children only issues or the two adults only issues). Credit card orders are not accepted at this time. Libraries and schools receive a 10% discount. Back-order status of an issue is set by CWW according to specific specifications.

22. Reading Fees are reasonable and available. Write, and include a self-addressed, stamped envelope, to CWW for information and fee.

23. Checks are made payable to: Brigitta Ludgate, Creative With Words Publications.

Creative With Words
Manuscript Submittal Form

(put NA, where not applicable)

Name of Author: ______________________________

Indicate whether ADULT:__________, or CHILD ____________

If child: Give age _________ or Grade Attending at School: _______

Full Home Address of Author: ______________________________

____

____

If child, Name of Teacher/Sponsor: ______________________________

If child, Name of School: ______________________________

If child, Full address of School: ______________________________

____

____

Name of Local Library: ______________________________

Full address of Local Library: ______________________________

____

____

Name of Local Newspaper: ______________________________

Address of Local Newspaper: ______________________________

____

____

Name of CWW Project (if known) to which manuscript is submitted:

____

If child, Verification of authenticity (by responsible adult): ______

____

Statement of Senior Citizen Status: ______________________________

____

Statement of Disability (handicapped), Shut-In: ______________________________

____

To qualify, a self-addressed, stamped envelope must be enclosed.

Thank you for submitting your manuscript to Creative With Words Publications (CWW). Manuscripts will be placed in appropriate theme file and processed after deadline of theme. You will be notified one way or the other within two or four weeks after deadline.

CRIME WRITERS OF CANADA

Crime Writers of Canada
3007 Kingston Road
Box 113
Scarborough, Ontario M1M 1P1 Canada
Phone (416) 461-9876; Fax (416) 461-4489
Email ap113@freenet.toronto.on.ca
Website www.crimewriterscanada.com

Deadline: January 31, 2001

2001 ARTHUR ELLIS AWARDS
The Crime Writers of Canada are calling for submissions for the 2001 Arthur Ellis Awards, this country's premier award for excellence in the crime genre. The Arthur Ellis Awards, established in 1984 and named after the nom de travail of Canada's official hangman, are awarded annually by the Crime Writers of Canada for published works.

Guidelines
Four (4) copies of any work submitted for an Arthur Ellis Award (please include a cover letter telling us what category and name of publisher's imprint) must be received by the CWC no later than the close of the business day on January 31, 2001 at the address above. (Short stories, include a photocopy of the original published issuance).

Submissions are taken in the following categories: best crime novel (by a previously published author), best true crime, best first crime novel (by a previously unpublished novelist), best crime short story, best crime genre criticism/reference/anthology, best play with a criminous theme (including film scripts or electronic media duly performed or qualified as published), best juvenile crime fiction, and a new category, best crime publication in French (fiction, true crime or related subjects).

To qualify, a work must be in one of the above categories and fall under the following criteria: first publication, regardless of language, in the preceeding year (2000) by a writer, regardless of nationality, resident in Canada or by a Canadian writer resident abroad.

"Crime" is defined as: crime, detective, espionage, mystery, suspense, and thriller. Fictional or factual accounts of criminal doings, including literary novels with a criminous theme.

If less than three titles are submitted in any category, the appropriate award will be postponed until three titles have been submitted. The judges decisions are final.

No entry fee is charged, and winners and those on the short list will be notified by mail, fax or e-mail, depending on the circumstances.

The short list will be announced on or around April 15, 2001 with the Arthur Ellis Awards Dinners being held in Toronto and Vancouver in May.

DANA AWARDS

Mary Elizabeth Parker, Chair
Dana Awards in Poetry, Short Fiction, and the Novel
7207 Townsend Forest Court
Browns Summit, NC 27214
E-mail danaawards@pipeline.com
Website http://danaawards.home.pipeline.com

Deadline: October 31, 2001 postmark
Michael Dana, non-Southerner living in the South, wed to poet and novelist Mary Elizabeth Parker, wants to continue to encourage good work with the sixth annual Dana Awards. Awards: Dana Award in the Novel is $1,000; Dana Award for Literary/Mainstream Short Fiction is $500; Dana Award for Speculative Short Fiction is $500; and Dana Award for Poetry is $500.

The purpose of the Dana Awards is monetary encouragement for work that has not yet been recognized, so all work submitted should be unawarded, unpublished, and not under promise of award or publication at the time it's submitted to us. This rule excludes any novel, short story, or group of poems which has been awarded/published even in part, EVEN IF YOU SUBMIT A DIFFERENT PART/ARRANGEMENT TO US — because under our definition the work has already received some recognition.

DANA AWARD IN THE NOVEL.
Award: $1,000 for the first 50 pages of a novel either completed or in progress (in progress submissions should be as polished as possible). First 50 pages only. All types of novels accepted (this is a change from previous years). Literary excellence is the only criterion. No novels for or by children/young adults. Typed, double-spaced.

DANA AWARD FOR LITERARY/MAINSTREAM SHORT FICTION.
Award: $500 for the best short story. Fiction only, no memoirs. No stories for or by young children/young adults. Up to 10,000 words maximum if you must, but due to volume, we'd be grateful for stories of 3,000 words maximum. Typed, double-spaced.

DANA AWARD FOR SPECULATIVE FICTION.
Award: $500 for the best speculative short story (sci-fi, fantasy, horror, surrealism). Includes sci-fi, horror, fantasy, and surrealism. But please, no slasher-gore, or pornographic stories. No stories for or by children/young adults. Up to 10,000 words maximum if you must, but due to volume we'd be grateful for 3,000 words maximum. Typed, double-spaced.

DANA AWARD FOR POETRY.

Award: $500 for the best group of five poems. Five (5) poems per entry. No light verse or verse for or by children/young adults. Poems may be thematically related but need not be. No length restrictions, although poems of more than 100 lines are discouraged. Typed single or double-spaced (single preferred).

Submission Guidelines

Entry fees: $10 per five poems, $10 per short story, $20 per novel entry.

Please make checks payable to Dana Awards.

Each submission must include a separate cover sheet listing name, address, phone number, title(s) of work(s) submitted, category for each work (crucial, especially to differentiate speculative from literary/mainstream short fiction). Author's name and address must not appear on manuscript.

Authors may enter in any or all categories, with more than one submission in each category, but each submission must have a separate cover sheet and entry fee.

It is crucial to include a self-addressed, stamped envelope for competition results only. All manuscripts will be recycled.

Because we don't publish (we're working on that problem), you may submit the same work simultaneously to other competitions, journals, publishers, and still be eligible for Dana Awards.

THE DAYTON PLAYHOUSE FESTIVAL OF NEW WORKS

Attn: Managing Director
1301 E. Siebenthaler Avenue
Dayton, OH 45414

Deadline: August 1, 2001 – September 30, 2001 postmark

FUTUREFEST 2001
The entry to the 12th annual Dayton Playhouse Festival of New Works FutureFest 2002 MUST be a full-length play. Musicals and children's plays WILL NOT be accepted.

Three full scale selections, as well as three reader's theater selections, will be presented during FutureFest weekend in July 2002. All playwrights will be given travel and lodging expenses to attend the weekend.

Invited adjudicators will view the six productions, critique the shows in front of the audience after each performance with the playwright on stage and in private sessions, and select a winner.

The winner will be awarded a $1,000 cash prize with the other five participants receiving $100.00 each. More award money is pending.

The winning manuscript may be produced by The Dayton Playhouse as part of 2001-2002 season.

Rules for Submission
The entry must be an original work, and must not have been published or previously produced where admission was charged. However, staged readings and/or workshop productions would not be disqualifying factors.

There is no restriction of subject, style, treatment, etc., but, a word of caution on overuse of raw and explicit language. Content should have broad rather than restrictive audience appeal.

A playwright may submit more than one entry.

A playwright must submit one typewritten, bound copy of the script with a title page containing:

1. title
2. author's name
3. mailing address and phone number.

Character descriptions and an act/scene synopsis also may be included. The playwright must also include a resume.

The script must be neatly typed according to standard norms and IT MUST BE FIRMLY BOUND IN ONE OF TWO ITEMS: a report folder or a three-ring binder. UNBOUND SCRIPTS WILL BE DESTROYED.

Scripts will not be returned unless accompanied by a self-addressed, stamped envelope.

The winning playwright awards The Dayton Playhouse the option to produce the winning play on its main stage in Dayton, Ohio.

Entries must be postmarked no earlier than August 1, 2001 no later than September 30, 2001. No plays may be withdrawn from the contest after September 30, 2001.

The judges reserve the right to withhold the award if, in their opinion, no entry merits it. Adjudicators will consist of National Theater and/or Literature specialists.

Send manuscripts to: The Dayton Playhouse, Attn: Managing Director, 1301 E. Siebenthaler Ave., Dayton, Ohio 45414

DePAUL UNIVERSITY

Theatre School
2135 North Kenmore Avenue
Chicago, IL 60614-4111

Deadline: December 1, 2001 postmark

THE CUNNINGHAM PRIZE FOR PLAYWRITING
Prize: $5,000. The competition was established as an endowment gift from the Cunningham Family in honor and memory of Rev. Donald Cunningham, a Chicago priest, playwright, and lover of the theatre.

The purpose of the prize is to recognize and encourage the writing of dramatic works which affirm the centrality of religion, broadly defined, and the human quest for meaning, truth and community. It is the intent of the endowment to consider submissions of new dramatic writing in all genres, including works for children and young people. The prize is awarded annually in March, except in those years when it is the determination of the judges that none of the submissions merit final consideration. The winner will be notified on or before March 1, 2002.

Eligibility
All genres are eligible. The focus for the awarding of the prize is Metropolitan Chicago. The candidates for the award must be writers whose residence is in the Chicago area, defined as within 100 miles of the Loop. Scripts must be submitted by the author(s). Playwrights who have won the award within the last five years are not eligible. Graduates, students and employees of The Theatre School are not eligible until they have been absent from the school for five years.

Rules
Script(s) must be submitted by the author(s). Scripts must be original, full-length, and the sole property of the author(s).

Scripts must be typewritten and copied onto 8-1/2 x 11 inch white bond paper. Do not submit original manuscript. Ensure that copy is legible. There is no application form. The author's name, address, and telephone number must be clearly displayed on the front cover or on the first page and be able to be removed for anonymous submission of the script to the judges. A brief statement about the submission, making the connection to the purpose of the prize, should accompany the script.

In all matters, the decisions of the judges are final.

Scripts and other materials will not be returned unless accompanied by a self-addressed, stamped envelope.

Scripts remain at all times the property of those owning them, and DePaul University assumes no rights or obligations whatsoever.

Send all submissions to Cunningham Prize Selection Committee at the above contest name and address.

DELACORTE PRESS BOOKS FOR YOUNG READERS

c/o Bantam Doubleday Dell Books for Young Readers
1540 Broadway
New York, NY 10036

Deadline: October 1, 2001 – December 31, 2001 postmark

THE DELACORTE PRESS CONTEST FOR A FIRST YOUNG ADULT NOVEL

Delacorte Press Books for Young Readers is pleased to announce the 18th Annual Delacorte Press Contest for a First Young Adult Novel. The prize of a book contract (on the publisher's standard form) for a hardcover and a paperback edition, including an advance and royalties, is awarded annually to encourage the writing of contemporary young adult fiction. The award consists of $1,500 in cash and a $6,000 advance against royalties. Contest results will be announced no later than April 30, 2002.

Eligibility

1. The contest is open to U.S. and Canadian writers who have not previously published a young adult novel.
2. Foreign-language manuscripts and translations are not eligible.
3. Manuscripts submitted to a previous Delacorte Press contest are not eligible.
4. Manuscripts sent to Delacorte Press may not be submitted to other publishers while under consideration for the prize.
5. Authors may not submit more than two manuscripts to the Delacorte Press competition; each must meet all eligibility requirements.

Submission Guidelines

1. Submissions should consist of a book-length manuscript with a contemporary setting that will be suitable for readers ages 12 to 18.
2. Manuscripts should be no shorter than 100 typewritten pages and no longer than 224 typewritten pages. Include a brief plot summary with your covering letter.
3. Each manuscript should have a cover page listing the title of the novel, the author's name, address, and telephone number; and a note stating whether or not the manuscript need be returned. The title should also appear on each manuscript page.
4. Manuscripts should be typed double spaced on 8-1/2 x 11 inch

good quality white paper, and pages should be numbered consecutively. The type should be at least 10 point. The author should retain a copy of any manuscript submitted.

5. Photocopies are acceptable if readily legible and printed on good quality white (not gray) paper.
6. Do not submit manuscripts in boxes. A padded envelope will do. Please do not enclose checks for postage. The publisher cannot guarantee the return of any manuscript, and is not responsible for late, lost, misdelivered, or misplaced submissions.
7. If your manuscript need not be returned, enclose a business-size, stamped, self-addressed envelope for notification. Manuscripts that need not be returned will be destroyed by Bantam Doubleday Dell. If your manuscript is to be returned, it must be accompanied by a stamped, self-addressed envelope or book mailer large enough to accommodate the manuscript; otherwise, the manuscript cannot be returned. Please check current postal regulations regarding manuscripts which weigh more than one pound.
8. Send manuscripts to: Delacorte Press Contest, c/o Bantam Doubleday Dell Books for Young Readers, 1540 Broadway, New York, New York 10036

Judging

1. The judges are the editors of Delacorte Press Books for Young Readers.
2. The judges reserve the right not to award a prize.
3. The decision of the judges will be final.
4. The editors of Delacorte Press Books for Young Readers will not be able to offer critiques of manuscripts or enter into correspondence about the manuscripts other than with the winning author.
5. Contest results will be announced no later than April 30, 2001.

ALSO SEE Bantam Doubleday Dell, for another contest for books for young readers.

"DISCOVERY"/THE NATION

c/o The 92nd Street Y Unterberg Poetry Center
1395 Lexington Avenue
New York, NY 10128
Recorded Guidelines (212) 415-5759

Deadline: Late January 2001 postmark

THE JOAN LEIMAN JACOBSON POETRY PRIZES
Now in its 27th year, the "Discovery"/*The Nation* Contest, co-sponsored by The 92nd Street Y Unterberg Poetry Center and *The Nation* magazine, is designed to attract large audiences to poets who have not yet published a book of poems. Each of the four winners will be awarded $300, a reading at The Poetry Center in May 2001, and publication in *The Nation.*
Grace Schulman, Poetry Editor at *The Nation,* is contest coordinator. Each year three different leading poets are invited to be judges.

Guidelines

1. The contest is open to poets who have not published a book of poems (chapbooks, self-published books included). Individual poems which have been or will be published elsewhere may be submitted.

2. A $5.00 entry fee must accompany the submission. Please make checks or money orders payable to the "92nd Street Y," and attach them to your cover letter. Do not send cash.

3. Submit four identical sets of a typed ten-page manuscript. The manuscript is not to exceed 500 lines in length for the ten pages. Include no more than one poem per page. Each set is to contain the same ten pages in the same order. No double submissions.

4. Each set of the ten-page manuscript must be stapled in the upper left-hand corner. Do not use paper clips. All pages of the manuscript must be numbered.

5 No personal identification or copyright attributions for previously published poems should appear on any of the poems. Enclose ONE cover letter including your name, address, and day and evening telephone numbers, as well as a list of the submitted poems in the order in which they appear, with copyright attributions for published poems. Biographical information is not necessary. Do not attach the cover letter to the manuscripts.

6. Photocopied manuscripts are acceptable. However, in the case of previously published poems, do not send photocopied pages of the periodical or book in which the poem(s) originally appeared.

7. All poems must be original and in English (no translations).

8. No corrections can be accepted after receipt of the contest submission.

9. Entries must be postmarked late January. Please do not include return postage; the large number of entries we receive makes it impossible for us to return manuscripts. If you wish to receive confirmation of receipt of your manuscript, please enclose a stamped, self-addressed postcard. Allow several weeks for its return. Winners will be contacted by telephone in April 2001; all contest entrants will be mailed the names of winners and of the judges shortly thereafter.

10. Due to the large number of applicants, no phone queries can be taken. If you wish to hear a recording of the guidelines or to receive another set of these guidelines in the mail call (212) 415-5759. Call for exact deadline.

Mail to: "Discovery"/*The Nation* 2001, c/o The 92nd Street Y Unterberg Poetry Center, 1395 Lexington Avenue, New York, NY 10128.

DOGWATCH RESCUE AND WELFARE

M. Edridge
267 Hillbury Road
Warlingham, Surrey, ENGLAND CR6 9TL

Deadline: September 1, 2001 – September 30, 2001 postmark

DOGWATCH OPEN POETRY COMPETITION
First Prize £50, Second Prize £30, Third Prize £20.

Rules and Guidelines

1. Only unpublished work is to be submitted: poems up to 40 lines, open style and theme. It is preferred that entries are typed.
2. No identification should appear on poems. Entry Form must be attached. No poems will be returned but results will be sent if you enclose a self-addressed, stamped envelope.
3. Copyright remains with the author.
4. Winning poems will appear in the DOGWATCH Newsletter (sent to all winners).
5. No correspondence will be entered into.
6. Entry fee is £2 for the first entry, and £1 for all further entries. Checks should be made out to DOGWATCH. All entries must be postmarked September 2000.
7. Send entries to: M. Edridge, 267 Hillbury Road, Warlingham, Surrey, ENGLAND CR6 9TL

DOGWATCH Open Poetry Competition Entry Form

I submit 1 POEM at £2 (First Entry) ________

I submit (______) POEMS at £1 (All Further Entries)

I enclose a self-addressed, stamped envelope for results ______

I would like to know more about DOGWATCH and enclose a self-addressed, stamped envelope ______

I accept the Competition Rules.

Signed ____

NAME (In block letters) ____

ADDRESS ____

____

____

TELEPHONE ____

THE DONNER PRIZE

Prize Manager, The Donner Prize
112 Braemore Gardens
Toronto, Ontario M6G 2C8 Canada
Phone (416) 652-7179; Fax (416) 658-5205
E-mail meisner@interlog.com

Deadline: November 30, 2001
In 1998, the Donner Canadian Foundation created Canada's newest literary award, The Donner Prize, for best book on Canadian public policy. The only prize of its kind, The Donner Prize will award $25,000 to the winning author and $5,000 each to two runners-up.

Eligibility
All entries must be published in English or French between January 1, 2000 and December 31, 2000.

Each submission should deal with significant issues in Canadian public policy. Priority will be given to books that provide information to an informed readership through new ideas, perspectives and analysis.

Criteria for content is broad; for instance, "issues in Canadian public policy" may include historical examinations of public policy in Canada, biography and autobiography.

A collection of essays by one author is considered eligible if the essays are on a single theme, and if the work in its entirety has not been reproduced elsewhere. Please note that a collection of essays by more than one author is not eligible.

Posthumously published works, pamphlets and conference papers, and subsequent or revised editions are not eligible.

Books published outside Canada are eligible providing the author is a Canadian citizen, the book is published in English or French and the theme is relevant to Canadian public policy.

In early April, 2001, a short list will be announced, with the winner and runners-up being announced at the end of that month. The winning author and the two runners-up are required to attend the awards ceremony in May, 2001 and to address the audience.

The jury reserves the right not to award the prize.

The rules for eligibility shall be interpreted and may be revised from time to time at the discretion of the Board of Directors of the Donner Canadian Foundation.

Guidelines

All titles must be submitted by the publisher. No other entries will be accepted.

Six copies of each title must be delivered to the Prize Manager by November 30. For titles published between November 30, 2000 and December 31, 2000, the publisher may submit bound galleys or bound typescripts.

Each submission must include a publication or release date and a general overview of its contents.

The earliest possible submission of books is recommended.

Receipt of each candidate title will be acknowledged by the Prize Manager in a letter that will also set out the responsibilities of the publisher and the author should their title be short-listed or chosen for the Prize.

About the Prize

Good public policy — which embraces the vital themes of regulatory and legal reform, public finance, environment, urban affairs, health care, educational reform, youth issues and social policy —is vital to a healthy economy and country. The prize aims to recognize the fundamental importance of public policy and to reward excellent work in this field.

"We are very pleased that the Donner Canadian Foundation can extend its mandate of promoting research into social and economic issues affecting Canadians," said Patrick Luciani, Executive Director of the Foundation. "We believe that the prize will encourage an open exchange of ideas, and hope that it will provide a spring-board for authors who may not necessarily be well-known, but who can make an innovative and meaningful contribution to policy discourse."

The Donner Canadian Foundation, established in 1959 by businessman and philanthropist William H. Donner, supports projects that advance the common good in Canada by encouraging private initiative, independence and individual responsibility. In 1967 the Foundation embarked on a course of professional grant-making that has contributed over $80 million to more than 600 projects across Canada.

DRURY COLLEGE

c/o Sandy Asher, Writer-in-Residence
900 North Benton Avenue
Springfield, MO 65802
Phone (417) 865-8731

Deadline: Call or write for next deadline.

THE DRURY COLLEGE ONE-ACT PLAYWRITING COMPETITION
The 9th biennial Drury College One-Act Playwriting Competition offers a first prize of $300 and two honorable mentions of $150 each. Winning plays will be considered for production at Drury College and will receive special recommendation to The Open Eye Theater.

Rules and Guidelines

1. Competition is open to all playwrights. Scripts are to be original, unpublished, and unproduced. Staged readings or workshop productions will not disqualify a script. Musicals, monologues, children's plays, adaptations, film and TV scripts are ineligible.

2. Preference will be given to small cast, one-set shows with running times of no less than twenty and no more than forty-five minutes.

3. No more than one script is accepted from any author.

4. All scripts are to be typewritten and firmly bound.

5. Scripts cannot be acknowledged or returned unless accompanied by a self-addressed envelope with sufficient postage.

6. No written or verbal critiques will be tendered.

7. The decisions of the judges are final. Drury College reserves the right to produce any of the three winning plays royalty-free, to withhold production, and to modify cash awards as deemed necessary by the judges.

8. Drury College does not assume any responsibility for the loss, damage, or return of scripts. All reasonable care will be taken.

9. Submit entries to: Drury College Playwriting Competition, c/o Sandy Asher at the address above.

DUBUQUE FINE ARTS PLAYERS

Jennie G. Stabenow, DFAP One-Act Playwriting Contest Coordinator
1321 Tomahawk Drive
Dubuque, IA 52003
Phone (319) 583-6748

Deadline: January 31, 2001

DUBUQUE FINE ARTS PLAYERS
NATIONAL ONE-ACT PLAYWRITING CONTEST
The Dubuque Fine Arts Players (DFAP), in existence since 1977, invites submissions of original manuscripts for its annual National One-Act Playwriting Contest. The top three winning playwrights will be awarded cash prizes of $600, $300, and $200. In addition, the winning plays may be staged in full production, if they can be produced in Dubuque.

Concentrate on character, relationships, and a good story. Large cast, multiple sets and scenes, and prop-heavy shows are strongly discouraged, but not prohibited.

Rules and Guidelines

1. Each play submitted must be accompanied by: 1) a completed entry form; 2) an entry fee of $10 per play submitted (one check may be written to cover all the plays you submit, but must total $10 per play, $20 for 2 plays, etc.); and 3) two (2) copies (each in a separate folder) of each play submitted.

2. Send a self-addressed, stamped envelope to receive evaluations and suggestions from our readers. If you want your plays returned as well, send a self-addressed, stamped envelope with enough postage. It may be simpler and about the same cost to keep a copy of your play, to be recopied if you need it later, and send us only a regular size self-addressed, stamped envelope for results of the contest and evaluations of your play.

3. Entries must be original, unproduced one-acts of no more that 35 pages (or 40 minutes running time). No children's plays, musicals, or adaptations of works not in the public domain (unless the playwright has written permission from the original author for the adaptation) will be accepted.

4. Each copy of each entry should be in a protective folder (cheap paper folders with pockets or fasteners are fine). The playwright's name, address, etc., should not appear anywhere on the script or folder. Plays will be number coded for the purposes of evaluation.

5. Please include a one-paragraph synopsis of the play and/or your reasons for writing it.

6. Entries must be postmarked no later than January 31, 2001 to be entered in the 2001 contest.

7. During the contest no inquires about the status of a play will be answered. If a self-addressed, stamped envelope or postcard is sent with the play/or plays, we will return it to acknowledge receipt of your manuscript(s).

8. The DFAP shall have first rights to produce the winning entries, as well as the right to use photographic and video materials made during production of the winning plays for the promotion of future contests, without the payment of royalties or licensing fees, so long as direct profits are not made from said photos or videos.

9. An individual may enter more than one script and win more than one prize in one year, but may win no more than three consecutive contests.

10. The DFAP reserves the right to turn down any play entry for not following these guidelines, or for subject matter or language that our readers find totally unsuitable for an average Dubuque audience.

Important Criteria in Our Evaluation of Plays

Plot: Does the play tell an interesting, well-developed story? Do events lead to a plausible, satisfying climax? Is the reason for the conflict clear?

Characters: Are they real, engaging, and worth the audience's time? Do they grow or change in believable ways?

Theme: Is it universal? Does it motivate or involve all the characters?

Style: Does the style of the play fit the ideas you want to get across? Is it built around a gimmick and nothing else? Does it work?

Economy of Production: Is the cast workable (two to five cast members)? How many scenes (one or two preferred) or sets (one preferred)? How long will it run (less than 40 minutes)?

Address all entries and correspondence to: Jennie G. Stabenow, DFAP One-Act Playwriting Contest Coordinator, 1321 Tomahawk Drive, Dubuque, IA 52003.

Dubuque Fine Arts Players National One-Act Playwriting Contest Entry Form

PLAY TITLE:

AUTHOR:

TELEPHONE ( ) (a.m.) ( ) (p.m.)

ADDRESS:

CITY: STATE: ZIP:

CHECKLIST: Do you have the following?

1. Two copies of each play in folders.
2. A synopsis and a check for $10 for each play.
3. A self-addressed, stamped envelope to send to you our evaluation sheets and anything else you want returned. Please check one:
   __Send reader's evaluations only
   __Send plays only
   __Send both plays and evaluations
4. Be sure your name and address appear nowhere on the script or its folder.

How did you find out about the Dubuque Fine Arts Players One-Act Playwriting Contest?

I acknowledge that I have read the contest rules and guidelines, and affirm that my manuscript is an original, previously unproduced work. I further affirm that if my work is an adaptation of any other person's work, I have confirmed that the copyright of said work is no longer in force or I have gotten written permission to use the work and will produce such permission upon request.

(signature) (date)

Please do not write in space below.

E

P

G

EMPORIA STATE UNIVERSITY

English Department
Emporia, KS 66801
Website www.emporia.edu/bluestem/index.htm

Deadline: March 1, 2001

THE BLUESTEM AWARD- A NATIONAL POETRY AWARD
Prize: $1,000 and publication

Guidelines
For an original book-length collection of poems in English. A typed manuscript of original work, at least 48 pages long, with two title pages. One title page should include author's name, address and phone number. This information should not appear elsewhere. Also include a $15 reading fee (checks payable to Bluestem) and a #10 self-addressed, stamped envelope for notification of contest winner (manuscripts will not be returned).

Manuscripts may include poems previously published in periodicals but not in full-length, single-author collections. The judge for the final selection will be announced at the end of the competition.

Send manuscripts to: The Bluestem Award, Department of English, Box 4019, Emporia State University, Emporia, KS 66801-5087.

THE FARGO-MOORHEAD COMMUNITY THEATRE

NPC Administrator
333 4th Street South
Fargo, ND 58103-1913

Deadline: May 1, 2002 – July 1, 2002

THE FARGO-MOORHEAD COMMUNITY THEATRE'S
NATIONAL PLAYWRIGHTS' COMPETITION
The Fargo-Moorhead Community Theatre (FMCT), a civic theatre located in Fargo, North Dakota and Moorhead, Minnesota, announces its 16th Biennial Playwrights' Competition.

Award is $500 plus travel/housing to and from Fargo for the playwright during rehearsal/production period or, if a winning play is not selected for production, $1,000 to the winning playwright.
Material submitted must be a one-act play (less than one hour playing time) unpublished and unproduced, suitable for performance in the 372-seat Thrust House. FMCT may enter the winning one-act in the National AACT (American Association of Community Theatres) Festival. Playwrights are encouraged to avoid large casts and scenic/costume-intensive subjects. ONE SUBMISSION PER PLAYWRIGHT.

Submission Guidelines

1. Manuscripts must be typed, with author's name(s), address, and telephone number appearing on the title page only.
2. Manuscripts must be accompanied by a cover letter and a brief resumé or biography, including any writing/publishing credits.
3. Only COMPLETE manuscripts will be considered.
4. A self-addressed, stamped envelope is required if the author wishes the return of the manuscript. Scripts unaccompanied by a self-addressed, stamped envelope will NOT be returned. (FMCT is not responsible for lost and or damaged manuscripts.)

Material will be accepted from May 1, 2002 through July 1, 2002 ONLY. Regardless of postmark, script must be on site at FMCT on or before July 1, 2002. Scripts received before May 1, 2002 will be returned. The winner will be notified by January 1, 2003 via telephone and mail.

Please note: The Theatre reserves the right to extend the competition and/or change notification dates at its DISCRETION.

Send entry to: FMCT, Attn: NPC Administrator, 333 4th Street South, Fargo, ND 58103-1913.

FLYWAY LITERARY REVIEW

Department of English
Iowa State University
206 Ross Hall
Ames, IA 50011

THE FLYWAY LITERARY REVIEW AWARDS

Deadline: March 20, 2001 postmark

Poetry Prize – $500 Award
Send up to three poems; a $10 reading fee is required. (fee is waived for new subscriptions.)

Deadline: April 30, 2001 postmark

Short Fiction Prize – $500 Award
Send short fiction, up to 7,500 words. Entrants may submit more than one story. A $10 reading fee per story is required. (One fee is waived for new subscriptions).

Deadline: September 25, 2001

Creative Non-fiction Prize – $300 Award (with publication)
Send short memoir, personal essays, autobiography, reportage, or travel writing up to 5,000 words. No limits on subject matter. We are also interested in non-fiction submissions that stretch the parameters of what non-fiction can be by fusing genres or challenging the limits of memory or experience. A $10 reading fee per submission is required. (One fee is waived for new subscriptions).

Winning entries and honorable mentions will be published in the Fall and Winter 2001 issues.

Send work to: *Flyway Literary Review*, Department of English, Iowa State University, 206 Ross Hall, Ames, IA 50011.

FOLIO

Department of Literature
Gray Hall
The American University
Washington, DC 20016

Deadline: September 1, 2001 – March 15, 2002, Manuscripts
September 1, 2001 – March 1, 2002, Art

Folio is a nationally recognized literary journal sponsored by the College of Arts and Sciences at American University in Washington, DC. We showcase outstanding stories, poetry, art and translations by burgeoning and established artists. Previous contributors include Jean Valentine, Linda Pastan, Henry Taylor, and William Stafford. We also award annual prizes for original fiction, poetry and art. Awards: Payment for published work is two copies of the issue in which your work appears. Annual contest winners also receive a $100 prize.

Guidelines for Fiction and Poetry

Written submissions must be unpublished and typed (preferably double-spaced).

Simultaneous submissions are fine, but please inform us immediately should your work be accepted elsewhere.

Please limit fiction submissions to 4,500 words and poetry to five poems.

All submissions should be accompanied by a cover letter in which contact information, a brief bioiography, and title(s) of the enclosed work are included.

You must also send a self-addressed, stamped envelope for return of manuscripts or art. Rejected work without a self-addressed, stamped envelope will be discarded.

Be sure to retain a copy of all work submitted.

Folio is not responsible for lost or damaged work.

All of our published submissions are automatically considered for awards.

Manuscripts are read between September 1, 2001 and March 15, 2002. Materials received during summer will be returned or discarded.

Guidelines for Art
Send up to 15 black and white slides or (preferably) camera-ready images.

All of our published submissions are automatically considered for awards.

Art is reviewed between September 1, 2001 and March 1, 2002.

If you have not seen a recent issue of *Folio*, we encourage you to do so in order to determine the compatibility of the magazine and your work. Back issues are available for $5, except the most recent issue, which is $6. Subscriptions run $12 per year.

THE FORMALIST
A JOURNAL OF METRICAL POETRY

320 Hunter Drive
Evansville, IN 47711

Deadline: June 15, 2001 postmark

THE HOWARD NEMEROV SONNET AWARD
The 7th annual Howard Nemerov Sonnet Award is sponsored by *The Formalist,* A Journal of Metrical Poetry. The winner receives a $1,000 prize and publication in the Fall/Winter issue.

Rules and Guidelines

1. Sonnets must be original and unpublished. No translations. Writers may enter as many sonnets as they wish. Sonnet sequences are acceptable, but each sonnet will be considered individually. Entry fee is $3 per sonnet. Author's name, address, and phone number should be typed on the back of each entry.

2. The winning poem and eleven finalists will be published in the Fall/Winter 2001 issue of *The Formalist*. The final judge is to be announced.

3. Entries must be sent to the address below and postmarked no later that June 15, 2001. Enclose a self-addressed, stamped envelope if you would like to be notified of the contest results by September 2001. Entries cannot be returned. For another copy of these rules, send a self-addressed, stamped envelope to: Howard Nemerov Sonnet Award, *The Formalist*, 320 Hunter Drive, Evansville, IN 47711.

FRENCH-AMERICAN FOUNDATION

41 E 72nd Street, 2nd Floor
New York, NY 10021
Phone (212) 829-8800; Fax (212) 829-8810
E-Mail French-AmerFdn@msn.com

Deadline: July 1, 2001

The French-American Foundation is now seeking submissions for its fourteenth translation Prize. This prize, which carries a $5,000 award, will be presented to the translator for the best translation of a prose work from French to English. Translations for consideration must either have been published or have a scheduled publication date in the United States between January 1, 2001 and December 31, 2001.

All categories of prose work are eligible with the exception of poetry, technical, scientific and reference works, and children's literature. Books or galleys must be submitted in duplicate and accompanied by the French original work by July 1, 2001. The award, presented to the translator, will be announced in late October or early November 2001.

Send submissions to: Violaine Lenoir, The French-American Foundation, 509 Madison Avenue, Suite 310, New York, NY 10022.

FRIENDS OF AMERICAN WRITERS CHICAGO

Literary Awards Committee
Jane Larson, Chairman
400 E. Randolph, #2123
Chicago, IL 60601
Phone (312) 856-1147

Deadline: December 1, 2001

FRIENDS OF AMERICAN WRITERS BOOK AWARDS PROGRAM
Friends of American Writers was organized in 1922 for the study of American literature and for the encouragement of American writers. Since 1929 monetary awards have been made annually for outstanding books of fiction or non-fiction. The 71st annual book awards program offers a first place award of $1,600 and a second place award of $1,000.

We invite you to participate in our annual program of awarding promising midwestern authors by arranging to have two copies of eligible books sent to the above address as soon as possible. Each book is read and reviewed by a designated committee. To be eligible:

1. A book of fiction or non-fiction of good quality writing must have been published during the year 2001 and must be received by December 1, 2001.

2. The author must be a resident (or previously been a resident for five years) of Arkansas, Illinois, Indiana, Iowa, Kansas, Michigan, Minnesota, Missouri, North Dakota, South Dakota, Nebraska, Ohio, or Wisconsin; or the locale of the book must be in those regions.

3. The author shall not have published more than three books under his/her own pen name and we prefer honoring the first and second books written.

No application is necessary. The winner must attend the award banquet in May at his own expense. We do need to have two (2) copies of each book as early as possible, along with biographical material of the author. All books and correspondence should be sent to the above address by December 1, 2001.

FRIENDS OF AMERICAN WRITERS JUVENILE LITERATURE AWARDS

Juvenile Literature Awards Committee
Minnie Orfanos, Chairman
680 North Lake Shore Drive, Apt. L208
Chicago, IL 60611-4402
Phone (312) 664-5628

Deadline: December 31, 2001

The Juvenile Literature Awards Committee of the Friends of the American Writers invites you to submit books for consideration for our year 2002 awards. No entry fee is required. To qualify for consideration, a book must meet these criteria:

1. It must have been published in 2000.

2. It must be the first, second or third book published by the author in the young people's categories of preschool, elementary, intermediate, or secondary school readership.

3. The author must be a native of, or a current resident of, or have lived for five years in, or the setting of the book must be in one of these states: Arkansas, Illinois, Indiana, Iowa, Kansas, Michigan, Minnesota, Missouri, Nebraska, North Dakota, Ohio, South Dakota, or Wisconsin.

4. It must be prose, either fiction or non-fiction.

To enter send two (2) complimentary review copies of each book to the above address.

Judging begins August 1, 2001. To insure complete careful consideration, please submit entries as soon as possible. The deadline for receiving books is December 31, 2001.

FRIENDS OF THE CHICAGO PUBLIC LIBRARY

Chair, Carl Sandburg Awards
400 S. State Street, #10S-7
Chicago, IL 60605
Phone (312) 747-4907; Fax (312) 747-4077
E-mail FRIENDSCPL@aol.com

Deadline: August 15, 2001

THE CARL SANDBURG LITERARY AWARDS
The Friends of the Chicago Public Library is accepting entries from publishers and Metropolitan Chicago authors for the 23rd annual Carl Sandburg Literary Award in the following categories: Fiction, Non-fiction, Poetry, and Children's Literature (fiction and non-fiction).

A prize in the amount of $1,000 will be awarded to the winner of each category at the Friends of Chicago Public Library awards ceremony.

Eligibility and Submission Guidelines

1. Native or resident of the six-county Chicago Metropolitan area (includes Cook, Lake, McHenry, Will, DuPage, and Kane)

2. Published books only.

3. Publication date of June 1, 2000 through May 31, 2001.

4. Two (2) copies, including publication date, submitted NO LATER than August 15, 2001.

5. A $25 entry for fee for each title submitted. Please make check payable to the Friends of the Chicago Public Library.

Submit entries to: Chair, Carl Sandburg Awards, Friends of the Chicago Public Library, 400 S. State Street, #10S-7, Chicago, IL 60605.

For more information, please call (312) 747-4907, fax us at (312) 747-4077, or e-mail your question to: FRIENDSCPL@aol.com.

23rd Annual Carl Sandburg Literary Awards

Please duplicate this form as necessary.

Author's Name:

Address:

City: State: Zip Code:

Work Phone Number: Home Phone Number:

E-mail:

Signature:

Publisher:

Division of:

City: State: Zip Code:

Phone Number: E-Mail:

Awards Coordinator/Marketing Rep:

Signature:

Title:

Publishing Date:

Publication date of June 1, 2000 through May 31, 2001.

Please feel free to include a press release with copies of the book.

_ Fiction _ Non-Fiction _ Poetry _ Children's Literature

_ $25.00 entry fee enclosed. Please make your check payable to the Friends of Chicago Public Library.

Has the novel won other awards? Please state:

Has the author won other awards? Please state:

Author is: _ Native of Chicago Metropolitan area
_ Current resident of Chicago Metropolitan area
_ Not sure

FRIENDS OF THE SACRAMENTO PUBLIC LIBRARY

828 1 Street, Room 309
Sacramento, CA 95814
Phone (916) 264-2880 call will be returned
Website www.saclibrary.org — then click on friends

Deadline: August 6, 2001 postmark

15TH ANNUAL FOCUS ON WRITERS' CONTEST.
Winners will be announced at the day-long Focus on Writers' 2001 Conference on Saturday, October 24, 2001 in Sacramento.

Prizes
First- $100; Second- $50; Third- $25
Honorable Mention winners will receive certificates; winners will be notified before the conference and invited to attend as guest.

Contest Categories
1. Short story (2,500 word maximum)

2. First chapter of a novel (5,000 word maximum) with 1- page summary of plot

3. Poetry (two-page maximum per poem; each poem is a separate entry)

4. Non-fiction article (2,500 word maximum)

5. Story/Picture Book for younger children (2,500 word maximum)

6. First chapter of a novel for older children (5,000 word maximum) with 1-page summary of plot

Contests Rules
All Northern California writers are eligible. Must enter on or before deadline. Contestants may enter up to a total of five unpublished manuscripts ($5 per entry).

All prose entries must be typed and double spaced. If you wish acknowledgment of receipt, enclose self-addressed, stamped postcard.

Mail entries to : Writer's Contest 2001 at above address

Do not show author's name on entry. Do attach a 3x5 inch card to each entry with author's name, address, phone number, title of entry and category. Enclose a check covering the $5 (per entry) fee made payable to Friends of the Sacramento Public Library (or FSPL).

Manuscripts cannot be returned, so please do not send a return envelope. Authors retain all rights to their manuscripts. Manuscripts may be disqualified if the above procedure are not followed.

All entrants will receive information on the conference.

All entrants will receive a coupon entitling them to a $5 reduction in the conference admission fee.

FUND FOR INVESTIGATIVE JOURNALISM, INC.

Executive Director, Peg Lotito
5120 Kenwood Drive
Annandale, VA 22003
Phone (703) 750-3849
E-mail Fundfij@aol.com

The Fund for Investigative Journalism gives grants to financially struggling and often unknown reporters working outside the backing of major news organizations. These grants range from $500 to $5,000 for newspaper and magazine articles and up to $10,000 for books and television documentaries.

There is no application form. The applicant must write a letter outlining the story, what he or she expects to prove, how this will be done, and the sources for the proof. The letter must be supported by a resumé, budget, writing samples, and a letter of commitment from an editor or publisher to consider publishing or broadcasting the final product. Though we recognize that publication is not guaranteed, the commitment underlies the intent and increases the likelihood the story will get out.

All materials should be submitted on paper no larger than 8-1/2 x 11 inches.

Our funds are limited to journalists seeking help for original investigative work involving corruption, malfeasance, incompetence and societal ills in general and are global in nature. The fund also gives grants for media criticism. The board meets three times a year, in March, July and November.

THE GILMAN & GONZALEZ-FALLA THEATER FOUNDATION

109 East 64th Street
New York, NY 10021
Phone (212) 734-8011; Fax (212) 734-9606

Deadline: September 30, 2001

THE GILMAN & GONZALEZ-FALLA THEATER FOUNDATION AWARD
The amount of the award is $25,000, and its use will be unrestricted. Applicant(s) will be judged on the totality of their submitted materials. In order to qualify for the award, applicants must satisfy the following criteria:

Eligibility

A. Applicant must have the written recommendation of a member in good standing of one of the following organizations: The League of American Theaters and Producers, The League of Off Broadway Theaters and Producers, or a professional non-profit theater.

B. The applicant must have at least one musical produced in the U.S. in either a commercial theater or professional non-profit theater. Stage readings, workshops, and developmental production and performances in universities or college theater departments, and amateur or civic community theaters will not be considered.

C. The award was created to support and encourage lyricists, book writers, and composers who are involved in the creation of the American Musical Theater. A person can apply by himself or with a creative team.

Submission Guidelines

The application package must contain two copies of the following:

1. A brief biography or resumé.

2. A complete list of produced and unproduced works, including names of producing organizations, locations, and dates when applicable.

3. Any scripts, narrative outlines, and tapes of either complete works or excerpts which the applicant considers the best representation of his *oeuvre.* Musical scores or sheet music should not be sent.

4. Include information, if available, on the most recent work or work in progress including book and/or script, list and description of dramatic personae, tape with music and lyrics, and plans for its production.

5. Proof of U.S. Citizenship or legal residence in the U.S.

6. No less than two letters of recommendation (in addition to the letter described in "A" above) by theater professionals.

7. Please be sure to include a self-addressed, stamped envelope to ensure return of one's materials.

All submissions must be in the Foundation office on or before September 30, 2001. The winner of the award shall be notified by the President of the Foundation immediately following the Board's decision in the Spring of 2002.

For further information, please contact the Gilman & Gonzalez-Falla Theater Foundation, 109 East 64th Street, New York, NY 10021; phone (212) 734-8011; Fax (212) 734-9606.

GLIMMER TRAIN PRESS

Linda Burmeister Davies, Contest Director
710 SW Madison Street, Suite 504
Portland, OR 97205-2900
Phone (503) 221-0836; Fax (503) 221-0837
Website http://www.glimmertrain.com

Deadline: April 1, 2001 – July 31, 2001 postmark

VERY SHORT FICTION SUMMER AWARD
Offered to encourage the art of the very short story. Open to all writers. Send your unpublished very short story with a $10 reading fee per story. Word count is 2,000 maximum. Entries must be postmarked between April 1 and July 31, 2001. Cover letter is optional. First page of story to include name, address, phone, word count, and "VSF." "VSF" must also be written on the outside of the envelope. Winners will be called by November 1. For a list of winners, include a self-addressed, stamped envelope with your story. First place is $1,200, publication in *Glimmer Train Series* (circulation 13,000), and 20 copies of that issue. First/second runners-up receive $500/$300, respectively, and consideration for publication.

Deadline: November 1, 2001 – January 31, 2002 postmark

VERY SHORT FICTION WINTER AWARD
Offered to encourage the art of the very short story, include a $10 reading fee per story. Word count is 2,000 maximum. Entries must be postmarked between November 1, 2001 and January 31, 2002. Cover letter is optional. First page of story to include name, address, phone, word count, and "VSF." "VSF" must also be written on the outside of the envelope. Winners will be called by May 1. For a list of winners, include a self-addressed, stamped envelope with your story. First place is $1,200, publication in *Glimmer Train Series* (circulation 13,000), and 20 copies of that issue. First/second runners-up receive $500/$300, respectively, and consideration for publication.

Deadline: August 1, 2001 – September 30, 2001 postmark

FALL SHORT STORY AWARD FOR NEW WRITERS
The contest is open to any writer whose fiction hasn't appeared in a nationally-distributed publication with a circulation over 5,000. Send your unpublished short story (1,200-8,000 words) with a $12 reading fee for each story entered. Entries must be postmarked between August 1 and September 30, 2001. First page of story to include name, address, phone, and "Short Story Award for New Writers." "SHORT STORY AWARD FOR NEW WRITERS" must also be written on the

outside of the envelope. No need for a self-addressed, stamped envelope as materials will not be returned. Winners will be called by January 2. First place is $1,200, publication in *Glimmer Train Stories* (circulation 13,000), and 20 copies of that issue. First/second runners-up receive $500/$300, respectively, and consideration for publication. All applicants receive a copy of the issue in which winning story is published and runners-up announced.

Deadlines: February 1, 2001 – March 31, 2001 postmark

SPRING SHORT STORY AWARD FOR NEW WRITERS
The contest is open to any writer whose fiction hasn't appeared in a nationally-distributed publication with a circulation over 5,000. Send your unpublished short story (1,200-8,000 words) with a $12 reading fee for each story entered. Entries must be postmarked between February 1 and March 31, 2001. First page of story to include name, address, phone, and "Short Story Award for New Writers." "SHORT STORY AWARD FOR NEW WRITERS" must also be written on the outside of the envelope. No need for self-addressed, stamped envelope as materials will not be returned. Winners will be called by July 1. First place is $1,200, publication in *Glimmer Train Stories* (circulation 13,000), and 20 copies of that issue. First/second runners-up receive $500/$300, respectively, and consideration for publication. All applicants receive a copy of the issue in which winning story is published and runners-up announced.

Deadlines: May 1, 2001 – June 30, 2001 postmark

FICTION OPEN
The contest is open to all writers. Send your unpublished short story with a $15 reading fee. There are no theme or word count limitations. Entries must be postmarked between May 1 and June 30, 2001. Cover letter is optional. First page of story to include name, address, phone, and "Fiction Open." "FICTION OPEN" must also be written on the outside of the envelope. Winners will be called by October 15. For a list of winners, include self-addressed, stamped envelope with your story. First place is $2,000, publication in *Glimmer Train Stories* (circulation 13,000), and 20 copies of that issue. First/second runners-up receive $1,000/$600, respectively, and consideration for publication.

Deadline: October 1, 2001 – October 31, 2001 postmark

OCTOBER POETRY OPEN
The contest is open to all poets. Send up to three poems with a $10 reading fee. There are no subject or form restrictions. Entries must be postmarked in October. Cover letter is optional. Include name, address, and phone number on each poem. Please write "POETRY OPEN" on the outside of the envelope. Winners will be called by March 1. For a list of winning entries, include a self-addressed, stamped envelope with your poems. First place is $500, publication in *Glimmer Train Stories* (circulation 13,000), and 20 copies of that issue. First/Second runners-up receive $250/$100, respectively, and consideration for publication.

Deadline: April 1, 2001 – April 30, 2001 postmark

APRIL POETRY OPEN
The contest is open to all poets. Send up to three poems with a $10 reading fee. There are no subject or form restrictions. Entries must be postmarked in April. Cover letter is optional. Include name, address, and phone number on each poem. Please write "POETRY OPEN" on the outside of the envelope. Winners will be called by September 1. For a list of winning entries, include a self-addressed, stamped envelope with your poems. First place is $500, publication in *Glimmer Train Stories* (circulation 13,000), and 20 copies of that issue. First/second runners-up receive $250/$100, respectively, and consideration for publication.

Submit all entries to the above address.

GOODIN WILLIAMS GOODWIN LITERARY ASSOCIATES

V.R. Williams
P.O. Box 8863
Springfield, MO 65801

Deadline: July 31, 2001 postmark

GOODIN WILLIAMS GOODWIN LITERARY ASSOCIATES
WRITING CONTEST FOR CHILDREN'S WRITERS
The 6th annual Writing Contest For Children's Writers offers a first place award of $80; second place award of $40; third-place award of $20; and fourth award of $10.

Categories are Fiction and Non-fiction with a 1,000 word limit (unpublished). Entries should be appropriate for children and not be illustrated or in rhymes.

Submission Guidelines
All entries must be typed, double-spaced.

Entries must be accompanied by a completed entry form. You may send multiple entries. Include a separate entry form for each entry. Please print the required information on the form.

Send a check or money order for $5.00 with your first entry, and $2.50 for each additional entry. (All payments in U.S. funds.)

Send a self-addressed, stamped envelope with sufficient postage for return of manuscript and/or list of winners. Judging will be the sole responsibility of Goodin Williams Goodwin & Associates.

We will not be responsible for manuscripts lost or damaged in the mail.

Entries must be postmarked no later than July 31, 2001. Winners will be notified four to six weeks after deadline.

Submit entries to: Writing Contest, P.O. Box 8863, Springfield, MO 65801. (No purchase is necessary to enter contest.)

Our Booklet, TIPS ON WRITING FOR CHILDREN, is still available for $3.00 (plus $1.05 S/H), $2.00 plus S/H if accompanied by a contest entry. Make check or money order payable to V.R. Williams.

Goodin Williams Goodwin & Associates
Entry Form

[ ] Contest [ ] Booklet

Name: ______________________________

Address: ______________________________

____

____

____

THE GREAT PLAINS PLAY CONTEST

Delbert Unruh
Director of The University Theatre
317 Murphy Hall
University of Kansas
Lawrence, KS 66045
Phone (785) 864-3381; Fax (785) 864-5251
E-mail dunruh@falcon.cc.ukans.edu

Deadline: September 1, 2001

THE GREAT PLAINS PLAY CONTEST
The goal of this contest is to encourage the development and production of full-length dramatic works or musicals, for either adult or youth audiences, about life on the Great Plains. Playwrights and/or composers are encouraged to submit scripts dealing with any historical or contemporary aspect of the human story on the Great Plains. Specifically, the competition seeks to identify, develop, and produce, as a part of The University Theatre Season, full-length dramatic works or musicals featuring Kansas themes. Priority will be given to works that deal with these themes.

This competition is an annual event with the goal of identifying plays for possible production by The University Theatre.

Awards may be given in two categories:

1. A "Development Award" of $500, total, may be given to the playwright(s) and/or composer(s) of a dramatic work or musical. This award will be given to encourage the further development of a promising work. Details concerning the development process will be specified at the time of the award. This award gives the University Theatre a production option on the work.

2. A "Production Award" of $2000, total, may be given to the playwright(s) and/or composer(s) of a dramatic work or musical. Works given this award will be produced by The University Theatre and the award includes all royalties for the production by The University Theatre. A total of $500 will also be given to the playwright(s) and/or composer(s) receiving a "Production Award" to enable them to participate in the production process. Specific details will be worked out at the time of the award.

Guidelines
Submit a single, typewritten copy of the script and/or score.

Include a self-addressed, stamped envelope if you want the script returned. Scripts will not be returned if the self-addressed, stamped envelope is not included.

Eligibility
The contest is open to any person.

Scripts submitted must be full-length.

Scripts submitted must be the original work of, or an original adaptation by, the author(s) and must not have had a prior production by a professional company or must not have had more than two prior productions by amateur or educational companies.

Scripts submitted may be either dramatic works or musicals intended for adult or youth audiences.

Judging will be done by a committee appointed and chaired by the Director of Theatre.

The University Theatre will reserve the right to publish winning works in an anthology of The Great Plains Play Contest winners.

Submit scripts by September 1, 2001 for consideration for production in the 2002-2003 season.

Scripts submitted after the September 1, 2001 deadline will automatically be considered for production in following seasons.

GREAT PLATTE RIVER PLAYWRIGHTS' FESTIVAL

Jeffrey Green
UNK Theater Department
Kearney, NE 68849
Phone (308) 865-8406; E-mail green@ platte.unk.edu

Deadline: January 1, 2001 – April 1, 2001 postmark

This will be the 13th season producing new works for the Great Platte River Playwrights' Festival (GPRPF). Festival dates are June through July. Categories are: Adult – Drama or Comedy; Children – Drama or Comedy; Musical – Drama or Comedy; and Historical – Drama or Comedy.

Winners will receive production/development of script, lodging and travel stipend, and cash awards of $500, $300, and $200.

Rules and Guidelines
Open to all types of subject matter. (Great Plains themes are of particular interest.)

Plays must be original and unpublished in play form. Works in progress are encouraged.

Submit duplicate (with a self-addressed, stamped envelope if return desired). Send tape for musicals. Do not send original or only copy!

The Festival reserves the right to developmental readings and staging of submitted plays without payment of royalties. Cash awards serve as royalties for initial full productions.

Scripts are accepted after January 1, 2001. Postmarked deadline is April 1, 2001 and winners will be announced by July 31, 2001.

The Festival reserves the right to withhold awards in any category.

Send entries to: Artistic Director, GPRPF Theater, UNK, Kearney, NE 68849.

GULF COAST POETRY AND SHORT STORY CONTEST

Gulf Coast (Genre) Prize
English Department
University of Houston
Houston TX 77204-3012

Deadline: February 15, 2001 postmark
Awards: $500 each and publication for the winning poem and short story.

Guidelines
Submit one short story or up to five poems.

Reading fee of $15 includes one year subscription.

Include a self-addressed, stamped envelope for results.

We are also currently accepting and reading submissions for our regular Fall of 2001 issue. We seek fiction (short stories), poetry, and nonfiction (creative and personal essays). Please send to the above address, labeled *Gulf Coast* (Genre) submission.

HARRISBURG AREA COMMUNITY COLLEGE

T.H.S. Wallace, Director
The Wildwood Prize in Poetry
Rose Lehman Art Center 213-E
Harrisburg Area Community College
1 HACC Drive
Harrisburg, PA 17110
Phone (717) 780-2300

Deadline: September 30, 2001 – November 15, 2001

THE WILDWOOD PRIZE IN POETRY
Harrisburg Area Community College announces the annual Wildwood Prize in Poetry. This prize, consisting of a $500 cash award and publication in the *Wildwood Journal*, will be awarded for the best unpublished poem of 100 lines or less by a submitting poet. Poets are invited to submit up to three poems for consideration. There are no restrictions on the kind of poetry or subject matter, although translations are not accepted. The winner will be announced and the prize awarded in March 2002.

Submission Guidelines
Poems are accepted between September 30 and November 15, 2001. Those received after the 15th will go unread.

All submissions must be typewritten, and on one side of the paper only. Clean photocopies are acceptable. Two (2) copies of each submission should be submitted, one without name, address, and telephone number.

A $5.00 non-refundable reading fee must accompany the poems. Please make checks payable to Harrisburg Area Community College. For acknowledgment of receipt of poems, enclose a stamped, self-addressed postcard. Poets should retain copies of their work since submissions will not be returned.

The final selection will be made by a distinguished poet who will remain anonymous until choosing the winner.

All manuscripts and correspondence should be sent to: T.H.S. Wallace, Director, The Wildwood Prize in Poetry, Rose Lehman Art Center 213-E, Harrisburg Area Community College, 1 HACC Drive, Harrisburg, PA 17110.

HELICON NINE EDITIONS

3607 Pennsylvania Avenue
Kansas City, MO 64111
Phone (816) 753-1095; Fax (816) 753-1016

Deadline: May 1, 2001 postmark

11TH ANNUAL POETRY AND FICTION AWARDS

2001 MARIANNE MOORE POETRY PRIZE
Prize: $1,000 for an original, unpublished poetry manuscript of at least 48 pages.

Deadline: May 1, 2001

2001 WILLA CATHER FICTION PRIZE
Prize: $1,000 for an original, unpublished manuscript of fiction (novella or short story collection) between 150-300 double-spaced pages.

Selection Process: Ten finalists in each competition will be chosen by an advisory panel and submitted to a distinguished writer for final selection. Winning manuscripts will be published by Helicon Nine Editions or participating presses. Winners and judges will be brought to The Writers Place in Kansas City for a joint reading.

Submission Guidelines
Each manuscript should be accompanied by a separate cover letter stating the author's name, address, telephone, title of manuscript, acknowledgments, and a brief biography. Author's name must not appear anywhere on the manuscript itself. We regret that manuscripts cannot be returned. Writers may submit more than one manuscript, but each submission must be accompanied by a $15 reading fee.

Both competitions are open to all poets and writers residing in the United States and its territories. The editors retain the right to grant no award in a given year. For contest results, please enclose a self-addressed, stamped envelope.

Send all submissions to Literary Prizes, Helicon Nine Editions at above address.

HEMINGWAY DAYS FESTIVAL

P.O. Box 993
Key West, FL 33041
E-mail calico2419@aol.com

Deadline: June 15, 2001

2001 LORAIN HEMINGWAY SHORT STORY COMPETITION
Award: $2,000 in cash prizes
The literary competition is open to all writers whose fiction has not appeared in a nationally distributed publication with a circulation of 5,000 or more.

The first-place winner will receive $1,000 in cash, while the second- and third- place winners will receive $500 each. Judges will also award honorable mentions to other entrants whose work demonstrates promise.

The Lorain Hemingway Short Story Competition was created in 1981 to support and encourage the efforts of writers who have not yet achieved major-market success. Formerly called the "Hemingway Days Short Story Competition," it was renamed in 1997 in honor of its longtime director Lorain Hemingway, the granddaughter of Ernest Hemingway, and the author of the critically-acclaimed novel *Walking into the River* and the National Book Award nominee *Walk on Water*.

Guidelines and Eligibility
Stories must be original, unpublished, typed and double spaced, and 3,000 words or less. There are no theme restrictions, but only works of fiction will be considered. Writer's names should not appear on the stories, and manuscripts will not be returned. Copyright remains the property of the author. Each story should be accompanied by a cover sheet with the writer's name, complete address, phone number, and title of the piece.

The entry fee is $10 for each story postmarked by June 1, 2001 and $15 for each story postmarked between June 1 and June 15, 2001. Entries postmarked after June 15, 2001 will not be accepted.

Winners will be announced on July 23, 2001, at the end of the Hemingway Days Festival in Key West, Florida. All entrants will receive a letter from Lorain Hemingway and a list of winners by October 1, 2001.

The Lorain Hemingway Short Story Competition has a nineteen year history of literary excellence, and its organizers are dedicated to supporting the efforts of emerging writers of short fiction.

All manuscripts should be submitted to above contest name and address.

HEMINGWAY WESTERN STUDIES CENTER

Tom Trusky, Editor
Boise State University
1910 University Drive
Boise, ID 83725
Phone (208) 385-1999; Fax (208) 385-4373
E-mail rentrusk@idbusu.idbsu.edu

ROCKY MOUNTAIN ARTISTS' BOOK COMPETITION
The Hemingway Western Studies Series at Boise State University is pleased to announce the 7th annual Rocky Mountain Artists' Book Competition.

The *Hemingway Series* publishes multiple edition works relating to public issues (such as gender, race, environment) of special concern to Rocky Mountain readers. Artists may address a topic (such as clear cutting) which not only relates to but also transcends regional concerns.

Proposals specifying offset, copier, or silkscreen printing on commercial papers will be favored. Works may consist of text and/or visual content and may have been previously published in unique or limited editions.

Authors and artists whose works are selected for publication in the *Hemingway Series* receive $500 prize monies and standard sale royalties.

Previously published letterpress or limited edition works, mock (dummy) copies, or detailed proposals should be sent with a self-addressed, stamped envelope to: Tom Trusky, Editor, Hemingway Western Studies Center, Boise State University, Boise, ID 83725.

For further information contact Mr. Trusky by phone (208) 385-1999; fax (208) 385-4373.

HIGHLIGHTS FOR CHILDREN

Highlights for Children
803 Church Street
Honesdale, PA 18431

Deadline: January 1, 2001 – February 28, 2001

HIGHLIGHTS FOR CHILDREN FICTION CONTEST
Topics are to be announced. Please write for guidelines. All topics are fair game this year, but here's the catch: we want thrilling stories, laugh-out-loud stories, moving stories, and most of all, memorable stories – stories that go beyond the norm.

There are three prizes of $1,000 each. The three winning entries will be announced in June of 2000. These stories will then become the property of *Highlights for Children* and will be published by Highlights. All other submissions will be considered for purchase by Highlights. Manuscripts not purchased will be returned in June with a list of the winners.

Guidelines
Stories may be any length up to 900 words. Stories for beginning readers should not exceed 500 words. Indicate the word count in the upper right-hand corner of the first page of your manuscript. No crime, violence, or derogatory humor. Manuscripts or envelopes should be clearly marked for Fiction Contest. Those not so marked will be considered as regular submissions to Highlights. Enclose a self-addressed, stamped envelope with each entry. No entry form or fee is required.

All entries must be postmarked between January 1 and February 28, 2001.

Send entries to: FICTION CONTEST, Highlights for Children, 803 Church Street, Honesdale, PA 18431.

THE HISTORIC NEW ORLEANS COLLECTION KEMPER AND LEILA WILLIAMS FOUNDATION

Dr. Jon Kukla, Director
533 Royal Street
New Orleans, LA 70130-2179
Phone (504) 523-4662

Deadline: January 15, 2002

THE WILLIAMS PRIZE FOR EXCELLENCE IN RESEARCH AND WRITING ABOUT LOUISIANA HISTORY

The Kemper and Leila Williams Prize, named for the founders of The Historic New Orleans Collection, offers a cash award of $1,500 for the best work on Louisiana history published between January 1 and December 31, 2001. Works about all aspects of Louisiana history and culture are eligible, as are works placing Louisiana subjects in regional, national, or international contexts.

All submissions must be made IN QUADRUPLICATE: Four (4) copies of the nominated work AND four (4) copies of the entry form.

The Williams Prize Committee welcomes nominations at this time and throughout the year. The final deadline for all 2002 Williams Prize submissions is January 15, 2002.

Nominations should be addressed to: Chair, Williams Prize Committee, The Historic New Orleans Collection, 533 Royal Street, New Orleans, Louisiana 70130-2179.

Williams Prize Entry Form

Please complete and submit four (4) copies of this form and four (4) copies of the nominated work by January 15, 2001, to Chair, Williams Prize Committee, The Historic New Orleans Collection, 533 Royal Street, New Orleans, Louisiana 70130-2179.

Date Submitted ____________________

Author's Name ____________________

Address ____________________

____

Telephone (   ) ____________________

Title of published work ____________________

____

ISBN (if applicable) ____________________

Publisher ____________________

ATTN: ____________________

Address ____________________

____

____

Telephone (   ) ____________ Fax (   ) ____________

The Williams Prize Committee is appointed annually by the Louisiana Historical Association. It reserves the right to amend its award procedure and determine eligibility of entries without prior notice. The committee chair must receive all nominations in quadruplicate by January 15, 2002.

Signature of applicant ____________________

Please complete and submit four (4) copies of this form and four (4) copies of the published work by January 15, 2002.

HODDER FELLOWSHIP

Council of the Humanities
122 East Pyne
Princeton University
Princeton, NJ 08544-5264

Deadline: November 1, 2001

Prize: Approximately $45,000

Candidates are invited to submit a resume a sample of previous work (ten-page maximum, not returnable), a project proposal of two to three pages, and a self-addressed, stamped envelope for acknowledgment. Letters of recommendation are not required. Preference is given to individuals outside of academia, and candidates for the Ph.D. degree are not eligible.

The Hodder Fellow spends an academic year in residence at Princeton University, pursuing an independent project in the humanities. Twenty eight individuals in various writing fields have received the fellowship in the past fifty-four years.

The appointment of the Hodder Fellow is made each February by the President of Princeton University on the recommendation of the Committee on Humanistic Studies. An announcement of the award is sent at that time to all applicants.

Send submissions to the above address.

HOLLYWOOD DISCOVERY AWARDS

Columbus Screenplay & Manuscript Discovery Awards
433 N. Camden Drive, Suite 600
Beverly Hills, CA 90210
Phone (310) 288-1882; Fax (310) 475-0193
E-mail writing@screenwriters.com

Deadline: November 1, 2001
Submissions are accepted monthly

SCREENPLAY AND MANUSCRIPT DISCOVERY AWARDS
Submissions are accepted MONTHLY. The final deadline for all awards is November 1 of every year.

Criterion is based on execution, originality, and salability. Winner(s) will be selected ONLY if screenplay or book manuscript meets our quality standards. Those selected will be contacted within 120 days from submission date. Due to our selection process, we suggest that you send us your screenplay or book manuscript AS SOON AS POSSIBLE.

SCREENPLAY DISCOVERY OF THE MONTH AWARD
Feedback and access; honoring the best screenplay for each month. One open genre screenplay will be selected monthly, if it meets our quality standards. Stories receive rewrite notes from one of our experienced script consultants. Selected screenplay(s) will be introduced to key decision makers in the entertainment industry. Selected screenplay(s) are automatically finalists for our "Discovery of the Year Award."

Our script consultants include: Linda Seger (*Making A Good Script Great*) and Christopher Vogler (*The Writer's Journey*).

SCREENPLAY DISCOVERY OF THE YEAR
Options and access, up to $10,000 per option. First, second, and third place winners will be offered film rights options by the Hollywood Network, Inc. Scripts will be introduced to major studios.

First, second, and third place winners will get a one year registration to the HollywoodNet Inner Circle. The membership provides access to agents, financing sources, Hollywood executives, and products. The HollywoodNet.com includes Pitch rooms, Logline rooms, Dealmaking desks, and Opportunity desks.

First, second, and third place winners will receive VIP passes to the Hollywood Film Festival and a signed copy of *Opening The Doors To Hollywood: How To Sell Your Idea,* by Carlos Abreu and Howard Jay Smith, from Crown Publishers.

OPUS MAGNUM DISCOVERY AWARDS
BOOK MANUSCRIPT DISCOVERY OF THE YEAR
First, second, and third place winners winners will be offered film rights options by the Hollywood Network, Inc.

First, second, and third place winners winners will get a one year registration to the HollywoodNet Inner Circle. The membership provides access to agents, financing sources, Hollywood executives, and products. The HollywoodNet.com includes Pitch rooms, Logline rooms, Dealmaking desks, and Opportunity desks.

First, second, and third place winners winners will receive VIP passes to the Hollywood Film Festival and a signed copy of *Opening The Doors To Hollywood: How To Sell Your Idea,* by Carlos Abreu and Howard Jay Smith, from Crown Publishers.

Submission Guidelines

1. ONLY non-produced, non-optioned screenplays or book manuscripts may be submitted.

2. Writers are allowed to submit more than one screenplay or book manuscript.

3. Application/Release Form and Fee MUST be sent with each screenplay or book manuscript. For forms, write to the above address.

4. A non-refundable registration fee of $55.00 per script, or $75.00 per book manuscript, is required.

5. Screenplays and book manuscripts that are FINALISTS in other contests are NOT ELIGIBLE for submission. Semi and quarter finalists are accepted.

Send entries to: Columbus Screenplay & Manuscript Discovery Awards, 433 North Camden Drive, Suite 600, Beverly Hills, CA 90210.

L. RON HUBBARD'S WRITERS OF THE FUTURE

P.O. Box 1630
Los Angles, CA 90078

Deadline: Quarterly – March 31, June 30, September 30, and December 31, 2001 postmark

L. RON HUBBARD'S WRITERS OF THE FUTURE CONTEST
L. Ron Hubbard's Writers of the Future Contest is an international search for new and amateur writers of new short stories or novelettes of science fiction or fantasy.

No entry fee is required. Entrants retain all publications rights. All awards are adjudicated by professional writers. Prizes awarded every three months are $1,000, $750, and $500. The annual grand prize is $4,000 additional!

Rules and Guidelines

1. No entry fee is required, and all rights to the story remain the property of the author. All types of science fiction and fantasy are welcome; every entry is judged on its own merits only.

2. All entries must be original works of science fiction or fantasy written in English. Plagarisms will result in disqualification. Submitted works may not have been previously published in professional media.

3. Eligible entries must be works of prose, either short stories under 10,000 words or novelettes under 17,000 words in length. We regret we cannot consider poetry, or works intended for children.

4. The Contest is open only to those who have not professionally published a novel or short novel, more than three short stories, or more than one novelette.

5. Entries must be typewritten and double spaced with numbered pages (computer-printer output is O.K.). Each entry must have a cover page with the title of the work; the author's name, address, and telephone number; and an approximate word count. The manuscript itself should be titled and numbered on every page, but the AUTHOR'S NAME SHOULD BE OMITTED to facilitate fair judging.

6. Manuscripts will be returned after judging. Entries MUST include a

self-addressed return envelope. U.S. return envelopes MUST be stamped: others may enclose international postal reply coupons.

7. There will be three cash prizes in each quarter: First Prize of $1,000, Second Prize of $750, and Third Prize of $500, in U.S. dollars or the recipient's locally equivalent amount. In addition, there shall be a cash prize of $4,000 to the Grand Prize winner, who will be selected from among the First Prize winners for the period of October 1, 2000 through September 30, 2001. All winners will also receive trophies or certificates.

8. The contest will continue through September 30, 2001 on the following quarterly basis:
   October 1 – December 31, 2000
   January 1 – March 31, 2001
   April 1 – June 30, 2001
   July 1 – September 30, 2001

   Information regarding subsequent contests may be obtained by sending a self-addressed, stamped, business-size envelope to the above address. To be eligible for the quarterly judging, an entry must be postmarked no later than Midnight on the last day of the Quarter.

9. Each entrant may submit only one manuscript per Quarter. Winners in a quarterly judging are ineligible to make further entries in the Contest.

10. All entrants, including winners, retain all rights to their stories.

11. Entries will be judged by a panel of professional authors. Each Quarterly judging and the Grand Prize judging may have a different panel. The decisions of the judges are entirely their own, and are final.

12. Entrants in each Quarter will be individually notified of the results by mail, along with the names of those sitting on the panel of judges.

Don't delay! Send your entry to: L. Ron Hubbard's Writers of the Future Contest, P.O. Box 1630, Los Angles, CA 90078.

HUDSON RIVER CLASSICS, INC.

Keith Hedrick, President
P.O. Box 940
Hudson, NY 12534
Phone (518) 851-6840; Fax (518) 851-2631

Deadline: March 1, 2001 – June 1, 2001

ANNUAL PLAYWRITING CONTEST
New ideas and new plays are what the Hudson River Classics, Inc. (HRC) is looking for in its Annual Playwriting Contest.

The contest is open to new, aspiring, or established playwrights throughout New York State and the Northeast who have previously unpublished works they would like to submit. The play should run between 60 to 90 minutes and be suitable for presentation as a reading by professional actors.

Entries should be submitted to Hudson River Classics, Inc., P.O. Box 940, Hudson, New York 12534 by June 1st for review by a panel of distinguished playwrights, actors, and authors.

The winning playwright will receive a $500 award that will be presented in the Fall, when the play will be given a concert reading by professional actors.

Anyone interested in entering the contest should submit their play, along with a short biography, and a $5 non-refundable processing fee. Writers wishing materials returned should send a self-addressed stamped envelope.

Entries should be received between March 1st and June 1st.

For further information on the contest, contact Keith Hedrick, President, at (518) 828-1329 (telephone and fax).

HUTTON PUBLICATIONS

P.O. Box 2907
Decatur, IL 62524

Deadline: November 1, 2000 postmark

HUTTON PUBLICATIONS RHYME TIME CONTEST

Hutton Publications invites you to enter our annual no-fee contest for poems of any length, in any style. You may submit only one poem. It must be typed in proper format with your name and address in one corner. Handwritten poems or envelopes will be discarded.

Previously published work is acceptable. The postmark deadline is November 1 each year. Be sure to include a #10 typed, self-addressed, stamped envelope for winner's list. A sample copy of *The Rhyme Time Poetry Journal*, published quarterly since 1981, is $4. RT publishes only subscribers' work.

Deadline: September 15, 2001

MYSTERY MAYHEM CONTEST

Here's your chance to write as terribly as you can. Just produce one sentence, of any length, as the worst opening sentence of the murder mystery you plan to write someday. The awfullest entry will receive $10 and be published in *Mystery Time*, as well as in a special flyer of mayhem by Hutton Publications. You can order the flyer of previous winners for $1 and a #10 typed, self-addressed, stamped envelope.

The annual deadline is Agatha Christie's birthday: September 15. No entry fee; one entry per person; entry must be typed. All envelopes must be typed.

Submit with a #10 typed, self-addressed, stamped envelope to Mystery Mayhem, P.O. Box 2907, Decatur, IL 62524.

Deadline: February 14, 2001

ROTTEN ROMANCE CONTEST

Here's your chance to write as terribly as you can. Just produce one sentence, of any length, as the worst opening sentence of the romance novel you plan to write someday. The awfullest entry will receive $10 and be published in a special Rotten Flyer by Hutton Publications. You can order the flyer of previous winners for $1 and a #10 typed, self-addressed, stamped envelope.

The annual deadline is Valentine's Day. No entry fee; one entry per person; entry must be typed. All envelopes must be typed.

Submit with #10 typed, self-addressed, stamped envelope to Rotten Romance, P.O. Box 2907, Decatur, IL 62524.

NOTE: Handwritten envelopes and/or entries will be discarded.

Rhyme Time Contest
Entry Form

Hutton Publications, P.O. Box 2907, Decatur, IL 62524

Your Name ______________________________

Your Address ______________________________

____

____

INTERNATIONAL TRAINING SYSTEMS

3600 South Harbor Blvd. Suite 74
Channel Islands Harbor, CA 93035
Phone/fax (805) 382-2323
E-mail ITS3232@aol.com

Deadline: June 1, 2001 postmark

2001 RAINER MARIA RILKE INTERNATIONAL
POETRY COMPETITION

Prize: $1,000 first prize and publication in *ArtLife* magazine, a limited edition monthly journal of fine art and poetry.

Guidelines

Contributors should send up to 5 poems with a $10 entry fee.

To maintain anonymity before the judges, poets should include a separate index card bearing the poem title(s), author's name, address and phone number. To receive a copy of winning poems, please enclose a self-addressed, stamped envelope.

Send submissions to above contest name and address.

IOWA STATE UNIVERSITY
CREATIVE WRITING FELLOWSHIP

203 Ross Hall
Department of English
Iowa State University
Ames, IA 50011
Phone (515) 294-2477; Fax (515) 294-6814
E-mail englgrad@iastate.edu

Deadline: February 1, 2001

PEARL HOGREFE FELLOWSHIP IN CREATIVE WRITING
The Pearl Hogrefe Fellowship supports graduate study toward a degree program that will involve and emphasize creative writing. The major field for the degree need not be in English.

Fellowships are granted for a nine-month academic year, subject to students maintaining adequate grades. The fellowship carries a basic stipend of $950 per month and, in combination with other available university funds, provides for payment of university fees.

Persons who have a master's degree in English or Creative Writing, or who will receive one during the 2000-2001 academic year, are not eligible. Holders of Pearl Hogrefe Fellowships cannot concurrently have another university appointment, such as a teaching assistantship.

Normally, Hogrefe Fellows will be expected to carry nine (9) university credits of course work each term. During the fellowship year, holders must complete a minimum of six (6) semester credits in creative writing or otherwise demonstrate substantial progress in creative writing under the direction of a member of the creative writing staff of the Department of English.

Applicants for the fellowship should submit letters of application explaining their aims and objectives concerning their proposed study at the university. Each applicant should also submit a fellowship application form, a resumé, three letters of recommendation, and a portfolio of no more than 25 pages of his or her creative writing.

In addition, to be considered for a fellowship, applicants must have submitted all materials required for admission to the Graduate College. Hogrefe Fellows must meet the requirements for unrestricted admission to graduate study at Iowa State University. Applications for admission and all transcripts are to be submitted to the Office of Admissions.

The deadline for applications for the 2001-2002 fellowship and for admission to the Graduate College will be February 1, 2001. Announcement of awards will be made about March 31. Check all dates.

Fellowship applications or queries should be sent to: Hogrefe Fellowship Committee, 203 Ross Hall, Department of English, Iowa State University, Ames, IA 50011; phone: (515) 294-2477; fax: (515) 294-6814; e-mail: englgrad@iastate.edu.

For applications for admission to the Graduate College, please write to: Office of Admissions, Alumni Hall, Iowa State University, Ames, IA 50011.

ALSO SEE University of Iowa Press Publication Awards.

ITALIAN AMERICANA

University of Rhode Island
College of Continuing Education
80 Washington Street
Providence, RI 02903-1803
Phone (401) 277-5306

Deadline: Ongoing

THE JOHN CIARDI AWARD
The $1,000 John Ciardi Award for lifetime contribution to Italian American poetry is awarded annually. The recipient must have published at least two books of poetry (excluding chapbooks).

Send submissions to above address.

This organization offers two other awards for those who have published in Italian Americana. Phone for exact details.

THOMAS JEFFERSON UNIVERSITY PRESS

100 E. Normal Street
Kirksville, MO 63501-4221
Phone (800) 916-6802; Fax (660) 785-4181
Voice (660) 785-4525
E-mail tjup@truman.edu
Website www2.truman.edu/tjup

DEADLINE: OCTOBER 31, 2001 FOR 2002 AWARD

T.S. ELIOT PRIZE FOR POETRY
Prize: The winner receives $2,000 and publication of the collection. The four finalists will also be considered for publication. New Odyssey Press, an imprint of Thomas Jefferson University Press, publishes contemporary poetry, including translations, critical works in poetry and sponsors the T.S. Eliot Prize for poetry. It is an annual award for the best unpublished book-length collection of poetry in English regardless of a poet's nationality, reputation, stage in career, or publication history.

Guidelines
Manuscripts should be between 60 and 100 typed pages of original poetry in English. Each poem should begin on a separate page. Include two title pages: one with your name, address, phone number, and manuscript title; one with only your manuscript title. (Your name must not appear in the manuscript, since the poet's identity should not be known to the judge.) Include a table of contents and a list of acknowledgments for previously published individual poems, if applicable.

Enclose a self-addressed, stamped envelope if you want to be notified when we receive your manuscript. (No other postage-paid envelopes are necessary.) All entrants will receive notice of the results. Manuscripts will not be returned. Please do not send your only copy. Include $25 for the reading fee. Make checks payable to New Odyssey Press. If you prefer to pay by Visa or MasterCard include your credit card number, expiration date, and signature.

Manuscripts must be sent to: T.S. Eliot Prize, New Odyssey Press, Truman State University, 100 East Normal Street, Kirksville, MO 63501.

Each entrant will receive a copy of the winning book.

To place orders for publications: visit website, call, write to address above, fax, or e-mail.

JEWEL BOX THEATRE

Charles Tweed, Production Director
Craig Pruitt, Public Relations Director
Kate Leader, Jewel Box Under the Stars Artistic Director
3700 N. Walker
Oklahoma City, OK 73118-7099
Office Phone (405) 521-1786
Public Relations Phone (405) 528-3108
Fax (405) 525-6562

Deadline: October 6, 2000 – January 15, 2001

JEWEL BOX THEATRE PLAYWRIGHTS' COMPETITION
The Jewel Box Theatre, for 41 years a highly successful community theatre in Oklahoma City, invites all playwrights to submit original manuscripts for its year 2001 competition. Scripts will be accepted October 6, 2000 through January 15, 2001. Sponsored by the First Christian Church.

Criteria for judging include establishment of plot, character, setting, consistency, and credibility.

The winner will be announced in June, 2001 and a cash award of $500 will be presented at the Gem Awards banquet. In addition, the season selection committee will consider the play for full production in the 2001-2002 season.

Plays should be of a strong ensemble nature with emphasis on character rather than spectacle. There is no censorship of subject matter for the competition.

Submission Guidelines

1. Entries must be postmarked no later than January 15, 2001. Hand delivered entries must be checked into the Jewel Box business office at 3700 N. Walker, Oklahoma City, OK 73118 by 5:00 p.m. January 15, 2001.

2. No more than one entry may be submitted by an author. A $5.00 entry fee (check or money order) must accompany the script.

3. Each submission must include two (2) copies of the script with no mention of the author's name or address on any page. Scripts may be bound or in folders but no staples, please.

4. Scripts will be returned if accompanied by a self-addressed, cor-

rectly stamped mailer large enough to accommodate both copies. Score sheets will accompany returned scripts.

If you desire just the score sheets, include a legal size, stamped, self-addressed envelope. Unreturned plays will be destroyed after July 1, 2001.

5. Please use an accepted script format, neatly typed, and include in each script a full character list with description of each character (age, relationship to other characters, etc.) to aid the judges.

6. Only full-length unproduced plays will be considered. Studio production/readings during the writing of the play are not considered full productions. Translations from another language must be submitted by the original author.

7. No children's shows, musicals, or multimedia works can be considered.

8. A COMPLETED AND SIGNED ENTRY FORM/INFORMATION SHEET AND A PLAYWRIGHT'S AGREEMENT STATEMENT MUST ACCOMPANY ALL SUBMISSIONS.

9. Send entries, including entry fee, to: Jewel Box Theatre Playwrights' Competition, 3700 N. Walker, Oklahoma City, OK 73118-7099.

THE JAMES JONES LITERARY SOCIETY

c/o Department of English
Patricia Heaman, Department Chairperson
Wilkes University
Wilkes-Barre, PA 18766

Deadline: March 1, 2001 postmark

THE JAMES JONES LITERARY SOCIETY FIRST NOVEL FELLOWSHIP
The James Jones Society announces that the 8th annual James Jones First Novel Fellowship will be awarded to an American author of a first novel in progress. Novellas (up to 150 pages) and collections of closely linked short stories may also be considered for the competition.

The award is intended to honor the spirit of unblinking honesty, determination, and insight into modern culture exemplified by the late James Jones, author of *From Here to Eternity* and other prose narratives of distinction. Jones was himself the recipient of aid from many supporters as a young writer, and his family, friends, and admirers have established this award of $3,000 to continue this tradition in his name.

The judges are Kaylie Jones, his daughter and a novelist; Kevin Heisler, a writer; J. Michael Lennon, one of his biographers; Patricia Heaman, Chairperson of the English Department of Wilkes University, Wilkes-Barre, Pennsylvania; and Liz Szabla, a fiction writer and editor.

The competition is open to all American writers who have not previously published novels. Manuscripts may be submitted for publication simultaneously, but the Society must be notified of acceptance elsewhere. Officers of the James Jones Society are not eligible for the award.

Entries must be postmarked no later than March 1, 2001. The winner will be notified by September 1, 2001. Winners must accept the award at the James Jones Literary Society Conference to be held in November in Illinois. Transportation funding will be provided.

Submission Guidelines

A two page (maximum) outline of the entire novel and the first 50 pages of the novel-in-progress should be submitted. It should be typed, double spaced. Name, address, and telephone number should be on the title page, but nowhere else on the manuscript. Pages should be numbered. If a manuscript is selected for the final round, its author will be asked to send up to 50 additional pages. Submissions will be acknowledged only if accompanied by a self-addressed, stamped postcard. No manuscripts will be returned. Failure to comply with manuscript guidelines may disqualify entries.

An entry fee of $15 per entry, payable to Wilkes University, must accompany each entry.

All entries must be sent to The James Jones First Novel Fellowship, c/o Department of English, Wilkes University, Wilkes-Barre, PA 18766.

JUNIPER PRIZE POETRY PROGRAM

Juniper Prize
University of Massachusetts
P.O. Box 429
Amherst, MA 01004

Deadline: May 1, 2001 – September 30, 2001

JUNIPER PRIZE
The Juniper Prize for Poetry is awarded annually for an original manuscript of poems. In alternating years, the program is open to poems either with or without previously published books.

In 2001, we will consider only manuscripts by writers whose poems may have appeared in literary journals and/or anthologies, but have not been published or accepted for publication in book form (with the exception of chapbooks under 30 pages in length). Submissions will be accepted between May 1 and September 30, 2001. The award winner will be announced in April/May 2002, and publication scheduled for Spring 2002. Entries for the 2001 prize must be postmarked no later than September 30, 2001.

In the Fall of 2002, we will consider only manuscripts whose authors have had at least one full length book or chapbook or poetry published or accepted for publication. Chapbooks must be at least 30 pages in length, and self-published work does not meet the requirement. Submissions must include the following information about previously published volumes: title, page count, publisher, and year of publication. Entries for the 2002 prize must be postmarked no later than September 30, 2002.

Guidelines
Manuscripts must be paginated and must not exceed 60 pages in typescript (generally 50-55 poems).

Include the following along with your manuscript:

1. Paginated contents page.

2. A list of acknowledgments for poems in the manuscript that have been published or are slated for publication in literary journals and/or anthologies.

3. If applicable, the following information about previously published books: title, page count, publisher, and year of publication.

4. Payment of a $10 nonrefundable entry fee (check or money order payable in U.S. dollars to Juniper Prize, University of Massachusetts Press).
5. A self-addressed, stamped envelope and/or mailer for notification letter and/or return of manuscript. If you wish, you may also include a self-addressed, stamped post card for confirmation of receipt.

The press and the board assume no responsibility for lost or damaged manuscripts, and suggest that you retain a copy for your protection.

Manuscripts by more than one author, entries of more than one manuscript within the same year, translations, and manuscripts from employees and students of the University of Massachusetts or from former Juniper Prize winners are ineligible for submission.

KALLIOPE

3939 Roosevelt Boulevard
Jacksonville, FL 32205
Phone (904) 381-3511

Deadline: November 1, 2001 postmark

THE SUE SANIEL ELKIND POETRY CONTEST
The Sue Elkind Poetry Contest, co-sponsored by *Kalliope*, a journal of women's art, and *Papier Mache,* offers an annual first prize award of $1,000. The winning poem by a woman will be published in *Kalliope*; runners-up will be considered for publication. Judges are to be announced.

Submission Guidelines
Poetry may be in any style and on any subject. Maximum poem length is 50 lines. Entry fee is $5.00 per poem or three (3) poems for $12.00. Payment must accompany submission. Any number of poems may be submitted. Poems that have been previously published, have received monetary awards, or are under consideration elsewhere are not eligible. Manuscripts must be typed. Submit two (2) copies of each poem, one copy with the author's name, address, and phone number TYPED on the upper right corner. The author's name, address, and phone number or identification must NOT appear on the other copy which will be used in the judging. (Strict adherence to guidelines is required. Failure to follow these rules will disqualify entry!) Manuscripts will not be returned. Winner will be announced in Spring 2002.

For an announcement of winners, include a self-addressed, stamped envelope. (If you want to be notified of receipt of your manuscript, include a self-addressed, stamped postcard.)

Submit poetry and check or money order (no cash) to: Kalliope, Sue Saniel Elkind Poetry Contest, FCCJ, 3939 Roosevelt Blvd., Jacksonville, FL 32205.

THE JOHN F. KENNEDY CENTER FOR THE PERFORMING ARTS

2700 F Street, N.W.
Washington, DC 20566
Phone (202) 416-8024
Fax (202) 416-8205
Website http:/kennedy-center.org

Deadline: May 1, 2001

THE JOHN F. KENNEDY CENTER FOR THE PERFORMING ARTS FUND FOR NEW AMERICAN PLAYS AWARDS

We are pleased to announce the 14th year of operation of the Kennedy Center Fund for New American Plays and to present guidelines for the 2001 grant proposal submissions. Please read the guidelines carefully this year, even if you are a regular applicant to the Fund, as we have attempted to define terms, eligibility, and conditions a bit more specifically to avoid confusion. Please also note the addition this year of a specific application form to be included with your submission.

We look forward to your submissions for 2001. If you have any questions, or need application forms, please don't hesitate to call (202) 416-8024 or fax us at (202) 416-8205.

Program Overview
The Fund for New American Plays provides grants in three different categories:

THEATER GRANTS
Theater Grants are awarded to theaters to underwrite specific or extraordinary expenses relating to:

Creative Support – for expenses related to hiring and maintaining the creative team that exceed the theater's budget allocation; and for expenses that permit the playwright's choice of director or designer.

Actor Support – for the costs of guest artists that exceed the theater's budget allocation and for those productions that have larger casts than the producing theater can usually support.

Production Support – for the living and travel expenses of playwrights during the rehearsal and performance, in order to guarantee a minimum of a four-week rehearsal period, and to give the author the opportunity to remain at the theater for rewriting during the run of the play.

Please note: Funding for sets, costumes, lighting, props, or other physical production needs will be considered only under special circumstances. If you are applying for physical production assistance, please explain in your application why you believe such circumstances are special. We do not fund publicity, marketing, payroll taxes, box office, theater overhead, or other non-artistic aspects of a production budget.

The amount of the theater grant is dependent upon the theater's submitted production budget and the total amount available to the Fund for the year and is determined by the Artistic Advisory Committee at its sole discretion.

PLAYWRIGHT GRANTS
Playwright Grants are awarded to the winning playwright in addition to production support for the theater. This award is in the amount of $10,000.

THE ROGER L. STEVENS AWARD
This award is a separate incentive grant in the amount of $2,500 given from time to time to a playwright whom the Artistic Advisory Committee believes has shown exceptional promise, even though the play did not win a theater/playwright grant in that particular year.

MOST PROMISING COMEDY WRITER AWARD
Please take notice that the 2000 Kennedy Center Fund for New American Plays competition now has a new award category. The new annual award will be given to the most promising comedy writer and will be in the amount of $5,000. Please call for details.

If you have any questions, or need application forms, please don't hesitate to call (202) 416-8024 or fax us at (202) 416-8205.

Eligibility

THEATERS
Any non-profit professional American theater company may apply for financial support for one new play that will open on stage in its world premiere no earlier than November 1, 1999, and no later than December 31, 2000. Professional may be loosely defined as any theater which:

1) maintains a regular annual mainstage season;
2) employs a professional administrative staff and professional actors; and
3) presents each of its shows for a standard run of at least 16 performances.

Non-professional theater companies, for the purpose of this grant, would include community theaters, dinner theaters, summer stock, college/high school theaters, and similar organizations. Non-profit status must be proven by submission of a copy of the theater company's 501(c)(3), as outlined in the application requirements.

Co-productions between more than one theater are allowed, but all parties must sign and be obligated to the terms of the final contract. Theaters participating in a co-production submissions may not submit another separate proposal in the same year.

PLAYS

The play submitted must be written by a U.S. citizen. The play may not have been produced before, but may have had readings and workshop productions preparatory to full production. Any previous production which included standard set, lighting, and costume elements, and was shown before a paying audience, would be considered a full production, and would therefore render the play ineligible for this award.

Adaptations of novels or other forms of literature, foreign and domestic, are permitted, but translations of foreign plays are not. All copyright issues related to such adaptations must be resolved by the playwright before submission to the Fund.

Since funding decisions are based primarily on the artistic excellence and merit of the play, it is imperative that the script sent be in a completed form (realizing, of course, that the script will be constantly reworked and fine-tuned throughout the final production process). Partial scripts or outlines are not acceptable. A series of one-act plays intended to be shown together on the same evening is eligible as one submission, but the plays must be written by the same playwright.

In theory, this grant is intended for plays for adult audiences. While plays for young people are not ineligible, please be aware that they may suffer by comparison to other adult works simply because of differences in style, length, and available resources. The Kennedy Center also sponsors a separate bi-annual competition entitled New Visions/New Voices, which is intended to assist theaters in producing new works for young audiences. For further information on the 2001 competition, please call (202) 416-8880, or e-mail them at yfp@mail.kennedy-center.org, or visit the Center's home page at http:/kennedy-center.org.

How to Apply

All applications for grants must be submitted by a theater company. No submissions from individual playwrights will be accepted. If the application is for a co-production, please have one theater serve as a primary representative and send the submission through that theater. The submission package must contain the following items:

1. A completed application form.

2. A production budget. This must be arranged in a three-column format (call or write us for a sample). THE PURPOSE OF THIS PROJECT IS TO HELP SUPPORT A PARTICULAR PLAY; HENCE, YOUR REQUEST FOR FUNDING SHOULD NOT REFLECT OVERHEAD OR ANNUAL COSTS OF RUNNING THE THEATER. We are, however, interested in all costs concerning the submitted production, including those line items and operating costs for which we do not provide funding. If you are submitting a request for costumes, sets, lighting, and other unusual production expenses, please note special circumstances. Please be sure to include the theater, author's name, and title of the play on your submission budget.

3. Five non-returnable copies of the play. Please "blind" three of the copies by removing the name of the playwright and the theater, and leave one of the remaining two copies unbound in case additional copies are needed.

4. A brief history of the theater organization, including an overview of its mission and standard programming offerings.

5. Proof of non-profit status. This should be in the form of an official 501(c)(3) tax exemption letter issued by the U.S. Department of Treasury.

6. A copy of the exclusive arrangement between the playwright and theater stating that, should the play receive a grant, no other theater may produce the play prior to the funded theater's production.

7. A history of readings, workshops, and other development work associated with the submitted play.

8. Disclosure of any encumbrances to the script (i.e., adaptation rights have been obtained verbally, but the written agreement is not yet finished).

9. Disclosure of any co-production agreements with other theaters or producers in regard to the submitted play.

10. Press materials as follows (to be used immediately should the play be chosen for a grant): short biographies of the theater, its artistic director, the playwright, and any artist for whom financial support is being requested; TWO black-and-white headshots (photos) of the playwright; and a short synopsis of the play as you would like it to appear in a press release.

All submission packages must be RECEIVED in our office by Monday, May 1, 2001. Due to the very quick turnaround time necessary to get the plays read, NO LATE SUBMISSIONS WILL BE ACCEPTED. A package postmarked by May 1st but not received by that date will be considered late and NOT ACCEPTED.

Mail or deliver to: Fund for New American Plays, The John F. Kennedy Center for the Performing Arts, 2700 F Street, N.W., Washington, DC 20566.

Please don't hesitate to call our office for an application form, or if you have any questions or need assistance; phone (202) 416-8024; fax (202) 416-8205.

KEY WEST THEATRE FESTIVAL

The Red Barn Theatre, San Carlos Institute, Tennessee Williams Fine Arts Center, and Waterfront Playhouse
Phil Lindsay, Event Administrator
P.O. Box 992
Key West, FL 33041
Phone (305) 292-3725; Fax (305) 293-0845

Deadline: none

THE KEY WEST THEATRE FESTIVAL
The 10th annual Key West Theatre Festival accepts play submissions all year. We are particularly looking for one-act and full-length scripts preferably with single sets and a maximum cast of eight. We are also looking for musicals and children's plays.

All scripts should be submitted by an agent/and or accompanied by two letters of recommendation. Submissions must be unproduced. Please include a self-addressed, stamped envelope if you would like your script returned. Please include a one-page synopsis of your play.

If your play is selected for production, you will receive airfare and accommodation in Key West for part of the rehearsal period and opening of the play.

Now in its tenth year, the annual ten-day festival produces new original plays from around the country, incorporating our island's theatre venues and talent to bring the pieces to life.

The festival has enjoyed a steady increase in national recognition and attendance, and in the quality of plays submitted. Several plays have gone on to script publication with Samuel French and some have been produced in major cities, with notable success and positive critical response.

THE LEDGE

78-44 80th street
Glendale, NY 11385

Deadline: April 30, 2001

THE LEDGE 2001 POETRY AWARD COMPETITION
Prize: $1,000 and publication in *The Ledge*

Guidelines
No restrictions on length, form or content. Excellence is the only criterion. Unpublished poems only. Simultaneous submissions are acceptable.
Entry Fee: $9 for the first three poems; $3 for each additional poem.

$12 subscription gains free entry (for the first three poems) to the competition. All poems will be considered for publication in *The Ledge.*

Include name and address on each poem. Include a self-addressed, stamped envelope for notification or manuscript return. Winner will be announced in September, 2001.

Send submissions to above contest name and address.

Deadline: October 31, 2001

THE LEDGE PRESS 2001 AND EIGHTH ANNUAL
POETRY CHAPBOOK COMPETITION
Prize: $1,000 and 50 copies of typeset, professionally printed chapbook.

Guidelines
Submit 16-28 pages of poetry with title page, biography and acknowledgments, if any. Simultaneous submissions are acceptable and poets may enter as many manuscripts as they wish.

No restrictions on form or content. Excellence is the only criterion.

Include a self-addressed, stamped envelope for results or manuscript return. Winner will be announced in April, 2002 and winning chapbook will be published in the Fall of 2002.

$12 entry fee includes a copy of the winning chapbook.

Send submissions to above contest name and address.

LE SAND PUBLICATIONS

1252 Terra Nova Boulevard
Pacifica, CA 94044-4340

Deadline: November 30, 2001

LINES IN THE SAND SHORT FICTION CONTEST
The Lines in the Sand Short Fiction Contest offers First, Second, and Third Prizes of $50, $25, $10, respectively. All winning stories including, honorable mentions, will be published in the year 2002 January/February Awards Edition of *Lines In The Sand.*

Submission Guidelines
Submit two double-spaced typed copies any genre, 2,000 words maximum. A $5 reading fee is required for each manuscript submitted. (Be sure to print your name on first page of the manuscript.) Include a brief biography with your entry. Manuscripts are not returned. Submission deadline is November 30, 2001.

Mail entry fee to: Le Sand Publications, 1252 Terra Nova Blvd, Pacifica, CA 94044-4340.

There is no critique on Contest Stories. We reserve the right to cancel and return all entry fees if response is inadequate to cover cash prizes.

General Publication Guidelines
Le Sand publications accept all types of fiction up to 2,000 words, and all poetry up to 20 lines. Authors receive a copy of the issue in which their story appears. Manuscripts should by typed double spaced on white paper. Submit seasonal material six months in advance. Send a brief biography with your submission. Remember, be sure to include a self-addressed, stamped envelope for return of your manuscript. For an optional personal critique, submit $5.00 along with your manuscript.

Subscription Information

SINGLE ISSUE $3.50 (Outside U.S.A. $4.50)
Send for an issue to see what kind of stories we publish. Include your name, address with zip code, and check or money order, and mail to: Le Sand publications, 890 Southgate Avenue, Daly City, CA 94015.

LINCOLN COLLEGE

c/o Janet Overton
300 Keokuk Street
Lincoln, IL 62656-1699

Deadline: May 31, 2001 postmark

THE BILLEE MURRAY DENNY POETRY AWARD
Lincoln College announces the 21st annual contest for the Billee Murray Denny Poetry Award. First Prize is $1,000, Second Prize is $500, and Third Prize is $250.

Rules and Guidelines

1. Contestants may submit one, two, or three original poems that have not been published previously by a commercial, university, or small press with a circulation greater than 250.

2. Contestants may not have previously published a book of poetry with a commercial or university press. This rule does not apply to chapbooks with a circulation less than 250.

3. Lincoln College will not discuss Rules 1 and 2 or any other aspect of this contest by mail, phone, or in any other way with contestants.

4. No comments will be made regarding any of the entries

5. Poems may not exceed 100 lines in length.

6. Entries must be typed on 8-1/2 x 11 inch white paper.

7. Contestant's name and address must not appear on either the front or the back of the typewritten sheet.

8. Entries of more than one page should be stapled in the upper left corner. Do not staple two or more entries together.

9. Contestants should keep a copy of all entries as they will not be acknowledged or returned.

10. Poems may be written on any subject, using any style. The Denny will stipulates that the official contest rules must state that winning poems cannot contain any vulgar, obscene, suggestive, or offensive word or phrase. This stipulation should not be interpreted to imply that the judges will use anything other than accepted contemporary literary standards when evaluating entries.

11. The entry form (or facsimile) must be accompanied by an entry fee of $10 (U.S. currency) per poem; limit three poems per entrant ($30). Checks should be payable to "Poetry Contest – Lincoln College." Poems submitted without the entry fee will not be considered or returned. Entry fees for poems withdrawn by a contestant after submission will not be returned. Checks returned for insufficient funds will result in immediate disqualification of the entry.

12. Winners will be notified on or before September 30, 2001. To receive a list of the contest winners, enclose a self-addressed, stamped envelope marked "Winners." No phone inquiries please.

13. All prizes, including a selected number of honorable mentions, will be awarded at the sole discretion of the judges.

14. Lincoln College will have the right to publish the winning poem, including selected honorable mention winners, in *The Denny Poems* anthology. Exclusive rights to publication will not be held by Lincoln College any longer than one year.

15. All entries must be postmarked no later than May 31, 2001.

16. Copies of *The Denny Poems – 1998-99*, an anthology of the 1998 and 1999 contest winners and honorable mentions, are available for $5 each from Lincoln College.

17. Mail entries or requests for books to Poetry Contest, c/o Janet Overton, Lincoln College, 300 Keokuk Street, Lincoln, Illinois 62656-1699.

Contest Entry Form

Mail entry form to Poetry Contest, c/o Janet Overton, Lincoln College, 300 Keokuk Street, Lincoln, Illinois 62656-1699.

Name ______________________________

Address ______________________________

Telephone ( ) ______________________________

City ______________________________

State ______________ Zip Code ______________

Poem Title

1. ______________________________

Poem Title

2. ______________________________

Poem Title

3. ______________________________

I certify that all works submitted to the Billee Murray Denny Poetry Contest represent my original and unpublished work and that I meet the eligibility requirements stipulated in the contest rules. By entering this contest. I grant full permission to Lincoln College and to anyone authorized by Lincoln College to publish and publicize my entry, including my name, address, and photograph.

SIGNATURE ______________________________

[illegible]

Name

Address

Telephone

City

State Zip Code

Occupation

Poem Title

Poem Title

[illegible]

SIGNATURE

LINDBERGH FOUNDATION

Executive Director
708 South 3rd Street, Suite 110
Minneapolis, MN 55415-1141
Phone (612) 338-1703; Fax (612) 338-6826
E-mail lindfdtn@mtn.org

Deadline: November 1, 2002

ANNE SPENCER LINDBERGH PRIZE
Prize: $5,000. The Anne Spencer Lindbergh Prize in Children's Literature will be offered on a biennial, rather than annual, basis. The program recognizes children's fantasy novels written in the English language judged to be the best published during the year.

Deadline for entries in the 2001-2002 program is November 1, 2002.

Four copies of each book along with a $25 submission fee should be sent to the above address.

Judges will be a panel of writers, editors, librarians and teachers prominent in the field of children's literature.

Announcement of award is January 2003.

Past winner was Joan Aiken for her novel, *Cold Shoulder Road*.

THE ANNUAL LITERAL LATTÉ FICTION AWARDS

61 East 8th Street
Box 240
New York, NY 10003
Phone (212) 260-5532
E-mail litlatte@aol.com
Website www.Literal-Latte.com

Deadline: January 19, 2001 postmark

LITERAL LATTÉ FICTION AWARDS
Stimulating stories, essays, and poetry. Awards: First Prize, $1,000; Second Prize, $200; Third Prize, $100; up to 7 Honorable Mentions; and winning stories published in *Literal Latté*.

Guidelines
Send previously unpublished stories up to 5,000 words

Include name, address, and telephone number on cover page only.

Include self-addressed, stamped envelope for notification (and return of manuscript if desired).

Include $10 reading fee per story, or $15 for entry for one story and 1 year/6 issue subscription (if renewal, please note).

Make check or money order payable to *Literal Latté*, or include Visa/MasterCard or American Express number, expiration date and signature.

Winners will be notified by April 15.

Deadline: July 19, 2001 postmark

THE ANNUAL *LITERAL LATTÉ* POETRY AWARDS
Awards: First Prize, $1,000; Second Prize, $200; Third Prize, $100; up to 7 Honorable Mentions; and winners published in *Literal Latté.*

Guidelines
Send previously unpublished poems (all styles, up to 2,000 words each).

Include name, address, and telephone number on cover page only.

Include self-addressed, stamped envelope for notification (and return of manuscript if desired).

Include $10 entry fee for each set of up to six poems, or $15 which includes entry for one set of poems plus a one year/6 issue subscription (if renewal, please note).

Make check or money order payable to *Literal Latté*, or include Visa/MasterCard or American Express number, expiration date and signature.

Winners will be notified by September 15, 2001.

Literal Latté publishes 25,000 copies, six times a year.

LITTLE THEATRE OF ALEXANDRIA

Chairman, Playwriting Competition
Little Theatre of Alexandria
600 Wolfe Street
Alexandria, VA 22314

Deadline: September 1, 2001 – February 29, 2002 postmark

LITTLE THEATRE OF ALEXANDRIA
NATIONAL ONE-ACT PLAYWRITING COMPETITION
Entries to the 25th LTA National One-Act Playwriting Competition must be unpublished (not available to amateur or professional theatres for royalty payments) and unproduced (not staged for paying audience as of date of entry). No adaptations or translations are accepted.

Scripts will be judged on concept, dramatic action, characterization, dialogue, and technical requirements.

Winning playwrights will receive cash awards: First – $350, Second – $250, and Third – $150.

Submission Guidelines
All scripts should be legibly typed, firmly bound and of standard size. Send a duplicate copy, not the original. Only one entry per playwright.

Scripts will be returned only if accompanied by manuscript-size, self-addressed, stamped envelope. Do not use metered postage on return envelope.

Scripts should include the name, address and telephone number of author on title page. A cast of characters with descriptions and a brief synopsis should be attached as part of play. Number all pages.

Scripts may be held until the winner is announced in September or October 2002.

All production and publication rights remain the property of the playwright.

The Little Theatre of Alexandria (LTA) shall have the right to produce selected scripts without payment of royalties. LTA reserves the right to withhold any or all awards. Production will be at the discretion of LTA.

Only stage plays will be judged. Film and TV scripts will not be accepted. Critical analysis of scripts will not be provided.

Experience has shown that judges are favorably inclined towards scripts that have a running time of 20 to 60 minutes, where the scenes are few, only one set is used, and when a precis of the play precedes abstract works.

All scripts must be postmarked by February 29, 2002.

Send scripts and $5.00 submission fee to: Chairman, Playwriting Competition, Little Theatre of Alexandria, 600 Wolfe Street, Alexandria, VA 22314.

THE LONGMEADOW JOURNAL LITERARY COMPETITION

c/o Robert and Rita Morton
6750 Longmeadow Avenue
Lincolnwood, IL 60646
Phone (312) 726-9789

Deadline: December 31, 2001

THE LONGMEADOW JOURNAL LITERARY COMPETITION
FOR SHORT STORY WRITERS BETWEEN THE AGES OF 10 AND 19

We shall annually publish twenty short stories and award the following prizes: First prize $175; Second prize $100; and five Third prizes of $50. If you mention a teacher, librarian, dean, or advisor (with mailing addresses) who encouraged you to enter your short story, and you win a cash prize, we will recognize that person with a special award of $50.

Submission Guidelines

Manuscript must be typed, double-spaced, less than 3,000 words, and submitted before December 31, 2001 with a self-addressed, stamped envelope. The writer's name, age, and address, and the name of the school he or she attends must appear.

The editors will be the final judge of all submissions and reserve the right of first publication.

All winners will be notified by June 2001.

Entries should be sent to: The Longmeadow Journal, c/o Robert and Rita Morton, 6750 Longmeadow Avenue, Lincolnwood, IL 60646. Telephone inquiries may be made to (312) 726-9789.

THE MADISON REVIEW

University of Wisconsin – Madison
Department of English
Helen C. White Hall
600 N. Park Street
Madison, WI 53706

Deadline: September 1, 2001 – September 30, 2001

The Madison Review announces annual prizes for Poetry and Fiction submitted in an open national competition.

THE PHYLLIS SMART YOUNG PRIZE IN POETRY
The Phyllis Smart Young Poetry Award and publication in *The Madison Review* will be awarded to the best group of three unpublished poems.

THE CHRIS O'MALLEY PRIZE IN FICTION
The Chris O'Malley Prize in Fiction and publication in *The Madison Review* will be awarded to the best unpublished short story.

Submission Guidelines
Submissions must be accompanied by business-sized, self-addressed, stamped envelope for contest results. Manuscripts will not be returned. Multiple or previously published submissions are ineligible. Submissions must arrive at *The Madison Review* between September 1 and September 30. All entries will be considered as submissions to *The Madison Review*, the literary journal of The Program in Creative Writing of the University of Wisconsin – Madison. Submissions are limited to one short story, or three poems (of no more than four, typed, double-spaced pages for each poem) from each author. Author's name, address, and phone must appear on each poem or story. Winners will be announced in December. Due to heavy submissions, there will be an Entry Fee of $3.00. Submissions without entry fee and self-addressed, stamped envelope will not be considered for the contests.

Send manuscripts and queries to: The Madison Review/Phyllis Smart Young Prize in Poetry or The Madison Review/Chris O'Malley Prize in Fiction, Department of English, 600 N. Park Street, Helen C. White Hall, University of Wisconsin – Madison, Madison, WI 53706.

Make all checks payable to: The Madison Review.

THE MARLBORO REVIEW

Ellen Dudely, Editor
The Marlboro Review, Poetry Prize
P.O. Box 243
Marlboro, VT 05344
Website www.marlbororeview.com

Deadline: January 15, 2001

THE MARLBORO PRIZE IN POETRY
Awards: Winner will be awarded a $1,000 honorarium. The winning poem(s) will be published in the Spring 2001 issue.

Guidelines
Please submit up to five poems (any length) and a $10 reading fee.

Make checks payable to The Marlboro Review, Inc.

Winner will be notified by March 15, 2001.

Judge's decision is final although all submissions will be considered for publication.

Include self-addressed, stamped envelope for contest results or visit our website.

The Marlboro Prize in Poetry Application Form

Please list poems below; no name should appear anywhere on the poems.

Name: ____________________

Address ____________________

City, State, Zip ____________________

List Poems by title:

1. ____________________

2. ____________________

3. ____________________

4. ____________________

5. ____________________

MAXIM MAZUMDAR NEW PLAY COMPETITION

Kevin Stevens, Literary Manager
Alleyway Theatre
1 Curtain Up Alleyway
Buffalo, NY 14202-1911
E-Mail AlleywayTH@aol.com
Website www.alleyway.com

Deadline: July 1, 2001

The annual international competition was founded in 1989 by Alleyway Theatre in memory of Canadian actor and playwright Maxim Mazumdar (1953-1988). Mr. Mazumdar's many contributions to the early growth of Alleyway Theatre were artistically invaluable and instrumental in shaping a continuing relationship with Canadian Theatre. It was at Alleyway Theatre that Mr. Mazumdar gave his final performance in the premiere of his original musical LUPERCAL on March 27, 1988.

Awards: In addition to modest cash prizes in each category, the winning full-length will receive its premiere production at Alleyway Theatre in the following season which begins ten months after the announcement of winners. The winning one-act will receive its premiere in the annual Buffalo Quickies Festival. The winning play for children receives first consideration for premiere by K!dSHowCo., Alleyway Theatre's children's company. Finalists will be announced October 1st; winners will be announced November 1st.

Guidelines

Entry fee of $5 US funds per playwright covers entry in all three categories, money order or check made out to Alleyway Theatre, Inc. There is no entry form.

Self-addressed, stamped envelope required if playwright wishes script returned.

Musicals must be accompanied by audio tape of complete score.

Please include character breakdown, including doubling.

Entry in the competition constitutes the author's agreement that, in the event of being declared a winner, he or she must grant first production rights to Alleyway Theatre under the terms of the Alleyway Theatre Standard Production Agreement (sample available upon request, additional terms will not be negotiated).

Eligibility

The competition is open to anyone of any age and citizenship, but entrants are limited to one submission per category per year.

Although an entry may be of any style, preference will be given to scripts which are uniquely theatrical.

Entries must not be previously produced (staged readings excepted) and must be withheld form production during the period of the competition.

Categories

Full-Length: play or musical not less than ninety minutes in length, any style, no more than 10 performers. Collections of one-acts are not eligible.

One-Act: Play not more than forty minutes in length, any style, no more than six performers.

Play for Children: play or musical not more than sixty minutes in length, no more than five performers.

THE MID-AMERICAN REVIEW

Department of English
Bowling Green State University
Bowling Green, OH 43403
Phones (419) 372-2725 and (419) 372-2576
Senior Editor: Robert Early
Editor-in-Chief: George Looney
Poetry Editor: David Hawkins
Translation Editor: Amy Withrow
Non-fiction Editor: George Looney
Fiction Editor: Michael Czyzniejewski

THE MID-AMERICAN REVIEW

THE SHERWOOD ANDERSON PRIZE FOR FICTION

THE JAMES WRIGHT PRIZE FOR POETRY

The Mid-American Review (MAR) awards the Sherwood Anderson Prize for fiction and the James Wright Prize for poetry to manuscripts published in regular editions of MAR. There is no application form nor is there an entrance fee. The awards are given when funding is available.

Submission Guidelines

Stories, poems, and articles will generally be returned or accepted within one to four months. Please include a self-addressed, stamped envelope.

Payment to authors is $10.00 per page (pending funding) for fiction, poetry, translations, and non-fiction with a maximum payment of $50; contributing authors receive two complimentary copies. Sample copies of MAR are $5.00, current issues $7.00, and rare back issues $10.00.

All rights revert to the author upon publication. Manuscripts are not read from June through August. MAR does not consider simultaneous submissions or work which has previously appeared elsewhere.

Poetry

Poetry Editor: David Hawkins

Poems should emanate from textured, evocative images; use language with an awareness of how words sound and mean; and have a definite sense of voice. Each line should help carry the poem, and an individual vision must be evident. We encourage new as well as established writers. There is no length limit on individual poems, but please send no more than six poems.

Translation

Translation Editor: Amy Withrow

All submissions must include the original as well as the translated work. Chapbooks (approximately 10-15 poems) are designed to provide readers with an introduction to a single contemporary poet or a group of poets. An introductory essay of 300-500 words outlining the historical context of the poetry is encouraged. Translations of contemporary fiction are also welcome and should follow these guidelines as well as those listed under Fiction.

Non-fiction

Non-fiction Editor: George Looney

The Mid-American Review seeks essays and critical articles which focus on contemporary authors and topics of current literary interest. Contributions should generally not exceed 15-20 pages and should follow standard MLA style. We also seek short (500-1,000 words) book reviews of current works of poetry, fiction, and non-fiction prose, published within the last one to two years. Address book reviews to the Non-fiction Editor.

Fiction

Fiction Editor: Michael Czyzniejewski

The Mid-American Review prefers quality fiction which is both character and language oriented; we are open to experimental work, but discourage juvenilia and genre-type fiction. Do not submit more than one story at a time. *The Mid-American Review* usually prints stories 10-20 pages in length; authors submitting manuscripts of over 30 pages should query first with a self-addressed, stamped envelope.

Submit all entries to: Department of English, Bowling Green State University, Bowling Green, Ohio 43403.

MIDLAND COMMUNITY THEATRE, INC.

2000 W. Wadley
Midland, TX 79705
Phone (915) 682-2544

Deadline: December 1, 2000 – January 31, 2001

MCLAREN MEMORIAL COMEDY PLAYWRITING COMPETITION
Enter your original, unproduced comedy scripts for the stage. We are seeking comedy scripts only.

Plays submitted should be unproduced. We do not count previous "readings" as productions and we will consider plays produced once in a non-profit setting. Length, number of characters, and setting are not limited. The playwright retains all rights to the work submitted.

The winning play may be presented as a full production in the following MCT membership season. The winning playwright will receive a $400 cash prize.

Submission Guidelines
Scripts will be accepted between December 1 and January 31 for the annual competition.

Scripts should be typed and bound, or in a folder.

Scripts will not be returned unless accompanied by a self-addressed, stamped envelope.

Semi-finalists will be selected by April 1st. Finalists will be selected by May 15th. The finalists will be presented in a festival format. The winning play will be announced by September 1st. Non-winning finalists will be designated, but no prizes will accompany such designations.

A $5.00 entry fee per script is required.

Send your script and entry fee to: McLaren Memorial Comedy Playwriting Competition, Midland Community Theatre, 2000 W. Wadley, Midland, Texas 79705.

MID-LIST PRESS

4324-12th Avenue South
Minneapolis, MN 55407-3218
Website www.midlist.org

MID-LIST PRESS FIRST SERIES AWARDS

Deadline: October 1, 2000 – February 29, 2001 postmark

FIRST SERIES AWARD FOR THE NOVEL

Guidelines for Novelists
Since 1990, Mid-List Press has sponsored the First Series Award for the Novel for writers who have yet to publish a novel. Manuscripts must be at least 50,000 words in length. The award includes publication and a $1,000 advance against royalties. Submissions are accepted between October 1 and February 1. Writers who have yet to publish a novel may only submit manuscripts through the first series. Previously published novelists should query first with a representative sample from the manuscript.

Deadline: April 1, 2001 – July 1, 2001 postmark

FIRST SERIES AWARD FOR SHORT FICTION

Guidelines for Writers of Short Fiction
Since 1995, Mid-List Press has sponsored the First Series Award for Short Fiction for writers who have yet to publish a book-length collection of short fiction (short stories, novellas). Manuscripts must be at least 50,000 words in length. The award includes publication and a $1,000 advance against royalties. Submissions are accepted between April 1 and July 1. Writers who have yet to publish a collection of short stories and/or novellas may only submit manuscripts through the First Series. Writers who have previously published a collection of short fiction should query first. The query should include at least one story or novella.

Deadline: April 1, 2001 – July 1, 2001 postmark

FIRST SERIES AWARD FOR CREATIVE NON-FICTION

Guidelines for Writers of Creative Non-fiction
Since 1996, Mid-List Press has sponsored the First Series Award for Creative Non-fiction for writers who have yet to publish a book of creative non-fiction (either a collection of essays or a single book-length work). "Creative non-fiction" includes (but is not limited to) memoir, autobiography, nature writing, travel writing, personal essay, literary journalism, social commentary, and cross-disciplinary work.

Manuscripts must be at least 50,000 words in length. The award includes publication and a $1,000 advance against royalties. Submissions are accepted between April 1 and July 1. Writers who have yet to publish a book-length creative non-fiction may only submit manuscripts through the First Series. Writers who have previously published a book of creative non-fiction should query first. The query should include at least one essay or sample chapter.

Deadline: October 1, 2000 – February 1, 2001 postmark

FIRST SERIES AWARD FOR POETRY

Guidelines for Poets
Since 1990, Mid-List Press has sponsored the First Series Award for Poetry for poets who have yet to publish a book of poetry. (A chapbook is not considered a book of poetry.) Manuscripts must be at least 60 pages in length, numbered, and single spaced. The award includes publication and a $500 advance against royalties. Submissions are accepted between October and February. Poets who have yet to publish a book of poetry may only submit manuscripts through the First Series. Poets who have previously published a book of poetry should query first. The query should include a representative sample from the collection.

General Guidelines for Submission
An official entry form and a $15 reading fee must accompany each submission. (Please photocopy the entry form if submitting for more than one award.) Make checks payable to Mid-List Press. There are no special formatting requirements other than those noted above. Submit the entire manuscript. Only one submission per person per award. Simultaneous submissions are acceptable.

Manuscripts may be submitted for the First Series Award for the Novel and the First Series Award for Poetry beginning October 1, 2000, and must be postmarked by February 1, 2001. Manuscripts may be submitted for the First Series Award for Short Fiction and the First Series Award for Creative Non-fiction beginning April 1, 2001, and must be postmarked by July 1, 2001.

Manuscripts will not be returned, so submit a disposable copy. Include a #10 business self-addressed, stamped envelope for notification. We will acknowledge receipt of the manuscript only if you also enclose an optional self-addressed, stamped postcard.

Mail manuscripts to: First Series Awards, Mid-List Press, 4324-12th Avenue South, Minneapolis, MN 55407-3218.

No submissions or queries of any kind will be returned or responded to without a proper self-addressed, stamped envelope. At this time Mid-List Press does not consider children's books, young adult fiction, general non-fiction, or photographic essay material.

Mid-List Press is not responsible for any manuscripts that do not follow these submission guidelines.

We reserve the right to select no winner for any given award in any given year.

Mid-List Press First Series Award
Entry Form

Please type or print.

Name ______________________________
Last First Middle

Address ______________________________
(Apt. No)

City ______________________________

State ______________ Zip ______________

Phone ______________________________

Title of Work ______________________________

____

____

Category ______________________________

MILL MOUNTAIN THEATRE

One Market Square, S.E.
Second Floor
Roanoke, VA 24011-1437
Phone (540) 342-5749

Deadline: October 1, 2001 – January 1, 2002

THE 2001 MILL MOUNTAIN THEATRE NEW PLAY COMPETITION
Sponsored by Norfolk Southern Foundation
Prizes: First Place: $1,000 and a staged reading with the possibility of a full production. Second Place: $500

Submission Guidelines
Open to any playwright living in the United States. Eligible scripts are ones that are unproduced, unpublished theatrical scripts in English.

One submission per author per year. Script must be agent-submitted or recommended by a director, literary manager or dramaturg. Subject matter and character variations are open. No film or television scripts.

No translations or adaptations. Plays that have received developmental workshops are permitted. One-acts are permitted (minimum running time: 25-35 minutes). Musicals permitted if accompanied by a demo tape. Previous submissions are permitted only with substantial structural revisions.

Scripts must be legibly typed, firmly bound, on standard letter-sized paper and accompanied by:

- name, address and phone number of author on a title page.
- author's biography and history of play.
- brief synopsis of scenes.
- self-addressed, stamped postcard if arrival acknowledgment is needed.
- self-addressed, stamped envelope (manuscript-sized) with First Class postage if return desired.

By submitting to this contest, entrants agree to:

- accept all conditions of the submission guidelines.
- production of winning script(s) by Mill Mountain Theatre.
- sign a statement of authenticity declaring it is an original work and not under consideration for publication prior to the scheduled contest production dates.

Mill Mountain Theatre:

- maintains the exclusive right to declare no winner and withhold prizes if no script of merit is found.
- assumes no responsibility for lost or damaged scripts.
- relinquishes all right to the author(s) of the winning script(s) after the scheduled contest production dates.

Submissions should be addressed c/o Literary Manager at the above contest name and address.

Finalists will be announced by August 1, 2002.

MILTON CENTER

Kansas Newman University
3100 McCormick Avenue
Wichita, KS 67213-2097
Phone (316) 942-4291; Fax: (316) 942-4483
Milton Center Fax (316) 942-9658
E-mail miltonc@newmanu.edu
Website www.newmanu.edu

Deadline: March 1, 2001

Fellowship: $11,000 stipend for each fellowship winner. These fellowships are designed to offer new writers of Christian commitment the opportunity to complete their first book-length manuscript of fiction, poetry, or creative nonfiction.

The Milton Center exists to encourage work by writers who seek to animate the Christian imagination, foster intellectual integrity and explore the human condition with honesty and compassion. Each fellowship provides a $11,000 stipend, disbursed over nine months.

Those awarded fellowships should be prepared to take up residence in Wichita, Kansas, by September 1, 2001. Fellows will share in the ongoing work of the Center, such as planning conferences, grant-writing, etc. This work will entail approximately ten hours per week. Experience with computers, software and e-mail is very desirable. A supportive community of writers will meet in a weekly workshop which will provide peer review of manuscripts in progress.

The Center also invites fellowship recipients to be a part of the worshipping community at Newman University while they are here. The Milton center is not concerned with promoting a particular religious dogma. Of the nine Fellows we've had to date, four have been Catholic, two Baptists, one Eastern Orthodox, one Mennonite, and one Episcopalian.

Selection of the post-graduate fellows will be based on the viability of the project proposed, the quality of the writing displayed, and the applicant's demonstrated ability to carry through a complete writing project. We are looking for writers whose projects are well under way or are clearly formulated. The Milton Center will give professional assistance in placing the manuscript with appropriate publishers.

MISSISSIPPI VALLEY POETRY CONTEST

Max Molleston, President
P.O. Box 3188
Rock Island, IL 61201
Phone (319) 359-1057

Deadline: January 1, 2001 – September 1, 2001

MISSISSIPPI VALLEY POETRY CONTEST

Under the auspices of the North American Literary Escadrille the annual Mississippi Valley Poetry Contest began in 1972 and has grown to become one of the premier contests in the U.S. and abroad. Open to all poets, the contest especially wishes to encourage student participation.

The Mississippi Valley Poetry Contest (MVPC) is certified non-profit by the Illinois Secretary of State's Office. Contests are practically funded by donations, grants, and private sponsors. The MVPC operates under auspices of a non-profit parent organization, the North American Literary Escadrille. Both groups are operated by non-paid volunteer poets, writers, and artists. The Escadrille also sponsors workshops, writing contests, and lectures. Top poetry contest winners are selected by outstanding poetry judges. Our purpose is to encourage the writing and appreciation of poetry everywhere.

Special Categories

If you do not choose to enter one or more of the special categories, mark your entry "Adult General."

1. Mississippi Valley: Poems best describing any aspect of the Mississippi Valley, historically or in the present. Award $50.
2. Senior Citizen: Poems on any subject by any poet 60 or over. Award $50.
3. Jazz: Poems on any aspect of jazz, past or present. Award $50.
4. Religious: Poems on any religious theme. Award $50.
5. Humorous: Any form of humor, but no jingles, please. Award $50.
6. Haiku: Best poem in this style. Award $50.
7. Rhyming: Poems on any subject. Award $50.
8. Ethnic: Any aspect of ethnic culture, customs, or history. Award $50.
9. History: Any aspect of regional, U.S., or world history, early or recent. Award $50.

There also will be awards of merit and honorable mentions that do not include cash prizes.

Student Awards

High School: Award of $75.
Junior High School: Award of $75.
Elementary School: Award of $50.

Adult General Category Awards

First Prize Award of $100.
Second Prize Award of $75.
Third Prize Award of $50.

Major/Grand Prize Awards

Entrants in the Adult General Category are also considered for the Grand Prizes. Grand prizes are:

First Grand Prize Award of $175.
Second Grand Prize Award of $125.

Submission Guidelines

1. The contest is open to poets of all ages.

2. Each poet may submit from one to five poems, maximum 50 lines per poem, for a flat fee of $5.00 The entry fee remains just $5.00 whether you submit one poem or five.

3. Poems entered in the contest must not have been previously published. Do not submit the same poem in more than one category.

4. Type or write clearly each poem. Place your name and address in the top left-hand corner of the title page and list the category you are entering (such as "Adult General"). Clip together poems of more than one page.

5. If you are a student, you should include your grade and the name of your school as of September of the year in which you are entering. IMPORTANT: Students may enter only the student division. One to five poems on any subject may be entered for $3.00.

6. Include fee (cash or check) with poems you submit. Poems that do not include the fee cannot be considered. Fees help defray the considerable costs of printing, mailing, advertising, and other expenses.

7. Mail poems to Mississippi Valley Poetry Contest, (MVPC), P.O Box 3188, Rock Island, IL 61201.

8. The entry period for poems is from January 1, 2001 to September 1, 2001. No entries can be accepted for this contest period after this date.

9. Poems cannot be returned. Authors retain full publication rights to their work.

10. IMPORTANT: When requesting rules or asking that a list of winners be sent, include a business-size, self-addressed, stamped envelope or we cannot honor your requests.

11. ANY POEM ENTERED IN THE ADULT GENERAL CATEGORY CANNOT BE ENTERED IN THE SPECIAL CATEGORIES.

12. Winners will be notified by mail in advance of Awards Night. We strongly urge winners to be present for awards whenever possible.

Winning poems are read by professional readers. Awards Night and the reception that follows are free and open to the public. We sincerely hope that you will enter the Mississippi Valley Poetry Contest. We are certain that, in one way or another, each of you will be a winner.

For more information call: Max Molleston, President; Telephone: (319) 359-1057.

THE MISSOURI REVIEW

University of Missouri Columbia
1507 Hillcrest Hall MU
Columbia, MO 65211

Deadline: Postmark by October 15, 2001

11TH ANNUAL EDITOR'S PRIZE IN FICTION AND ESSAY
FIFTH ANNUAL LARRY LEVIS EDITOR'S PRIZE IN POETRY
Prizes: $1,500 for Fiction, $1,500 for Poetry, and $1,000 for Essay. One winner and three finalists will be chosen in each category. Winners will be published and finalists announced in the following spring's issue of *The Missouri Review.* Finalists in all categories will receive a minimum of $100, or consideration for publication at regular rates.

Guidelines
Fiction and essay entries are not to exceed 25 typed, double-spaced pages. Poetry entries can include any number of poems up to ten pages. Each story or essay constitutes one entry.

Entry fee is $15 for each entry (checks made payable to *The Missouri Review*). Each fee entitles entrant to a one-year subscription, or a gift subscription (a $4 savings from the regular subscription price). Please indicate your choice and enclose a complete address for subscription.

Outside of the envelope must be marked "Fiction," "Essay," or "Poetry." Each entry in each category must be mailed in a separate envelope. Enclose an index card with the author's name, address, and telephone number in the left corner and the work's title in the center of the card if fiction or essay. The author's name may also appear on the manuscript but does not need to. Entries must be previously unpublished and will not be returned. Send a #10 self-addressed, stamped envelope for announcement of winners only.

Entries must be clearly addressed to: *Missouri Review* Editors' Prize and sent to above address.

MR. CHRISTIE'S BOOK AWARD PROGRAM

Marlene Yustin
Mr. Christie's Book Award Program
2150 Lakeshore Boulevard West
Toronto, Ontario M8V 1A3 Canada

Deadline: January 31, 2001
The purpose of the twelfth annual Mr. Christie's Book Award Program is to honour excellence in the writing and illustration of Canadian children's literature and to encourage the development and publishing of high quality children's books that will promote a love of reading.

One award of $7,500 will be awarded in the following categories: Best English Children's book for young children (approx. newborn to 7 years); Best English Children's book for middle readers (approx. 8 to 11 years); Best English book for young adults (approx. 12 to 16 years); Best French Children's book for young children (approx. newborn to 7 years); Best French Children's book for middle readers (approx. 8 to 11 years); and Best French book for young adults (approx. 12 to 16 years).

Guidelines
The book must first be published in Canada during the January 1 to December 31 period within each calendar year.

The author and illustrator must be Canadian and not employees of Christie Brown & Co., its associated companies, agents, judges and judging chairpersons and members of their immediate families living in the same household.

A Canadian is defined as a person having Canadian citizenship or having landed immigrant status at the time of his/her book's publication.

For a winning picture book both author and illustrator will share equally in the prize. A picture book is defined as a book in which the illustrations are integral to the work and the text and illustrations bear substantially equal weight. The sponsor's decision with respect to this is final and without appeal.

Prize money will be allocated as agreed in this document. Christie Brown accepts no responsibility for honouring Terms/Agreements or Contracts agreed to between other parties (i.e. publishers, authors and illustrators).

Translations of previously published books are ineligible for this program.

By entering this contest, entrants agree that in the event that their entry is chosen as one of the winning books they will place the Mr. Christie's Book Award seal on the cover. In order to be declared the winner of a prize, a selected entrant must sign an appropriately worded document obliging it to place the Mr. Christie's Book Award seal on future printing and publishings of the winning book, and also acknowledging that it has the legal right to do so.

Submitted books will become the property of the Mr. Christie's Book Award program and will not be returned.

Deadline: six copies of eligible submissions must be received at the above address no later than January 31, 2001.

All decisions made by panel of judges are final. Mr. Christie's Book Award program will notify the short listed candidates. Otherwise no correspondence will be forthcoming.

MIXED BLOOD THEATER COMPANY

1501 So. 4th Street
Minneapolis, MN 55454

Deadline: February 1, 2001

Award: a cash prize of $2,000 if Mixed Blood chooses to produce the winning script, or $1,000 if Mixed Blood declines production.

The contest is specifically designed for full-length, contemporary comedies; particularly comedies about race, sports or containing a political edge (or similar theme musical comedies). Scripts must be at least 65 pages in length. No translations or adaptations will be accepted. Revisions will not be accepted after initial entry of script.

Eligibility

The contest is open to all American playwrights who have had at least one of their works produced or work-shopped. All scripts entered in the contest must remain unproduced as of September 1, 2000. Produced is defined as any production to which tickets are sold.

Number of entries: Limit of two submissions per author; dual entries must be sent under a separate cover. Previously entered scripts in the "Mixed Blood Versus America" playwriting contest are ineligible for entry in this contest, even if revised.

Script requirements: All scripts must be firmly bound and legibly typed or word processed. The playwright must be an American citizen to enter; a playwright resume is optional. Be sure to include the playwright's name, address and phone number on the title page of the script. A self-addressed, stamped envelope is required for return of submitted materials.

Rules

Mixed Blood Theater Company reserves the right to produce the world premiere of the winning play and will assume the playwright understands and recognizes this right at the time his/her script is submitted to the contest. Mixed Blood Theater company reserves the right to withhold the prize and not declare a winner if no play of merit is found.

Submit contest scripts to: "We Don't Need No Stinkin' Dramas" at above address. Note: This contest replaces "Mixed Blood Versus America" playwriting contest. Mixed Blood encourages and seeks out the emerging playwright.

NATIONAL ASSOCIATION OF SCIENCE WRITERS

P.O. Box 294
Greenlawn, NY 11740
Phone (516) 757-5664

Deadline: July 1, 2001 postmark

SCIENCE-IN-SOCIETY JOURNALISM AWARDS
The National Association of Science Writers (NASW) established the Science-in-Society Journalism Awards to provide recognition – without subsidy from any professional or commercial interest – for interpretive reporting about the sciences and their impact for good and bad. NASW especially wants to encourage the kind of critical, probing article that would not receive an award from an interest group. The awards are for outstanding writing, for material published or broadcast about science and its impact on the quality of life.

Separate prizes of $1,000 and Certificates of Recognition will be awarded for writing judged best in each of these three categories: 1. Newspapers, 2. Magazines, 3. Television and Radio. Publishers and Broadcasters of awarded material will also receive Certificates of Recognition.

Eligibility
Any writer (or team) is eligible to submit not more than three entries in each category. Material may be a single article or broadcast, or a series. Series will be considered to be single entries. Books and digests are not eligible. Work must be written, or spoken, in English, intended for the lay person, and published or broadcast in North America between June 1, 2000 and May 31, 2001. (The publication date on the periodical or the broadcast date will be governing.) The original of a story transmitted by a news service will be eligible. Winners of last year's awards are not eligible.

Rules for Submission
Entries must meet purpose stated above. Material about advances in sciences, however significant and well-written, is not eligible unless it also tells WHY IT MATTERS. Any person, including the author, may submit material.

Submit ten (10) copies of each entry. Attach to each copy a copy of the entry blank. Only one copy of printed material need be a tearsheet or an original. One radio tape or 1/2-inch VHS cassette, videotape or broadcast material should be accompanied by ten (10) copies of typed or printed scripts. Attach a copy of the entry blank to each copy of the printed script. The substance, not the method of presentation, of submitted material is judged.

Deadline for submission: Entries must be postmarked by July 1, 2001. (ATTACH ONE ENTRY BLANK, FRONT SIDE ONLY TO EACH COPY OF ARTICLES/SCRIPT)

NASW
Science-in-Society Journalism Award

Description of Entry

Category: Newspaper Magazine Broadcast

Title of Entry: ______

Name and present position
of author (or authors) ______

______

Periodical or station: ______

Publication or broadcast
date(s): ______

Address of periodical or station:

______

______

Phone #: ______

Address of author if different from above:

______

______

Home Phone #: ______

National Association of Science Writers
P.O. Box 294, Greenlawn, NY 11740
(516) 757-5664

I submit the enclosed material, described on the reverse side of this entry form, for consideration in the Science-in-Society Journalism Award.

Name of Submitter: ______

Position and address: ______

______

Date ______

Signature ______

NATIONAL FEDERATION OF STATE POETRY SOCIETIES, INC.

Alan and Claire van Breemen Downes
1206 13th Avenue, S.E.
St. Cloud, MN 56304

Deadline: March 15, 2001

NATIONAL FEDERATION OF STATE
POETRY SOCIETIES, INC. CONTESTS
National Federation of State Poetry Societies, Inc. (NFSPS) is a non-profit organization, exclusively educational and literary. Its purpose is to recognize the importance of poetry with respect to national cultural heritage. It is dedicated solely to the furtherance of poetry on the national level and serves to unite poets in the bonds of fellowship and understanding. NFSPS was organized in Baton Rouge, LA, October 17, 1959; its constitution was adopted in Philadelphia, PA, June 18, 1960; and incorporated in Madison, WI, July 15, 1966. Each year NFSPS sponsors fifty national contests and conducts an annual convention, hosted by one of its affiliated states.

1. NFSPS FOUNDERS AWARD (To honor Mary B. Wall)
   Any subject, any form, 100 line limit. Open to all poets. Entry fee to all, $5 per poem. Limit, four poems per contestant. First prize $1,500; second prize $500; third prize $250.

2. WINNERS' CIRCLE AWARD
   Any subject, any form, 80 line limit. Sponsored by previous winners in the NFSPS Founders Award category. Bailey, Chambers, Fasel, Glancy, Golightly, Lazzeroni, Morrise, Rewey, Socwell, Stodghill. First prize $300; second prize $200; third prize $100.

3. POETRY SOCIETY OF TEXAS AWARD
   Any subject, any form, 40 line limit. Sponsored by the Poetry Society of Texas. First prize is $125; second prize $50; third prize $25.

4. NFSPS PAST PRESIDENTS' AWARD
   Any subject, any form, 40 line limit. Sponsored by Russell and Grace Ferrall. First prize $125; second prize $50; third prize $25.

5. THE JACK MURPHY MEMORIAL AWARD
   In memory of Jack Murphy who served as the president of NFSPS and the Poetry Society of Texas. Any subject, any form, 40 line limit. Sponsored by Pat and Don Stodghill. First prize $100; second prize $60; third prize $40.

6. FUTURISTIC AWARD
Optimistic, sensitive, and persuasive concerning 2048 A.D. May be imaginative. Form: traditional meter and rhyme, 32 line limit. Sponsored by Walt Morgan. First prize $100; second prize $60; third prize $40.

7. POWER OF WOMAN AWARD
Subject: Power of Woman, any form, 50 line limit. Sponsored by Barbara Stevens and Susan Chambers. First prize $100; second prize $75; third prize $25.

8. NEVADA POETRY SOCIETY AWARD
An aubade (poem of lovers parting at dawn), any form, 60 line limit. Sponsored by Sam Wood, Dolores van Keuren, and Gordon Holladay. First prize $100; second prize $60; third prize $40.

9. UTAH STATE POETRY SOCIETY AWARD
Any subject, any form, 50 line limit. First prize $100; second prize $50; third prize $30.

10. FLORIDA STATE POETS ASSOCIATION, INC. AWARD
Any subject, any Rondeau/Rondel form, 25 line limit. Sponsored by the Florida State Poets Association. First prize $100; second prize $50; third prize $25.

11. BEYMORLIN SONNET SCROD MEMORIAL AWARD
In memory of Marjorie Lees Linn, and Carl and Isabel Morton. Sonnet, Shakespearean or other form, with rhymes at end of lines as usual, but also with another set of rhymes, not necessarily the same form, at the beginning of each line, within the first two syllables to allow for feminine rhymes; i.e., a separate rhyme scheme follows through each line at the beginning and also the ending of each line. Sponsored by Richard Beyer. First prize $75; second prize $50; third prize $25.

12. ALABAMA STATE POETRY SOCIETY AWARD
A love poem concerning loftier aspects (no trite sentimentality), any form, 40 line limit. Sponsored by the Alabama State Poetry Society. First prize $75; second prize $50; third prize $25.

13. THE JOSEPH V. HICKEY MEMORIAL AWARD
Sponsored by his wife, Madelyn Eastlund. Subject: American History (excepting the Civil War), narrative, 40 line limit. First prize $75; second prize $50; third prize $25.

14. INDIANA STATE FEDERATION OF POETRY CLUBS AWARD
Any subject, any form, 40 line limit. Sponsored by Indiana State Federation of Poetry Clubs, Poets' Study Club of Terre Haute, and

Anderson Poetry Club. First prize $50; second prize $35; third prize $25.

15. EDNA MEUDT MEMORIAL AWARD
Narrative subject, any form, 40 line limit. Sponsored by the Wisconsin Fellowship of Poets. First prize $50; second prize $35; third prize $15.

16. ALICE MORREY BAILEY MEMORIAL AWARD
Any subject (serious or humorous) any form, 40 line limit. Sponsored by friends of Alice Morrey Bailey: Blaisdell, Carroll, Cook, Jennings, Socwell. First prize $50; second prize $30; third prize $20.

17. POETS CLUB OF CHICAGO AWARD
Any subject, any form, two-page limit. Sponsored by Lake Shore Publishers. First prize $50; second prize $25; third prize $15; two honorable mentions $5 each.

18. THE NEW YORK POETRY FORUM AWARD
Subject: The Art of Poetry, any form, 40 line limit. First prize $50; second prize $30; third prize $20.

19. JOAN ROBBINS HONORARY AWARD
Subject: Theater, any form, 40 line limit. Sponsored by Jerry Robbins. First prize $50; second prize $30; third prize $20.

20. THE LEAGUE OF MINNESOTA POETS AWARD
Any subject, free verse, 32 line limit. Sponsored by the League of Minnesota Poets. First prize $50; second prize $30; third prize $20.

21. PLAINS POETS AWARD
Subject: Coffee, any form, 30 line limit. Sponsored by Sy and Carlee Swann. First prize $50; second prize $35; third prize $15.

22. WEST VIRGINIA POETRY SOCIETY AWARD
Subject: West Virginia (history, heritage, home life, personages, or gifts of nature), any form, 40 line limit. Sponsored by West Virginia Poetry Society. First prize $50; second prize $30; third prize $20.

23. MORTON D. PROUTY, JR., MEMORIAL AWARD
In memory of Morton D. Prouty, Jr., who served as NFSPS treasurer and Poet Laureate of Alabama. Nature poem, any form, 40 line limit. Sponsored by Elsie S. Prouty. First prize $50; second prize $25; third prize $15.

24. LOUISIANA STATE POETRY SOCIETY AWARD
Any subject, any form, 32 line limit. Sponsored by Louisiana State Poetry Society. First prize $36; second prize $26; third prize $13.

25. ARIZONA STATE POETRY SOCIETY AWARD
In memory of Dorothy Greenlee. Any subject, any form, 32 line limit. Sponsored by Arizona State Poetry Society. First prize $35; second prize $25; third prize $15.

26. DONALD D. DUNGLEY MEMORIAL AWARD
Subject: Flying or Aviation, any form, 40 line limit. Sponsored by Melba Dungy. First prize $30; second prize $20; third prize $15.

27. AMELIA REYNOLDS LONG MEMORIAL AWARD
Subject: On the Light Side, any form, 32 line limit. Sponsored by the Pennsylvania Poetry Society and Henrietta Palmer Bequest. First prize $30; second prize $20; third prize $10.

28. VERSE WRITERS GUILD OF OHIO AWARD
Any subject, any form, 40 line limit. Sponsored by Verse Writers Guild of Ohio. First prize $25; second prize $20; third prize $15.

29. SAVE OUR EARTH AWARD
In memory of David F. Balph. Subject: Environmental issues, any form, 40 line limit. Sponsored by Martha H. Balph. First prize $25; second prize $15; third prize $10.

30. WYOMING POETS AWARD
Any subject, any form, 40 line limit. Sponsored by the Wyoming Poets Association. First prize $25; second prize $15; third prize $10.

31. ARKANSAS AWARD
Any subject, any form. 36 line limit. Sponsored by Poets' Roundtable of Arkansas. First prize $25; second prize $15; third prize $10.

32. POETRY SOCIETY OF OKLAHOMA AWARD
Humorous subject in good taste, any form, 20 line limit. Must be funny. Sponsored by the Poetry Society of Oklahoma. First prize $25; second prize $15; third prize $10.

33. SOUTH DAKOTA POETRY SOCIETY AWARD
Any serious theme, any form, 12 line limit. Sponsored by the South Dakota Poetry Society. First prize $25; second prize $15; third prize $10.

34. HUMOROUS POETRY AWARD
Any subject, rhymed, 16 line limit. Sponsored by Irene Warsaw and Colleen Stanley Bare. First prize $25; second prize $15; third prize $10.

35. MUSIC AWARD
A sonnet expressing the spiritual impact of great music. Sponsored

by Pearl Hand Cockrell. First prize $25; second prize $15; third prize $10.

36. WISCONSIN POETRY AWARD
Theme: Nature and Human Values, any form, 40 line limit. Sponsored by the Wisconsin Fellowship of Poets. First prize $25; second prize $15; third prize $10.

37. POETRY SOCIETY OF NEW HAMPSHIRE AWARD
Any subject, any form, 40 line limit. First prize $25; second prize $15; third prize $10.

38. PERRYMAN-VISSER NATIONAL POETRY AWARD
Form: The Visser Sonnet. Like Italian (Petrarchan) sonnets except that most of the rhymes are not at the end of the lines but scattered internally. Please underline all rhymes. Sponsored by Audrae Visser. First prize $25; second prize $15; third prize $10.

39. MASSACHUSETTS STATE POETRY SOCIETY AWARD
Any subject, any form, 40 line limit. Sponsored by Massachusetts State Poetry Society. First prize $25; second prize $15; third prize $10.

40. POETS AND FRIENDS AWARD
Any subject, traditional rhyme and meter, 32 line limit. Sponsored by Missouri Poets and Friends. First prize $25; second prize $15; third prize $10.

41. OUR NATIVE AMERICAN HERITAGE AWARD
Subject: Any that relates to Native Americans, any form, 24 line limit. Sponsored by New Mexico State Poetry Society. First prize $25; second prize $15; third prize $10.

42. KENTUCKY STATE POETRY SOCIETY AWARD
Any subject, any form, 28 line limit. First prize $25; second prize $15; third prize $10.

43. MINUTE AWARD
A minute is a 60-syllable, 12-line poem written in strict iambic meter, syllable count 8,4,4,4,8,4,4,4,8,4,4,4, and rhymed a, a, b, c, c,d,d,e,e,f,f, capitalized and punctuated like prose and capturing a minute in time. Sponsored by Verna Lee Hinegardner. First prize $25; second prize $15; third prize $10.

44. THE MANNINGHAM AWARD
Subject: Humor, light verse; rhymed, 12 line limit. Sponsored by Howard and Mary Manningham. First prize $25; second prize $15; third prize $10.

45. POETRY SOCIETY OF MICHIGAN AWARD
Any subject, form: Villanelle. Sponsored by Poetry Society of Michigan. First prize $25; second prize $15; third prize $10.

46. LIGHTEN YOUR LIFE AWARD
Any humorous subject, any rhyming form, up to 12 lines. Sponsored by Wanda Blaisdell. First prize $25; second prize $15; third prize $10.

47. LOSS AWARD
Subject: Loss, grief; any form; 40 line limit. Sponsored by E.K.W. Occasional Poetry. First prize $25; second prize $15; third prize $10.

48. IOWA POETRY ASSOCIATION AWARD
Subject: Poetry for Children, any form, 32 line limit. Sponsored by Iowa Poetry Association. First prize $25; second prize $15; third prize $10.

49. SESTINA AWARD (IN MEMORY OF WYLIE F. SMITH)
Any subject. Sponsored by Grace Haynes Smith. First prize $25; second prize $15; third prize $10.

50. STUDENT AWARD
No fee required. Any subject, any form, 32 line limit. Grades 9 through 12. (Indicate age and class on entry.) Sponsored by Kay Kinnaman and Ralph Hammond. First prize $40; second prize $20; third prize $15; $5 to each of seven honorable mentions.

Rules and Guidelines

The contests are open to all. Any violation of the rules will disqualify entry.

1. Any poem submitted must:
   a. be the original work of the contestant, unpublished in any form, not under consideration or accepted for publication, not having been presented in public performance live or in filmed/taped broadcast. (Award will be recalled if a winning poem is found to be in violation of rules before publication in *Prize Poems* anthology, and lower awards and honorable mentions will move up in classification.)
   b. be written in English, be titled (unless a haiku) but not use the exact words of category subject or theme as poem title.
   c. have a 40 line limit for all categories not stating line limit.
   d. be typed or computer-generated (not handwritten or hand-printed), without illustrations.
2. An eligible poem may not be withdrawn after submission.
3. Except as indicated in NFSPS Founders Award, contestants may submit only one entry for any award, and may not submit the same

poem for any other award.

4. Check or money order enclosed must be made out to NFSPS, Inc. (initials sufficient) rather than to any individual.
   a. Non-members may enter contests at $1.00 each poem (except $5.00 each for NFSPS Founders Award entries).
   b. Members may enter all categories for $8.00 total fee (except for NFSPS Founders Award at$5.00 for each entry).
   c. Entrants from outside U.S. (except Canada) must send checks drawn on U.S. banks or branches, payable in U.S. funds, or send U.S. currency.

5. First place NFSPS Founders Award (contest #1) winner is not eligible to enter the following year. NFSPS Founders Award only.

6. Judges will be selected by NFSPS, Inc. and their decisions will be final. No ties will be awarded.

7. Contest Deadline: entries must be postmarked by March 15, 2001.

8. "Member" is eligible if a paid-up member of a state society, listed in alphabetical membership roll sent to Contest Chairman by January 15, 2001.

9. Only those poems receiving cash awards of over $10 will be held for possible first printing in *Prize Poems* anthology. Prize winning poems will be printed at the discretion of the editor who may exclude any poem deemed to be inappropriate. Printed poems are released after anthology is published. Honorable mentions are merely listed (without titles). No poems will be returned, so copies should be retained by poets.

10. A list of winners will appear in 3rd quarter *Strophes* (August). All prize winners will be notified, and others may obtain a list of winners by sending $1 and a #10 self-addressed, stamped envelope to Linda Banks, 2912 Falls Church, Mesquite, TX 75149 after August.

11. How to submit poems:

    Send two clear copies of the poem, typed single spaced, and photocopied or computer-generated on 8-1/2 x 11 inch white paper (no onionskin or tissue). If the poem runs longer than one page, staple together all pages of each copy. On both copies, place the number and the name of the award in the upper left corner.

On second copy only, place the name and address of the poet, and state society membership or "NON-MEMBER NFSPS" in upper right corner. If the poem is over one page, number pages also on upper right corner (both copies).

Separate originals from duplicates and stack in numerical order (1–50) with originals on top. Include a 3 x 5 file card with name, address, society membership (or "non-member") and specify the numbers of the contests entered.

Mail all entries at one time, unfolded, in a large envelope; include file card and entry fee with poems. Send first class or priority mail only (not Special Delivery or Registered) to Claire van Breemen Downes, Contest Chairman, after January 1, 2001. Do not send entries to any other NFSPS officer.

Mail entries to: Claire van Breemen Downes, Contest Chairman, 1206 13th Avenue, S.E., St. Cloud, MN 56304

NFSPS, Inc., will not assume mailing costs and will not be responsible for any manuscripts lost or delayed in the mails.

FOR FURTHER INFORMATION, send a 9-1/2 x 4-1/4 inch (#10) self-addressed, stamped envelope to one of the following:

For information about contests and submitting entries: Alan and Claire van Breemen Downes, 1206 13th Avenue, S.E., St. Cloud, MN 56304.

For information on how to sponsor a contest: Clarence P. Socwell, 2727 N. 650 East, Ogden, UT 84414.

For information about ordering copies of the contest brochure: Linda Banks, 2912 Falls Church, Mesquite, TX 75149.

NOTE: Any poetry group located in a state not already affiliated but interested in affiliating with the NFSPS is invited to contact Membership Chairman Sy Swann, 2712 Scott Avenue, Fort Worth, TX 76103. In a state where no valid group exists, help also may be obtained by interested individuals in organizing a poetry group for future affiliation.

THE NATIONAL FEDERATION OF THE BLIND WRITERS

Deadline: May 1, 2001 postmark

THE NATIONAL FEDERATION OF THE BLIND WRITERS
POETRY, FICTION, AND ESSAY CONTESTS
The National Federation of the Blind Writers announces its Poetry, Fiction, and Essay contests for 2001. All three contests are now open.

Guidelines for Submissions
All entries must be accompanied by a $5 entry fee per piece; a self-addressed, stamped envelope; and a cover page with your name, address, and phone number.

POETRY
Send previously unpublished poetry to: Lori Stayer, 2704 Beach Drive, Merrick, NY 11566. Poems may be up to 36 lines. Entries must be typed.

FICTION
Send your previously unpublished fiction, typed, double spaced, 2,000 words or less, to: Tom Stevens, 1203 S. Fairview Rd., Columbia, MO 65203.

PERSONAL ESSAY
Send your previously unpublished personal essays, 1,000 words or less, to: Dr. Patricia Morrow, 1900 Vassar Drive, Columbia, MO 65203.

Entrants are asked not to submit contest entries elsewhere while the contest is running, or for six months after it ends if the entry wins. Prizes are $40, $25, and $15 for each contest. Winning entries may be published in *SLATE & STYLE*.

Caution: Entries must be postmarked by the contest deadline. Please do not send your first draft. Proofread your work.

Winners will be notified separately. Otherwise, winning entries will be announced in the July 2001 issue of *SLATE & STYLE*.

THE NATIONAL LEAGUE OF AMERICAN PEN WOMEN, INC.

NLAPW-Simi Valley Branch
P.O. Box 1485
Simi Valley, CA 93062

Deadline: July 30, 2001 postmark

THE DOROTHY DANIELS ANNUAL HONORARY WRITING AWARD
The Dorothy Daniels Annual Honorary Writing Award offers a First Prize of $100 in the categories of Poetry, Fiction, and Non-fiction.

Rules and Guidelines
Any person except Simi Valley Pen Women, interns, and their immediate families are eligible.

Entries must be original, unpublished (not currently submitted elsewhere), and must have received no prior awards. There is no limit on number of entries.

SHORT FICTION – 2,000 words maximum. Any genre, but no essays or journal entries.

POETRY – 50 lines maximum. Free verse or traditional, single or double spaced, one poem per page.

NON-FICTION – 1,500 words maximum. Any subject. Entries must develop and maintain focus, and have a recognizable conclusion.

Name and address must not appear on manuscript. Entries must be typewritten, double-spaced, on one side of 8-1/2 x 11 inch white paper. Entries MUST be titled.

On a separate cover page, type name, address, phone number, title and category of each entry, and word or line count for each entry.

Enclose a $3.00 entry fee per poem; $5.00 fee per fiction or non-fiction entry. Do not send cash. Make checks payable to NLAPW-Simi Valley. Any deviation from these rules will disqualify entries.

Judges' decisions are final. WINNERS WILL BE NOTIFIED BY MAIL ON OR BEFORE NOV. 1, 2001. Entries will NOT be returned; keep copies. We do not publish. Writers retain all rights.

Optional
For the list of winners send a self-addressed, stamped envelope marked "Winners List." Include a note on your entry cover page telling how you learned about this contest. Include a note on your entry cover page with name and address of one newspaper we can notify if you win.

NATIONAL ORGANIZATION FOR WOMEN

Des Plaines/Park Ridge NOW
Department L
P.O. Box 2440
Des Plaines, IL 60018

Deadline: August 31, 2001 postmark

FEMINIST WRITERS' CONTEST
The Des Plaines/Park Ridge NOW announces its annual Feminist Writers' Contest for Fiction and Non-fiction Essay. Awards in each category are $100 for First Place and $50 for Second Place. Winners will be notified in November 2001.

Guidelines for Submission
Work must reflect feminist perspectives. It should not endorse or promote sexism, racism, agism, or homophobia.

Short stories or essays may not exceed 3,000 words.

Manuscripts should be typed, double spaced on 8-1/2 x 11 inch white paper. Please send two (2) photocopies.

Each entry must be accompanied by the entry form (or facsimile) and a $15 entry fee.

Author's name must not appear anywhere on the entry.

Manuscripts will not be returned.

Winners will be notified in November 2001. Enclose a self addressed, stamped envelope if you wish to receive a list of winners.

Enclose $15 for entry. Make check payable to Des Plaines/Park Ridge NOW. Proceeds from the contest will be used to support our work on women's issues.

Mail entry with completed form to: Des Plaines/Park Ridge NOW Contest, Department L, P.O. Box 2440, Des Plaines, IL 60018.

National Organization of Women Feminist Writers' Contest Entry Form

I wish to enter the enclosed manuscript in the 2001 Des Plaines Park Ridge/NOW Feminist Writers' Contest.

(Check one):__________Essay__________Short Story

__________I have enclosed the $15 entry fee.

__________I have enclosed a self-addressed, stamped envelope for a winner's list.

Please print legibly:

Title of entry ____

____

Name ____

Address ____

City/State/Zip ____

Phone with area code ____

Your source of information on the contest

____

Name/Address of local newspaper for winner's publicity

____

____

Mail entry with completed form to:
Des Plaines/Park Ridge NOW Contest
Department L, P.O. Box 2440, Des Plaines, IL 60018.

THE NATIONAL POETRY SERIES

NPS Coordinator
P.O. Box G
Hopewell, NJ 08525

Deadline: January 1, 2001 – February 15, 2001 postmark

POETRY BOOK PUBLICATION COMPETITION
The National Poetry Series (NPS) was established in 1978 to ensure the publication of five books of poetry each year. Winning manuscripts are selected by means of an annual open competition, judged by five distinguished poets. Each winning poet receives a $1,000 cash award in addition to having his or her manuscript published by a participating trade, university, or small press publisher. Publishers currently include Sun and Moon Press, Graywolf Press, The University of Illinois Press, Viking Penguin, and W.W. Norton.

The National Poetry Series seeks book-length manuscripts of poetry written by American citizens. All manuscripts must be previously unpublished, although some or all of the individual poems may have appeared in periodicals. Translations, chapbooks, and books previously self-published are not eligible, nor are single poems or small groups of poems. Manuscript length is not limited; however, a 48–64 page limit is suggested.

Manuscripts, accompanied by an entrance fee of $25.00 (per manuscript), made payable to The National Poetry Series, will be accepted at The National Poetry Series, P.O. Box G, Hopewell, NJ 08525, between January 1 and February 15, 1999, but postmarked no later than February 15, 1999.

Guidelines for Submission
Manuscripts must include two (2) cover pages. The first cover page should include the title of manuscript, and author's name, address, and telephone number. This should be the only page with author's identification. The second cover page should include the title of the manuscript only.

Manuscripts must be typed on standard white paper, on one side of the page only. The manuscript should be paginated (include a table of contents). Use paper clips to bind document as more permanent bindings are very difficult to deal with!

DO NOT INCLUDE acknowledgments, explanatory statements, resumé, autobiographical statements, photographs, illustrations, or art-

work. These will not be considered.
We regret that manuscripts cannot be returned. No additions, deletions, or substitutions are accepted once a manuscript is submitted.

Finalists will be requested to submit six (6) copies of their original submission.

Winning authors will be given the opportunity to make final changes prior to publication.

Please include a self-addressed, stamped postcard if you would like confirmation that your manuscript has been received. Include a self-addressed, stamped envelope if you would like notification of the National Poetry Series winners (announced in July).

If you require any additional information, please write to the National Poetry Series, Coordinator, P.O. Box G, Hopewell, NJ 08525.

NATIONAL REPERTORY THEATRE FOUNDATION

The Annual National Play Award
P.O. Box 286
Hollywood, CA 90078

Deadline: January 1, 2001 – March 31, 2001 postmark

THE ANNUAL NATIONAL PLAY AWARD
The Annual National Play Award is presented by the National Play Award Committee of The National Repertory Theatre Foundation. Awards: $5,000 cash and production or staged reading of winning script. $500 cash to Four Runners-up.

Guidelines
Entries must be full-length original plays conceived for production on the living stage – no musicals, translations, or adaptations.

Entries must not have been previously submitted to the National Play Award, published, produced on the professional stage (with a paid Equity cast), or have already won a major play award by date of submission.

Scripts must be submitted in a professional format: securely bound, letter-quality typeface (no smaller than 10 pt) or typewritten and legibly photocopied.

Each script submission must be under separate cover.

Enclose entry fee of $25 (make check payable to the National Repertory Theatre Foundation). Mail check with script.

Reading: all entries are pre-screened by a staff of professional readers. Each eligible entry is evaluated by at least two readers. Entries selected as finalists are then sent on to our panel of judges.

Finalist will be announced September 1, 2001. Winner will be announced by December 31, 2001. Prizes must be claimed by June 30, 2002.

Entries will not be returned unless accompanied by a self-addressed, stamped envelope. To receive acknowledgment of receipt, enclose a self-addressed, stamped post card.

NATIONAL WOMEN'S STUDIES ASSOCIATION

7100 Baltimore Avenue, Suite 301
College Park, MD 20740
Phone (301) 403-0525

The National Women's Studies Association (NWSA) offers various awards, fellowships, and scholarships that are intended to expand the boundaries and possibilities of women's studies scholarship and are available to people of all ages whose qualifications are compatible with the requirements of each award. Submission deadlines for each award are available from: National Women's Studies Association (NWSA), 7100 Baltimore Ave, Suite 301, College Park, MD 20740, (301) 403-0525. With the exception of the Pat Parker Poetry Award and the Audre Lorde Memorial Prose Prize, all applications/entries must be postmarked no later than February 15, 2001. All applicants who are NSWA members will be given special preference.

Deadline: February 15, 2001 postmark

NWSA GRADUATE SCHOLARSHIP IN LESBIAN STUDIES
The NWSA Scholarship of $500 Award will be awarded to a graduate student who in the fall of 2001 will be doing research for or writing a Master's thesis or Ph.D. dissertation in Lesbian studies.

Deadline: February 15, 2001 postmark

GRADUATE SCHOLARSHIP IN JEWISH WOMEN'S STUDIES
The NWSA Award of $500 in Jewish Women's Studies will be given in 2001 to a graduate student who is enrolled for the fall semester and whose area of research is Jewish Women's Studies.

Deadline: May 1, 2001 – July 1, 2001 postmark

PAT PARKER POETRY AWARD
This award of $250 is given for an outstanding narrative poem or dramatic monologue by a Black, lesbian, feminist poet. Submitted poems can be up to 50 lines in length and on a topic that addresses the concerns of African American women, lesbians, and feminists; or the life and work of poet Pat Parker. Special preference will be given to poems that inspire, enlighten, or encourage. If no suitable entry is received, no award will be made. Submissions will be accepted from May 1 to July 31, 2001.

Deadline: September 1, 2001 – November 17, 2001 postmark

AUDRE LORDE MEMORIAL PROSE PRIZE
The Audre Lorde Memorial Prose Prize is an award of $250 and publication by Woman in the Moon Press. The contest is sponsored by Women in the Moon Press and is open to all feminist writers. Submissions may be either fiction or non-fiction, and all works must be original and never before published. Non-fiction essays should consist of an intellectual response to any theme found in Lorde's writing; fiction work should illustrate a condition or ideal found in Lorde's fiction or prose. We accept applications for this award between September 1 and November 17, 2001, with a grace period at the end of the month of November. The winning submission will be announced on February 18, 2002, Lorde's birthday.

Guidelines for Submissions

1. The work must be no less than 500 words and no more than 7,000 words in typewritten form, double spaced, and in triplicate. The applicant's name must not appear anywhere on the manuscript.

2. Applicants must include a self-addressed, stamped envelope and one index card with the name of the piece, and the writer's own name, address, and phone number.

3. A submission fee of $20 is required, made out to Women in the Moon Press.

4. A sealed envelope with a photo and resumé would be helpful to have on hand to speed promotion once the winner has been announced.

Send complete applications to: The National Women's Studies Association, 7100 Baltimore Avenue, Suite 301, College Park, MD 20740.

NATIONAL WRITERS ASSOCIATION

3140 South Peoria Street, #295
Aurora, CO 80014

The National Writers Association (NWA) offers annual prizes and publication awards in the categories of Poetry, Non-fiction, Short Story, Screenplay, and the Novel.

Deadline: July 1, 2001 – October 1, 2001 postmark

NATIONAL WRITERS ASSOCIATION POETRY CONTEST

The purpose of the National Writers Association Poetry Contest is to encourage the writing of poetry, as an important form of individual expression which has a limited commercial market.

Judging will be based on originality, technique, adherence to poetic style, and emotional value. Copies of the judges' evaluation sheets will be sent to entrants furnishing a self-addressed, stamped envelope with their entry. First through fourth place awards will be presented at the year 2002 NWA Conference. Other winners will be notified by January 2002. First Prize is $100; Second Prize is $50; Third Prize is $25; Fourth Prize is $15; and Fifth through Tenth Places will receive a book of the winner's choice. Honorable mentions receive a certificate.

Rules and Guidelines

Only unpublished poems are eligible. All poetry forms and styles are eligible as long as they do not exceed 40 lines. Authors retain all rights and may submit their entries to publishers while the contest is in progress. Anthology rights will be requested for the first through third place winners.

Entries must be accompanied by the entry form (photocopies are acceptable) and an entry fee of $10 per poem. Include a return self-addressed, stamped envelope if you wish the poem and rating sheets returned. POEMS WILL NOT BE RETURNED WITHOUT SELF-ADDRESSED, STAMPED ENVELOPE. The U.S. Postal Service will not allow us to use your metered postage unless it is undated. Receipt of your entry will not be acknowledged without a self-addressed, stamped, return postcard. The author's name and address must appear on the first page of each manuscript.

The entry fee per submission is $10. If you wish to have your poem critiqued, please request this on the entry form and include an evaluation fee of $16. Entry fees are used to pay judges and prize money.

Submit entries to: NWA Poetry Contest, 3140 South Peoria Street #295, Aurora, CO 80014.

NWA Poetry Contest Form

Entry # ______________________________

To: Poetry Contest
National Writers Association
3140 South Peoria Street, #295
Aurora, CO 80014

Return postage ____ Y ____ N

Date ______________________________

Amount ______________________________

Please enter the enclosed poem (title) ______________________________

____

in the NWA Poetry Contest.

_____My entry fee $10 is enclosed OR

_____Please charge my:

Mastercard# ____________ Visa# ____________ Exp date ______

NAME (PLEASE PRINT) ______________________________

ADDRESS ______________________________

CITY, STATE, ZIP ______________________________

TELEPHONE# ______________________________

_____You may retain my poem for a critique after judging. I am enclosing an additional $16 for evaluation.

I have read and understand these rules. Signature ______________________________

Deadline: October 1, 2001 – December 1, 2001 postmark

NATIONAL WRITERS ASSOCIATION NON-FICTION CONTEST

The purpose of the National Writers Association Non-fiction Contest is to encourage the writing of non-fiction and recognize those who excel in this field.

Judging will be based on originality, marketability, research, and reader interest. Copies of the judges' evaluation sheets will be sent to entrants furnishing a self-addressed, stamped envelope with their entry. First through fifth place awards will be presented at the year 2002 NWA Conference. Other winners will be notified by January 2002. First Prize is $200 (and Clearinghouse representation if the winner is a book proposal); Second Prize is $100; Third Prize is $50; and Fourth through Tenth Places will receive a book of the winner's choice. Honorable mentions receive a certificate. Anthology rights will be requested for the first through third place winners.

Rules and Guidelines

Only unpublished works may be submitted. Non-fiction entries in the following areas will be accepted as follows:

> ARTICLES. Submissions should include query letter, first page of manuscript, and a separate sheet citing five (5) possible markets.
>
> ESSAY. Entries should include the complete essay and five (5) possible markets on a separate sheet.
>
> NON-FICTION BOOK. Entries should include the proposal including query letter, chapter by chapter outline, first chapter, biography, and market analysis.

Those unsure of proper manuscript format should request Research Report #35.

Entries must be accompanied by the entry form (photocopies are acceptable) and an entry fee of $18 per submission; and return a self-addressed, stamped envelope if you wish the submission and rating sheets returned. SUBMISSIONS WILL NOT BE RETURNED WITHOUT A SELF-ADDRESSED, STAMPED ENVELOPE. The U.S. Postal Service will not allow us to use your metered postage unless it is undated. Receipt of entry will not be acknowledged without a self-addressed, stamped, return postcard. Author's name and address must appear on the first page.

The entry fee per submission is $18. If you wish to have your submission critiqued, please request this on the entry form and enclose a $20 evaluation fee. Entry fees are used to pay judges and prize money.

Submit entries to: NWA Non-fiction Contest, 3140 South Peoria Street #295, Aurora, CO 80014.

NWA Non-fiction Contest Form

Entry # ____________________

To: Non-fiction Contest
National Writers Association
3140 South Peoria Street, #295
Aurora, CO 80014

Return postage ____ Y ____ N

Date ____________________

Amount ____________________

Please enter the enclosed entry (title) ____________________

____

in the NWA Non-fiction Contest.

_____My entry fee $18 is enclosed OR

_____Please charge my:

Mastercard# Visa# Exp date ____________________

NAME (PLEASE PRINT) ____________________

ADDRESS ____________________

CITY, STATE, ZIP ____________________

TELEPHONE# ____________________

_____You may retain my non-fiction entry for a critique after judging. I am enclosing an additional $20 for evaluation.

I have read and understand these rules. Signature ____________________

Deadline: April 1, 2001 – July 1, 2001 postmark

NATIONAL WRITERS ASSOCIATION SHORT STORY CONTEST
The purpose of the National Writers Association Short Story Contest is to encourage the development of creative writing skills, and recognize and reward outstanding ability in the area of short story writing.

Judging will be based on originality, marketability, research, and reader interest. Copies of the judges' evaluation sheets will be sent to entrants furnishing a self-addressed, stamped envelope with their entry. First through fifth place awards will be presented at the year 2002 NWA Conference. Other winners will be notified by January 2002. First Prize is $250; Second Prize is $100; Third Prize is $50; and Fourth through Tenth Places will receive a book of the winner's choice. First through third place winners will be asked to grant one-time anthology rights for publication in Winning Works book. Honorable mentions receive a certificate.

Rules and Guidelines

Any genre or category of novel manuscript may be entered. Only unpublished works may be submitted. All manuscripts must be typed, double spaced, in the English language. Maximum length is 5,000 words. Those unsure of proper manuscript format should request Research Report #35.

Entries must be accompanied by the entry form (photocopies are acceptable) and an entry fee of $15 per submission. Include a return self-addressed, stamped envelope if you wish the poem and rating sheets returned. SUBMISSIONS WILL NOT BE RETURNED WITHOUT A SELF-ADDRESSED, STAMPED ENVELOPE. The U.S. Postal Service will not allow us to use your metered postage unless it is undated. Receipt of entry will not be acknowledged without a self-addressed, stamped, return postcard. Author's name and address must appear on the first page. Entries remain the property of the author and may be submitted during the contest as long as they are not published before the final announcement of winners.

The entry fee per submission is $15. If you wish to have your poem critiqued, please request this on the entry form and enclose an evaluation fee of $5 per 1,000 words of manuscript. Entry fees are used to pay judges and prize money.

Submit entries to: NWA Short Story Contest, 3140 South Peoria Street #295, Aurora, CO 80014.

NWA Short Story Contest Form

Entry # ______________________

To: Short Story Contest
National Writers Association
3140 South Peoria Street, #295
Aurora, CO 80014

Return postage ____ Y ____ N

Date ______________________

Amount ______________________

Please enter the enclosed entry (title) ______________________

____

in the 1999 NWA Short Story Contest.

_____My entry fee $15 is enclosed OR

_____Please charge my:

Mastercard# __________ Visa# __________ Exp date __________

NAME (PLEASE PRINT) ______________________

ADDRESS ______________________

CITY, STATE, ZIP ______________________

TELEPHONE# ______________________

______You may retain my submission for a critique after judging. I am enclosing an additional $5 per thousand words for the critique.

I have read and understand these rules. Signature ______________________

Deadline: December 1, 2000 – April 1, 2001 postmark

NATIONAL WRITERS ASSOCIATION NOVEL CONTEST

The purpose of the National Writers Association Novel Contest is to encourage the development of creative writing skills and recognize and reward outstanding ability in the area of novel writing.

Judging will be based on originality, marketability, research, and reader interest. Copies of the judges' evaluation sheets will be sent to entrants furnishing a self-addressed, stamped envelope with their entry. First through fifth place awards will be presented at the 2001 NWA Conference. First Prize is $500 and Clearinghouse representation; Second Prize is $250; Third Prize is $150; and Fourth through Tenth Places will receive a book of the winner's choice. Honorable Mentions receive a certificate.

Rules and Guidelines

Any genre or category of novel manuscript may be entered. Only unpublished works may be submitted. All manuscripts must be typed, double spaced, in the English language. Maximum length is 100,000 words. Those unsure of proper manuscript format should request Research Report #35.

Entries must be accompanied by the entry form (photocopies are acceptable) and an entry fee of $35 per submission. Include a return self-addressed, stamped envelope if you wish the poem and rating sheets returned. SUBMISSIONS WILL NOT BE RETURNED WITHOUT A SELF-ADDRESSED, STAMPED ENVELOPE. The U.S. Postal Service will not allow us to use your metered postage unless it is undated. Receipt of entry will not be acknowledged without a self-addressed, stamped, return postcard. Author's name and address must appear on the first page. Entries remain the property of the author and may be submitted during the contest as long as they are not published before the final announcement of winners.

The entry fee per submission is $35. If you wish to have your submission critiqued, please request this on the entry form and enclose an evaluation fee of $1.50 per 1,000 words of manuscript. Entry fees are used to pay judges and prize money.

Submit entries to: Novel Contest, 3140 South Peoria Street #295, Aurora, CO 80014.

NWA Novel Contest Form

Entry # ____________________

To: Novel Contest
National Writers Association
3140 South Peoria Street, #295
Aurora, CO 80014

Return postage ____ Y ____ N

Date ____________________

Amount ____________________

Please enter the enclosed entry (title) ____________________

____

in the NWA Novel Contest.

_____My entry fee $35 is enclosed OR

_____Please charge my:

Mastercard# ________ Visa# ________ Exp date ________

NAME (PLEASE PRINT) ____________________

ADDRESS ____________________

CITY, STATE, ZIP ____________________

TELEPHONE# ____________________

______You may retain my submission for a critique after judging. I am enclosing an additional $1.50 per thousand words for the critique.

I have read and understand these rules. Signature ____________________

Deadline: October 1, 2001 – December 31, 2001 postmark

NATIONAL WRITERS ASSOCIATION SCREENPLAY CONTEST
The purpose of the National Writers Association Screenplay Contest is to encourage the writing of screenplays, an emerging field of individual expression which has an increasing commercial market.

Judging will be based on originality, technique, adherence to correct script format. Copies of the judges' evaluation sheets will be sent to entrants furnishing a self-addressed, stamped envelope with their entry. First through fifth place awards will be presented at the NWAF Conference. Other winners will be notified by April 1. First Prize is $400 and a presentation of work to a major Hollywood production company; Second Prize is $200; Third Prize is $75; and Fourth through Tenth Places will receive a book. Honorable Mentions receive a certificate.

Rules and Guidelines
Only unpublished/unproduced/unoptioned screenplays are eligible. Screenplays are eligible for any length features or TV film. Authors retain all rights and may submit their entries to production companies or agents while the contest is in progress.

The entry must be accompanied by entry form (photocopies are acceptable), entry fee of $35 per screenplay, and self-addressed, stamped envelope if you wish the script and rating sheets returned. Scripts will be destroyed if adequate postage is not included. SUBMISSIONS WILL NOT BE RETURNED WITHOUT A SELF-ADDRESSED, STAMPED ENVELOPE. The U.S. Postal Service will not allow us to use your metered postage unless it is undated. Receipt of entry will not be acknowledged without a self-addressed, stamped, return postcard. Author's name and address must appear on the cover sheet.

The entry fee per submission is $35. If you wish to have your submission critiqued, please request this on the entry form and enclose an evaluation fee of $175. Entry fees are used to pay judges and prize money.

Submit entries to: Novel Contest, 3140 South Peoria Street #295, Aurora, CO 80014.

NWA Screenplay Contest Form

Entry # ______________________________

To: Screenplay Contest
National Writers Association
3140 South Peoria Street, #295
Aurora, CO 80014

Return postage __ Y __ N

Date ______________________________

Amount ______________________________

Please enter the enclosed title ______________________________

____

in the NWA Screenplay Contest.

_____My entry fee $35 is enclosed OR

_____Please charge my:

Mastercard# __________ Visa# __________ Exp date __________

NAME (PLEASE PRINT) ______________________________

ADDRESS ______________________________

CITY, STATE, ZIP ______________________________

TELEPHONE# ______________________________

____You may retain my submission for a critique after judging. I am enclosing an additional $175 for the critique.

I have read and understand these rules.

____
Signature

NATIONAL WRITERS UNION

P.O. Box 2409
Aptos, CA 95001

Deadline: September 30, 2001

NATIONAL WRITERS UNION NATIONAL POETRY COMPETITION
The Santa Cruz/Monterey Local of the National Writers Union (NWU) announces its 17th annual National Poetry Competition. The competition begins in June 2001 and winners will be announced on November 30th, 2001. Winners also will be published in the National Writers Union Local newsletter.

The NWU celebrates multi-cultural creativity; all subject matter is welcome. Prizes are $200 for First Place, $100 for Second, and $50 for Third. Poets may enter any number of poems.

Submission Guidelines
Each poem submitted to the competition should be typed, double spaced on 8-1/2 x 11 inch paper; no longer than three pages; and accompanied by a $3.00 entry fee per poem. Entries must include a cover page with author's name, address, phone number, and a list of entry titles. The author's name must not appear on the poems.

Categories ineligible for submission are: translations, published poems (including self-published), and unpublished award winners. Winners may be published in NWU newsletters, website, and *Poetry Flash.*

The deadline for submissions is September 30, 2001. Entries are not returned. Included a self-addressed, stamped envelope for a list of winners. Proceeds from the competition go to support National Writers Union programs.

Mail poems, cover sheet, check, and a self-addressed, stamped envelope to: C-NWU, P.O. Box 2409, Aptos, CA 95001.

THE NEBRASKA REVIEW

University of Nebraska at Omaha
College of Fine Arts
Omaha, NE 68182-0324

Deadline: November 30, 2001

2001 AWARDS IN FICTION AND POETRY
Prize: Fiction $500 Poetry $500

Fiction story of 5,000 words or less. Poetry, for the best poem or group of poems (not to exceed 5 poems or 6 pages). The winners selected by the editors will be published in the Spring issue of *The Nebraska Review*. No restrictions on style or content.

Entry fee: $10. Each entrant will receive a one-year subscription to *The Nebraska Review* to begin with the Fall/Winter issue. Each entrant may enter as many times as desired. Each entry must meet length restrictions and be accompanied by the $10 fee, which must be drawn on US funds. (Please note whether additional fees are to be applied to extend subscription or for a gift subscription.) Entries not selected as winners will be considered for publication.

Submit original, previously unpublished work (with fee and self-addressed, stamped envelope) to either Fiction Prize or Poetry Prize to above address.

NEWBURYPORT ART ASSOCIATION

Sam Sargent Gallery
65 Water Street
Newburyport, MA 01950

NAA Poetry Contest Coordinator
12 Charron Drive
Newburyport, MA 01950

Deadline: January 1, 2001 – March 13, 2001 postmark

NEWBURYPORT ART ASSOCIATION POETRY CONTEST
Newburyport Art Association (NAA) is pleased to announce its annual Poetry Contest. All poets sixteen years of age or over are invited to enter work. Poems will be judged anonymously by a judge to be announced. Prizes are: First Prize $200; Second Prize $100; Third Prize $50; and Honorable mentions certificates. All winners, including honorable mention poets, are invited to read their own entries at the Awards Day Reading.

All poems awarded prizes and honorable mention certificates will be read at the Newburyport Art Association's historic Sam Sargent Gallery, 65 Water Street, Newburyport, MA. The day's events include a reception with light refreshments, an opportunity to read the winners and all other entries which will be on display at the gallery, and a brief reading by the judge.

Submission Guidelines
Poems in any style, on any theme, no more than three pages per poem in length, typed single or double spaced may be entered. No work that is hand-written, previously published, or untitled may be submitted.

Send two (2) copies of each poem: one with poet's name, address, and phone number in upper right-hand corner; and one with no identification of the poet. Be sure to keep copies of your poems, as entries cannot be returned. More than one entry may be mailed in a single envelope.

Each poem (not each copy, but each separate poem) must be accompanied by a $3 entry fee, payable by check made out to "NAA Poetry Contest." If you enter several poems, please send a single check for the entire amount.

Please enclose a self-addressed stamped envelope with your poems, so we can notify you of contest results. Poems not entered in accordance with the guidelines cannot be accepted.

Mail entries to: NAA Poetry Contest Coordinator, 12 Charron Drive, Newburyport, MA 01950.

NEW DELTA REVIEW

Department of English
Louisiana State University
Baton Rouge, LA 70803-5001

Deadlines: February 28, 2001 Spring/Summer Issue
September 30, 2001 Fall/Winter Issue

The New Delta Review (NDR) is a national literary journal that has made *USA Today's* list of notable books and is regularly consulted by anthologies like Best New Stories from the South, Best American Short Stories, Best American Poetry, and the Pushcart Prize.

New Delta Review represents a balance of fiction and poetry by established, up-and-coming, and promising writers, and we expect even better work in the journal over the coming year.

Ann Rice, W.D. Snodgrass, Lee Smith, Richard Ford, Olen Butler, and many other recognized authors are featured in interviews that discuss writing and the writing life.

We published Wendy Brenner's first story, winner of the Flannery O'Connor Short Story Award in 1996, and a story by Brian Griffin, who in 1996 won the Mary McCarthy Prize in Short Fiction, selected by Barry Hannah. Griffin's collection, *Sparkman in the Sky and Other Stories*, was just published by Sarabande Books. Millicent Borges, who won an NEA Grant for $20,000, and George Looney, Editor of the *Mid-American Review*, have both published poems in NDR. Looney's first book, *Animals Housed in the Pleasure of Flesh*, won the Bluestem Award.

The Editors are currently planning a *Best of New Delta Review* issue, collecting poetry and fiction from the whole range of award-winning writers published in our pages, and an Interview issue, collecting our best interviews, along with new conversations about writing.

The judges for the Prizes change with each issue. Previous judges include Robert Olen Butler, Lee Smith, Edward Falco, Elizabeth Dewberry, and Michael Martone.

Each winner in fiction and poetry receives $50, publication in NDR, and acknowledgment as the prize-winner in the issue in which their work appears.

Guidelines
New Delta Review accepts fiction and poetry, particularly from new or

previously unpublished writers, and, on occasion, we also publish reviews and essays. Please do not let our address mislead you into believing that we only like works that reflect Southern regionalism; our only absolute criterion for publication is quality.

We ask that you submit no more than three poems at one time or one story in standard format with a maximum of 7,500 words. Please specify on the outside of the envelope whether you are submitting fiction or poetry, and all manuscripts should specify the author's name, address, phone, and social security number.

Include a self-addressed, stamped envelope if you wish to receive notification of editorial decisions or your returned manuscript. The submission deadline for the Fall/Winter issue is September 30, and for the Spring/Summer issue, February 29. We read year round, although replies will be slightly delayed during the summer.

THE EYSTER PRIZE

If your fiction or poetry is chosen for publication, it will automatically be considered for the *New Delta Review* Eyster Prize, which honors author and teacher Warren Eyster, who taught at Louisiana State University for many years. In addition to the fiction and poetry prizes, one poem and one story are selected from each issue to win the Eyster Prize.

Submit entries to: *New Delta Review*, Department of English, Louisiana State University, Baton Rouge, LA 70803-5001.

NEW ENGLAND POETRY CLUB

Virginia Thayer, Contest Coordinator
11 Puritan Road
Arlington, MA 02174

Deadline: April 1, 2001 – June 30, 2001

NEW ENGLAND POETRY CLUB CONTESTS
The New England Poetry Club (NEPC) Contests are open to all members in good standing (except board members). Non-members may enter by paying $10 for up to three (3) poems and $5 per additional poem. No charge for students. (For membership Information, contact Victor Howes, 137 West Newton Street, Boston, MA 02118.)

Members-only Contests

THE ROSALIE BOYLE/NORMA FARBER AWARD
A poem in traditional form, including sonnet, villanelle, and sestina, $100.

THE GRETCHEN WARREN AWARD
The best published poem by a member in the previous year. Send two (2) copies (up to 4 poems) dates, and names of publication. No cash award.

Contest Open to Members and Non-members

THE DANIEL VAROUJAN AWARD
For an unpublished poem, not a translation, worthy of Varoujan, a poet killed by the Turks at the onset of the genocide which decimated three-quarters of the Armenian population, $500.

THE BARBARA BRADLEY AWARD
For a lyric poem under 21 lines written by a woman, $200.

THE JOHN HOLMES AWARD
For a poem by a New England college student, $100. Send poems in duplicate with student's name, name of school, and school year on one copy.

THE FIRMAN HOUGHTON AWARD
For a lyric poem worthy of the former NEPC president, $250.

THE ERIKA MUMFORD AWARD
For a poem in any form about foreign culture or travel, $250.

THE MAY SARTON AWARD
Given intermittently to a poet whose work is an inspiration to other poets, $250.

THE DER-HOVANESSIAN
For a translation from any language, $100. Send a copy of the original with the poem.

THE GOLDEN ROSE
Given annually since 1920 to a poet who has done the most for the art during the last year or in a lifetime. Chosen by board members.

SHEILA MARGARET MOTTON PRIZE
For a book of poems published in the last two years, $500.

Rules and Guidelines
One poem may be entered in each contest. There is no charge for students or members.

Entries should be original unpublished poems in English.

No poem may be entered in more than one contest, nor should it have won a previous contest.

No entries will be returned and there will be no correspondence regarding poems or contest decisions.

Judges are well-known poets, sometimes winners of previous NEPC contests.

Mark the names of the contests on the envelope before sending to: Virginia Thayer, 11 Puritan Road, Arlington, MA 02174

NEW ISSUE PRESS

The Green Rose Prize in Poetry
Department of English
1201 Oliver Street
Western Michigan University
Kalamazoo, MI 49008
Website http://www.wmich.edu/english/fac/nipps

Deadline: September 30, 2001

THE GREEN ROSE PRIZE IN POETRY
Award: $1,000 and publication for a book of poems by an established poet. The edition of the prize winning manuscript will consist of at least 1500 paperbound, and 250 clothbound books.

Guidelines
Poets writing in English who have published one or more full-length collections of poetry. We will consider individual collections and volumes of new and selected poems as well.

A $20 reading fee must accompany each manuscript. Checks should be made payable to New Issue Press Poetry Series.

A manuscript may be submitted that is being considered elsewhere but New Issue should be notified upon the manuscript's acceptance elsewhere.

Please do not bind the manuscript. A manilla folder or metal clasp will do. Include a brief biography and relevant publication information, cover page with name, address, phone number, and title of the manuscript. Please include a table of contents.

Enclose a self-addressed, stamped postcard for notification that the manuscript has been received, or your cancelled check may be used as a notification of receipt. For notification of title and author of the winning manuscript enclose a self-addressed, stamped envelope. Notifications will be made in January 2002.

Manuscripts may be submitted between May 1 and September 30 2001. The winning manuscript will be published in the Fall of 2002.

Manuscripts in addition to the winner will be considered for publication from this competition – as many as three. New Issue does not consider manuscripts outside the context of its competitions.

Send manuscripts and queries to above address.

New Issue Poetry books are designed and produced by the Design Center, Department of Art, Western Michigan University.

New Issue nominates its books for all relevant national awards. In 1998 Rebecca Reynolds' book *Daughter of the Hangnail* published by New Issue Press won the Norma Farber Book Award of the Poetry Society of America. There are currently 16 titles in print and by Spring of 2000 there should be 22 titles.

Deadline: November 30, 2001

NEW ISSUE POETRY PRIZE
Award: $1,000 and publication for a first book of poems

Guidelines
U.S. residents writing in English and U.S. citizens living abroad who have not previously published a full-length collection (48 plus pages) of poems in an edition of 500 or more copies.

Submit a manuscript at least 48 pages in length, typed on one side, single spaced preferred. Photocopies acceptable. Please do not bind manuscript. A manila folder or metal clasp will do. Include a brief biography and relevant publication information, cover page with name address, phone number, and title of manuscript. Please include a table of contents. It is not necessary to send additions, revisions, deletions, etc. after you manuscript has been submitted.

A $12 reading fee must accompany each manuscript. Checks should be made payable to New Issue Press Poetry Series.

A manuscript may be submitted that is being considered elsewhere but New Issues should be notified upon the manuscript's acceptance elsewhere.

Enclose a self-addressed, stamped postcard for notification that the manuscript has been received, or your cancelled check may be used as a notification of receipt. For notification of title and author of the winning manuscript enclose a self-addressed, stamped envelope.

New issue Press publishes three to six first books of poems per year. Manuscripts in addition to the winner will be considered for publication.

The winning manuscript will be named in April 2002 and published January 2003.

Manuscripts will be recycled.

For other book orders call 1-877-885-book.

NEW JERSEY COUNCIL FOR THE HUMANITIES

28 West State Street, Sixth Floor
Trenton, NJ 08608
Phone (609) 695-4838; Fax (609) 695-4929

Deadline: May 1, 2001

NEW JERSEY COUNCIL FOR THE HUMANITIES BOOK AWARD

The New Jersey Council for the Humanities (NJCH) is proud to announce its 13th annual Book Award Competition. For each title nominated (publishers may nominate more than one title), please submit the following: application form (enclosed); and four (4) reading copies (hardcover whenever possible, please). The award is $1,000 to the author. Presentation will be made in the Fall of 2001.

Guidelines and Criteria

1. The author will have a New Jersey connection either by birth, by residence, or by occupation at the time of submitting the manuscript OR the book concerns itself primarily with a significant New Jersey subject. In either case, the author must clearly possess and display scholarly knowledge of the subject, though the author need not have an academic affiliation.

2. The subject of the book is in one or several of the humanities fields as defined by the National Endowment for the Humanities including, but not limited to: literature, language, aesthetics, jurisprudence, history, philosophy, archaeology, comparative religion, and ethics; and those aspects of the social sciences which have humanistic content and imply humanistic methods.

3. The book is a non-fiction title written in a way that invites critical reflection and makes scholarly knowledge available and exciting to a general audience.

4. In 2001, the deadline for nominations is April 1 for books published between January 1, 2000 and December 31, 2000.

5. Normally, no edited or multiple authored works are accepted.

6. A book published in a foreign language is only eligible if it is avail-

able in English translation.

7. Reprints may only be nominated if they were not nominated in the year that they were originally published.

Note: The Award is annual and is granted to a single book. The NJCH reserves the right to make no award in a year in which no book is considered worthy of the Award.

New Jersey Council for the Humanities
Book Award Nomination Form

For each title nominated, please mail this form along with four (4) reading copies to the above address by April 1, 2001.

Publisher

Contact Person: ____________________

(name and title)

Company Name: ____________________

Address: ____________________

____

Phone: __________ Fax: __________ E-mail: __________

Author

Name: ____________________

N.J. Affiliation: ____________________

(If appropriate.)

Nominated Book

Title: ____________________

N.J. Subject: ____________________

(If appropriate, explain briefly)

Date of Publication: ____________________

Month Day Year

List Price:

Hardcover: __________ Softcover: __________

Humanities discipline(s) featured in the book:

____history (including art and music history)
____philosophy
____linguistics
____comparative religion
____literature
____jurisprudence
____ethics
____language
____archaeology
____art theory/criticism
____other:____________

any of the following social science BUT with humanistic content:

____political science
____psychology
____economics
____sociology
____anthropology

Enclosures (Nomination Deadline: April 1, 2001)

1. Reading copies are: ____enclosed or ____being sent under separate cover. (Four (4) per nominated title. Please submit hardcover copies whenever possible.)
2. Brief description of the book and a statement showing why it deserves this award.

NEW MILLENNIUM

Room W
P.O. Box 2463
Knoxville, TN 37901
Phone (423) 428-0389

Deadlines: January 31 and June 15, 2001 postmark

THE NEW MILLENNIUM WRITING AWARDS
The New Millennium Writing (NMW) Awards offer $6,000 in cash prizes, plus publication: Best Fiction, $1,000; Best Poetry, $1,000; and Best Non-fiction (essay, humor, interview, memoir, travel, etc.),$1,000 awarded each Spring and Fall. Judges are Fred Brown, Lisa Coffman, David Hunter, Marilyn Kallet, Jon Manchip White, Allen Wier, and Don Williams, Editor.

Guidelines

1. There are no restrictions as to style, content, format, or number of submissions. Keep fiction and non-fiction entries to 6,000 words or less. Keep poetry submissions to five pages and three poems or less per entry.

2. No previously published material is accepted; simultaneous and multiple submissions OK.

3. Deadline is January 31 for Spring/Summer issue and June 15 for Fall/Winter issue (entries should be postmarked by then).

4. Send a $10 check payable to 'NMW' with each submission. This fee includes the price of the journal in which winning entries will appear, and which all contestants will receive.

5. Each piece of fiction or non-fiction is counted as a separate submission and requires a separate entry fee. Each poetry submission may include up to three poems and five pages.

6. Include name, phone number, address, and category entered on a cover letter or title page only. Winners will be notified.

7. Manuscripts will not be returned except in hardship cases (e.g., printer broken? No computer?) and then only if a self-addressed, stamped envelope is included (we do recycle).

8. Mail entries to: NMW, Room W, P.O. Box 2463, Knoxville, TN 37901.

NEW RIVERS PRESS

Jim Cihlar, Managing Editor
420 North Fifth Street, Suite 910
Minneapolis, MN 55401
Phone (612) 339-7114; Fax (612) 339-9047
Website www.mtn.org/newrivpr

Deadline: January 15, 2001 – April 1, 2001 postmark

THE MINNESOTA VOICES PROJECT COMPETITION
New Rivers Press announces the 20th annual competition for new and emerging writers of poetry, short fiction, novellas, personal essays, memoirs, and other forms of creative prose. Two prose and two poetry manuscripts will be selected as winners. Each winning author will receive $500 and publication of her or his work by New Rivers Press.

Eligibility

1. This competition is open only to current residents of Minnesota. (Note: This is a new policy. A second contest, the Headwaters Literary Competition, will be open to residents of neighboring states. Call or write New Rivers Press for more information.)
2. No author who has had creative work published by a commercial house or a major university press series (Pittsburgh, Carnegie Mellon, Louisiana State University, etc.) will be eligible.
3. Authors who have more than two books published (exclusive of chapbooks) by small independent presses in the genre they would like to compete in will not be eligible.
4. No author may submit more than one manuscript in each year's competition, even if the manuscripts are in different genres.
5. No children's books, or books for juveniles, are eligible.
6. Winners of previous Minnesota Voices Project Competitions will be eligible to enter again after three years, providing they meet the other requirements.
7. All entrants must fill out and return an official entry form.

Guidelines

1. If your manuscript is accepted elsewhere during the judging period, you must notify New Rivers Press in writing as soon as possible that you wish to withdraw your work from consideration. If we do not receive such notification and your manuscript is selected, your signature below gives New Rivers Press the right to proceed with publication.
2. Send two (2) complete copies of your manuscript. Each must be placed in a sturdy folder or binder, with your name and address on the outside as well as on the title page. Pages must be numbered.
3. Manuscripts must be typed (or word processed) on 8-1/2 x 11 inch

sheets. Use one side of the sheet only. Fiction and other prose must be double spaced. Poetry may be single spaced but no more than one poem should appear per page. No photocopies of magazine publications will be accepted.

4. Work previously published in magazines or anthologies is acceptable but must be acknowledged.

5. Prose submissions should be between 100-200 pages. Poetry submissions should be between 40-60 pages of text.

6. No manuscripts will be returned after the competition. Retain a copy for your files.

7. Required: Enclose a stamped, self-addressed, business-size number 10 envelope (9-1/2 x 4 inch) to be notified of results.

   Optional: Enclose a stamped, self-addressed post card to be notified of receipt of your submission.

8. Notify New Rivers Press in writing of any change in your address or phone number.

9. Only manuscripts written by individual authors will be considered. Manuscripts by two or more individuals will not be considered.

10. Mixed genre (poetry and prose) manuscripts are eligible for this competition.

11. Manuscripts must be postmarked by April 1, 2001.

12. Please do not submit manuscripts prior to January 15, 2001. No hand delivery of manuscripts will be accepted.

13. The contest will be judged by a panel including the publisher.

14. All entrants will receive letters notifying them of the panel's decisions. The results will not be announced prior to October 1, 2001. Please, no phone inquiries prior to the announcement of the winners. Winning manuscripts will be published in calendar year 2002. Authors are paid after publication.

Deadline: September 16, 2001 postmark

NEW RIVERS PRESS SOUTHEAST ASIAN ANTHOLOGY
Although the Southeast Asian American community has a long history and a rapidly growing population, there are a few books that feature the poetry, fiction and creative non-fiction of the established and emerging authors of this community.

We are soliciting fiction, creative non-fiction, and poetry created by Southeast Asian Americans, for a literary anthology of previously unpublished work. By Southeast Asian Americans we mean residents of the United States with Brunei, Burmese (Myanmar), Cambodian, Filipino, Hmong, Indonesian, Laotian, Malaysian, Singaporean, Thai, or Vietnamese heritage, including recent immigrants as well as second, third, fourth, etc., generation writers. Subject matter is not limited. The work may, for instance, explore such ideas as community, memory, locations, genders, the subject of the artist and language – and may do so in creative writing that celebrates, records, preserves, explores, questions, problematizes, invents and defines – and would do so for an audience who may be both familiar and unfamiliar with Southeast Asian Americans.

Guidelines

1. All submissions must be typed/word processed, double spaced on 8-1/2 x 11 inch paper on one side of the sheet. Submit no more than ten (10) pages for poetry, thirty for prose.

2. Submit three (3) copies [original plus two (2) photocopies] of each piece.

3. We will not be able to return your work, so please keep another copy for yourself. Send a self-addressed, stamped envelope for notification of results.

4. Author's name, address, and phone number must appear at the top of the first page, and author's name and page number should appear on each following page.

5. Include a brief resumé (no more than two pages) with mention of author's Southeast Asian heritage.

6. Authors should keep us informed of any address changes.

7. Only previously unpublished work will be considered.

Send submissions postmarked by September 16, 2001 to: New Rivers Press, Jim Cihlar, Managing Editor, 40 North Fifth Street, Suite 910, Minneapolis, MN 55401.

Minnesota Voices Project Competition
Entry Form

1. I have read the guidelines for the 2001 Minnesota Voices Project Competition and understand them.

2. My creative work has not been published in book form by any commercial publishing house (i.e., Dell, Random House, etc.) or by a major university press, and qualifies as the work of a "new and emerging author."

3. All of the material included in this submission is of my own composition and is free from copyright restrictions. I understand that, should I win the competition, I will be responsible for securing releases.

Signature and Date: ____________________

Name: ____________________

Address: ____________________

City/State/Zip: ____________________

Telephone:(   ) ____________________

Poetry: ____________________

Prose: ____________________

Title of Manuscript: ____________________

____

Send your submission and this completed entry form to:
New Rivers Press
Attn: Jim Cihlar, Managing Editor
420 North Fifth Street, Suite 910
Minneapolis, MN 55401

NEW YORK UNIVERSITY PRESS PRIZES

70 Washington Square South 2nd Floor
New York, NY 10012-1091

Deadline May 2, 2001

NEW YORK UNIVERSITY PRESS PRIZE FOR FICTION

NEW YORK UNIVERSITY PRESS PRIZE FOR POETRY

Prize: $1,000, publication and will be honored in person at New York University. All submissions must be in the English language. Submissions will be accepted from any country in the world. Winners will be notified in Fall 2001. Only winners will be notified. Manuscripts will not be returned. Please no telephone inquires.

Guidelines
One type written copy of a book-length manuscript. Include a one page support letter on letterhead from a qualified reader, teacher, agent, editor, etc., and a cover sheet with your name, address and daytime telephone number. Send a self-addressed, stamped postcard to enable us to acknowledge receipt.

Send submissions to above address, “Attn: Poetry” or “Attn: Fiction.”

NIMROD INTERNATIONAL JOURNAL

The University of Tulsa
600 S. College
Tulsa, OK 74104-3189
Phone (918) 631-3080

Deadline: April 30, 2001

Prizes: First: $2,000 and publication; Second: $1,000 and publication.

Poetry: either a long single poem (min. approx. 500 words) or a collection of 5-10 shorter poems. Fiction: 7500 words maximum. No previously published works or works accepted for publication elsewhere. Author's name must not appear on manuscript. Include a cover sheet containing major title and subtitles, author's name, address, phone and fax numbers and e-mail. "Contest Entry" must be on envelope. Manuscripts will not be returned. *Nimrod* retains the right to publish any submission. Works not accepted for publication will be released. Send a self-addressed, stamped envelope for results only.

Entry/Subscription fee: $20 includes both entry and subscription covering 2 issues. Writers submitting both prose and poetry need send only one entry fee. Make $20 check payable to *Nimrod* and send to above address.

96 INC.

Bruce P. Rossley Literary Awards
P.O. Box 15559
Boston, MA 02215

Deadline: August 1, 2001 – September 30, 2001

THE BRUCE P. ROSSLEY LITERARY AWARD
The Bruce P. Rossley Literary Award is presented in even years by *96 Inc.,* a magazine, a resource, and artists' collaborative. The award is given biennially to a writer of poetry, fiction, or non-fiction in New England. There are no specific publication requirements for nominating a writer. The award is intended to give greater recognition to a writer of merit. A panel of judges from the fields of publishing, writing, and teaching will select the recipient of this monetary prize of $1,000. The writer's work will be celebrated at a reception at the Lansdowne Street Playhouse on November 24, 2001. In addition to writing, the writer's accomplishments in the fields of teaching and community service will also be considered.

THE BRUCE P. ROSSLEY NEW VOICE AWARD
The founding judges were unanimous in their belief that a young writer cannot be compared to someone who is older and has had more time to achieve and accomplish, and therefore they established the Bruce P. Rossley New Voice Award. The New Voice Award has been presented for the past three years. This award will be considered each year based on the type and merit of the nominations. This offers a cash prize of $100, and follows the same guidelines as the Bruce P. Rossley Literary Award.

Submission Guidelines

1. Writers may be nominated by anyone familiar with his or her work.
2. The letter of nomination should be approximately one page and should be accompanied by a *vitae* or a short profile of the nominee. Include six (6) copies of all materials.
3. Samples of the writer's work may be submitted. (Please submit six (6) copies of a sample of the writer's work. If the sample is in the form of a book or a long work, then please select a chapter, or excerpt, and submit six (6) collated copies (maximum 20 pages please).
4. Open to all writers in New England.
5. Nominations, along with a $10.00 reading fee payable to 96 Inc, should be mailed to: The Bruce P. Rossley Literary Award (or The Bruce P. Rossley New Voice Award), P.O. Box 15559, Boston, MA, 02215, between August 1, 2001 and September 30, 2001.

NORTHEASTERN UNIVERSITY PRESS

Guy Rotella, Editor
English Department, 406 Holmes Hall
Northeastern University
Boston, MA 02115

Deadline: September 15, 2001 postmark

SAMUEL FRENCH MORSE POETRY PRIZE
The Morse Poetry Contest Prize is publication of the winning manuscript by Northeastern University Press and an award of $1,000.

Guidelines

The contest is open to manuscripts of first or second books of poems by U.S. poets. Chapbooks and "vanity" publications are not considered previously published books. Members of the Northeastern University community are not eligible.

Manuscripts must contain between 50 and 70 pages of poetry, exclusive of front matter, section dividers, and other material. Manuscripts must be typed or "word processed." Clear photocopied copies are acceptable.

One copy of the entry should be submitted. It should be held together by a binder clip in order to permit handling without scattering or loss (paper clips are insufficient). The manuscript should be accompanied by a list of acknowledgments (if appropriate) and by a brief biography of the entrant on a separate page(s). Those materials should not be attached to the manuscript. The poet's name should not appear on the title or table of contents pages, or on any of the poems themselves.

A reading fee of $15.00 must accompany each entry submitted. Checks or money orders must be made payable to the English Department, Northeastern University.

Manuscripts will not be returned. Be sure to retain a copy. Enclose a self-addressed, stamped envelope for notification of contest results. For acknowledgment of receipt of your manuscript, include a self-addressed, stamped postcard.

Manuscripts will be judged anonymously. After an initial screening by a faculty panel, finalists' manuscripts will be sent to a distinguished poet for judging. Final selection is set for mid-January of 2002.

Contest correspondence must be postmarked no later than August 1, 2001 for inquiries; and September 15, 2001 for submissions.

Manuscripts and requests for information should be addressed to: Guy Rotella, Editor, Morse Poetry Prize, English Department/406 Holmes Hall, Northeastern University, Boston, MA 02115

OGLEBAY INSTITUTE'S TOWNGATE THEATRE

Oglebay Institute's Stifel Fine Arts Center
1330 National Road
Wheeling, WV 26003

Deadline: March 15, 2001 postmark

OGLEBAY INSTITUTE'S TOWNGATE THEATRE
PLAYWRITING CONTEST FOR COLLEGE STUDENTS

The winning playwright of the Oglebay Institute's Towngate Theatre 5th annual Playwriting Contest will receive a prize of $100. There will be a limited run of the play by the Parcel Players in the summer of 2001. The Parcel Players is comprised of high school and college students.

Guidelines for Submission

All full-length non-musical plays that have never been professionally produced or published are eligible.

Play entry deadline is March 15, 2001. No script postmarked after that date will be considered.

Contestants may submit more than one play for consideration.

Plays in which two or more authors have collaborated are acceptable; however, the prize money remains the same.

All contestants will be notified of the winning play no later than June 1, 2001.

Oglebay Institute reserves the right to withhold the award if, in the opinion of the judges, no entry merits it.

Applicants' plays will be returned only if accompanied by a self-addressed mailer with sufficient postage.

All plays must be controlled exclusively by the playwright. The playwright will retain all rights to the winning play.

Oglebay Institute, in collaboration with the author, reserves the right to determine the final staging of the play. All matters pertaining to production and promotion will be the responsibility of Oglebay Institute.

Authors should take into consideration the following limitations of Towngate Theatre when planning special effects that are absolutely necessary to the production. Theatre seating capacity is 166. Stage dimensions are 27-1/2 foot proscenium, and 30 foot depth. There is no grid or fly space. There is one trap door. Lighting is adequate for all but the most elaborate plots demanding special effects.

Send manuscripts to: Towngate Theatre Playwriting Contest for College Students, Oglebay Institute's Stifel Fine Arts Center, 1330 National Road, Wheeling, WV 26003.

OHIOANA LIBRARY ASSOCIATION

Attn: Linda Hengst
65 South Front Street, Suite 1105
Columbus, OH 43215-4163
Phone (614) 466-3831; Fax (614) 728-6974
E-Mail ohioana@winslo.state.ohio.us

Deadline: December 31, 2001

THE OHIOANA BOOK AWARDS

Sponsored by the Ohioana Library Association, the Ohioana Book Awards began in 1942. Their purpose is to bring state and national attention to Ohio authors and their books. The Ohioana Book Awards provide recognition and encouragement each year in the categories of Fiction, Non-fiction, Juvenile Books, Poetry, and Books about Ohio or an Ohioan.

Eligibility

Any book of general interest has been written or edited by a person born in Ohio or who has lived in Ohio for at least five years, with the exception of a "Book about Ohio or an Ohioan," which may be authored by an non-Ohioan.

Any book considered for an award must be received by the Ohioana Library Association during the calendar year prior to the year the award is given and must have a copyright date within the last two calendar years. A book is ordinarily considered only once for an award.

Books shall be judged by their literary merit and the overall importance of the work. Juvenile books will be judged by the same criteria, plus appeal to the intended audience of children or young adults.

Deadline: December 31, 2001

OHIOANA AWARD FOR CHILDREN'S LITERATURE
ALICE WOOD MEMORIAL

The Alice Wood Memorial is sponsored by the Ohioana Library Association. The Ohioana Award for Children's Literature was established in 1990 and is made possible by a bequest from Alice Louise Ridenour Wood. The award of $1,000 is given to an Ohio author of children's literature for a body of work or for a lifetime of contributions to children's literature.

Eligibility

The recipient must have been born in Ohio or lived in Ohio for a minimum of five years.

The recipient must have established a distinguished publishing record of books for children and young people.

The body of work has made, and continues to make, a significant contribution to the literature for young people.

Through the recipient's work as a writer, teacher, administrator, or through community service, interest in children's literature has been encouraged and children have become involved with reading.

It's desirable for the recipient to be present at Ohioana Day to receive the award.

Deadline: January 31, 2001 postmark

OHIOANA WALTER RUMSEY MARVIN GRANT

Sponsored by The Ohioana Library Association, the Walter Ramsey Marvin Grant was established by Dr. Marvin's family to encourage young writers. Dr. Marvin served as the Director of the Ohioana Library Associates from 1954 to 1965. The Marvin Grant is a $1,000 award given to an author under 30 years of age who has not had a book published.

A panel of three qualified judges will review and rank each entry on a scale of 0 to 100. Judges shall select the work of the person whose writing they consider best in overall quality. Judges reserve the right not to award the grant if, in their opinion, no submission merits a grant.

Eligibility

Applicant must have been born in Ohio or have lived in Ohio for a minimum of five years.

Applicant must be no older than 30 years of age on January 31 of the year the award is given.

Applicant must not have had a book published.

Guidelines

Entries submitted may consist of up to six pieces of prose.

No submission may total more than sixty pages nor less than ten pages.

Entries will not be returned.

Entries must be accompanied by the completed entry form or a letter stating the total length of time, dates, and the place of residence of the applicant, or the date and location of Ohio birth and the applicant's birth date, and a statement that the applicant has not published a book.

Entries must be postmarked no later than January 31 of the year in which the award is given.

Ohioana Library Association Book Awards

NOMINEE GENERAL INFORMATION: (Use one copy of the form for each title nominated. Forms may be photocopies. Individuals may nominate as many titles as they wish. Forms may be found at www.oplin.lib.oh.us/OHIOANA/)

Title of book: ______________________________

Publisher: ______________________________

____

____

Copyright date: ______________________________

Category:

Fiction Non-fiction Juvenile Book Poetry

About Ohio or an Ohioan

Author's Name: ______________________________

Address: ______________________________

City, State, Zip: ______________________________

Day telephone: ( ) ______________________________

Date and place of birth ______________________________

Place and length of a residence in Ohio ______________________________

____

NOMINEE QUALIFICATIONS: On a separate sheet, please describe why this book qualifies and should be considered for an Ohioana Book Award. Please submit one copy of the book you nominate.

Nominated by: ______________________________

Address: ______________________________

____

City, State, Zip ______________________________

Telephone: ( ) Fax: ______________________________

E-mail: ______________________________

Signature: Date: ______________________________

Please return to: Ohioana Library Association, Attn: Linda Hengst, 65 South Front Street, Suite 1105, Columbus, OH 43215-4163.

Ohioana Award for Children's Literature

NOMINEE GENERAL INFORMATION:

Name: ______________________________

Address: ______________________________

City, State, Zip: ______________________________

Day telephone: (   ) ______________________________

Date & place of birth ______________________________

Place and length of a residence in Ohio ______________________________

____

NOMINEE QUALIFICATIONS: On a separate sheet, please describe the nominee's special qualifications for the Ohioana Award for Children's Literature. Describe the nominee's publishing record and significant contributions to children's literature. Please include brief biographical information (maximum two pages) and supplemental materials such as samples of work and reviews. Please limit supplemental material to not more than ten pages.

Nominated by: ______________________________

Address: ______________________________

City, State, Zip ______________________________

Telephone: (   ) ______________ Fax: ______________

E-mail: ______________________________

Signature: ______________ Date: ______________

Please return to: Ohioana Library Association, Attn: Linda Hengst, 65 South Front Street, Suite 1105, Columbus, OH 43215-4163.

Ohioana Walter Rumsey Marvin Grant

ENTRY APPLICATION

Name: ______________________________

Address: ______________________________

City, State, Zip: ______________________________

Day telephone: (   ) ______________________________

Date and place of birth ______________________________

Place and length of a residence in Ohio ______________________________

____

I, ______________________________

have not published a book.

Signature: ______________________________ Date: __________

Please return to: Ohioana Library Association, Attn: Linda Hengst, 65 South Front Street, Suite 1105, Columbus, OH 43215-4163.

OHIO STATE UNIVERSITY PRESS

Bill Roorbach
David Citino, Poetry Editor
Ohio State University Press
1070 Carmack Road
Columbus, OH 43210-1002

Deadline: January 1, 2001 – January 31, 2001 postmark

THE SANDSTONE PRIZE IN SHORT FICTION
Sponsored by the Ohio State University and the MFA Program in Creative Writing at OSU.

An independent judge will select one manuscript for this annual award. The winning author will receive a cash prize of $1,500, publication under a standard book contract, and an invitation to direct a creative writing program and to perform a public reading. The winner will be announced in May 2001.

Eligibility
Submissions may include short stories, novellas, or a combination of both.

The competition is open to all writers in English, published or unpublished. Current students and employees of The Ohio State University are ineligible.

Manuscripts must be between 150 and 300 typed pages (approximately 40,000 to 80,000 words). Novellas must not exceed 125 pages (approximately 35,000 words).

Submission Guidelines
Manuscripts must be typed, double spaced, on quality white paper, 250 to 300 words per page, one side only, pages numbered consecutively. Crisp photocopies are acceptable.

Judging is anonymous, so please include the following: a cover sheet with name, street address; e-mail address; and phone numbers. Also include an acknowledgment page with publication history for any previously published work; and a title page listing title and approximate word count. A table of contents page listing only the stories and/or novellas and page number.

Include a self-addressed, stamped envelope so we can notify you of the contest results. Also include a self-addressed, stamped postcard if you wish to receive confirmation of receipt of your manuscript.

Ohio State University Press assumes no responsibility for lost or damaged manuscripts.

Manuscripts must be postmarked in the month of January and be accompanied by a non-refundable fee of $20. Send check or money order (no cash) made payable to Ohio State University.

Mail entries to: Bill Roorbach, Ohio State University Press, 1070 Carmack Rd, Columbus, OH 43210-1002.

Deadline: September 1, 2001 – September 30, 2001 postmark

THE JOURNAL AWARD IN POETRY
The Journal, the literary magazine of Ohio State University, selects one full-length manuscript of poetry each year for publication by the Ohio State University Press. The award carries with it a $1,000 cash prize. The winning entry will be announced by January 15, 2002.

Submission Guidelines
Entries of at least 48 typed pages of original poetry must be postmarked during the month of September 2001. Entries postmarked later than September 30, 2001 will be returned unread. Clear photocopies are acceptable. Manuscripts must be previously unpublished. Some or all of the poems in the collection may have appeared in periodicals, chapbooks, or anthologies, but these must be identified.

Include a nonrefundable handling fee of $20 with each manuscript (check or money order payable to Ohio State University). Entrants will receive a one-year subscription (two issues) to *The Journal.*

Include a stamped, self-addressed, business-sized envelope so we can notify you of the results. If you wish us to confirm receipt of your manuscript, also include a stamped, self-addressed postcard.

Ohio State University Press assumes no responsibility for lost or damaged manuscripts. Manuscripts will not be returned.

Mail entries to: David Citino, Poetry Editor, Ohio State University Press, 1070 Carmack Road, Columbus, OH 43210-1002.

THE OHIO UNIVERSITY PRESS

Scott Quadrangle
Athens, OH 45701

Deadline: October 31, 2001 postmark

THE 2000 HOLLIS SUMMERS POETRY COMPETITION
This competition invites writers to submit unpublished collections of original poems for both those who have not and who have published a book-length collection. Prize: $500 and publication by the Ohio University Press the following year.

Guidelines
Manuscripts of 60 to 95 pages should be typed on standard size paper or be a clean photocopy. Do not send your only manuscript, as those not chosen will be recycled. Do not send a self-addressed, stamped envelope. All contestants will be notified following the final selection. Include a self-addressed, stamped postcard if you wish acknowledgment of receipt of material.

Name, address, and phone number should appear on a title page. Acknowledgments should appear on a separate page. Individual collections must be the work of a single author. Translations are not accepted. Manuscripts should be submitted in final form; revisions or emendations to acknowledgments will not be considered during the contest. Multiple submissions to other publishers are acceptable provided we are informed if the manuscript is accepted elsewhere.

The manuscript should be submitted in a plain 9 x 11-1/2 inch manilla folder. Please do not submit manuscripts bound in ring binders or plastic holders.

Submissions should include a check for $15 made out to Ohio University Press to help defray administrative costs. Judge will be named in April when winner is announced. Individual criticism of manuscript cannot be given.

Send submissions to: Hollis Summers Poetry Competition at the above address.

OHIO WRITER MAGAZINE

P.O. Box 91801
Cleveland, OH 44101

Deadline: June 30, 2001

BEST OF OHIO WRITERS WRITING CONTEST
The best of Ohio Writers Writing Contest is sponsored by *Ohio Writer* magazine. Categories include Fiction, Poetry, Creative Non-Fiction, and "Writers on Writing" (any genre). Prizes awarded in each category are $150 First Prize and $50 Second Prize. First Place winners are published in a special edition of *Ohio Writer.* Announcement of winners will be in the November/December issue of *Ohio Writer.*

Eligibilty
Competitors must reside in the state of Ohio. Unpublished manuscripts only, please. Entries will be judges anonymously; do not put your name on the manuscript pages. Attach entry form (or facsimile) to submission.

Guidelines
Fiction is not to exceed 2,000 words. Poetry is limited to three poems per entry; two typewritten pages per poem. Creative Non-Fiction is limited to 2,000 words. Writers on Writing entry should conform to appropriate genre length.

Submit in 8-1/2 x 11 inch paper only; do not staple entry. Put title of piece and page number on every page.

Entry fees are $10 per entry; for each additional entry in same category, add $2 (limit three). Please make check payable to *Ohio Writer*, and mail to: Best of Ohio Writers Writing Contest, P.O. Box 91801, Cleveland, OH 44101. All entrants will receive a one-year subscription or renewal to *Ohio Writer* with entry fee.

General Publication Guidelines for *Ohio Writer*
Ohio Writer magazine is looking for non-fiction articles that deal with any area of writing, including how-to's, profiles and interviews with Ohio writers, poets, and journalists. *Ohio Writer* is read by both beginning and experienced writers. We hope to create a sense of community among writers of different genres, abilities, and backgrounds. We want to hear a personal voice, one that engages the reader. We're looking for intelligent, literate prose that isn't stuffy.

Focus articles should be approximately 1,500 words. Payment is $25 on publication. Reprinted articles $15 on publication.

Feature articles should be approximately 2,000-2,500 words. Payment is $50 on publication.

Reviews are accepted on any publication or book by an Ohio writer or Ohio Press. Include the title, author, press, and city where published, year of publication, number of pages, and price. Occasionally we use reviews of events: conferences, readings, bookstores, etc. Length should be 400-600 words. Payment is $5-$10.

Include a short biographical statement with all submissions.

Unsolicited manuscripts and book reviews will be accepted, but a self-addressed, stamped envelope (with sufficient return postage) is necessary if you wish the manuscript to be returned.

Reporting time is four to six weeks.

We suggest that writers unfamiliar with the magazine order a sample copy. Back issues are available for $2.00 plus 50 cents postage.

We buy one-time rights, plus the right to reprint. Any editing, except copy editing, will be done with the author's approval.

We also accept announcements or notes concerning writing, writing opportunities, and the writing life in Ohio for publication in our "Notes, Previews, and Announcements" column. Suitable calendar listings are published without charge.

Ohio Writer is published by the Poets' League of Greater Cleveland. Address all correspondence to Ohio Writer, c/o Ron Antonucci, Editor, P.O. Box 2115, Hudson, OH 44236.

Best of Ohio Writers Writing Contest
Entry Form

(Please attach to entry. Do not put author's name on manuscript. Submit on 8-1/2 x 11 inch paper only; do not staple entry. Put title of piece and page number on every page.)

Name ______________________________

Address ______________________________

____

City/State/Zip ______________________________

Day Phone ______________ Eve. Phone ______________

Category of Entry:

______ Poetry ______ Fiction

______ Creative Non-Fiction ______ Writers on Writing

Title(s) of Work ______________________________

____

____

____

____

Entry fee attached $______($10 per entry, $2 for each additional entry in same category, limit three.)

Mail entries to: Best of Ohio Writers Writing Contest, P.O. Box 91801, Cleveland, OH 44101.

OKLAHOMA CENTER FOR THE BOOK

200 NE 18th Street
Oklahoma City, OK 73105
Phone (405) 521-2502, ext. 264

Deadline: January 12, 2001

OKLAHOMA BOOK AWARD
Any individual, organization, or company may enter in appropriate category. Books considered for this award must have been written by an author who resides or who has resided in Oklahoma, or have an Oklahoma-based theme. The book must have been published between January 1, 2000 and December 31, 2000. Books, hardcover or paperback, entered in previous Oklahoma Book Award competitions are not eligible. Entries are forwarded to judges upon receipt, please enter as soon as possible.

Submission Guidelines
Entries will be considered in each of the following categories (books may be entered in more than one category): Fiction, Non-fiction, Children/Young Adult (fiction, non-fiction, and poetry), Poetry, and Design/Illustration.

A panel of judges will consider all entries. Awards will be granted at the discretion of the judges. Panel members represent a broad spectrum of expertise in writing and publishing in the fields covered by the award categories. Entries in all except the design/illustration category are judged principally on the quality of writing, with organization and interpretation also playing a role in the decision.

Entries must be received by January 12, 2001. Finalists will be notified February 9, 2001. Winners will be announced at the awards ceremony March 14, 2001.

The completed entry form, along with six (6) copies of the book (non-refundable), must be provided to the awards committee for each category entered.

No entry fee is required. Entrants will be responsible for shipping charges; collect shipments will be refused. The awards committee reserves the right to change the category of an entry. All entries, book copies, and correspondence should be sent to: Oklahoma Center for the Book, 200 NE 18th Street, Oklahoma City, OK 73105.

Questions or comments can be made by calling:
(405) 521-2502, ext. 264

OLIVET COLLEGE

Linda Jo Scott, Contest Chairperson
Department of Humanities
Olivet College
Olivet, MI 49076
Phone (616) 749-7000; Fax (616) 749-7121

Deadline: February 9, 2001

THE ABBIE M. COPPS POETRY COMPETITION
First Prize is $150 and publication in the *Garfield Lake Review*. Winner to be announced in March.

Guidelines for Submission

1. Submit only unpublished poems, 100 lines or less.

2. Include in the submission envelope: the unsigned, typed poem. The entry fee of $2 per poem (no limit on number of entries). A sealed envelope containing the name, address, and phone number of the poet. On the outside of this enclosed envelope, please write or type the first line of the poem.

3. Send to: Linda Jo Scott, Contest Chairperson, Department of Humanities, Olivet College, Olivet, MI 49076.

THE ORIGINAL THEATRE WORKS

Cerritos College Department of Theatre
11110 Alondra Boulevard
Norwalk, CA 90650
Phone (562) 860-2451, ext. 2638

Deadline: September 1, 2001 postmark

The Original Theatre Works (TOTW) is looking for unproduced, original plays, performance pieces, musicals, extravaganzas, entertainments, etc., for its 15th anniversary celebration. Awards will range from $250 to $750 if your piece is selected. The winning entry(s) will either be fully produced or workshopped during our summer season. Sound good?

Anyone may enter this contest. However, preference will be given to previously UNPRODUCED pieces written by authors who can arrange to be with us at TOTW rehearsals and pre-production festivities. Special consideration will be given to plays which explore subjects and themes which focus on the diverse cultures and the under-represented who make up America. We enjoy working with good playwrights, and we think you'll enjoy working with us.

Submission Guidelines
Write a full-length play or theatre piece. If you happen to have one lying around, all the better.

Clearly mark 20 consecutive pages of your script identified for initial reading.

List pertinent background information including productions and any needed music.

Complete the enclosed application.

Include a large, self-addressed, stamped envelope for the return of your manuscript and a self-addressed, stamped postcard for acknowledgment of your entry.

Send all with two (2) marked copies of your script and a $5 application fee payable to Cerritos College.

Postmark your entry no later than September 1, 2001

Sit back and relax! We will let you know by April 1, 2002 if your play has been selected for production.
We reserve the right not to offer an award for any given year if it has been determine that a suitable play has not been found.

Mail application and $5 application fee for each play (payable to Cerritos College) along with your marked scripts, background information, and a self-addressed, stamped envelope to: Cerritos College, The Original Theatre Works, 11110 Alondra Blvd., Norwalk, CA 90650.

The Original Theatre Works Application

Name ____________________

Address ____________________

City, State, Zip ____________________

Telephone, Home: __________ Work: __________ Fax: __________

TITLE OF PLAY ____________________

____

Please Note: Script will be destroyed and the paper recycled if you choose not to include a self-addressed, stamped envelope for its return.

Short Biography: ____________________

____

____

____

____

____

____

I confirm that the above named materials are my own original development and will not infringe upon any other property rights of any person or entity.

Signed: ____________________

OVERSEAS PRESS CLUB OF AMERICA

Sonya Fry, Executive Director
320 East 42 Street, Mezzanine
New York, NY 10017
Phone (212) 983-4655; Fax (212) 983-4692

Deadline: January 30, 2001 postmark

OVERSEAS PRESS CLUB OF AMERICA AWARDS
Annual awards for international coverage in Newspapers, Wire Services, On-Line Publications, Magazines, Radio, Television, Cartoons, Books, and Photography. Work must be Published by U.S. based publications or broadcast during 2000. All awards include a certificate of $1,000 cash prize.

Each entry is to be accompanied by a check for $100 made payable to The Overseas Press Club. Entries cannot be returned. Entries will be destroyed after judging is completed.

Award Categories

CLASS ONE
THE HAL BOYLE AWARD
Sponsored by AT&T. Best Newspaper or Wire Service Reporting from abroad.

CLASS TWO
THE BOB CONSIDINE AWARD
Sponsored by King Features Syndicate. Best Newspaper or Wire Service Interpretation of foreign affairs.

CLASS THREE
THE ROBERT CAPA GOLD MEDAL AWARD
Sponsored by Life Magazine. Best Published Photographic Reporting from abroad requiring exceptional courage and enterprise.

CLASS FOUR
THE OLIVER REBBOT AWARD
Sponsored by Newsweek. Best Photographic Reporting from abroad in magazines and books.

CLASS FIVE
THE JOHN FABER AWARD
Sponsored by The Coca-Cola Company. Best Radio News or Interpretation of foreign affairs.

CLASS SIX
THE LOWELL THOMAS AWARD
Sponsored by ABC. Best Radio News or Interpretation of foreign affairs.

CLASS SEVEN
THE DAVID KAPLAN AWARD
Sponsored by Bell Atlantic. Best TV Spot News reporting from abroad.

CLASS EIGHT
THE EDWARD R. MURROW AWARD
Sponsored by CBS News. Best TV Interpretation or Documentary on foreign affairs.

CLASS NINE
THE ED CUNNINGHAM MEMORIAL AWARD
Sponsored by Lexis-Nexis. Best Magazine reporting from abroad.

CLASS TEN
THE THOMAS NAST AWARD
Sponsored by Newsday. Best Cartoons on foreign affairs.

CLASS ELEVEN
THE MORTON FRANK AWARD
Best Business Reporting from abroad in magazines.

CLASS TWELVE
THE MALCOLM FORBES AWARD
Sponsored by Forbes Magazine. Best Business Reporting from abroad in Newspapers or Wire Services.

CLASS THIRTEEN
THE CARL SPIELVOGEL AWARD
Sponsored by a supporter of the OPC. Best Business Reporting from abroad in the broadcast media.

CLASS FOURTEEN
THE CORNELIUS RYAN AWARD
Sponsored by the Anita Diamant Literary Agency. Best Non-fiction Book on foreign affairs.

CLASS FIFTEEN
THE MADELINE DANE ROSS AWARD
Sponsored by Madeline Dane Ross Fund. Best Foreign Reporting in any medium showing a concern for the human condition.

CLASS SIXTEEN
THE ERIC AND AMY BURGER AWARD
Sponsored by the Estate of Eric and Amy Burger. Best Reporting in any medium dealing with Human Rights.

CLASS SEVENTEEN
THE JOE AND LAURIE DINE AWARD
Sponsored by their sons, Philip and Kim Dine. Best Reporting in a print medium dealing with Human Rights.

CLASS EIGHTEEN
THE WHITMAN BASSOW AWARD
Sponsored by AT&T. Best Reporting in any medium on international Environmental Issues.

CLASS NINETEEN
THE ROBERT SPIERS BENJAMIN AWARD
Sponsored by The Robert S. Benjamin Fund. Best Reporting in any medium from Latin America.

Submission Guidelines
Entries must include two (2) copies of:

1. The work nominate.,
2. Application information – first page of the entry form.
3. Brief summary or statement explaining why the entry deserves consideration.

Each entry must be accompanied by a $100 check payable to The Overseas Press Club.

Multiple entries are possible, but each entry must have two copies of the work nominated, application, and statement, as well as a $100 entry fee per category. Multiple entry fees can be submitted on one check.

Material may be the work of an individual, group, or staff, but must be on one subject.

It is NOT necessary to submit biographies or photos of the nominee, but the winners are expected to send a photo (head-shot) within a week of notification of winning so that they can be featured in *Dateline*, the awards magazine published by the OPC.

PHOTO EXHIBITS
In these categories (Class three, four, and five), it is necessary to send only one photograph or one set of photographs with the name of the photographer and submitting organization clearly printed on the back. Photos should not be larger than 17 x 20 inches. Limit entry to ten slides or photographs; however, use only one format. Each exhibit should consist of the photographer's published work on one subject. Submit proof of publication, e.g., tearsheet from newspaper or copy of magazine article.

CARTOON

Limit entry to ten (10) cartoons. Submit two (2) copies of each cartoon and proof of publication, e.g., tearsheet from newspaper or copy from magazine.

ON-LINE

Material published only On-Line will be placed in the appropriate category by OPC judges. Submit two (2) hard copies of each entry.

TELEVISION

In VHS format. Groups or teams working one subject or show may submit an entry, but please state clearly on the form the number of people to be considered for the award. For example, Correspondent, Producer, Cameraperson, etc. Only the people listed on the form will appear on the award certificate.

Please remember that entries go through numerous hands during the judging process. Tearsheets should be arranged in sequence, bound or firmly anchored in a folder or scrapbook. Tapes, discs, and film should be labeled clearly as to sequence.

To avoid conflict, judges will excuse themselves from judging entries from their own organizations.

Judges usually confer one award and one citation in each category, but judges have the discretion to make dual awards.

Entries must be postmarked no later than January 30, 2001.

All information concerning the awards should be directed to: Sonya Fry, Manager, Overseas Press Club of America, 320 East 42 Street, Mezzanine, New York, NY 10017; phone (212) 983-4655, fax (212) 983-4692.

Overseas Press Club of America

Nominee ____________________

Organization Name ____________________

Nominee's Address and Phone # ____________________

____

____

____

City, State, Zip Code ____________________

Title of Entry ____________________

Category ____________________

Date(s) of Publication or Broadcast ____________________

Submitted by: ____________________

(Name, Address, Phone Number of Person and Organization) ____________________

____

____

____

Each entry is to be accompanied by a check for $100 made payable to The Overseas Press Club.

______

OWL CREEK PRESS

2693 S. West Camano Drive
Camano Island, WA 98292

Deadline: February 15, 2001 for Fiction and Poetry
August 15, 2001 for Chapbook

OWL CREEK PRESS PRIZES IN POETRY AND FICTION
Owl Creek Press now sponsors a Fiction Prize of $1,000 as well as its annual Poetry Prize each February and Chapbook Prize each August. Novels, novellas, collections of short stories – any book manuscript of fiction will be considered.

Owl Creek Press will also continue to sponsor The Green Lake Chapbook Prize of $500 each summer and The Owl Creek Poetry Prize of $750 for a full-length poetry manuscript each winter.

The Press has been publishing works of literary art for more than 18 years and awarding prizes for more than 16 years. All prizes are non-returnable advances against royalties and additional payments will be made if royalties exceed the prize money.

Deadline: August 15, 2001

GREEN LAKE (POETRY) CHAPBOOK PRIZE
Prize is $500. Entry fee is $10. Length should be under 40 pages.

Deadline: February 15, 2001

OWL CREEK POETRY PRIZE
Prize is $750. Entry fee is $15. Submission should be over 50 pages in length.

Deadline: February 15, 2001

OWL CREEK FICTION PRIZE
Prize is $1,000. Entry fee is $20. There is no page limit.

Submission Guidelines
Manuscripts will be returned only if a self-addressed, stamped envelope with sufficient return postage is provided. Please include a standard size envelope for contest results if you do not wish your manuscript returned.

Any combination of published (magazines and anthologies) or unpublished work is acceptable as long as the work has not appeared in a single author book.

There is no limit to the number of entries for any contest. Each will be considered separately. Translations are welcome if permission from the original publisher or author can be provided.

Submit entries to: Owl Creek Press, 2693 S. West Camano Drive, Camano Island, WA 98292.

PAINTBRUSH

Truman State University, MC 335
100 E. Normal Street
Kirksville, MO 63501 USA

Deadline: October 30, 2001

THE EZRA POUND POETRY AWARD
Prize: $2,000 and publication of manuscript in *Paintbrush*
The competition is open to all poets writing in English, nationality, reputation, or publication history notwithstanding.

Please submit a 32-page, typed or printed copy of the manuscript. Print no more than one poem on each page. Make sure that you are using letter-quality print. Include two title pages, one bearing the full title of the manuscript only for blind review, and the second showing the title of the submitted work, your full name, mailing address and telephone number. Your name must not appear anywhere else in the manuscript, save on the second title page which will be removed from your manuscript before it gets forwarded to the judge(s). Also include a table of contents showing titles and page numbers of all entered poems, and a separate acknowledgment page listing previously published poems.

A self-addressed, stamped envelope is necessary if you wish to be notified of the receipt of your manuscript. Please do not send your only copy. It will not be returned. A $25 reading fee payable to *Paintbrush*.

Results of the competition, along with the identity of the judge(s) will be released in the Spring 2002. If you wish to receive personal notification of the results, please include a self-addressed, stamped envelope marked "Results."

Send all submissions to: The Ezra Pound Poetry Award at the above address.

THE PARIS REVIEW

541 East 72nd Street
New York, NY 10021
Phone (718) 539-7085 (subscription)

Manuscripts are selected for awards from those submitted and published each year in the *Paris Review.*

Our prizes are awarded annually by the editors of *The Paris Review.* The winning selection for each prize is announced in the Winter issue. No formal application form is required: standard submission guidelines apply.

Fiction manuscripts should be submitted to the Fiction Editor, poetry to the Poetry Editor c/o *The Paris Review* at the above address.

We suggest to all who submit that they have read several issues of *The Paris Review* to acquaint themselves with the material the magazine publishes. Copies of *The Paris Review* are available in many public libraries. Sample copies can be ordered with the form below.

Submission Guidelines
While we welcome the submission of unsolicited manuscripts. we cannot accept responsibility for their loss. Manuscripts will not be returned unless accompanied by a self-addressed, stamped envelope.

Material must be in English and previously unpublished. Translations are acceptable and should be accompanied by a copy of the original text. A cover letter is not necessary. Please submit only one manuscript at a time.

THE ALGA KHAN PRIZE FOR FICTION
An award for the best previously unpublished short story published in *The Paris Review* during the year. Manuscripts must be a minimum of 1,000 words and a maximum of 10,000 words. All fiction manuscripts will be considered. The winner will be awarded $1,000. Submissions should be addressed to the Fiction Editor at the above address.

THE BERNARD F. CONNERS PRIZE FOR POETRY
The prize is awarded annually by the editors of *The Paris Review* for the finest unpublished poem over 200 lines published in *The Paris Review* during the year. The winner will be awarded $1,000. Submissions should be addressed to the Poetry Editor at the above address.

THE PARIS REVIEW DISCOVERY PRIZE
The prize is awarded annually for the best work of fiction or poetry published in *The Paris Review* that year by an emerging or previously unpublished writer.

THE JOHN TRAIN HUMOR PRIZE is no longer being awarded, but humorous submissions are still welcome.

Order back issues or subscriptions by phone (718) 539-7085 or by mail using the following order form. A one-year subscription (four issues) is $34. The 40th anniversary issue is $12; the commemorative 100th issue is $12; and one sample copy is $11.

NAME ____

ADDRESS ____

CITY/STATE/ZIP ____________________________________

MC/VISA NUMBER ________________________ EXP. ______

PASSIAC COUNTY COMMUNITY COLLEGE

Maria Mazziotti Gillan, Director
The Poetry Center
One College Boulevard
Patterson, NJ 07505-1179
Phone (973) 684-6555

Deadline: February 1, 2001

THE PATTERSON POETRY PRIZE
Award: $1,000 for a book of poems, 48 pages or more on length, selected by our judges as the strongest collection of poems published in 2000. The prize will be split evenly between the publisher and the poet. The poet will be asked to participate in an awards ceremony and to give a reading at the Poetry Center.

Guidelines
Minimum press run: 500 copies

Each book submitted must be accompanied by an application form.

Publishers may submit more than one book for prize consideration.

Three copies of each book should be sent to: Maria Mazziotti Gillan, Director.

Books entered in the competition will be donated to the Poetry Center Library at Passaic County Community College. Books cannot be returned.

For a list of the winners, include a self-addressed, stamped envelope labeled "Paterson Poetry Prize."

Announcements of winners will be placed in the *Poets & Writers Newsletter*.

The Patterson Poetry Prize
Application Form

Name of Author ______________________________

Home Address ______________________________

____

To receive a timely notification use your own address (c/o publisher's address may result in delays).

Phone Number ______________________________

Social Security Number ______________________________

Name of Book ______________________________

____

Name of publisher ______________________________

Publisher's Address ______________________________

____

Phone Number ______________________________

I understand that books cannot be returned.

Deadline: February 1, 2001

Send three copies of each book with application to:
Maria Mazziotti Gillan, Director
The Poetry Center
Passiac County Community College
One College Boulevard
Patterson, NJ 07505-1179

Deadline: April 1, 2001

2001 ALLEN GINSBERG POETRY AWARDS
Awards: First, $500; Second, $200; and Third, $100. Winners will be asked to participate in a reading to take place in Patterson's Historic District. The winning poems will be published in the *Patterson Literary Review*.

Guidelines
Up to five poems per person will be accepted for consideration. Four copies of each poem should be submitted for distribution to the judges. No poem should be more than two manuscript pages. Since the poems will be judged anonymously sheets which contain the poems should not have the poet's name on them. Instead, a separate sheet with the poet's name, address, phone number, and the titles of the poems should be included. Poems cannot be returned.

Only unpublished poems may be submitted to the contest.

Submissions should be sent to: Maria Mazziotti Gillan, Director. A check for $13 payable to PCCC must accompany submission (in the memo section of the check write "poetry contest").

Awards and winners will be announced in June 2001.

Contests entrants are asked not to call the college in reference to the contests results. Winners will be notified by mail. Winner's names will also appear in newspaper announcements. Please include a self-addressed, stamped envelope for list of winners.

The entry fee of $13 for the Allen Ginsberg Poetry Awards covers the cost of a subscription to the *Patterson Literary Review*.

Deadline: March 15 2001

THE PATTERSON PRIZE FOR BOOKS FOR YOUNG PEOPLE
Award: $500 in each category. In each category one book will be selected, which in the opinion of our judges, is the most outstanding book for young people published in 2000.

Guidelines
The categories are Pre-K to Grade 3, Grade 4 to 6, and Grade 7 to 12.

Each book submitted must be accompanied by an application form.

Publishers may submit more than one book for the prize consideration.

Submissions should be sent to: Maria Mazziotti Gillan, Director.

Books entered will be donated to the Poetry Center Library at Passaic County Community College. Books cannot be returned.

For a list of winners, include a self-addressed, stamped envelope labeled: "Patterson Prize. (Young People's Book award).

Announcement of winners will be placed in the *Poets & Writers Newsletter.*

The Patterson Prize for Books For Young People Application Form

Name of Author ______________________________

Home Address ______________________________

____

To receive a timely notification use your own address (c/o publisher's address may result in delays).

Phone Number ______________________________

Social Security Number ______________________________

Name of book ______________________________

____

Category: Pre K – Grade 3 __Grades 4 – 6 __Grades 7 – 12 __

Name of Publisher ______________________________

Publisher's Address ______________________________

____

Phone Number ______________________________

Date of Application ______________________________

I understand that books cannot be returned.

Deadline: March 15, 2001

Send three copies of each book with application to:
Maria Mazziotti Gillan, Director
The Poetry Center
Passiac County Community College
One College Boulevard
Patterson, NJ 07505-1179

[illegible]

Author's Website ______________________________

Deadline: April 1, 2001

THE PATTERSON FICTION PRIZE
Award: $500 for a novel or collection of short fiction which, in the opinion of our judges, is the strongest work of fiction published in 2000.

Guidelines
Each book must be accompanied by an application form.

Publisher may submit more than one book for prize consideration.

Three copies should be sent to: Maria Mazziotti Gillan, Director.

Books entered in the competition will be donated to the Poetry Center Library at Passaic County Community College. Books cannot be returned.

For a list of winners, include a self-addressed, stamped envelope labeled "Patterson Prize."

Announcements of winners will be placed in the *Poets & Writers Newsletter*.

The Patterson Fiction Prize
Application Form

Name of Author ______________________________

Home Address ______________________________

____

To receive a timely notification use your own address (c/o publisher's address may result in delays).

Phone Number ______________________________

Social Security Number ______________________________

Name of Book ______________________________

____

Name of publisher ______________________________

Publisher's Address ______________________________

____

Phone Number ______________________________

I understand that books cannot be returned.

Deadline April 1, 2001

Send three copies of each book with application to:
Maria Mazziotti Gillan, Director
The Poetry Center
Passiac County Community College
One College Boulevard
Patterson, NJ 07505-1179

PAVEMENT SAW PRESS

PO Box 6291
Columbus, OH 43206

Deadlline: June 1, 2001 – July 15, 2001 postmark

Each year Pavement Saw Press will seek to publish at least one book of poetry and/or prose poems from manuscripts received during this competition. Selection is made anonymously through a competition that is open to anyone who has not previously published a volume of poetry or prose. The author receives $1000 and a percentage of the press run. The judge of the competition is Bin Ramke. All poems must be original, all prose must be original, fiction or translations are not acceptable. Writers who have had volumes of poetry and/or prose under 40 pages printed or printed in limited editions of no more than 500 copies are eligible. Submissions are accepted during the month of June and until July 15, 2001 postmark.

Guidelines
Manuscripts should be at least 48 pages and no more than 64 pages in length. A cover letter which includes a brief biography, the book's title, your name, address, and telephone number, your signature, and, if you have e-mail, your e-mail address. It should also include a list of acknowledgments for the book.

The manuscript should be bound with a single clip and begin with a title page including the book's title, your name, address, and telephone number, and, if you have e-mail, your e-mail address. The second page should have only the title of the manuscript. There are to be no acknowledgments or mention of author's name from this page forward. A table of contents should follow the second title page. The manuscript should be paginated, beginning with the first page of poetry.

There should be no more than one poem on each page. The manuscript can contain pieces that are longer than one page. Your manuscript should be accompanied by a check in the amount of $15 made payable to Pavement Saw Press. All US contributors to the contest will receive at least one book provided a 9 x 12 inch, self-addressed, stamped envelope with $3.20 in postage is provided. Add appropriate postage for other countries. Include a self-addressed, stamped postcard for notification of manuscript arrival. For notification of results include a business-sized, self-addressed, stamped envelope.

A decision will be reached in September 2001. Book(s) will be published before January 31, 2002. Do not send the only copy of your work. All manuscripts will be recycled, and individual comments on the manuscript cannot be made.

Send all submissions to Transcontinental Award Entry at the above address.

PEARL

3030 E. Second Street
Long Beach, CA 90803

Deadline: May 1, 2001 – August 1, 2001 postmark

POETRY CONTEST
Prize: $1,000, publication, 25 copies, and a Foreword by the finalist judge. The winner will be announced and manuscripts will be returned at the end of the year. Judge 2001: to be announced

Manuscripts should include a title page with the author's name, address, and phone number; an acknowledgment page listing previously published poems; 48-64 pages of original poetry; and a self-addressed, stamped envelope for reply or return of manuscript.

Manuscripts should be typed, pages numbered, and name should appear on title page only. Clear photocopies and computer print-outs are acceptable. We will consider simultaneous submissions, but ask that you notify us if your manuscript is accepted elsewhere.

A $20 entry fee includes a copy of the winning book. All other proceeds go to the continuing publication of *Pearl*.

The selection of manuscripts for final judging will be made by the editors of *Pearl*. All entries are read anonymously. Send submissions to: *Pearl* Poetry Prize at above address.

Deadline: December 1, 2000 – March 15, 2001 postmark

SHORT STORY CONTEST
Prize: $100, publication in *Pearl* and 10 free copies of the issue the story appears in. The winner is announced and manuscripts returned in June.

Manuscripts should be typed, double spaced, with name and address on first page. Clear photocopies and computer printouts are acceptable. Please include a self-addressed, stamped envelope for reply or return of manuscripts. We will consider simultaneous submissions, but ask that you notify us if your story is accepted elsewhere. Previously unpublished stories only. Length: 4000 words maximum (about 15-16 manuscript pages).

Entry fee is $10 per story, payable to *Pearl* Magazine, and includes a copy of the magazine featuring the winning story. All other proceeds go to the continuing publication of *Pearl.*

Judging: the winning story is selected by the editors of *Pearl.* Although we are open to all types of fiction, we look most favorably upon coherent, well crafted narratives that contain interesting, believable characters and meaningful situations.

All submissions are considered for publication in *Pearl's* annual fiction issue. Send submissions to *Pearl* Short Story Contest at above address.

PERISHABLE THEATRE

Mark J. Lerman, Artistic Director
Kibbe Reilly, President, Board of Directors
95 Empire Street
Downtown Providence
P.O. Box 23132
Providence, RI 02903
Phone (401) 331-2695; Fax (401) 331-7811

Deadline: December 31, 2001

PERISHABLE THEATRE'S
WOMEN'S PLAYWRITING FESTIVAL
Each year the Women's Playwriting Festival receives well over three hundred submissions from women. This is an international festival and we have received submissions from the United States, Canada, France, Singapore, and Japan. Due to the overwhelming number of submissions we have recently received and a limited staff for the festival we have decided to implement a small entrance fee of $5 per playwright. (Note: this fee is per playwright not per play.) We hope that this nominal fee will not hinder your submission(s) to the festival.

Three winning playwrights each will be awarded a $250 cash prize and production. The dates for the 9th Annual Women's Playwriting Festival are to be announced. The festival is now accepting submissions.

Submission Guidelines
Plays must be written by women and be approximately 10–30 minutes in length.

Submit plays that have not had previous professional production.

There is a two play submission limit per author. Submission deadline is December 31, 2001.

Include a self-addressed, stamped envelope if you would like your play returned.

Enclose a $5.00 per playwright entrance fee in the form of a check or money order payable to: Perishable Theatre.

Send submissions to: Vanesa Gilbert, Perishable Theatre, P.O. Box 23132, Providence, RI 02903.

PEW FELLOWSHIPS IN THE ARTS

Melissa Franklin, Director
Christine Miller, Program Assistant
The University of the Arts
230 South Broad Street, Suite 1003
Philadelphia, PA 19102
Phone (212) 875-2276; Fax (215) 875-2276
Website www.pewarts.org

Deadline: December of the year preceding discipline
Call for exact date.

Fellowship: $50,000. Up to 12 fellowships are awarded each year. The Pew Fellowships in the Arts provides financial support directly to artists so that they may have the opportunity to dedicate themselves wholly to the development of their artwork for up to two years. A goal of the Pew Fellowships in the Arts is to provide such support at a moment in an artist's career when a concentration on artistic development and exploration is most likely to contribute to personal and professional growth.

Guidelines

Call or write for application and guidelines (available in mid-September) or go to the Pew Fellowship website: www.pewarts.org.

Eligibility: Application is not restricted to US citizens. Open only to Pennsylvania residents of Bucks, Chester, Delaware, Montgomery, or Philadelphia country for two years or longer at the time of application. Applicants must be 25 years of age or older. Matriculated students, full or part-time, are not eligible.

Application Procedure: Panel review by artists and arts professionals; first level of review is discipline based, second level of review is interdisciplinary, final selection of candidate is based on the applicant's accomplishments or promise in his or her discipline, and the degree to which the fellowship will address a critical juncture in the artist's career and/or artistic development.

Eligible Art Forms: Three fields of application are selected each year. In previous years, fields of application have included choreography, craft arts, literature (fiction, creative nonfiction, poetry), media arts (audio, film, video), music composition, script works (play writing, screen writing), visual arts (2-D: painting, photography, printmaking, design), and visual arts (3-D: sculpture, conceptual work, installation).

Winners will be notified by letter. A formal report of the grant is required.

THE PHOENIX THEATRE

749 North Park Street
Indianapolis, IN 46202
Phone (317) 635-PLAY; Fax (317) 635-0010

Deadline: February 28, 2001 postmark
Prize: $750 for full-length plays and $325 for one-acts. Deadline: Postmarked by February 28, 2001.

Guidelines and Criteria
Play should be sent to: F.E.A.T Competition at above address. Please do not send before December 31, 2000. A $5 entry fee must accompany each submission. Make check or money order payable to the Phoenix Theater.

Full-length and one-act original works are accepted. Synopsis or sample scenes are not eligible for critique. There are no restrictions on the type of submissions. Scripts must be bound; please do not send looseleaf scripts. Plays must not have been previously produced by a professional theater. Second productions are welcomed.

The Phoenix Theater has two intimate stages: a 150-seat house and a 75-seat house. Cast size and scenic elements must be adaptable to these environments.

Each script must include: A one to two page play synopsis, production history of the play and playwright's personal biography/resumé.

A judge's critique will be returned if you submit a business-sized, self-addressed, stamped envelope. Submit a 9x12 inch self-addressed, stamped envelope if the script is to be returned with the judge's critique. Limit: two scripts per playwright. Family members of the Phoenix Theatre's staff and/or its board of directors may not submit scripts for consideration in the F.E.A.T. Series.

Announcement and notification of winners will be made in June 2001. Playwrights are encouraged to participate in the production and rehearsal process; the availability of the playwright may be considered.

Critically acclaimed, the Phoenix Theatre produces contemporary, issue-oriented plays. Over the past 15 seasons, 46 original plays have been staged.

Send submissions to the above address.

PIG IRON PRESS

P.O. Box 237
Youngstown, OH 44501
Phone (330) 747-6932

Deadline: for Poetry January 2001 – December 31, 2002
for Fiction January 2003 – December 31, 2004

KENNETH PATCHEN FICTION AND POETRY COMPETITIONS
A bi-annual competition for paperback publication in an edition of 1,000 copies. Genre: Alternates between poetry and fiction. Prize: $500, publication and 20 free author copies.

Guidelines
Open to any writer, any age, any location, writing in the English language. Length: Poetry: 75 – 175 pages; Fiction: 100 – 300 pages.

Clear photocopies acceptable. Unbound manuscripts preferred. Author's name in cover letter, with title of manuscript; no author name in manuscript. Include a self-addressed, stamped envelope with sufficient return postage if you want your manuscript returned.

Short fiction collections eligible; long poem manuscripts eligible.

Entry Fee: $10 is required for eligibility. Make check payable to Pig Iron Press. Submit manuscripts to above contest name and address.

Rights and Rules
Copyright in the Author's name

Judging is anonymous

All entrants notified of results, winner in September after deadline

5% royalty on net sales

Author retains future rights to work

Author may purchase additional copies at 40% list price

PIONEER DRAMA SERVICE, INC.

P.O. Box 4267
Englewood, CO 80155-4267
Phone (303) 779-4035; Fax (303) 779-4315
Toll Free (800) 333-7262
E-mail piodrama@aol.com
Website www.pioneerdrama.com

Deadline: March 1, 2001 postmark

SHUBERT FENDRICH MEMORIAL PLAYWRITING CONTEST
Deadline: Postmarked by March 1, 2001. Manuscripts received with a later postmark will be considered for the following year's contest.

Prize: $1,000 royalty advance in addition to publication. The winner will be announced June 1, 2001.

Contest Guidelines and General Guidelines
Individuals currently published by Pioneer Drama Service are not eligible for this contest. Pioneer Drama Service employees and their families are also excluded. Contest entries should indicate "Playwriting Contest" on the envelope and must be accompanied by the following completed application.

Plays must be between 20 and 90 minutes. The running time should be indicated in the manuscript. All plays accepted for publication will be considered contest finalists and in competition for the award. Plays must be unpublished and have had at least one production. Since new plays are created for the purpose of production, the editors feel this fundamental field test is necessary before a play can be considered for publication. Plays can be on any subject, but both subject and language must be appropriate for family-oriented amateur groups, such as schools and community theaters. Plays with flexible cast favoring female roles and minimal set requirements are preferred due to the needs of our customers. Please keep in mind that our plays are often produced by groups with limited resources. Plays with strict set or costume requirements will not be as appealing.

Submission Requirements
Query letters are preferred; however, unsolicited manuscripts will be accepted. We strongly recommend that you are familiar with what we publish before submitting a query letter or an unsolicited manuscript. To learn more visit our website.

Query letters require a self-addressed, stamped envelope for reply.

Submissions will not be returned unless a self-addressed, stamped envelope of sufficient size and postage is provided. Response time on queries is about two weeks and on submissions about four months.

The following information must accompany your manuscript: Title and synopsis, cast list and breakdown, running time, proof of production (i.e. review, program, etc.) number of sets and or scenes and musical score or tape, if applicable.

Please send your query or submission, accompanying information, and cover letter or resume to the Editorial Staff at the address listed above.

Writers not previously published by Pioneer Drama Service are eligible to enter our playwriting contest with their submissions. Follow the guidelines.

Pioneer Drama Service, Inc.
Contest Application

Title of Play: ______________________________

Author: ______________________________

1. How did you hear about this contest?

____

2. What is your theatre/writing background? Have you published other plays? If so, please list the name of the plays and the publishers. You may attach a resume if you wish.

____

____

____

____

____

3. Do you belong to any drama or writer's organizations? If so, which ones?

____

____

4. How do you see your play meeting Pioneer Drama Service's needs?

____

____

____

____

____

PLAYBOY

Playboy College Fiction Contest
680 North Lake Shore Drive
Chicago, IL 60611
Website
http://www.playboy.com/whatsnew/ficitoncontest/fiction-contest.html

Deadline: September 1, 2001 – January 1, 2002 postmark

Prizes: First Prize $3,000 and publication in October 2002 issue; Second Prize $500 and a year's subscription.

Guidelines and Rules
Contest is open to all college students—no age limit. Employees of Playboy Enterprises, Inc. and their families, its agents and affiliates are not eligible.

To enter, submit your typed double-spaced manuscript of 25 pages or fewer with a 3x5 inch card listing name, home address and phone number to *Playboy* College Fiction contest at above address. Decisions of the judges are final. *Playboy* reserves the right to withhold prizes if no submitted entries meet its usual standard of publication.

Winners will be notified by mail and may be obligated to sign and return an affidavit of eligibility within 30 days of notification. By acceptance of their prize, winners consent to the use of their names, photographs or other likeness for purpose of advertising, trade and promotion on behalf of Playboy Enterprises, Inc. without further compensation to the winners, unless prohibited by law. *Playboy* reserves the right to edit the first-prize-winning story for publication. *Playboy* reserves the right to publish winning entries in U.S. and foreign editions of *Playboy* and to reprint or incorporate them in any electronic or print English-language or foreign edition anthologies or compilations of *Playboy* material. Void where prohibited by law. All manuscripts become the property of *Playboy* and will not be returned.

Taxes on prizes are the responsibility of the winners. The list of winners will be posted on the above website; for a printed list, send a self-addressed, stamped envelope with submission to above address.

THE PLAYWRIGHTS' CENTER

2301 Franklin Avenue East
Minneapolis, MN 55406-1099
Phone (612) 332-7481

Deadline: February 1, 2001 postmark

THE PLAYWRIGHTS' CENTER'S MCKNIGHT ADVANCEMENT GRANTS

The Playwrights' Center's McKnight Advancement Grants recognize playwrights whose work demonstrates exceptional artistic merit and potential, and whose primary residence is in the state of Minnesota. The grants are intended to significantly advance the recipients' art and careers, and can be used to support a wide variety of expenses, including but not limited to writing time, artistic costs of residency at a theater or arts organization, travel/study, production, or presentation.

Three Advancement Grants of $8,500 each will be awarded in 2001-2002 Additional funds of up to $1,500 per grant recipient are available for workshops and readings using the Center's developmental program or may be designated to a partner organization for joint development and/or production purposes anywhere in the world. These grants are funded by the Minneapolis-based McKnight Foundation as part of its Arts Program.

The Playwrights' Center will evaluate each application, forwarding the finalists to a diverse panel of three judges from the national theater community.

Recipients will be selected on the basis of artistic excellence, professional achievement, and proposed residency plans. Selection panels are also guided by The Playwrights' Center's mission statement:

> The Playwrights' Center fuels the theater by providing services that support playwrights and playwriting. The Playwrights' Center is committed to the following core values: artistic excellence; playwright initiative and leadership; the practice of cultural pluralism; the discovery of emerging artists; advocacy of playwrights and their work; and new visions of theater.

Eligibility

Applicant must have been a citizen or permanent resident of the United States and a legal resident of Minnesota since August 1, 1998 and must maintain residency in Minnesota during the fellowship year.

Applicant must have had a minimum of one work fully produced by a professional theater at the time of application. "Fully produced by a professional theater" is defined as a production for which the author and/or primary artists (actors, directors, creative collaborators) were compensated and received at least three public performances. University, college, secondary school, amateur, and Equity showcase/waiver productions are not considered full productions.

Applicant may not have received a McKnight Advancement Grant from The Playwrights' Center since 1997.

Applicant may not be a Playwrights' Center staff member.

Conditions and Requirements
Grant recipients may not receive any other Playwrights' Center fellowships or grants during the grant year.

Minnesota artists may apply to more than one of the seven organizations offering fellowships that are sponsored by McKnight Foundation funds; however, no Minnesota artist may receive more than $45,000 in McKnight Foundation fellowship support in any three year period.

Recipients are required to designate two months of the grant year in which they plan to participate actively in Center programs. This must include weekly attendance and critical participation in readings or workshops of other members' work.

Submission Guidelines
Please submit four (4) sets items one through six:

1. A completed application form.

2. One script, securely bound, with your name and play title on the front cover and/or one video or audio tape if work is non-textual. (One per set, four total.)

3. A representative list (maximum two pages) of production credits, indicating whether productions were professional, non-professional, or academic; and listing name, address, and phone number of each producer/ presenter. (Indicate production which satisfies eligibility requirement.)

4. A list of fellowships, grants, prizes, and honors you have won, listing the most recent first. List award name, inclusive dates, and amount for each. Include any individual artist grants in any disci-

pline received within the past two years that were funded by the McKnight Foundation.

5. A brief (maximum two pages) autobiographical narrative of career history emphasizing artistic and professional accomplishments.

6. A description of plans (maximum two pages) for the grant year with specific reference to the residency period. (See Conditions and Requirements.)

Optional: Please include four appropriately sized self-addressed, stamped envelopes if you would like your materials returned. Receipt of applications will not be acknowledged and materials without a self-addressed, stamped envelope will not be held or returned. While care will be taken, The Playwrights' Center is not responsible for the safe return of application materials.

Mail to: McKnight Advancement Grants, The Playwrights' Center, 2301 Franklin Avenue East, Minneapolis, MN 55406-1099.

Application must be postmarked by February 1, 2001. Grant recipients will be announced by May 1, 2001. The grant year beings July 1, 2001 and ends June 30, 2002. All grant requirements must be met during that time.

Questions? Call The Playwrights' Center at (612) 332-7481.

Deadline: January 15, 2001 postmark

THE PLAYWRIGHTS' CENTER'S MCKNIGHT FELLOWSHIPS
The Playwrights' Center offers two $10,000 McKnight Fellowships annually to recognize American playwrights whose work has made a significant impact on the contemporary theater. The program supports continuing artistic development with significant financial underwriting and a one-month working residency at The Playwrights' Center. During their residencies, fellows develop new work while sharing their time and leadership with the Center's artistic community. Additional funds of $2,000 per fellow are available for workshops and staged readings of fellows' scripts. Funds are also available for travel, housing, and living expenses in the Twin Cities for fellows residing outside a 150 mile radius of the Twin Cities.

The Playwrights' Center will evaluate each application, forwarding the finalists to a diverse panel of three judges from the national theater community.

Recipients will be selected on the basis of artistic excellence, professional achievement, and proposed residency plans. Selection panels are also guided by The Playwrights' Center's mission statement:

> The Playwrights' Center fuels the theater by providing services that support playwrights and playwriting. The Playwrights' Center is committed to the following core values: artistic excellence; playwright initiative and leadership; the practice of cultural pluralism; the discovery of emerging artists; advocacy of playwrights and their work; and new visions of theater.

Eligibility

Applicant must have been a citizen or permanent resident of the United States.

Applicant must have had a minimum of two different works fully produced by a professional theater at the time of application. "Fully produced by a professional theater" is defined as productions for which the author and/or primary artists (actors, directors, creative collaborators) were compensated and received at least three public performances. University, college, secondary school, amateur, and Equity showcase/waiver productions are not considered full productions.

Applicant may not have received a McKnight Fellowship from The Playwrights' Center since 1997.

Applicant may not be a Playwrights' Center staff member.

Conditions and Requirements

Fellows may not receive any other Playwrights' Center fellowships or grants during the grant year.

Minnesota artists may apply to more than one of the seven organizations offering fellowships that are sponsored by McKnight Foundation funds; however, no Minnesota artist may receive more than $45,000 in McKnight Foundation fellowship support in any three year period.
Fellows will spend one month or more in residence at The Playwrights' Center between July 1, 2001 and June 30, 2002.

During the residency period, fellows will have at least one public reading of their work and may make use of the Center's developmental programs to that end. Creative partnerships with other Twin Cities arts organizations are encouraged.

During the residency period, fellows will lead or participate in an introductory workshop or roundtable with Center Members. Fellows also will be expected to attend or participate in at least one reading or workshop of a Center writer's work each week of their residency.

Fellows are responsible for securing their own housing and travel arrangements during the residency period. A Playwrights' Center staff liaison will provide assistance as needed.

Submission Guidelines
Send four (4) sets of items one through six:

1. A completed application form.

2. A representative list (maximum two pages) of production credits, indicating whether productions were professional, non-professional, or academic; and listing name, address, and phone number of each producer/presenter. (Indicate productions which satisfy eligibility requirement.)

3. A list of fellowships, grants, prizes, and honors you have won, listing the most recent first. List award name, inclusive dates, and amount for each. Include any individual artist grants in any discipline received within the past two years that were funded by the McKnight Foundation.

4. A brief (maximum two pages) autobiographical narrative of career history emphasizing artistic and professional accomplishments.

5. A description of plans (maximum two pages) for the fellowship year with specific reference to the residency period. (See Conditions and Requirements.)

6. A work sample (maximum thirty pages) with contextual synopsis (may include more than one work) and/or one video or audio tape if work is non-textual. (One per set, four total.)

Optional: Please include four appropriately sized self-addressed, stamped envelopes if you would like your materials returned. Receipt of applications will not be acknowledged and materials without a self-addressed, stamped envelope will not be held or returned. While care will be taken, The Playwrights' Center is not responsible for the safe return of application materials.

Mail to: McKnight Fellowship, The Playwrights' Center, 2301 Franklin Avenue East, Minneapolis, MN 55406-1099.

Applications must be postmarked by January 15, 2001. Fellowship recipients will be announced by April 15, 2001. The fellowship year beings July 1, 2001 and ends June 30, 2002. All fellowship requirements must be met during that time.

Questions? Call The Playwrights' Center, (612) 332-7481.

McKnight Advancement Grant Application Form

NAME: ____________________

PLAY TITLE: ____________________

ADDRESS: ____________________

CITY/STATE/ZIP/ ____________________

DAY PHONE: ____________________ EVENING PHONE: ____________________

E-MAIL: ____________________

Number of years as a Minnesota resident: ______

Please list the names of three (3) people whom the Selection Panel may consult for a recommendation of your work, especially in relation to your grant proposal. All references are held confidential. (Please let your references know that the panel may be contacting them.)

NAME	PHONE	POSITION (FULL TIME)	ADDRESS

(Optional) The McKnight Advancement Grant selection panel's membership changes every year. Please use this space to nominate leaders in the American theater whom you would like to recommend to serve on future panels. (They may be playwrights, dramaturges, directors, artistic directors, or other theater artists.) Please include addresses and phone numbers if possible. Use a separate sheet if necessary.

____

____

____

____

I hereby certify that the information in this application is true and correct to the best of my knowledge.

Signature ____________________ Date ____________________

About Playwright Membership. Playwright Members automatically receive applications for all Center competitions, and *Subtext*, the Center's national bi-annual journal; eligibility for playwright developmental opportunities such as the Playwright Members' Roundtable; notification of all Center events and opportunities; member news bulletins; listings of members' accomplishments in *Subtext*; and discounts on theater tickets, Center space rental, and special events. Membership is not required to apply for Center competitions.

__ I would like to become a Playwright Member and have enclosed a check for $40.

THE APPLICATION POSTMARK DEADLINE IS FEBRUARY 1, 2001.

McKnight Fellowships
Application Form

NAME: ______

PLAY TITLE: ______

ADDRESS: ______

CITY/STATE/ZIP/ ______

DAY PHONE: ______ EVENING PHONE: ______

E-MAIL: ______

Number of years as a Minnesota resident: ______

Please list the names of three (3) people whom the Selection Panel may consult for a recommendation of your work, especially in relation to your fellowship proposal. All references are held confidential. (Please let your references know that the panel may be contacting them.)

NAME PHONE POSITION (FULL TIME) ADDRESS

______

______

______

______

(Optional) The McKnight Advancement Fellowship selection panel's membership changes every year. Please use this space to nominate leaders in the American theater whom you would like to recommend to serve on future panels. (They may be playwrights, dramaturges, directors, artistic directors, or other theater artists.) Please include addresses and phone numbers if possible. Use a separate sheet if necessary.

______

______

______

I hereby certify that the information in this application is true and correct to the best of my knowledge.

Signature ______ Date ______

About Playwright Membership. Playwright Members automatically receive applications for all Center competitions, and *Subtext*, the Center's national bi-annual journal; eligibility for playwright developmental opportunities such as the Playwright Members' Roundtable; notification of all Center events and opportunities; member news bulletins; listings of members' accomplishments in *Subtext*; and discounts on theater tickets, Center space rental, and special events. Membership is not required to apply for Center competitions.

__ I would like to become a Playwright Member and have enclosed a check for $40.

THE APPLICATION POSTMARK DEADLINE IS JANUARY 15, 2001.

PLAYWRIGHTS' PREVIEW PRODUCTION

17 East 47th Street
New York, NY 10017-1920
Phone (212)-1380; Fax (212) 421-1387
David Sheppard, Literary Manager (212) 421-1380

PLAYWRIGHTS' PREVIEW PRODUCTION
EMERGING PLAYWRIGHT AWARD
Established in 1986, Urban Stage's Emerging Playwright Award is presented to the best of new, innovative playwrights whose works speak to the whole of our society.

Plays that are finalists are presented as staged and workshop readings. These readings are a collaboration between playwright and director. Finalists are first included as part of Urban Stage's Fall or Spring reading series. A cash prize of $500 (in lieu of royalties) will be awarded, plus a staged production of the play in New York. The award is usually announced in the spring.

Eligibility
The competition is open to playwrights in the United States. Plays may have been developed elsewhere, but never produced in New York. Full-length plays or related one acts are preferred. There is no limit to submission. Subject matter and character variations are open but cast size is limited to no more than nine. No translations or adaptations.

Submission Guidelines
Submissions are received throughout the year.

Name, address, and phone number of the author should be on the title page. Include a biography and/or author's history of the play. Provide the cast of characters and brief description. All scripts must be firmly bound. No changes or revisions accepted after submission.

The play should be accompanied by a manuscript-size self-addressed, stamped envelope to return the play. Do not include loose cash, stamps, labels or metered postage. A self-addressed, stamped postcard should be included if you want acknowledgment of arrival. It usually takes from one to four months for us to read and process your script.

All scripts will be handled with care, but Playwrights' Preview Production will not assume responsibility for lost or damaged scripts. RETAIN A COPY OF YOUR SCRIPT.

Before production of the award winning play, a contract will be signed between the playwright and the company. This contract is approved by the Dramatist Guild.

Playwrights' Preview Production reserves the right to withhold the prize and not declare a winner if no play of merit is found.

Direct inquiries to: David Sheppard, Literary Manager (212) 421-1380.

Please send manuscripts to: PLAYWRIGHTS' PREVIEW PRODUCTION, 17 East 47th Street, New York, NY 10017-1920.

POCKETS MAGAZINE

Upper Room Pockets
Lynn Gilliam
1908 Grand Avenue
P.O. Box 189
Nashville, TN 37202-0189

Deadline: March 1, 2001 – August 15, 2001 postmark

Prize: $1,000 Fiction Contest Written for Children
The purpose of *Pockets* magazine is to open up the fullness of the Gospel of Jesus Christ to children and to help children grow in their relationship with God. The magazine emphasizes that God loves us and that God's grace calls us into community. Through this community of God's people we experience God's love in our daily lives.

The magazine is for children six through eleven. Our readers include persons of many cultures and ethnic backgrounds. These differences should be reflected in the references which are made to lifestyles, living environments (suburban, urban, rural, reservation), families (extended families, single parent homes), and individual names. Stories should show appreciation of cultural differences and not leave the impression that one way is better than another. Stories should contain lots of action, use believable dialogue, be simply written, and be relevant to the situations faced by this age group in everyday life.

Children need to be able to see themselves in the pages of the magazine. The tone should not be "preachy" or didactic. Use short sentences and paragraphs. When possible, use concrete words instead of abstractions. However, do not "write down" to children. It is no longer common practice to use such terms as man, mankind, men in the familiar generic sense. Substitute terms that are inclusive of everyone (e.g., humankind, persons, human beings, everyone). Historical fiction is not eligible.

Guidelines
Returned only if accompanied by a self-addressed, stamped envelope with sufficient postage (1-5 pages, postage for 1 ounce, if 6-11 pages, send postage amount for second ounce).

Word count 1,000 to 1,600 words. Write word count on the cover sheet (we do adhere to our word parameters). Stories are to be unpublished.

Designate "Fiction Contest" on the envelope and on a cover sheet.

There is no entry fee. The winner will be notified by November 1, 2001 and will receive a $1,000 award. Since the purpose of the contest is to discover new writers, previous winners are not eligible.

Send submissions to above contest and address.

POETRY

Joseph Parisi, Editor
60 West Walton Street
Chicago, IL 60610
Phone (312) 255-3703
Website www.poetrymagazine.org

Deadline: none

Founded in 1912 by Harriet Monroe, *Poetry* has no special manuscript needs, and no special requirements as to form or genre. We examine in turn all work received and accept that which seems best. We can accept nothing which has been previously published or accepted for publication, anywhere, in any form, either in this country or abroad. Nor can we consider poems scheduled for book publication within a year. We do not consider simultaneous submissions. We regret that the volume of submissions received and the small size of our staff do not permit us to give individual criticism.

Several prizes, awarded annually, are announced each November for the best work printed in *Poetry* during the preceding year. Only poems already published in the magazine are eligible for consideration, and no formal application is necessary.

THE RUTH LILLY POETRY PRIZE
The Ruth Lilly Poetry Prize is also given each year to a poet whose published work merits special recognition. The selection is made by a panel of judges and no applications are accepted. Two Ruth Lilly Poetry Fellowships are awarded annually to students who have not yet received the M.A. or M.F.A. degree, based on work submitted. Students must be nominated by their program directors or department chairs.

Submission Guidelines
Submissions should be limited to four (4) poems or fewer, typed single spaced, not exceeding ten pages total. Manuscripts are usually reported on within 12 to 14 weeks from the day of receipt. All manuscripts must be accompanied by a stamped, self-addressed envelope. Stamps alone are not sufficient. Writers living abroad must enclose a self-addressed envelope together with enough postage in international reply coupons for at least sea mail return.

Manuscripts should contain the author's name and address on every page. Avoid oversized envelopes. Please wait at least one year after our reply before submitting again. Do not send revisions unless they have been specifically requested by the editors. Inquiries about the status of a manuscript should be avoided, but when necessary must be in writing. Payment is made on publication at the rate of $2 per line. *Poetry* is copyrighted for the protection of its contributors. The author, the author's agents or heirs, and no one else, will be given transfer of copyright when they request it for purposes of republication in book form.

Anyone contemplating a submission to *Poetry* is encouraged to examine the magazine before sending a manuscript. To that end, *Poetry* offers subscriptions to writers at a professional discount. You can use the coupon below to purchase a year-long subscription (12 monthly issues) at the special rate of $24.50. Sample copies cost $3.00 plus $1.50 for postage and handling.

Send inquiries to: Poetry, 60 West Walton Street, Chicago, IL 60610.

Please Send __Sample Copy ($4.50); __1 year subscription (12 monthly issues, $24.50; $31.50 foreign)

Name: ______________________________

Address: ______________________________

City/State/Zip ______________________________

__My check or money order is enclosed. (Checks should be made out to *Poetry*.)
__Please charge my __Visa __MasterCard #__________________

Exp. date ______________________________

Signature ______________________________

Please allow six weeks for subscription to begin.

POETS' DINNER COMMITTEE

Dorothy V. Benson
2214 Derby Street
Berkeley, CA 94705
Phone (510) 841-1217

Deadline: January 26, 2001 postmark

POETS' DINNER COMMITTEE CONTEST
Dust off your dactyls, trot out your trochees, write a poem for the 74th annual Poets' Dinner contest. Theme poem this time around is to be announced. Other categories are Beginnings and Endings, Humor, Nature, Love, Spaces and Places, People, and Poet's Choice. There is no charge to enter.

The Dorothy Tyrrel Grand Prize of $50 is chosen from the first three winners in each category. There are also six awards for each category: First $25, Second $15, and Third $10; plus three honorable mentions. The Ad Schuster Annual Citation for last year's Grand Prize Winner will also be awarded.

Winning poems and honorable mentions will be kept for a possible future anthology. Others will be destroyed after the contest.

Submission Guidelines
Each entry must be original, unpublished, in English, and not a previous prize or honorable mention winner. Up to three (3) poems may be submitted, one (1) per topic. Maximum length is 40 lines, any form or style acceptable. The postmark deadline is January 26, 2001. No certified or registered mail, please.

Entries must be typed on one side only of white 8-1/2 x 11 inch paper; the topic shown in upper right-hand corner; and no author's name given. Three (3) clear copies of each poem go to the new chairperson to be announced.

The author's identity is revealed when winning poems are read at the Poet's Dinner March 26, 2001, at Spenger's in Berkeley, when cash and book prizes are awarded. Authors must be present to win.

Winning entries will be read and awards presented ONLY at the dinner. Use cards provided at the dinner to claim a winning poem immediately after it is read. If there is no claim, the prize will go to the next ranked submission. Judges' decisions are final.

Mail entries to: Contest Chair, 2214 Derby Street, Berkeley, CA 94705 Poetry book tables are available. Please arrange sale space for your books by contacting: Poetry Book Table Chair, Mel Smith (510) 933-9215 before February 26, 2001. Space is limited.

THE POPE FOUNDATION

Ms. Catherine Pope, Journalism Awards Program Director
211 West 56th Street
New York, NY 10019

Deadline: June 15, 2001 – November 1, 2001

THE POPE FOUNDATION JOURNALISM AWARDS
Intended to reward and encourage mid-careerists, The Pope Foundation Journalism Awards offer a total of three honorariums of $15,000 each to be used as working fellowships. Winners will be notified by mail, followed by formal presentation.

Mid-career status is determined not by age, but by experience with a minimum of ten years of journalistic background required for eligibility.

All entries are reviewed by a select panel of professionals acting as consultants to the Foundation. Special consideration will be given to entrants whose work displays investigative initiative for the greater social cause.

It is the Pope Foundation's wish to enable such seasoned professionals to use their talent as an instrument for social change.

The Pope Foundation, which for almost half a century has made significant philanthropic contributions in the areas of health, education, and welfare, is an independent, New York based, family coordinated enterprise.

Founded by Generoso Pope, Sr., its fields of interest have broadened over the years and its Journalism Awards are part of an ambitious philanthropic initiative created to benefit the cultural sector.

The awards are administered by Program Director, Catherine Pope, under the aegis of the Pope Foundation for the Arts.

Using the application form, please tell us exactly how you would use a $15,000 Pope Foundation Journalism Award. If you need more space, attach the proposal on a separate sheet of paper.

Please Note: In accordance with the Federal Tax Reform act of 1969, winners will be held accountable for a detailed summary of their fellowship activities and expenditures.

Application Guidelines
Applicants must submit four (4) separate packages of all entry materials. Each package must contain (copies of) the following.

1. Current *Curriculum Vitae*: It must come attached to the application form and it must contain: a) educational summary/academic and vocational; b) professional history, starting with current position and working backwards; c) list of organizations you belong to; d) a brief (one paragraph) biography telling us about yourself in your own words.

2. Materials: You may submit one book OR four published articles OR one video cassette containing produced-for-air material not to exceed 20 minutes in length. While we welcome relevant press reviews/interviews, we ask that you submit nor more than three clippings, photocopied, and attached to the application form.

Entries must be received no earlier than June 15th and no later than November 1st. Materials will not be returned unless accompanied by sturdy, stamped and self-addressed envelope. (Please be sure to include sufficient postage, and understand that The Pope Foundation is not responsible for damage or loss of materials.)

Send entry parcel to: Ms. Catherine Pope, Journalism Awards Program Director, The Pope Foundation, 211 West 56th Street, New York, NY 10019.

Please note: Awards must be given through a sponsoring institution with a 501(c) 3 status. Name and Federal ID # must accompany application.

The Pope Foundation Journalism Awards Application

Name (in full): ______________________

Address: ______________________

____

Telephone: ______________________

Place of birth: ______________________

Date of birth: ______________________

Sex: Citizenship: ______________________

If naturalized, give date and place of naturalization:

____

____

References (please list three, including name, address, telephone, and relationship):

1) ______________________

____

____

2) ______________________

____

____

3) ______________________

____

Have you received any other grant or fellowship?________

If you answered YES to the above, please give details:

____

____

____

____

____

POTATO EYES FOUNDATION

PO Box 76
Troy, ME 04987
Web Page www.litline.org/html/potatoeyes.html

Deadline: November 15, 2001 postmark

11TH ANNUAL WILLIAM & KINGMAN PAGE POETRY BOOK AWARD
Prize: $1,000 plus 25 copies of the winning book, in lieu of royalties.

Guidelines and Rules
An annual open competition for publication of a 48 page book of poetry. Submit up to 41 pages of poetry, maximum 43 lines per page, and a cover sheet with the title of the collection only. Do not place name or any other identification mark on any of these 41 pages or on the cover/title sheet.

On a separate sheet, list acknowledgments, the title of your manuscript, your name, address, and home and work telephone numbers.

Enclose a legal size self-addressed, stamped envelope for competition results; manuscripts will not be returned. You may include a self-addressed, stamped postcard for acknowledgment of receipt of your manuscript.

Manuscripts must be typed with no more than one poem per page. Simultaneous submissions are okay if so noted in the acknowledgments. Poems must be written by one person only and author is responsible for copyright clearance on any of the poems previously published.

Enclose a $12 check or money order as entry and reading fee, payable to The Potato Eyes Foundation.

All executive aspects of the competition reside with the Foundation, where qualified members will screen the manuscripts. The final judge will be designated at the close of the competition so as to avoid partiality and influence peddling. Announcement of the winning manuscript will be made on or before February 1st.

All short-listed poets receive one year free subscription to *Potato Eyes* literary arts journal.

Send submissions to above address.

PRAIRIE SCHOONER

Hilda Raz, Editor
201 Andrews Hall
University of Nebraska
Lincoln, NE 68588-0334
Phone (402) 472-0911

Deadline: September 1, 2001 – May 31, 2002

Prairie Schooner offers the following writing prizes annually, based on availability of funds. Only work published in *Prairie Schooner* is eligible for consideration. Awards for the year are announced in the spring issue of the following year.

THE LARRY LEVIS PRIZE FOR POETRY
For poetry published the previous year, $1,000.

THE LAWRENCE FOUNDATION AWARD
For the best short story published in *Prairie Schooner,* $1,000.

THE VIRGINIA FAULKNER AWARD
For fiction, non-fiction, poetry, or translations published during the previous year, $1,000.

THE STROUSSE AWARD
For the best poem or group of poems published during the previous year, $500.

THE BERNICE SLOTE AWARD
For the best work by a beginning writer published during the previous year, $500.

THE EDWARD STANLEY AWARD
For poetry published during the previous year, $500.

THE HUGH J. LUKE AWARD
Award open to any genre published the proceeding year, $250.

PRAIRIE SCHOONER/READER'S CHOICE AWARDS
Awarded on a year-to-year basis for work published during the previous year, $250 each. All genres of writing are eligible for these awards.

General Publication Guidelines for *Prairie Schooner*
Thank you for your interest in our magazine. *Prairie Schooner* publishes short stories, poems, interviews, imaginative essays of general interest, and reviews of current books of poetry and fiction. (Scholarly articles requiring footnote reference should be submitted to journals of literary scholarship.)

Prairie Schooner's intention is to publish the best writing available, from both beginning and established writers. In over 70 years of publication, we have printed the work of Eudora Welty, Octavio Paz, Tennessee Williams, Weldon Kees, Joyce Carol Oates, Rita Dove, Raymond Carver, Reynolds Price, Julia Alvarez, Sharon Olds, Cornelius Eady, plus scores of others.

All submissions to *Prairie Schooner* should be typed, double spaced (except for poetry), on one side of the paper only. Use margins of at least one inch, and be sure to put your name on each page of the manuscript.

A self-addressed envelope with adequate return postage must accompany each submission.

For poetry, we prefer a selection of five to seven poems, for fiction, essays, and reviews, we prefer you send only one selection at a time.

Send submissions to the attention of the editor at the address above. Please allow three to four months for a reply. *Prairie Schooner* does not read simultaneous submissions, and submissions must be received between September and May.

We encourage you to read *Prairie Schooner*. To subscribe or order a copy, fill out the form provided and send it with your payment to: Hilda Raz, Editor, *Prairie Schooner*, 201 Andrews Hall, University of Nebraska, Lincoln NE 68588-0334.

Please send:
(the prices listed below represent a professional discount for writers)
Sample copy $4_____
Current issue $6.50_____
1 year subscription $20_____
2 year subscription $35_____
3 year subscription $45_____

Name ______________________________

Address ______________________________

City/State/Zip ______________________________

PREMIO AZTLAN LITERARY PRIZE

English Department
University of New Mexico
Albuquerque, NM 87131

Deadline: December 15, 2001

THE 2001 PREMIO AZTLAN
Premio Aztlan is a literary prize established for the purpose of encouraging and rewarding writers at the onset of their writing careers. This $1,000 premio in literatura Chicana was begun in 1993.

Any writer or publisher may submit five copies of a work of fiction published in 2001. Writers at the beginning of their careers are defined as those who have only two books of fiction in publication. The 2001 publication may be the second book.

The writer's current vita must also be submitted. Books and vita must be received by deadline. The vita must clearly show all of the writer's publications.

The award will be made in the Spring of 2002, and the winner will present a public reading at the University of New Mexico.

Prior winners may not submit again. Any questions related to entries will be decided by judges. The judges may chose not to award a premio.

Please submit books and vita to Rudolfo Anaya/ Department of Languages and Literature/ Humanities Building at above address.

THE PRINCESS GRACE FOUNDATION

Ms. Toby E. Boshak, Executive Director
150 East 5th Street
New York, NY 10155
Barbara Horgan, Co-Chair, Arts Advisory Board
Eduardo Garcia, Co-Chair Arts, Advisory Board
Chair, Theater Panel
Phone (212) 317-1470; Fax (212) 317-1473
Website www.pgfusa.com
E-mail pgfusa@pgfusacom

Deadline: March 31, 2001 postmark

THE PRINCESS GRACE AWARDS PLAYWRIGHT GRANT
The Princes Grace Awards is a national program dedicated to identifying and assisting emerging young artists in theater, dance, and film to realize their career goals. One playwright will be selected to receive a grant in the amount of $7,500, and a ten week residency (including transportation cost) at New Dramatists, Inc., New York City, NY. The award winning script will be included in the New Dramatists' lending library and will receive national distribution to catalog subscribers for one year, and possible publication through the Dramatist Play Service.

Awards are based primarily on the artistic quality of the play submitted, and the appropriateness of the activities to the individual's artistic growth as well as the writer's potential future excellence.

We are please to accept applications for the 2001 Princess Grace Awards for playwright grants. Please note the applications' postmark deadline of March 31, 2001. The Princess Grace Foundation-USA will be unable to accept or review any applications postmarked after this date.

Please remember to include the attached application along with your play, resume, and letter of recommendation. Playwright applicants will be notified in September, 2001. Should you have any questions, please contact Ms. Toby E. Boshak, Executive Director of Princess Grace Foundation-USA at (212) 317-1470 between 9:30 and a.m. and 5:30 p.m., Eastern time.

We look forward to receiving this year's nominations.

Submission Guidelines
Under ordinary circumstances, nominees for playwright fellowships should be under 30 years of age at the time of application. All candidates

must be United States citizens or have permanent resident status.

In addition to the completed application, please attach the following required information:

1. Resumé of applicant, including a listing of other plays written and produced, when, and where.

2. One unproduced, unpublished play (there is no restriction to subject matter). No adaptations. Please submit the typed script in a binder, using accepted format.

3. Title and author should be on the cover of the play. If you would like the script returned, you must enclose a self-addressed, stamped envelope.

4. Applicant's personal statement: Please describe, in your own words, your views and expectations of your role as a theater artist now and in the future (not to exceed one page).

Although not required, applicants are encouraged to submit a letter of recommendation from a theater professional (Director, Dramaturge, etc.) addressing how the applicant has demonstrated his/her excellence in the field; promise as an outstanding young artist; and why he or she is deserving of a Princess Grace Award.

Applications must be postmarked no later than March 31, 2001 and should be addressed to: Toby E. Boshak, Executive Director, Princess Grace Awards, Princess Grace Foundation-USA, 150 East 5th Street, New York, NY 10155.

Princess Grace Awards Playwright Grant Application

You must submit the following information with your application:

Applicant's Name ____________________

Phone Number ( ) ____________________

Applicant's Current Address ____________________

____

____

Applicant's Birth date / / Hometown ____________________

____

Applicant's Social Security # ____________________

Applicant's Permanent Address ____________________

____

____

Date / / ____________________

Applicant's Signature ____________________

PRISM INTERNATIONAL

Creative Writing Program
University of British Columbia
Buchanan E462
1866 Main Mall
Vancouver, British Columbia CANADA V6T 1Z1
Website http://www.arts.cal/prisim/

Deadline: December 15, 2001 postmark

PRISM INTERNATIONAL ANNUAL FICTION CONTEST
PRISM International will award a First Prize of $2,000 and five (5) Runner-Up prizes of $200. All six stories will be published in the Summer Fiction Contest issue. Contest winners will also receive our normal payment for publication. All entrants receive a one year subscription to PRISM International. Current subscribers will receive a one year extension to their subscription.

The contest is open to anyone except students or instructors in the Creative Writing Program at the University of British Columbia.

Preliminary judging is by the PRISM International editorial board. The final Judge is to be announced.

Guidelines

1. Entries must be original, unpublished material, not under consideration elsewhere. We will purchase First North American serial rights for all work accepted for publication. Entries will not be returned.

2. Works of translation are eligible.

3. Entries must be typed, double spaced, on standard-sized 8-1/2 x 11 inch white paper, and must be no longer than 25 pages.

4. The entrant's full name, address, and the title of the story must appear on a separate cover page. The title of the story should appear on each page of the manuscript, but the author's name should not.

5. Entries must be postmarked no later than December 15, 2001. The entry fee is $20, plus $5 for each additional story.

6. Winners will be notified in June, 2002 and published in the Summer Fiction Contest issue. If you would like to receive a list of winners before the Summer Contest issue is published, please enclose a

self-addressed, stamped envelope with your entry, or check our Website at http://www.arts.cal/prisim/.

7. Send entry form, entry fees, and manuscript(s) to: PRISM International, 2001 SHORT FICTION CONTEST, Creative Writing Program, University of British Columbia, Buchanan E462, 1866 Main Mall, Vancouver, British Columbia CANADA V6T 1Z1.

PRISM International Short Fiction Contest Entry Form

SEND ENTRY FORM, ENTRY FEES, AND MANUSCRIPT(S) TO:
PRISM International 2001 SHORT FICTION CONTEST
Creative Writing Program, University of British Columbia, Buchanan E462, 1866 Main Mall, Vancouver, British Columbia CANADA V6T 1Z1

NAME: ______________________________

ADDRESS: ______________________________

____

____

____

Entry Fee with one story (Includes 1 yr. subscription) $20

Plus ___ Stories additional at $5 each + $_____

TOTAL enclosed $_____

How did you hear about our contest?

____

____

____

PRO DOGS NATIONAL CHARITY

Adult entries: M. Edridge
267 Hillbury Road
Warlingham, Surrey, ENGLAND CR6 9TL
Junior entries to: Y. Wheeler
45 Fleetway
Vange, Basildon, Essex, ENGLAND SS16 4UT

Deadline: October 1, 2001 postmak

PRO DOGS OPEN CREATIVE WRITING
AND PHOTOGRAPHIC COMPETITION
Prizes in each Adult Section: First £200, Second £150, Third £75.
Junior Section: First £50, Second £30, Third £20.

Results will be published in *Argos*, the journal of PRO DOGS, and winning entries will be published in a booklet. Winners will be announced and prizes given at the PRO DOGS Awards Luncheon in November 2001.

Submission Guidelines
Only unpublished work is to be submitted.

Poems may be up to 40 lines, any style or theme.

Stories may be up to 1000 words, any style or theme.

Photographs may be black-and-white or color, any theme.

Entries preferably should be typed, but legible handwritten entries are accepted. No identification is to appear on poems or stories. Please print your name and address on back of photographs. Each entry, or entries from the same person, should be accompanied by an entry form, attached to entries.

The copyright remains with the author.

The PRO DOGS National Charity reserves the right to publish any entries for which prize money is offered.

NO POEMS OR STORIES CAN BE RETURNED. PHOTOGRAPHS will be returned if a suitable self-addressed, stamped envelope is enclosed with entries. No correspondence will be entered into.

Closing date is October 1, 2001 postmark.

Entry is free to Juniors who are under 16 years of age at the closing date, October 1, 2001.

PRO DOGS 2001
Open Competition Entry Form

ADULT SECTION

I submit	1	Poem @ £3.00 1st Entry	£ __
I submit __		Poems @ £1.50 (subsequent entries)	£ __
I submit	1	Story @ £3.00 1st Entry	£ __
I submit __		Stories @ £1.50 (subsequent entries)	£ __
I submit	1	Photos @ £3.00 Entry	£ __
I submit __		Photos @ £1.50 (subsequent entries)	£ __

JUNIOR SECTION
Entrants must be under 16 years of age
at the closing date, October 1, 2001.

I submit __Poems FREE ENTRY	0
I submit __Stories FREE ENTRY	0

I would like to order the booklet of winners
at the special price of £3 each (Including postage)

Quantity __ @ £3 £ __

TOTAL AMOUNT ENCLOSED £ __

__ I enclose a self-addressed, stamped envelope for the return of photographs and/or results of competition.

__ I would like to know more about PRO DOGS and enclose self-addressed, stamped envelope.

NAME ______

ADDRESS ______

Post Code ______

Telephone ______

AGE (if Junior Section) ______

Please ask a Parent/Guardian or Teacher to sign here that the entry is your own work.

______
Teacher Signature

I am the owner of all rights, including copyright, of the submitted entries and agree to the rules of the competition.

______
Signature

Please make checks/postal orders (in sterling only) payable to PRO DOGS and submit Adult entries to: M. Edridge, 267 Hillbury Road, Warlingham, Surrey, ENGLAND CR6 9TL; submit Junior entries: Y. Wheeler, 45 Fleetway, Vange, Basildon, Essex, ENGLAND SS16 4UT.

[illegible]

NAME

ADDRESS

Post Code

Telephone

[illegible]

Teacher's Signature

[illegible]

Signature

[illegible]

PULITZER PRIZES

Administrator, Pulitzer Prize Board
709 Journalism Building
2950 Broadway, Mail Code 3865
Columbia University
New York, NY 10027
Phone (212) 854-3841 or (212) 854-3842
Website http://www.pulitzer.org/

Deadlines: July 1, 2001 postmark
for books published between January 1 and June 30, 2001

November 1, 2001 postmark
for books published between July 1 and December 31, 2001

PULITZER PRIZES IN LETTERS
Columbia University, on the recommendation of The Pulitzer Prize Board, annually awards the Pulitzer Prize in Letters of $5,000. The Pulitzer Prize Board acts on the nominations of distinguished committees of Pulitzer Jurors in accordance with the provisions established by the will of the first Joseph Pulitzer. Competition for prizes is limited to work done during the calendar year ending December 31. The prize winners are announced during the Spring. Winning entries will be included on The Pulitzer Prizes archival site on the World Wide Web at: http://www.pulitzer.org/.

Criteria and Guidelines
Books first published in the United States during 2001 are eligible for consideration. All entries must be published in book form and available for purchase by the general public. In the Fiction, Biography, and General Non-Fiction categories, authors must be American citizens. In the History category, the author may be of any nationality but the subject of the book must be U.S. history. In the Poetry category, the award is for original verse by an American author.

Anyone, including the author or publisher, may submit a book that is eligible. Entries must be submitted in writing and addressed to the Administrator of The Pulitzer Prize Board.

Entries should be postmarked by July 1, 2001 for books published between January 1 and June 30, and by November 1, 2001 for books published between July 1 and December 31.

Books that will not be published until November or December (published during the calendar year but after the entry deadline) should be submitted in galley or page-proof form by November 1, 2001.

Materials that make up a complete entry include:

1. A complete entry form, one biography and one photograph of the author.
2. Four (4) copies of the book.
3. A $50 handling fee per entry payable to Columbia University/Pulitzer Prizes. (Fees for multiple entries should be paid with one check.)

Books may be sent before other materials are ready. You may send books first and follow up with forms, fees, and other materials; however, please be sure to clearly indicate in which category the book should be entered. All entries must be completed by November 1, 2001.

Send books and entry materials to: Administrator, The Pulitzer Prize Board, 709 Journalism Building, 2950 Broadway, Mail Code 3865, Columbia University, New York, NY 10027. Photocopied entry forms are acceptable.

THE PULITZER PRIZES IN DRAMA AND MUSIC

For the Prize in Drama, works produced during the twelve months from March 2, 2001 through March 1, 2002 are considered. Entries shall be made while the work is being performed together with six (6) published or manuscript copies of each work. There is no entry fee for Drama.

For the Prize in Music, works given their American premiere during the twelve months from March 2, 2001 through March 1, 2002 are considered. Entries shall be accompanied by scores and recordings. Each entry in Music must be accompanied by a handling fee of $50, made payable to Columbia University/Pulitzer Prizes.

All entries should include biographies and pictures of entrants.

For complete information and deadlines for Prizes in Drama and Music, please call (212) 854-3841 or (212) 854-3842.

Entry Form for a Pulitzer Prize In Letters, Drama, or Music

(To be filed before July 1, 2001 or November 1, 2001 for Letters. See Criteria and Guidelines)

TITLE OF WORK ______

AUTHOR OR COMPOSER ______

HOME ADDRESS ______

PRESENT OCCUPATION AND ORGANIZATION ______

DATE AND PLACE OF ENTRANT'S BIRTH ______

PUBLICATION DATE (for books) ______

PREMIERE DATE AND LOCATION (for music) ______

PLEASE ENCLOSE (and check accordingly) ENTRANT'S

Biography ___ Photograph ___ $50 Handling Fee ___ (no fee for Drama entries)

The following awards will be made annually as Prizes in Letters. Except in the case of Drama, where production rather than publication shall be the criterion, eligibility for these awards shall be restricted to works first published in America during the year in book form and available for purchase by the general public.

	Check Box
(1) For distinguished fiction by an American author, preferably dealing with American life. Five thousand dollars ($5,000).	1.
(2) For a distinguished play by an American author, preferably original in its source and dealing with American life, Five thousand dollars ($5,000).	2.
(3) For a distinguished book upon the history of the United States, Five thousand dollars ($5,000).	3.
(4) For a distinguished biography or autobiography by an American author, Five thousand dollars ($5,000).	4.
(5) For a distinguished volume of original verse by an American author, Five thousand dollars ($5,000).	5.
(6) For a distinguished book of non-fiction by an American author that is not eligible for consideration in any other category, Five thousand dollars ($5,000).	6.
(7) For distinguished musical composition of significant dimension by an American that has had its first performance in the United States during the year, Five thousand dollars ($5,000).	7.

______

Signature of person sponsoring this entrant (may be self)

Name, title and organization (please print) ______

______

Address ______

______

Send entry materials to: The Pulitzer Prize Board, at 709 Journalism, 2950 Broadway, Mail Code 3865, Columbia University, New York, N.Y. 10027. Telephone: (212) 854-3841 or (212) 854-3842. Please make checks payable to Columbia University/Pulitzer Prizes.

PULLIAM JOURNALISM FELLOWSHIPS

The Indianapolis News
PO Box 145
Indianapolis, IN 46206
Phone (317) 633-9206

Deadline: July 1, 2001

EUGENE C. PULLIAM FELLOWSHIP
Prize: $30,000 for editorial writers, for travel and study. Honors an editorial writer by helping to broaden his or her journalistic horizons and knowledge of the world. Applicants must have at least three years of full-time editorial writing experience.

Contact: Society of Professional Journalists, PO Box 77, 16 S. Jackson St., Greencastle, IN 46135-0077; phone (765) 653-3333.

Deadline: March 1, 2001 postmark

PULLIAM JOURNALISM FELLOWSHIPS
Prize: $5,250 and a 10-week work study program in Indianapolis or Phoenix for 20 journalism college graduates. Applications are invited from graduates in the August 1999 – June 2000 classes who are newspaper journalism majors or liberal art majors with part-time or summer newspaper experience.

Contact: Russell B. Pulliam, Indianapolis, IN 46202-0145; phone (317) 633-9121.

There may be 5 early-admission winners. Their deadline is November 15, 2000. All other fellows must be postmarked by March 1, 2001.

PURDUE UNIVERSITY PRESS

1532 South Campus Courts E
West Lafayette, IN 47907

Deadline: April 15, 2001

VERNA EMERY POETRY PRIZE
Prize: $500 awarded upon publication plus royalty arrangements.

Guidelines
Manuscripts of 60 to 90 pages should be typed on standard sized paper or be a clean photocopy. Do not send your only copy. Name, address, and phone number should appear on the title page. Acknowledgments should appear on a separate page. Individual collections must be the work of a single author.

Translations are not accepted. Manuscripts should be submitted in final form; later revisions or emendations to acknowledgments will not be considered. Multiple submissions to other publishers are acceptable provided we are informed if the manuscript is accepted elsewhere.

The manuscript should be submitted in a plain 9x12 inch manilla folder. Please do not submit manuscripts bound in ring binders or plastic holders. Manuscripts submitted will not be returned; therefore, we request that you do not send a self-addressed, stamped envelope.

Announcement of winning entry will appear in a Fall 2001 issue of *American Poetry Review.*

You may include a self-addressed, stamped postcard if you wish acknowledgment of the manuscript's receipt. Submissions should include a check for $15 payable to Purdue University to help defray administrative costs.

The final judge for the competition will be named when the results of the competition are announced in September. Individual criticism of manuscripts cannot be given.

Send submissions to above address.

QUARTERLY REVIEW OF LITERATURE POETRY SERIES

26 Haslet Avenue
Princeton, NJ 08540

Deadline: May 1, 2001 – May 31, 2001

The QRL Poetry Series is a continuation of the Quarterly Review of Literature, publishing four to six prize-winning books in one volume and awarding $1,000 plus 100 books to each writer. Books are selected through international competition, presenting poetry book collections, long poems, poetic plays, and translations in a community of writing that has quality and diversity.

Biographical material, photographs, and an afterword about writing by the authors are included.

Submission Guidelines

Submission is in May only. Authors may submit a book of poems, a single long poem, a poetic play, or translations of one poet, 50 to 100 pages in length.

Manuscripts in English are invited from outside the U.S.

Only one manuscript per reading period may be entered.

Entries must be accompanied by a self-addressed, stamped envelope.

With your submission, we request a $20 subscription that entitles you to any combination of volumes adding up to that amount. The Series provides a remarkable bargain: eight to ten books in a two-volume paperback subscription for $20. Institutional and cloth price is $20 per volume. The QRL Poetry Series has a large, interested, readership and the attention of the reviewing world.

Mail entries to: QRL Poetry Series, 26 Haslet Ave., Princeton, NJ 08540

The QRL Poetry Series has been hailed as "the most significant publishing event in years for poetry," *(College Sun Times)*, applauded as "brilliant" *(New York Times)*, and determined to be "of the highest quality" and a "remarkable bargain" *(Publisher's Weekly)*.

"One of the ten best. [The QRL Poetry Series is] a thick, very professional product which is really several books by as many poets bound together and all first rate at the craft." (*The Reference Librarian*), "A national treasure." (*Parnassus*).

"The editors, whose eclectic, international taste is to be commended, continue to search for the best in current poetry." (*Library Journal*),

"One of our favorite books of the year. QRL publishes book-length manuscripts and pays authors real money." (*Voice Literary Supplement*).

QUARTERLY WEST

200 South Central Campus Drive, Room 317
University of Utah
Salt Lake City, UT 84112-9109
Phone (801) 581-3938

Deadline: October 1, 2001 – December 31, 2001 postmark

QUARTERLY WEST NOVELLA COMPETITION
Quarterly West offers two prizes of $500 each to the authors submitting the two best novellas. The winning manuscripts will be published in the Fall 2002 issue of *Quarterly West.*

Submission Guidelines

1. Manuscripts should be 50-125 pages in length, typed double spaced. Letter-quality computer printouts and photocopies are acceptable. The author's name should appear on a separate title page only.

2. Multiple entries by a single author are acceptable. Once a manuscript has been received, no corrections or rewrites will be considered during the competition.

3. No manuscripts will be returned.

4. All entries should be accompanied by a self-addressed, stamped postcard for notification of receipt; a self-addressed, stamped for notification of results; and a $20 reading fee. Checks should be made out to *Quarterly West.*

5. Entries must be postmarked between October 1, 2001 and December 31, 2001.

6. Final judging will be done by a writer of national reputation from a pool of finalists selected by the editors of *Quarterly West.*

7. Results will be available in the late Spring of 2002.

8. Two winning writers will receive a prize of $500, and the winning manuscripts will be published in *Quarterly West* in the Fall of 2001.

9. Send entries to: *Quarterly West* Novella Competition, University of Utah, 200 So. Central Campus Drive, Room 317, Salt Lake City, UT 84112-9109.

QUINCY WRITER'S GUILD

P.O. Box 433
Quincy, IL 62306-0433

Deadline: January 1, 2001 – April 1, 2001 postmark

QUINCY WRITER'S GUILD WRITING CONTEST
The aim of the Quincy Writer's Guild 12th annual Writing Contest is to encourage writers to create new works on a regular basis. Monetary prizes will be awarded to the First, Second, and Third Place winners in each category; honorables mentions will receive a certificate.

Submission Guidelines
Works must be original by the entrant and previously unpublished. NO prize-winning entry may be re-submitted in any subsequent year's contest.

Any number of entries may be made in one or all of the following categories:

Non-fiction, up to 2,000 words, $4 each entry.
Fiction, up to 3,500 words, $4 each entry.
Serious Poetry, any style or length, $2 each entry.
Light Poetry, any style or length, $2 each entry.

Appropriate fees MUST accompany all entries.

No personal identification may appear on manuscripts.

For each entry identification must appear on a 3x5 card that lists: author's name, address, city/state, and telephone number; and title of work and category.

Entries must be typed on one side only of 8-1/2 x 11 inch paper and, if prose, double spaced. Each page must be numbered, titled at the top, and unfastened to the other pages. Submit each entry in triplicate.

Only those entries accompanied by a self-addressed, stamped envelope will be returned. All other entries will be destroyed upon announcement of the winner.

Entries will be accepted beginning January 1, 2001 and must be postmarked no later than April 1, 2001.

Entrants are welcome to attend the Guild's annual meeting in July 2001 when the awards will be presented. Please notify the Guild of your intention to come to the meeting. Awards not claimed at that time will be mailed.

Quincy Writer's Guild reserves one-time rights for possible publication of winning entries.

Entries will be judged by a panel of qualified persons who are not members of Quincy Writer's Guild.

Mail entries to: Quincy Writer's Guild, P.O. Box 433, Quincy, Illinois 62306-0433.

THE MARY ROBERTS RINEHART FUND

William Miller
Mail Stop Number 3E4
English Department
George Mason University
Fairfax, VA 22030-4444
Phone (703) 993-1185

Deadlines: December 1, 2000 – November 30, 2001
Fiction and Poetry

December 1, 2001 – November 30, 2002
Non-fiction and Drama

THE MARY ROBERTS RINEHART AWARDS
To help aspiring authors, the late Mary Roberts Rinehart began the practice of giving money to writers whose work she felt showed promise. Since 1983 this Fund has been located at George Mason University. Each year in March, the Fund awards three grants to writers whose work is judged to merit such support. Grants are from $2,000 to $2,500 each. Grants are given to unpublished creative writers who need financial assistance to complete previously unpublished works of fiction, poetry, drama; or biography, autobiography, or history with a strong narrative quality.

Guidelines
For purposes of this award, the Fund considers "unpublished writers" to mean "having no book publications." A writer who has no book publications but who earns a living from work regularly appearing in prominent national magazines also would be debarred.

United States citizenship is not required to apply, but only works in English should be sent and awards will be made only in U.S. dollars.

A writer may apply only in one category in any given year. An author not granted an award one year may apply in succeeding years, but once a writer receives an award, he or she may not apply for another.

A writer must be nominated for a Mary Roberts Rinehart Award. Individual applications for grants are not accepted; that is to say a writer may not enter herself or himself. Instead a candidate must be nominated.

Many nominations come from writing program faculty around the country, but any unpublished writer may be nominated by a sponsoring writer, agent, or editor. There are no application forms, and strictly speaking, no formal written recommendation is necessary: the Fund will consider the submission of a candidate's work by an established writer or editor as a nomination. Candidates are requested, however, to provide their address, telephone number, and social security number with submissions. Candidates should also include a brief paragraph containing biographical information.

Submitted samples of a nominee's writing may be up to 30 pages in length for all categories. The decisions of the judges are final, and are based on the quality of the nominee's writing.

Nominations and manuscripts must be received at the office above by November 30 of each year. When November 30 falls on a Saturday or Sunday, the deadline is pushed forward to the following Monday. Manuscripts received without nominating letters and manuscripts received late will not be read. Grants will be announced by March 1 of the following year.

From December 1, 2000 to November 30, 2001, the fund will accept submissions of Fiction and Poetry.

From December 1, 2001 to November 30, 2002, the fund will accept submissions of Non-fiction and Drama.

Submit manuscripts to: William Miller, Mail Stop Number 3E4, English Department, George Mason University, Fairfax, VA 22030-4444.

RIVER CITY

Department of English
The University of Memphis
Memphis, TN 38152

Deadline: January 20, 2001 postmark

RIVER CITY WRITING AWARDS IN FICTION
Sponsored by the Hohenberg Foundation, *River City* offers three awards for best short story. First Prize is $2,000; Second Prize is $500; and Third Prize is $300.

Submission Guidelines
Any previously unpublished short story of up to 7,500 words is eligible. Writers may enter only one manuscript in the contest. NO simultaneous submissions are allowed.

All manuscripts should be typed, double spaced, and accompanied by a cover letter. The author's name should NOT appear anywhere on the manuscript itself.

All submissions should be postmarked by January 20, 2001.

All manuscripts must be accompanied by a $9.50 entry fee. This fee initiates a one year subscription to *River City.*

River City will publish the prize-winning story, and retains the right of first refusal to publish any contest entry.

Entries will be screened by members of the Creative Writing Faculty at the University of Memphis. Winners will be chosen from 15 finalists by a nationally known fiction writer.

Winner will be notified in April 2001.

All entrants will receive copy of the winning stories in the Winter 2001 issue of *River City.* No manuscripts will be returned.

River City is published twice a year at The University of Memphis. Single copies are available at $7 per copy. Subscriptions are $12 per year. A special subscription rate is available at three years for $24.

Make checks payable to The University of Memphis.

Send contest entries and subscriptions to: *River City*, Department of English, The University of Memphis, Memphis, TN 38152.

Publication Guidelines for *River City*

All manuscripts should be typed and double spaced (Poetry accepted in author's desired form).

All submissions should include a self-addressed, stamped envelope. Those not accompanied by a self-addressed, stamped envelope will not be returned or notified.

Submissions which engage a special topic should have the topic clearly marked on the envelope and cover sheet.

The editors recommend interested writers to obtain a copy of *River City*. Submissions should be sent to: River City, Department of English, The University of Memphis, Memphis, TN 38152.

ROME ART & COMMUNITY CENTER

308 W. Bloomfield Street
Rome, NY 13440

Deadline: July 1, 2001 – November 1, 2001 postmark

THE MILTON DORFMAN POETRY PRIZE
Sponsored by the Rome Art & Community Center, the 12th annual Milton Dorfman Poetry Prize offers a First Prize of $500; Second Prize of $200; and Third Prize of $100. Winning entries will be published in a Rome Art & Community Center publication and will be read at the Center during an awards ceremony. The Milton Dorfman Poetry Prize is open to the general public, with the exception of Rome Art & Community Center employees. The Judge is to be announced.

Submission Guidelines
Entries must be original poetry, unpublished at time of submission.

Entries must be typed on 8-1/2 x 11 inch paper.

The author's name, address and telephone number must appear on each entry.

Entries will be accepted starting July 1, 2001 and postmarked by November 1, 2001.

There is a reading fee of $5.00 per entry, U.S. funds only. Checks must be made payable to Rome Art & Community Center. There is $10 fee for any returned checks.

No entries will be returned.

Winners will be notified by February 1, 2001, by a representative of the Poetry Prize.

Mail entries and fees to: Milton Dorfman Poetry Prize, c/o Rome Art & Community Center, 308 W. Bloomfield St., Rome, NY 13440.

SALMON RUN PRESS

P.O. Box 672130
Chugiak, AK 99567-2130

Deadline: December 31, 2001 postmark

NATIONAL POETRY BOOK AWARD
Prize: $1,000 and publication

Submit book-length (48-96 pages) poetry manuscript with name and address on cover page only. One typed poem per page; any subject or style. Include $10 reading fee and a self-addressed, stamped envelope.

Winner's manuscript is published and nationally promoted.

Submit manuscripts to above contest name and address.

SALT HILL

Salt Hill
Syracuse University
Department of English
Syracuse, NY 13244
E-mail salthill@cas.syr.edu

Deadline: September 15, 2001 postmark

ANNUAL FICTION CONTEST
Awards: $500 first prize and publication; $250 second prize and publication; and $100 third prize and publication.

Guidelines
We are concerned primarily with excellence in style and craft. We show special interest in manuscripts that contain fresh imagery, original language, and tonal and structural experimentation.

Submit original, unpublished short/short fiction up to 1500 words.

Longer works (6,000 words maximum) are accepted.

Reading fee: $9 per story.

Name, address, phone, word count and story title should appear on separate cover sheet. No names on manuscript.

Enclose self-addressed, stamped envelope to have manuscripts returned.

Address envelope to Fiction Contest.

All entries considered for regular publication.

Deadline: May 1 postmark

ANNUAL POETRY CONTEST
Awards: $500 first prize and publication; $250 second prize and publication; and $100 third prize and publication.

Guidelines
We are interested in poetry that does more than simply deliver a tight, well-defined anecdote. We like to see the kind of intellectual and emotional engagement which is representative of a mature poetic imagination.

Submit original, unpublished poems.

Reading fee: $5 up to 150 lines (one to three poems). $3 extra every additional 100 lines. Send three to five poems. Write name, address and phone on poems.

Manuscripts will not be returned.

Address envelope to Poetry Contest.

All entries considered for publication.

General Guidelines
Submissions should be typed and one side to a page. Type name, address and phone on manuscripts.

Work should be previously unpublished.

Simultaneous submissions okay.

We report in two to six months. We publish two to eight months after acceptance.

We publish translations with permission of author.

Work accepted will be printed in *Salt Hill* and posted on the *Salt Hill* website.

Send manuscript, cover letter, and self-addressed, stamped envelope with sufficient postage. Address envelope to specific genre editor (Fiction, Poetry, Book Reviews).

In addition to fiction and poetry, we also accept hypertext, book reviews (900 words or less) and essays (3000 words or less). Each issue also features the work of on or more artists. Send a sheet of labeled slides, or a series of photographs with a biography and self-addressed, stamped envelope.

THE SAN FRANCISCO FOUNDATION

Administered by Intersection for the Arts
446 Valencia Street
San Francisco, CA 94013
Phone (415) 626-ARTS
Website intrsect@wenet.net

Deadline: November 16, 2000 – January 31, 2001 postmark

THE SAN FRANCISCO FOUNDATION LITERARY AWARDS
Applications from eligible young authors are invited for two $2,000 literary awards. The awards are made annually under the terms of the Joseph Henry Jackson Fund and the James D. Phelan Trust, housed at The San Francisco Foundation. A special fund, established by the author Mary Tanenbaum in memory of Joseph Henry Jackson, makes a third, $1,000 award available to encourage non-fiction writing.

Eligibility
Under the terms of the Jackson Fund and the Phelan Trust, the awards are intended to encourage young writers for an unpublished manuscript-in-progress. All applicants must, therefore, be between 20 and 35 years of age as of January 31, 2001.

JOSEPH HENRY JACKSON AWARD
Applicants for the 44th annual Joseph Henry Jackson Award must be residents of Northern California or the state of Nevada for three consecutive years immediately prior to the January 31, 2001 contest deadline. The unpublished work-in-progress submitted may be fiction (novel or short stories), non-fictional prose, or poetry.

JAMES DUVAL PHELAN AWARD
Applicants for the 64th annual James D. Phelan Award must have been born in the state of California, but need not be current residents. The unpublished work-in-progress submitted may be fiction, non-fictional prose, poetry, or drama.

SPECIAL AWARD IN NON-FICTION
Non-fiction writers who apply for either the Jackson or the Phelan award, but are not selected as winners, will be considered for the $1,000 Special Award for Non-fictional Prose. No separate application for this award is required.

Submission Guidelines
Eligible writers may submit one application form and manuscript to apply for either or both awards. No candidate may win more than one

award. Previous winners are ineligible to receive the same award again. Winners will be announced on or about June 15, 2001. Judges reserve the right to make no awards if, in their view, no manuscripts are worthy. All submissions must be postmarked by January 31, 2001.

The manuscript must be no longer than 100 double spaced pages (poetry need not be double spaced), typed on 8-1/2 x 11 inch paper, with a cover page that gives the work's title and the applicant's name and address. Manuscripts that are handwritten or are otherwise illegible will not be considered.

The manuscript must be forwarded, with a properly completed, official application form to: Jackson/Phelan Literacy Awards, Intersection for the Arts, 446 Valencia Street, San Francisco, CA 94103.

No application will be accepted without the applicant's signature, signifying agreement to the conditions of the competition and verifying the validity of all statements contained therein. Proof of birth, age, and residence may be required, and must be furnished within ten days if requested.

Award-winning manuscripts become the property of The San Francisco Foundation and will become part of the Foundation's permanent archives. Authors will retain full rights for the publication/distribution of their works. All other manuscripts submitted will be available for pickup between June 15 and July 15 at Intersection for the Arts, 446 Valencia Street, between 15th and 16th Streets in San Francisco, Mondays through Fridays, 10 a.m. to 5 p.m.

Manuscripts will only be returned if a self-addressed, stamped envelope is included at the time of submission. The envelope must be of a size which can accommodate the manuscript and must bear sufficient postage for its return.

The San Francisco Foundation Literary Awards Application Form

Please type or print neatly in ink.
Check award for which application is made:

____ Joseph Henry Jackson Award ____ James D. Phelan Award

Title: ______________________________

____

Genre: Poetry_ Fiction_ Non-fictional Prose_ Drama_

Brief description of work submitted (e.g., contents, degree of completion, projected plans):

____

____

____

Applicant Information:

____

Name - Last First Middle Initial

____

Current Address – Street/City/State/Postal Code

____

Permanent Address – Street/City/State/Postal Code

____

Telephone Evening Telephone Message/Other

____

Birthplace (City and State or, if foreign born, Country)

____

Age D.O.B.

For Jackson Award: Give addresses and dates of residency in Northern California or Nevada for the past three years.

1. ______________________________

Street Address City State

2. ______________________________

Street Address City State

3. ______________________________

Street Address City State

I affirm that the work submitted is my original creation, that I meet the age, residency, and/or place of birth requirements, and that none of the work is published as of this date.

____

Signature Date

SAN FRANCISCO STATE UNIVERSITY THE POETRY CENTER & AMERICAN POETRY ACHIVES

1600 Holloway Avenue
San Francisco, CA 94132
Center (415) 338-2227
Archives (415) 338-1056

Deadline: December 31, 2001

THE POETRY CENTER BOOK AWARD CONTEST
The Poetry Center invites submissions for its Annual Book Award. The Book Award has been given since 1980 to an outstanding book of poems published by an individual author in the current year. The award consists of a $500 cash prize and an invitation to read in the Poetry Center reading series.

To be eligible, books must be published and copyrighted in 2001. The award is for volumes by individual authors. Anthologies, collaborations, or translations are not accepted.

To enter a title, send one copy of the book and a $10 reading fee (per title) to the Poetry Center at the above address, marked Attn: Book Award. Reading fee MUST accompany the book.

Checks should be made payable to The Poetry Center. Please complete the attached form or include a cover letter listing the author's name, book title(s), name of person or publisher issuing check, and check number.

Announcement of the winner will be made in the summer of the following year. For further information, please call the Poetry Center: (415) 338-3132.

San Francisco State University
The Poetry Center Book Award Competition

Author's name: ______________________________

Address: ______________________________

____

Book title(s): ______________________________

____

____

____

Check issued by: ______________________________

Check number: ______________________________

SARABANDE BOOKS, INC.

P.O. Box 4999
Louisville, KY 40204

Deadline: January 1, 2001 – February 15, 2001 postmark

THE KATHRYN A. MORTON PRIZE IN POETRY
The Kathryn A. Morton Prize in Poetry includes a $2,000 cash award, publication of a full-length collection of poetry, and a standard royalty contract.

Eligibility
The contest is open to any writer of English who is a citizen of the United States. Employees and board members of Sarabande Books, Inc., are not eligible. Individual poems from the manuscript may have been published previously in magazines, chapbooks of less than 48 pages, or anthologies, but the collection as a whole must be unpublished. Translations and previously self-published books are not eligible.

Submission Guidelines
Please submit two (2) copies of the manuscript and our REQUIRED ENTRY FORM. For official entry forms, please write to the above address.

Manuscripts must be:

1. Anonymous, the author's name or address cannot appear anywhere on the manuscript (title page should contain the title only).
2. A minimum of 48 pages of poetry.
3. Typed on standard 8-1/2 x 11 inch white paper, one side of the page only.
4. Paginated consecutively with a table of contents and acknowledgments.
5. Machine copies – no dot-matrix please unless of letter quality.
6. Placed in two PLAIN FILE FOLDERS. No paper clips please.

All manuscripts must be accompanied by our entry form which contains all the necessary identifying information. Please DO NOT send your manuscript without this form.

Please retain a copy of your entry. We cannot return manuscripts.

Submission of more than one manuscript is permissible if each manuscript is accompanied by an entry form and handling fee. Once submitted, manuscripts cannot be altered. The winner will be given the opportunity to make changes before publication. Simultaneous submissions to other publishers are permitted, but Sarabande Books must be notified IMMEDI-

ATELY if manuscript is accepted elsewhere. The winner will be notified in early July. Sarabande Books will consider all finalists for publication.

There is a $15 handling fee, check made payable to Sarabande Books, Inc.

Manuscripts must be postmarked between and including January 1 and February 15, 2001.

Include a self-addressed, stamped postcard for notification that manuscript has been received. Also include a self-addressed, stamped, business-sized envelope for contest results.

Please send your manuscript in a plain or padded envelope. NO BOXES PLEASE. No Federal Express, Overnight Mail, or UPS. We strongly advise that you send your manuscript first class.

Please send entries to: The Kathryn A. Morton Prize in Poetry, Sarabande Books, Inc., P.O. Box 4999, Louisville, KY 40204.

For answers to additional questions, or for official entry forms, please write to the above address.

THE MARY MCCARTHY PRIZE IN SHORT FICTION
The Mary McCarthy Prize in Short Fiction includes a $2,000 cash award, publication of a collection of short stories or novellas, and a standard royalty contract.

Eligibility
The contest is open to any writer of English who is a citizen of the United States. Employees and board members of Sarabande Books, Inc., are not eligible. Submissions may include a collection of short stories, or one or more novellas (a novella may not exceed 150 pages), or any combination thereof. Works that have previously appeared in magazines or in anthologies may be included. Translations and previously self-published collections are not eligible.

Submission Guidelines
Please submit two (2) copies of the manuscript and our REQUIRED ENTRY FORM. For official entry forms, please write to the above address.
Manuscripts must be:

1. Anonymous, the author's name or address cannot appear anywhere on the manuscript (title page should contain the title only).
2. Between 150-300 pages in length.

3. Typed on standard 8-1/2 x 11 inch white paper, one side of the page only.
4. Paginated consecutively with a table of contents and acknowledgments.
5. Machine copies – no dot-matrix please unless of letter quality.
6. Placed in two PLAIN FILE FOLDERS. No paper clips please.

All manuscripts must be accompanied by our entry form which contains all the necessary identifying information. Please DO NOT send your manuscript without this form.

Please retain a copy of your entry. We cannot return manuscripts.

Submission of more than one manuscript is permissible if each manuscript is accompanied by an entry form and handling fee. Once submitted, manuscripts cannot be altered. The winner will be given the opportunity to make changes before publication. Simultaneous submissions to other publishers are permitted, but Sarabande Books must be notified IMMEDIATELY if manuscript is accepted elsewhere. The winner will be notified in early July. Sarabande Books will consider all finalists for publication.

There is a $15 handling fee, check made payable to Sarabande Books, Inc.

Manuscripts must be postmarked between and including January 1 and February 15, 2001.

Include a self-addressed, stamped postcard for notification that manuscript has been received. Also include a self-addressed, stamped, business-sized envelope for contest results.

Please send your manuscript in a plain or padded envelope. NO BOXES PLEASE. No Federal Express, Overnight Mail, or UPS. We strongly advise that you send your manuscript first class.

Please send entries to: The Mary McCarthy Prize in Short Fiction, Sarabande Books, Inc., P.O. Box 4999, Louisville, KY 40204.

For answers to additional questions, or for official entry forms, please write to the above address.

SASQUATCH BOOKS

Chinook Literary Prize
615 2nd Avenue, Suite 260
Seattle, WA 98104-2200
Phone (206) 467-4300; Fax (206) 467-4301
Website http://www.sasquatchbooks.com

Deadline: April 1, 2001 – June 1, 2001

CHINOOK LITERARY PRIZE
Prize: $10,000 advance and publication by Sasquatch Books.

This prize seeks to foster the regional literature of the Pacific Northwest. Submissions should be original work, fiction or nonfiction, that reflects the Pacific Northwest in either story, setting, theme or character. The winner will be announced by September 1, 2001.

Guidelines
Fiction submissions must be complete manuscripts. Nonfiction projects may be submitted in complete manuscript or in a detailed proposal accompanied by at least three complete chapters. Children's books and poetry are not being considered for this prize.

There is a $20 entry fee. If you entered a book in the 2000 contest, you don't have to pay an entry fee for 2001.

Please make submissions on single-sided copies, number every page in sequence, white letter-sized paper, double spaced.

Send submission to above contest name and address.

SCAVENGER

Janet Fox
519 Ellinwood
Osage City, KS 66523-1329
E-mail foxscav1@jc.net

Deadline: April 1, 2001 – July 1, 2001 postmark

SCAVENGER "KILLER FROG" CONTEST
Anyone may enter and there is no limit on the number of entries. Materials sent early will be filed until the contest officially begins; e-mail queries at foxscav1@jc.net are okay but no e-mail submissions are accepted.

Categories are Short Story, Short-Short Story, Poem, and Art.

Short Story must be 1,500-4,000 words (a play or script may be entered as a story).

Short-Short Story fiction may be up to 1,500 words.

Poems may be any length, any style.

Art: The winning drawing will be on the cover and the title of the anthology will be based on that drawing, so you may give it a title or letter the title into the design. The anthology will be half-legal size: 7 inches across by 8-1/2 down, so artwork should fit that. Inside art may or may not be reduced. Frogs have dominated the artwork for the contest thus far but the contest is not limited to frogs.

Prizes of $25 are awarded in each category, along with the "coveted" froggie statuette crafted by Victoria Rubottom for each category. The four Runners-Up in each category receive a year's subscription, or a year's extension to Scavenger's Newsletter.

All winners and runners-up will be published in an anthology and will receive a copy. The anthology is tentatively scheduled for September 2001.

Send photocopies for everything. Nothing will be returned. (Exceptions may be made if you have a good reason and are willing to provide return postage.)

Materials will be judged by the editor of Scavenger's Newsletter. You may write pseudonymously, if you wish, but I'll need your real name for the check.

There is no Entry Fee. If you want a list of winners, enclose a self-addressed, stamped envelope. If you want to buy a copy of the 2000 anthology at its pre-publication price, send $4. Additional copies of the anthology will be available after the contest at $4 for contest entrants and $4.50 for everyone else. The 2000 anthology is available as a sample (so you can check out winning entries from last year), $4.50 each, prepaid.

One-time rights are acquired only for use in the anthology. Rights revert to creators upon publication. The publisher reserves the right to keep the anthology in print until the next year's anthology is published. Artwork and excepts may be used in advertising.

Out of US Entries will be considered, but the entrants should know that awards will be given in U.S. funds or in SCAV products, your choice.

The contest is for adults, but porn-tinged material or profanity laced dialog that goes nowhere is not allowed. Offensive and gross is okay if an integral part of the tale, e.g., a horror poem, or story or artwork so overdone it becomes humorous. You may accompany your submission with a humorous cover letter, which may be published. Cover letter is optional.

Join the fun and send your "froggies" to the Scavenger's Killer Frog Contest beginning April 1, 2001.

Send your entries to: Janet Fox, 519 Ellinwood, Osage City, KS 66523-1329.

SCHOOL OF COMMUNICATION DESIGN
UNIVERSITY OF BALTIMORE

1420 North Charles Street
Baltimore, MD 21201-5779

Deadline: June 15, 2001

Prize: $500 and publication and honorable mentions will be published in Passager Poetry Contest for writers over 50.

Reading fee: $10.

Submit a brief biography and five poems, all previously unpublished and preferably under 30 lines each. Your name and address must appear at the top of each page. Poems will not be returned. Please include a self-addressed, stamped envelope with your submission for notification of the winner.

Send submissions to above address.

SEVENTEEN

850 Third Avenue
New York, NY 10022

Deadline: April 30, 2001

THE *SEVENTEEN* FICTION CONTEST
Give us your story! Enter the *Seventeen* fiction contest for young authors sponsored by Sally Hansen. We're looking for one fantastic piece of fiction. Our judging criteria are simple: make your story real. Make your story original. Give us the story you've always wanted to see in *Seventeen*. If your story wins, you'll receive $1,000 and a gift from contest sponsor Sally Hansen. Best of all, we'll publish your story in *Seventeen*! Second prize is $500; Third prize is $250; and five honorable mentions win $50 each. So what are you waiting for? Get to your keyboard and start writing!

Guidelines

Contestants must be between 13 and 21 years old as of April 30, 2001.

Fiction must not have been previously published in any form (except in school publications).

Manuscripts must be typed, double spaced on one side of each sheet of paper and should be no more that 4,000 words (about 16 pages).

Submit as many original stories as you like, but be sure to include your full name, address, telephone number, birth date, and signature in the top right-hand corner of the first page of each story. Your signature constitutes your acceptance of the contest rules.

Winners must sign an affidavit of compliance with rules, and a publicity release.

Deadline is April 30, 2001. All decisions of the judges are final. Prize winners will be notified by mail in late 2001. No phone calls please. K-III Magazine Corporation has the right to publish winning entries in a future issue of *Seventeen* and online. No manuscripts will be returned.

Mail entries to Seventeen, 2001 Fiction Contest, 850 Third Avenue, New York, NY 10022.

SHENANDOAH INTERNATIONAL PLAYWRIGHTS RETREAT

Robert Graham Small, Director
Kathleen Tosco, Managing Director
ShenanArts, Inc.
Route 5
Box 167-F
Staunton, VA 24401
Phone (540) 248-1868; Fax: (540) 248-7728

Deadline: February 1, 2001

Prize: Fellowship covers cost of retreat. Shenandoah International exists to provide young and established writers a stimulating, challenging environment to test and develop new work in a safe haven, free from the pressures of everyday living. Playwrights come from around the United States and the world. Each year the Retreat brings guest playwrights in this creative exploration. The writers work in close and intense collaboration with our multicultural company of dramaturgs, directors, and actors. What occurs is a simultaneous "on-the-feet/on-the-pagel" exploration of each play, culminating in a staged reading before an audience of invited professionals and advocates.

Guidelines

Competitive admission open to playwrights and screenwriters based on submitted work. Submissions should consist of two copies of completed draft of script to be worked on at retreat, personal statement of applicant's background as a writer and a self-addressed, stamped postcard for acknowledgment of receipt.

Entrants can call or write for further retreat information. Send for requested information to above address weeks before deadline.

Winners will be notified after June 10, 2001.

SIENA COLLEGE

515 Loudon Road
Loudonville, NY 12211-1462

Deadline: February 1, 2001 – June 30, 2001 postmark

SIENA COLLEGE INTERNATIONAL PLAYWRIGHTS' COMPETITION
The Biennial Playwriting Competition, sponsored by the Siena College Department of Creative Arts Theatre Program, seeks submission of previously unproduced, unpublished scripts for production during the college's 2001-2002 academic year. A $2,000 honorarium will be awarded to the winning playwright. A full production of the winning script will be mounted by the Siena College Theatre Program in the Spring of 2002 as part of its Theatre Series.

Living expenses and transportation to and from the college, up to a maximum of $1,000, will be awarded to the winning playwright for a four – six week residency in the Spring semester of 2002. During the residency, the playwright will participate in rehearsals, design conferences, public discussions, and the academic life of the Siena community.

Finalists and the eventual winner will be selected by a team comprised of the faculty and staff of the Siena College. Theatre Program and invited judges from other theatre faculties, the professional theatre, local media, or the Siena student body.

The decision of the team of adjudicators in final. The Siena College Theatre Program reserves the right to select no winner.

Submission Guidelines
Scripts must be original, unpublished, unproduced, and free of royalty and copyright restrictions. Musicals will not be considered. Plays which have had staged readings are acceptable, but workshop productions will disqualify entry.

Scripts must be full-length, require a unit set or minimal set changes, and feature an ensemble cast of three to ten actors. The age range of the ensemble should be suitable for undergraduate performers.

Scripts must be typed and bound. Manuscripts must be accompanied by an application form and a business-size, self-addressed, stamped envelope. Materials should be sent to: Siena International Playwrights Competition, Siena College, 515 Loudon Road, Loudonville, NY 12211-1462.

Playwrights who want scripts returned must include a script-size, self-addressed envelope with correct postage. Scripts without return envelopes and postage will be discarded at the conclusion of the contest. Please include one envelope for each script submitted. Siena College does not assume responsibility for loss, damage, or return of scripts. All reasonable care will be taken.

Scripts will be accepted beginning with a postmark of February 1, 2001. Deadline for entry is a postmark of June 30, 2001. The winner will be announced no later than September 30, 2001.

Finalists will be asked to submit educational and professional credentials and three references. A documented production history of the script also will be requested.

Siena College International Playwrights' Competition Application Form

Please photocopy additional forms if necessary.

Name ____________________

Institutional Affiliation (if any) ____________________

Mailing Address ____________________

City ____________ State ______ Zip ______

Phone H (   ) ____________ W (   ) ____________

E-Mail: ____________________

Play Title ____________________

____

Previous Production Yes __ No __

Staged Readings Yes__ No__

Unit Set Yes__ No__ If no, number of settings________

Number of characters________

Return with manuscript; business-size self-addressed, stamped envelope; and script-size, self-addressed stamped envelope (if return is desired) to: Siena International Playwrights' Competition, Siena College, 515 Loudon Road, Loudonville, NY 12211-1462.

SKIPPING STONES

P.O. Box 3939
Eugene, OR 97403
Phone (541) 342-4956
E-mail Skipping@efn.org

Deadline: January 15, 2001 postmark

SKIPPING STONES HONOR AWARDS
Skipping Stones invites entries for the 2001 Honor Awards. "Our global interdependence invites us to appreciate differences, and thus realize the potential inherent in diversity." (*Skipping Stones*)

Recognizing cultural and geological diversity to be essential components of our world, Skipping Stones Awards honor exceptional contributions to ecological and multicultural education. Books, magazines, and educational videos are considered under these categories:

Multicultural Books. Focuses on one or more of the following themes: Cultural and ethnic diversity within a country (such as indigenous societies), intercultural and international, global consciousness and social issues, peace and nonviolence, sustainable relationships between different cultures, understanding of religious differences, tolerance, and appreciation of languages.

Ecology and Nature Books. Promotes an awareness of the natural world; human, plant, and animal relationships; specific species and habitats; and environmental protection, conservation of resources, community projects, and sustainable living.

Educational Videos. We recognize that educational videos are being used frequently in today's schools and in home education programs; however, we concur with many educators who have expressed concerns about the quality and content of many of the videos available in the market. Through the Honor Awards we want to promote the production of educational videos that are truly exceptional, engaging, and revolutionary.

Our criteria for selecting a video will address the concern that watching videos can become a passive spectator activity, devoid of experiencing the self in tasks of 'doing and being' with others. We invite entries that are mindful that human interaction is vital for healthy, sustainable society.

The multicultural selection committee will be comprised of teachers, librarians, students, and *Skipping Stones* staff. The committee will look at various aspects of the entries in addition to their quality and contents: Does it promote positive human interaction? Does it engage us creatively? Does it promote constructive problem-solving approaches? Does it inspire us to think and act for the good of the society at large? Awards will be announced on the Spring Equinox, and reviewed in the Spring 2001 issue of *Skipping Stones.* The annual Skipping Stones Honor Awards, created in 1993, have recognized many outstanding books and educational videos produced by well-known international publishers, as well as small, nonprofit/independent publishers or producers.

At *Skipping Stones* we believe that our future depends on how we take care of our ecological riches, as well as how we understand each other's customs, cultures, languages, and thinking. Winner of the 1995 Golden Shoestring Award of *Ed Press*, *Skipping Stones* is a unique multicultural and nature magazine attempting to bridge the waters that separate people and nature, cultures and generations. The bimonthly magazine, now in its ninth year, is published by Skipping Stones, Inc., a nonprofit, tax-exempt organization. It encourages cooperation, creativity, and a celebration of cultural and ecological richness. Each issue features original art and writing in all languages, book reviews, and a Parent/Teacher Guide. Subscriptions are $35 for Institutions; $25 for Individuals.

All entries must be postmarked by January 15, 2001.

For more information or entry forms, contact: *Skipping Stones,* P.O. Box 3939, Eugene, OR 97403; phone (541) 342-4956.

Deadline: June 20, 2001 postmark

SKIPPING STONES YOUTH HONOR AWARDS
Recognizing youth, ages 7 to 17, for their contributions to multicultural awareness, nature and ecology, social responsibility and community building, peace and non-violence.

Writings and Artwork
Be as realistic or as creative as you choose to be. Your writing and art can include one or more of: social issues, cultural diversity, multilingual awareness, spirituality, religions and cultural celebrations, international understanding, appreciation of nature and/or sustainability issues.

Writings. Essays, interviews, poems, plays, short stories, songs, travelogues, etc., should be typed or neatly handwritten. Non-English or bilingual writings are welcome. Word length is limited to 750 words, poems to 30 lines.

Artwork. Drawings, cartoons, paintings, or photo essays with captions are limited to eight (8) frames. Please include your name, age, and city on the back of each artwork or photo. Black-and-white photos are especially encouraged.

Send your entries by June 20, 2001 with:

1. A cover letter (telling about yourself and your submission, your name, age, school and home addresses) and a self-addressed, stamped envelope.
2. A Certificate of Originality (from your parent or teacher).
3. A $3 entry fee. Low-income and subscribers, including schools, get one free entry. Everyone who enters receives a copy of *Skipping Stones* issue featuring the winning entries.

The top ten winning entries will be published in the Autumn issue of *Skipping Stones*. The winners will also receive an Honor Award Certificate, five multicultural or nature/ecology books, and a subscription to *Skipping Stones*. Other entries may be excerpted as part of a collage on this theme.

Youth Organizations

Using the same format as for Writings, tell us how your club or group works to:

1. Preserve the nature and ecology in your area.
2. Enhance the quality of life for low-income, minority, or disabled people.
3. Improve racial or cultural harmony in your community or school.

Skipping Stones always welcomes your submissions, suggestions and subscriptions ($25/yr., individuals; $35/yr., institutions). Please send your entries by June 20, 2001 to: Youth Honor Awards, *Skipping Stones Magazine*, P.O. Box 3939, Eugene, OR 97403-0930; phone (541) 342-4956; e-mail Skipping@efn.org.

Skipping Stones Honor Awards Entry Form

Instructions: To enter more than one title, please photocopy this form. Use separate forms for each entry. Please use typewriter or print legibly in block letters. Send four (4) copies of books/magazines; two (2) of videos. Include an entry fee of U.S. $50 per entr. (50% discount for low-income or small, non-profit publishers). Books/Magazines (with or without audio supplements) and Videos published between April 1999 - April 2000 are eligible. Entries must be mailed by January 15, 2001. Awards will be announced in the Summer 2002 issue. SEND TO: Skipping Stones Awards, 1309 Lincoln Street, Eugene, OR 97403-0939.

Please check all that apply to your entry:

___ Book ___ Magazine/Publication ___ Educational Video ___ Teaching Resource

Category (select one):

___ Multicultural and International ___ Ecology and Nature ___ Both

Title of Entry: ____________________

Author/Director: ____________________

Illustrator/Producer: ____________________

Publisher/Company Name: ____________________

Address: ____________________

City/State/Postal Code ____________________

Contact Person: ____________________

Tel. No.: (   ) ____________________

Publication/Release Date: (mo/yr) ____________ Price: ________

Press Run: ____________________

Entry Fees: $50 per entry; enclosed please find our check #___
for a sum of $____

Readership/Age level:

__ Elementary grades __Middle grades __ Upper grades __ All ages

Fifty word description of the entry:

____

____

____

____

____

____

____

____

SLEUTHHOUND MAGAZINE

A Whispering Willow Mystery Magazine
2517 South Central
PO Box 890294
Oklahoma City, OK 73189-0294
Phone (405) 239-2531; Fax (405) 236-0502
E-mail wwillows@telepath.com

Deadline: March 31, 2001

DAGGER AWARD
Prize: $200. Any good mystery will qualify.

Deadline: April 1, 2001

SLEUTH REPORTER AWARD
Prize: $100 prize and a *Sleuthhound* ball cap. This award is for the best interview for *Sleuthhound.* The word count limit is 1500.

Deadline: July 31, 2001

TRAVEL AWARD
Prize: $200. This mystery must have happened away from your protagonist's home.

Deadline: September 30, 2001

MYSTERY POETRY AWARD
Prize: $25 and the winner will be published in *Sleuthhound.* Any good mystery poem qualifies. The reading fee is $3.00 for each poem entered.

Deadline: October 31, 2001

BOOKMARK AWARD
Prize: $200. Any good mystery will qualify.

Deadline: December 31, 2001

SLEUTH AWARD
Prize: $250 Your protagonist must be an amateur sleuth.

Whispering Willow Mystery Magazine has a reading fee of $10 for each manuscript entered. The guidelines for contests are the same as the regular submissions (see below). Each winner receives a free copy of *Sleuthhound.* All of the winning stories are published in *Sleuthhound* WWMM.

Submission Guidelines

We accept simultaneous submissions, but we ask that you tell us when you are sending your manuscript to other publishers. Always keep a copy of your manuscript for your files. Editors for WWMM and *Sleuthhound* reserves the right to edit stories as needed for acceptance of manuscripts. *Sleuthhound* buys First North American Serial rights or one time rights. Manuscripts or art without proper return postage are discarded.

Send a clean manuscript that is typed, double spaced, on quality 8-1/2 x 11 inch white paper with margins of at least one inch on all sides. Do not use erasable bond. Good clear photocopies or computer printouts are acceptable. No e-mail or fax submissions please. We like to get the manuscript in on a computer disk, but that is not required. Our computers are PCs IBM-compatible.

The upper left of the page must have your name, address, and telephone number. On the upper right side of the first page beside the story title, place your approximate word count. Center the title of your story 10 spaces from the top. Each page thereafter must have your last name on upper left and numbered consecutively in upper right beside your title.

Please send only one story with each self-addressed, stamped envelope. We like to receive a cover letter, stating your writing credits. Query letters are not necessary, we prefer receiving the completed manuscript. After we are familiar with your writing we may purchase stories or interviews on assignment.

Limit your poetry submissions to three at a time.

Do not send original art work, only copies.

Sleuthhound is a quarterly magazine for writers that includes interviews, tips on writing, cartoons, short stories, poetry, and book reviews. We consider all quality writing from 500 to 5000 words. We pay from three to six cents a word, seventy-five percent of the published work is freelance. We are looking for stories that are in the genre of mystery, or mystery suspense. Interviews can be with any writer, living or deceased, who has made a success with his or her writing. Personal experiences do not have to be mystery. Poetry pays from $5 to $15. We pay on publication. We report from 8 to 12 weeks. The longer we keep the manuscript the better chance it will be purchased.

SLIPSTREAM DEPARTMENT

C Box 2071
Niagara Falls, NY 14301
Website http://wings.buffalo.edu/libraries/units/pl/slipstream

Deadline: December 1, 2001

Award: $1,000 plus 50 copies of winning poetry chapbook manuscript to poet.

Submission Guidelines
Send up to 40 pages of poetry – any style, format, theme (or no theme) along with a self-addressed, stamped envelope with correct return postage for return of your manuscript, and a $10 reading fee.

Simultaneous submissions are okay as long as you keep us informed of status. Previously published poems with acknowledgments and photocopies that are easy on the eyes are also acceptable.

All entrants receive a copy of winning chapbook and a one-issue subscription to *Slipstream Magazine*.

A winner is selected in the Spring at which time all manuscripts are returned. Winner will be featured on the "Grants and Awards" page of *Poets and Writers Magazine* as well as on the Slipstream website. Additional exposure of the winning chapbook will be included in all our catalogs, press releases, and promotional materials.

Submit to above address.

SNAKE NATION REVIEW

110 #2 West Force Street
Valdosta, GA 31601

Deadline: Submissions welcome throughout the year

Snake Nation Review appears three times a year: two contest issues and one non-contest issue.

We welcome submissions throughout the year. All well-written submissions on any topic in any form will be considered. Categories are: Fiction, 5,000 word limit; Poetry, 60 line limit; Essays, 5,000 word limit; and Art, pen & ink drawings and photographs.

Awards for Best Story are First Prize $300, Second Prize $200, and Third Prize $100. Awards for Best Poems are First Prize $100, Second Prize $75, and Third Prize $50. Payment for art is $100. Payments are given for entries published in the non-contest issues. Editors Choice for the non-contest issues wins $100 for each category. Entry fees are $5 for stories and essays and $1 for poems.

Deadline: February 15, 2001

VIOLET HAAS REED PRIZE
This yearly Poetry Contest offers a prize of $500 and publication. Manuscripts should be 50-75 pages in length. There is a $10 entry fee. Winner is determined by an independent judge.

Guidelines

1. List the author's NAME ON TITLE PAGE ONLY.
2. Previously published poems are eligible.
3. Simultaneously submissions are allowed with prompt notification if the piece is accepted elsewhere

Subscriptions are $20 individual; $30 institutions. Each sample copy is $6 (includes mailing). Subscription includes the contest poetry book.

Send submissions to: Snake Nation Press, 110 #2 West Force Street, Valdosta, GA 31601.

SOCIETY OF CHILDREN'S BOOK WRITERS AND ILLUSTRATORS

The Golden Kite Book Award
345 North Maple Drive, Suite 296
Beverly Hills, CA 90210

Barbara Karlin Grant Committee
c/o Larry Dane Brimner
3175 Lincoln Avenue
San Diego, CA 92104

Deadline: February 1, 2001 – December 31, 2001 year of publication

THE GOLDEN KITE BOOK AWARD
Four Golden Kite statuettes – one each for fiction, non-fiction, picture-book text, and picture-illustration – will be awarded each year to the most outstanding children's book published during that year and having been written or illustrated by members of the Society of Children's Book Writers and Illustrators. An Honor Book plaque in each category will be awarded as well. A certificate of acknowledgment will be presented to the author of the picture-illustrated award books.

Eligibility
Recipient must be a member of the Society of Children's Book Writers and Illustrators. For membership information, please contact the Society at 345 North Maple Drive, Suite 296, Beverly Hills, CA 90210.

Every book by a Society of Children's Book Writers and Illustrators member – writer, artist, or photographer – is eligible during the year of original publication. In case of co-authored books, both authors must be Society of Children's Book Writers and Illustrators members.

For the fiction and non-fiction awards, original works and single-author collections of stories or poems of which at least half are new and never before published in a book form are eligible; anthologies and translations are not. For the picture-illustration awards, the art or photographs must be original works (the texts, which may be fiction or non-fiction, may be original, public, domain or previously published).

Submission Guidelines
Three (3) copies of each book entered are to be submitted between February 1 and December 15 of the year of original publication. Galleys may not be submitted.

The panel of judges will consist of two children's book authors and a children's book artist or photographer.

All winners will be notified by April 15th.

Books to be entered, as well as further inquiries, should be submitted to: The Society of Children's Book Writers and Illustrators, 345 North Maple Drive, Suite 296, Beverly Hills, CA 90210

Deadline: April 1, 2001 – May 15, 2001

THE BARBARA KARLIN GRANT

The Barbara Karlin Grant has been established to recognize and encourage the work of aspiring picture book writers.

Eligibilty

The Grant is available to writers, both full and associate members of Society of Children's Book Writers and Illustrators, who have never had a picture-book published. It is not available for a picture-book text on which there is already a contract. One picture-book manuscript per applicant may be submitted. The text may be an original story, work of non-fiction, or a re-telling or adaptation of a fairytale, folktale, or legend.

One Grant, in the amount of $1,000 will be awarded annually. A runner-up grant, in the amount of $500 will also be awarded. The Grant Committee reserves the right to withhold either or both of the grants in any given year.

Acceptable uses of the Grant money are attendance at writing courses, conferences, or workshops; child care; rental of work space; supplemental basic support; other items deemed necessary to further the work of the writer.

Submission Guidelines

Complete four (4) copies of the Grant Application.

Prepare four (4) clearly reproduced copies of the picture-book manuscript, which may be no longer than eight typed, double spaced manuscript pages with adequate margins.

Your name, as listed by the Society of Children's Book Writers and Illustrators, must be the one used on the application form and must appear on the first page of the picture-book manuscript.

Each set of material must be collated, with the application on top, and stapled.

It is essential that these procedures be followed exactly; entries not in compliance will be declared ineligible.

Completed materials will be accepted beginning April 1st and must be received no later than May 15th. Materials will not be returned. Announcement of the Grant recipients will be published in the October/November issue of the Society of Children's Book Writers and Illustrators Bulletin. Individual notification is not possible.

Completed materials should be sent to: Barbara Karlin Grant Committee, c/o Larry Dane Brimner, 3175 Lincoln Avenue, San Diego, CA 92104.

The Society of Children's Book Writers and Illustrators Barbara Karlin Grant Application Form

Name ______________________________

Mailing Address ______________________________

____

Phone ______________________________

Career Summary or Background (please include bibliography of all published work):*

____

____

____

____

____

Plans for use of Grant Money:*

____

____

____

____

Have you applied for any other grants in connection with this work? If so, please list:*

____

____

____

*If additional space is required, use supplemental sheets and staple to the application.

SOMERSAULT PRESS

P.O. Box 1428
El Cerrito, CA 94530-1428
E-mail jisom@crl.com

Deadline: submissions accepted throughout the year

SIDE SHOW: A SHORT STORY ANTHOLOGY
Our aim is to broaden the base of fiction so that it includes writers all across the spectrum for an audience reading primarily for pleasure. We are looking particularly for accomplished writers who feel they have been excluded from publication for reasons other than their merits or those who feel their best work is not being published. Our interest is in promoting the short story form as an art as well as to showcase writers who write fiction with passion and conviction.

We will no longer be publishing our anthology as an annual. From now on, we will publish a book once we have received the requisite number of publishable stories (approximately 20-25). We will be accepting stories all year around. All stories received will be considered for the book (and contest) currently in production or for the next (if we already have a full complement of stories). We anticipate publishing every year and a half or two years. We hope in this way to allow ourselves the time to collect the very best stories being submitted, and also to avoid being bound to a fixed deadline and a commitment to publish a book even when we do not have enough material for it. The anthology will continue to be a good looking perfect-bound paperback book running 250-300 pages in length.

Awards: First prize, $200; Second prize, $100; and Third prize, $75 plus payment of $5 per printed page for all accepted stories.

Guidelines
No pornography, essays, or novels will be accepted. There are no restrictions on length, theme, subject, or style. Our sole criterion is excellence.

With your submission, send a $10 entry fee, which will also entitle you to a copy of the latest *Side Show*.

Multiple submissions are encouraged. One $10 entry fee covers any number of submissions, as long as they are all mailed together in one envelope. Submissions with self-addressed, stamped envelope will be critiqued if requested. All unaccepted manuscripts with self-addressed, stamped envelope will be returned to sender usually within a month of receipt.

Except for the change in publishing our anthology yearly rather than annually, our commitment to finding the best possible unpublished new fiction will remain the same and we hope our format (and payment terms) will make us even more attractive to writers of talent looking for a commensurate venue for their writing.

SONORA REVIEW

Department of English
University of Arizona
Tucson, AZ 85721

SONORA REVIEW WRITING CONTESTS

Deadline: July 1, 2001

POETRY CONTEST
First Prize is $500 and publication in *Sonora Review*. The entry fee is $10 per submission. All entrants receive a copy of *Sonora Review*.

Up to four (4) poems, five page maximum may be entered. Poems must be original and unpublished. No simultaneous submissions are allowed. Include a self-addressed, stamped envelope (required) for return of manuscript. The winner will be announced in *Sonora Review*.

Deadline: July 1, 2001

NON-FICTION CONTEST
First Prize is $150 and publication in *Sonora Review*. The entry fee is $10 per submission, or one year ($12) subscription to *Sonora Review*. All entrants receive a copy of *Sonora Review*.

Manuscripts must be original and unpublished. There are no simultaneous submissions allowed. Include a self-addressed, stamped envelope (required) for return of manuscript. The winner will be announced in *Sonora Review*.

Deadline: December 1, 2001

FICTION CONTEST
First Prize is $500 and publication in *Sonora Review*. The entry fee is $10 per submission. All entrants will receive a copy of *Sonora Review*.

Stories must be original and unpublished. No novel chapters or simultaneous submissions are allowed. Include a self-addressed, stamped envelope (required) for return of manuscript. The winner will be announced in *Sonora Review*.

Send all contest entries to: *Sonora Review*, Poetry, Fiction, or Non-Fiction Contest, Department of English, University of Arizona, Tucson, AZ 85721.

Publication Guidelines for *Sonora Review*

Send complete manuscript with a self-addressed, stamped envelope. Submissions without a a self-addressed, stamped envelope or proper postage will not be returned. A brief cover letter is helpful, but not necessary. We accept simultaneous submissions for publication (not for contest entries) and we always accept photocopied submissions. We report in about two to three months, but be forewarned that delays do occur. All manuscripts must be typed. Fiction and non-fiction must be double spaced, about 8,000 words maximum (with exceptions). Maximum length for poetry is about 12 pages. Payment (other than contest awards): two (2) copies. All rights revert to author on publication.

We are looking for literary work (stories, poems, memoirs, personal essays, creative non-fiction) of lasting value. Works that stay with you, linger, incite revelation. We generally do not consider genre work (i.e., romance, mystery, western, sci-fi, techno-spy-thriller) unless it somehow transcends the boundaries of the genre. We are open to all forms (traditional, experimental, etc.). We encourage you to send us only your best work. Work from our contributors has earned placement in the *O. Henry, Pushcart Prize, Best of the West,* and *Best American Poetry Anthologies.*

SONS OF THE REPUBLIC OF TEXAS

1717 8th Street
Bay City, TX 77414

Deadline: January 15, 2001 postmark

SUMMERFIELD G. ROBERTS AWARD
A cash award of $2,500 will be presented by the Sons of the Republic of Texas to the author of a work of creative writing on the Republic of Texas judged best by the Judging Committee. This award will be presented at the annual membership meeting in the Spring of 2002.

The purpose of this award is to encourage literary effort and research about historical events and personalities during the days of the Republic of Texas, 1836 – 1846, and to stimulate interest in this period.

The judges will determine which manuscript best portrays the spirit, character, strength, and deeds of men and women who lived in the Republic of Texas.

The manuscripts must be written or published during the calendar year for which the award is given. No entry may be submitted more than one time. There is no word limit on the material submitted for the award. The manuscript may be either fiction or non-fiction, poems, essay, plays, short stories, novels, or biographies.

The competition is open to all writers everywhere; neither they nor the publishers need reside in Texas. Judges this year will be winners of the award in the last three years.

Five (5) copies of each entry must be mailed to the General Office of the Sons of the Republic of Texas at the address below, postmarked no later than January 15, 2001. These copies will be used by the judges and added to the archives of the Sons of the Republic of Texas. No copies will be returned.

Submit entries to: General Office of the Sons of the Republic of Texas, 1717 8th Street, Bay City, TX 77414.

SOUTH CAROLINA FICTION PROJECT

South Carolina Arts Commission
1800 Gervais Street
Columbia, SC 29201

Deadline: January 15, 2001 postmark

The 18th Annual South Carolina Fiction Project will be sponsored by *The Post and Courier* and the South Carolina Arts Commission. The competition is open to any writer (except for the previous year's winners) who is a legal resident of South Carolina and 18 years of age or older at the time of application. Each writer whose work is selected will receive $500 from *The Post and Courier*, which purchases first publication rights.

Guidelines
The writing competition calls for previously unpublished short stories (approximately 1,000 to 2,500 words). Manuscripts must be postmarked no later than January 15, 2001 and must be typed, double spaced. (Dot matrix print must be at lest 24 pin.) Each writer must send four (4) copies of the manuscript. No manuscripts will be returned. Only one short story per writer will be accepted. Please note that 2000 winners will not be eligible to enter again until 2002.

The author's name should not appear anywhere on the manuscript or copies, but the story's title must be on the manuscript and copies. Attach a separate cover sheet (no copies) on which the following information is typed: the author's name, address, daytime telephone number, social security number, and the story's title.

Stories will be judged by a panel of professional writers; selection will be based on literary quality and suitability for a general newspaper audience. The stories do not need to be Southern, nor do they need to be set in South Carolina, although such stories are acceptable for consideration.

Up to 12 short stories will be accepted for publication; the author of each manuscript selected will be notified no later than June 1, 2001. All writers will be notified no later than July 1, 2001.

All manuscripts should be sent to: South Carolina Fiction Project, South Carolina Arts Commission, 1800 Gervais St., Columbia, SC 29201.

SOUTH CAROLINA PLAYWRIGHTS' FESTIVAL

Trustus Theatre
P.O. Box 11721
Columbia, SC 29211-1721

Deadline: January 1, 2002 – March 15, 2002
The selection process enables the playwright and company of actors to spend an entire year working on the winning script. For the 2003 festival submissions deadline is from January 1, to March 15, 2002. Award: $250 and a staged reading. For the next 12 months, Trustus will give the play several readings while it is being refined. The play will then receive a full production and the playwright will receive an additional $500, plus travel and lodging.

Guidelines
Full-length plays (80 minutes or more), preferably one set, maximum cast of 8, with minimum production needs.

Casting roles in the late 50s and over is difficult, but not impossible.

No musicals and no children's shows will be accepted.

Submission Guidelines
Along with the application submit a resumé and two synopsis of the play. Do not send your script. If Trustus decides to select your script for entry, you will be notified and invited to send it with a $15 entry fee, and a self-addressed, stamped envelope large enough to contain the script, with proper postage affixed thereto, for return to you once the winner is selected.

Submissions should be sent to above address.

THE SOUTHERN ANTHOLOGY

The Southern Prize
2851 Johnston Street, Suite123
Lafayette, LA 70503

Deadline: May 30, 2001 postmark

THE SOUTHERN PRIZE FOR FICTION AND POETRY
The Southern Anthology encourages both traditional and avant-garde writing. Submissions need not address "Southern" themes, and should reflect a 75,000 word count. The Grand Prize Award is $600 and publication. The six finalists will be published. Stipends are available for all finalists. Winners and finalists will be announced on December 15, 2001.

Eligibility
All entries should be written in English, regardless of the author's citizenship. Staff and employees of The Southern Anthology, and their families, are not eligible. No previously published work will be accepted.

Guidelines
Submit one story, one fiction excerpt, or three poems. A $10 entry fee is required, payable to "The Southern Prize." Include a self-addressed, stamped envelope and telephone number for notification. No entry forms are necessary.

Entries should be postmarked by May 30, 2001.

Manuscripts must be typed on 8-1/2 x 11 inch paper. Legible photocopies and computer print-outs are acceptable.

Authors should keep personal copies of submitted work. Manuscripts will not be returned.

Mail entries to: The Southern Anthology, The Southern Prize, 2851 Johnston St. #123, Lafayette, LA 70503.

THE SOUTHERN CALIFORNIA ANTHOLOGY MASTER OF PROFESSIONAL WRITING PROGRAM

WPH 404
University of Southern California
Los Angeles, CA 90089-4034

Deadline: January 1, 2001 – April 15, 2001

THE ANN STANFORD POETRY PRIZE
The 14th annual Ann Stanford Poetry Prize offers a First Place award of $750, Second Place award of $250, and a Third Place award of $100. The judge is to be announced. Winning entries will be published. All other manuscripts will be considered for publication.

Submission Guidelines
Send up to five (5) poems with a $10 reading fee payable to The Southern California Anthology. All entrants will receive a free issue of The Southern California Anthology.

All poems must be typed and previously unpublished.

Complete the entry form with your name, address, and titles of poems. No name or address should appear on the manuscript copy.

Include a self-addressed, stamped envelope for contest results.

Mail submissions to: Contest Entry, The Southern California Anthology Master of Professional Writing Program, WPH 404, University of Southern California, Los Angeles, CA 90089-4034.

The Southern California Anthology
Master of Professional Writing Program
Entry Form

Use the following form (photocopies are acceptable) and enter all the information requested. Please write or type clearly. Thanks.

ANN STANFORD POETRY PRIZE

Author Information:

Name ______________________________

Address ______________________________

____

____

Day Phone ______________________________

Night Phone ______________________________

Titles of Poems (limited to 5):

____

#1 ______________________________

#2 ______________________________

#3 ______________________________

#4 ______________________________

#5

Send your contest entry between January 1 and April 15, 2001. Be sure to include a check or money order for $10.00; entries without the fee will be returned unread. Due to the high number of entries, we cannot return manuscripts unless accompanied by a self-addressed, stamped envelope with sufficient postage.

SOUTHERN ENVIRONMENTAL LAW CENTER

Cathryn McCue, Communications Coordinator
Southern Environmental Law Center
201 West Main Street, Suite 14
Charlottesville, VA 22902-5065
E-mail cmccue@selcva.org

Deadline: March 1, 2001 postmark
PHILLIP D. REED MEMORIAL AWARD FOR OUTSTANDING WRITING ON THE SOUTHERN ENVIRONMENT
A prize of $1,000 will be awarded to the winner, announced the last week of May. The Southern Environmental Law Center requests submissions for our annual Phillip D. Reed Memorial Award for Outstanding Writing on the Southern Environment. The award seeks to enhance public awareness of the richness and vulnerability of the South's natural resources by recognizing and encouraging excellent writing on the region's environment. Past winners have explored a wide range of issues, including how the city of Atlanta and developers pollute the Chattahoochee River, how rapid proliferation of chip mills is devastating southern forests, and how fast-paced development in the Carolinas is detroying plant and animal life.

The award is named in memory of Phillip D. Reed, a founding trustee of SELC who helped guide our organization through the early years. A talented attorney, committed environmental activist, and discriminating editor of the widely read *Environmental Law Reporter*, Phil was known for his ebullient spirit and inquiring intellect. When he died unexpectedly in 1993 at age 47, SELC established the writing award in his honor.

Guidelines
Works published during calendar year 2000 only, will be considered.

Submissions must relate to the southern environment within or including at least one of the following states: Alabama, Georgia, North Carolina, South Carolina, Tennessee and Virgina.

Entries must be a significant, sustained effort such as a book, long article, monograph, or collection or series of newspaper stories.

Minimum length of 3,000 words for each entry. Entries must be submitted in their entirety.

The award will be made to an individual author or two co-authors. Submissions with more than two authors must indicate which two authors are being nominated. Each author must meet the minimum word requirement, or the submission will be disqualified.

Nominations can be made by the author or by others.

Send eight (8) copies, at least one of which must be in the format in which it originally appeared.

Please include name, address, and phone number of author.

All submissions become the property of SELC unless accompanied by a written request and appropriate return address information.

Nominees will be judged by a panel of distinguished writers and two Trustees of the Southern Environmental Law Center.

Nominations and/or inquiries should be sent to: Cathryn McCue, Communications Coordinator

SOUTHERN POETRY REVIEW

Ken Mclaurin, Editor
Advancement Studies
CPCC
Charlotte, NC 28235

Deadline: April 1, 2001 – April 30, 2001

THE GUY OWEN POETRY PRIZE
Established in memory of Guy Owen, poet, fiction writer, friend of the arts, and founder of *Southern Poetry Review*.

The Guy Owen Poetry Prize is $500, and the award-winning poem will be published in the Winter 2001 issue of *Southern Poetry Review*. All others will be considered for future publication. The final judge is Walter McDonald.

Guidelines
Submit three to five original, previously unpublished poems. There is no restriction on style or content. Entry fee is a subscription to *Southern Poetry Review* ($8.00) to begin with the Winter 2001 issue. Submissions should be mailed only during the month of April. The winner will be announced in July.

Submit entries in an envelope marked "Guy Owen Poetry Prize," accompanied by a self-addressed, stamped envelope.

Mail entries to: Ken Mclaurin, Editor, *Southern Poetry Review*, Advancement Studies, CPCC, Charlotte, NC 28235.

THE SOUTHERN REVIEW

Louisiana State University
43 Allen Hall
Baton Rouge, LA 70803-5005
Phone (504) 388-5108; Fax (504) 388-5098

Deadline: January 31, 2001

SHORT FICTION AWARD
Prize: $500 and the possibility of the winner being invited to the campus for a reading. Short Fiction Award for the best first collection of short stories by an American citizen published in the United States. Deadline for submissions to be considered for the 2001 prize will be January 31, 2001.

Two manuscript copies should be sent by the publisher to the editors of *The Southern Review*/LSU Short Fiction Award at the above address.

THE SOW'S EAR POETRY REVIEW

Larry K. Richman, Managing Editor
Mary Calhoun, Graphics Consultant
19535 Pleasant View Drive
Abingdon, VA 24211-6827
Phone (540) 628-2651
E-mail richman@preferred.com

ANNUAL CONTESTS

Deadline: March 1, 2001 – May 1, 2001 postmark

CHAPBOOK COMPETITION
Awards are First Place $500, 25 copies, publication, and distribution to subscribers; Second Place is $200; and Third Place is $100.

Submission Guidelines
Send 22-26 pages of poetry plus a title page and a table of contents, all without your name. On a separate sheet list chapbook title, your name, address, phone number, and publication credits if any. There is no length limit on poems, but put no more than one poem on a page. Send the manuscript in March or April 2001. Postmarked deadline is May 1. Simultaneous submission is OK, but if your chapbook is accepted elsewhere, you must withdraw from our competition. Poems previously published are acceptable if you hold publication rights. Reading fee is $10. Send a self-addressed, stamped envelope for notification. Entries will not be returned but will be recycled.

Deadline: September 1, 2001 – November 1, 2001 postmark

POETRY COMPETITION
Awards are First Place $1,000, Second Place $250, and Third Place $100, and the option of publication for approximately twenty finalists.

Submission Guidelines
Send unpublished poems (no length limit) to the above address. Please do not put your name on poems. Include a separate sheet with name, address, and titles of poems. Simultaneous submission is acceptable. (We will check with finalists on status of poems before sending to final judge.) Entering five (5) poems or more entitles you to a subscription. Send the manuscript in September or October. Postmark deadline November 1, 2001. The final judge will be announced later. Reading fee is $2 per poem. Include a self-addressed, stamped envelope for notification, which we will try to send in January. Entries will not be returned but will be recycled.

Subscriptions
A year's subscription is $10.00 ($15 Canada, $20 other) and includes three issues and the year's winning chapbook. Sample copies are available at $5 each.

Publication Guidelines for *Sow's Ear Poetry Review*
Send us one to five poems, a biographical note, and the usual self-addressed, stamped envelope. There is no length limit on poems. We welcome submissions from unpublished poets. We accept occasional reviews and interviews, but most are commissioned. We publish no fiction. We welcome submission of black-and-white art and photography.

The Sow's Ear Poetry Review is a component of The Word Process, a non-profit Virginia corporation, 19535 Pleasant View Dr., Abingdon, VA 24211-6827; phone (540) 628-2651; Larry K. Richman, Managing Editor; Mary Calhoun, Graphics Consultant.

SPOON RIVER POETRY REVIEW

4240 Department of English
Illinois State University
Normal, IL 61790-4240

Deadline: April 15, 2001 postmark

SPOON RIVER POETRY REVIEW EDITOR'S PRIZE CONTEST
Prize: One award of $500 and two runners-ups $100 each. All winning poems and selected honorable mentions will be published in the Fall issue of *Spoon River Poetry Review.*

Guidelines
Submissions must be two copies of three unpublished poems, maximum of ten pages total. The name, address, and phone number of the poet should appear on each page of one copy only.

There is an entry fee of $15; make check payable to *Spoon River Poetry Review*. Each entry fee entitles entrant to a one-year subscription to *Spoon River Poetry Review*, or an extension of their current subscription or may be used as a gift subscription. Please indicate your choice and a current address for subscription or gift subscription.

Entries will not be returned. Entries cannot be received by fax. Include a self-addressed, stamped envelope for notification of winners. If all guidelines are not exactly followed, entry must be disqualified.

Send submissions to above contest and address.

STANLEY DRAMA AWARD

Department of Theatre & Speech
Wagner College
631 Howard Avenue
Staten Island NY 10301

Deadline: October 1, 2001

STANLEY DRAMA AWARD
The Stanley Drama Award is presented as a memorial to Alma Timolat Stanley (Mrs. Robert C. Stanley). The Stanley Drama Award will offer a prize of $2000 for an original full-length play, musical, or one-act play sequence that has not been professionally produced or received trade book publication.

Guidelines
We will consider only one submission (a single full-length play, musical, or one-act sequence) per playwright. Plays entered previously in the competition may not be resubmitted. Former Stanley Award winners are not eligible to compete.

A reading fee of $20 must accompany the manuscript.

Only stage plays are considered for the Stanley Drama Award. Scripts designed for other media (e.g. screenplays, teleplays, radio plays, hypertext dramas) are not eligible. Writers of musicals are urged to submit music on cassette tapes (not reel-to-reel) as well as book and lyrics.

All scripts must be typed or word-processed. Handwritten manuscripts will not be accepted. In addition, please make sure your entry is easy to read – i.e., typed according to one of the standard formats, on plain white letter-sized paper, and printed clearly (no dot-matrix). If for any reason your script is difficult to read, it will be discarded unread.

Bind your manuscript in a simple report cover that fastens the pages securely together. Unbound manuscripts will not be read.

Enclose check or money order for $20 US funds, payable to "Wagner College".

Include a self-addressed, stamped post card if you wish to be advised that we have received your script. Include a self-addressed, stamped envelope if you wish to be notified of the winner of the Award. Unhappily, due to changes in postal regulations, we can no longer return manuscripts. (We do recycle, however).

All entries must be accompanied by a completed application form. This form may be photocopied; or you may obtain additional applications by writing to the Department of Theatre and Speech, Wagner College, 631 Howard Avenue, Staten Island, N.Y. 10301. If you do write, please enclose an self-addressed, stamped envelope.

STILL WATERS PRESS

459 Willow Avenue
Galloway Township, NJ 08201-4633

POETRY CHAPBOOK COMPETITIONS
Still Waters Press holds two poetry chapbook competitions annually. The winner of each competition receives professional publication of the chapbook, 25 free copies, the lifetime privilege of purchasing future copies of his or her chapbook at 50% off the retail price, review distribution, and a professional publicity package.

Deadline: February 28, 2001 postmark

THE WOMEN'S WORDS COMPETITION
Open to women only.

Deadline: September 30, 2001 postmark

THE WINTER COMPETITION
Open to men and women.

Submission Guidelines
Aside from the gender restrictions and the different deadlines, the guidelines and awards for both competitions are identical.

Length should be 24-28 manuscript pages maximum, including front and back matter (i.e., table of contents, brief biography, previous publication, credits).

Previous publication is not required, but if you do have "previous publication" history on any or all of the manuscript poems, you must provide a list of these credits and either your assurance that YOU hold the copyright on each, OR the permission from the previous publisher to reprint in the chapbook, if you win.

Page format is single spaced or double spaced, one poem (no matter how short!) per page, typed on the front of white, 8-1/2 x 11 inch paper. Number every page: Title every poem (if one poem is not titled, then NO poem should be titled. We have published some chapbooks in which poems have consecutive numbers only as titles). Do not send chapbooks already published in the chapbook form.

A self-addressed, stamped envelope is required. Enclose a self-addressed, stamped envelope with sufficient postage affixed for your manuscript's return, OR enclose a #10 stamped envelope for contest results if you do not need your manuscript returned.

A reading fee is required. Please include a $10 check or money order. No foreign checks or money orders, please (our bank charges $15.00 to process such instruments, so obviously, we don't want them). International submissions are welcome but please send fee in $10 U.S. funds via Certified Mail.

Simultaneous submissions are permited; however, please notify us immediately if a simultaneously submitted chapbook manuscript is placed with another publisher for publication in chapbook or book form. Such placement disqualifies it from the Still Waters Press Chapbook competition. The reading fee is not refunded in such a case.

Submit entries to: Still Waters Press, 459 Willow Avenue, Galloway Township, NJ 08201-4633.

Three helpful pamphlets are available from Still Waters Press at $3 each: 1. *What Is a Chapbook? How to Prepare a Winner*, 2. *Lyric Modes: Voices & Choices*; and 3. *The Poet & Her Persona.*

STATE UNIVERSITY OF NEW YORK AT FARMINGDALE

Margery L. Brown
English Department
Knapp Hall
SUNY at Farmingdale
Route 110
Farmingdale, NY 11735
E-mail brownml@farmingdale.edu

Deadline: September 15, 2001

THE PAUMANOK POETRY AWARD
The Visiting Writers Program at SUNY Farmingdale announces the 10th annual competition for The Paumanok Poetry Award. Awards include one First Prize of $1,000 and expenses for a reading in our year 2002 – 2003 series; and two Second Prizes of $500, and expenses for a reading in our series.

Submission Guidelines
Interested writers should send the following items to the above address: a cover letter; a one-paragraph biography; three to five of their best poems (no more than ten pages, total); and the required $12 entry fee.

Poems may be published or unpublished, and there are no restrictions on style, subject matter, or length of poems submitted: quality is the single criterion. Please note that the writer's name, address, and phone number should be clearly indicated on the cover page.

Only one entry per person will be accepted.

Make checks payable to SUNY Farmingdale VWP.

Poems will not be returned, but writers who want to know the results of the competition should enclose a business-size, self-addressed stamped envelope for results (notification by late December). Deadline is September 15, 2001.

Send entries to: Margery L. Brown, English Department, Knapp Hall, SUNY Farmingdale, Route 110, Farmingdale, New York 11735.

For further information, e-mail to Margery Brown:
brownml@farmingdale.edu.

STORY LINE PRESS

Three Oaks Farm
Brownsville, OR 97327-9718
Phone (541) 466-5352; Fax (541) 466-3200
E-mail /slp@ptinet.com/www.ptinet.com/-slp

Deadline: May 1, 2001 – October 15, 2001

NICHOLAS ROERICH POETRY PRIZE
The 15th annual Nicholas Roerich Poetry Prize is a first book contest. Poets who have not published a full-length volume (48 pages) are eligible.

The winner receives: book publication by Story Line Press in Fall 2002; a book launch at the Roerich Museum in New York City; and a monetary prize of $1,000. One runner-up earns a full scholarship to the Wesleyan Writers Conference in Middletown, CT, as the Nicholas Roerich/Story Line Press Fellow.

Submission Guidelines
Manuscripts must be typewritten, single or double spaced (clear photocopies acceptable). Poems may have been previously published in journals or anthologies. Manuscripts need not be "blind" and should include the author's name on title page.

Postmark should be between May 1 and October 15, 2001.

Send the following to Story Line Press:

1. A manuscript of original poetry in English of at least 48 pages. Poems may be of any length and style.

2. A biographical sketch, one paragraph in length.

3. A properly-sized, self-addressed stamped envelope for manuscript return (no meter strips accepted). If you do not want the manuscript returned, please include a business-sized, self-addressed, stamped envelope for announcement of winners. We will not return manuscripts without proper postage.

4. A $20.00 reading/handling fee, check payable to Story Line Press.

5. Applicants may receive a complimentary copy of the winning book. Include an envelope of at least 6 x 9 inches with $1.50 postage attached. Please mark envelope "For Winning Book."

Notification will be in February, 2001.

Potential applicants are strongly encouraged to familiarize themselves with previous winners. Titles from 1988–1995 are available for $5 each, 1996-1997 for $8 each. Add $2 shipping for the first book, $.50 for each additional book

Submit entries to: Three Oaks Farm, Brownsville, OR 97327-9718.

SUB-TERRAIN MAGAZINE & ANVIL PRESS PUBLISHERS

175 East Broadway, #204-a
Vancouver, British Columbia CANADA V5T 1W2
Phone (604) 876-8710; Fax (604) 879-2667
E-mail subter@pinc.com

THE INTERNATIONAL THREE-DAY NOVEL-WRITING CONTEST
The communal Home of The International Three-Day Novel-Writing Contest is now in its 23rd year! Every Labor Day weekend entrants participate from around the world. Research and outlines prior to the contest are permissible, but the actual writing must take place over the long weekend. For a complete copy of the rules, send a self-addressed, stamped envelope to the address above. Entry fee is $25.00. The winner is announced November 30th. The Grand Prize is an offer of publication from Anvil Press.

Deadline: January 1, 2001 – May 15, 2001

THE sub-TERRAIN SHORT STORY CONTEST
Formerly the Penny Dreadful, our short story contest is now in its 10th year. Any unpublished fiction of 2,000 words or less is eligible. There is a one-time, one-story entry fee of $15; additional stories may be submitted with a supplementary fee of $5 per story. The winner is announced by June 15th. Winners receive a cash prize of $500, plus publication in the Summer issue. Entrants receive a four-issue subscription to sub-TERRAIN. Entries are accepted between January 1st and May 15th each year.

Deadline: August 1, 2001 – January 31, 2002

THE LAST POEMS POETRY CONTEST
A maximum of four (4) poems per entry is allowed. A one-time entry fee is $15. The winner is announced March 1st. The winner receives a cash prize of $250, plus publication in the Spring issue. Entrants also receive a four-issue subscription to sub-TERRAIN. Entries are accepted between August 1st and January 31st each year.

Deadline: August 1, 2001

THE CREATIVE NON-FICTION CONTEST
Creative non-fiction doesn't report as much as tells. It's a story conveying not "just the facts, ma'am," but an experience, a tale complete with true events, utilizing the tools of fiction, if necessary, to present itself.

We all tell stories, and a simple account of "a day in the life" can be an extraordinary example of creative non-fiction.

Submissions are not limited to any specific topic or subject, but should be 2,000 to 4,000 words maximum. Entry fee is $15 per story. Deadline is August 1st. Award is a cash prize of $250, plus publication in the Fall issue of the magazine. All entrants receive a four-issue subscription to sub-TERRAIN.

Additional Guidelines
All submissions must be accompanied by a self-addressed, stamped envelope and typed on 8-1/2 x 11 inch paper, double spaced (no disks or e-mail submissions, please).

Published three times a year, subscriptions to sub-TERRAIN are available $18/four issues and $34/eight issues. Sample copies are $5 each, postpaid.

Send entries and subscriptions to: 175 East Broadway #204-a, Vancouver, BC, V5T 1W2 Canada.

SUNSET CENTER

P.O. Box 1950
Carmel, CA 93921
Phone (408) 624-3996 (Administration)
Phone (408) 626-1288 (Community Activities and Recreation)

Deadline: June 15, 2001 – August 31, 2001

FESTIVAL OF FIRSTS PLAY WRITING COMPETITION
Prize: Up to $1,000
Submissions accepted from June 15, 2001 to postmark August 31, 2001. Not before or after.

Guidelines
For the 22nd Annual Carmel by the Sea competition
All submissions must be an original, unproduced, full-length stage play. There is a $15 (non-refundable) registration fee for each script submitted. Scripts must include a cast list, synopsis, and an entry form.

No musicals or operas accepted. Scripts must be contained in a binder or something similar; no loose scripts will be considered. The Sunset Center reserves the right to produce the winning play in its premiere performance within four months of announcing the winner.

Include a self-addressed, stamped envelope with appropriate return postage if you wish manuscript to be returned. The judges of this competition reserve the right to withhold the awards. Send submissions to the above contest and address.

22nd Annual Carmel By The Sea Competition Entry Form

Please submit this entry form with script.

Name of Play ______________________________

____

Name ______________________________

Address ______________________________

City ______________ State ______ Zip ______

Phone ______________________________

Social Security Number ______________________________

Payment Enclosed $ _______

TENNESSEE WRITERS ALLIANCE

Box 120396
Nashville, TN 37212
Phone (615) 385-5685
E-mail Tnsal@aol.com.
Website www. Concerthall.com/t-w-a.html.

TENNESSEE WRITERS ALLIANCE LITERARY COMPETITIONS

Deadline: May 31, 2001 postmark

MARTHA WITMORE HICKMAN FICTION COMPETITION
Twenty finalists will be chosen, from which the first, second, and third prize winners will be selected. First Prize is $500, Second Prize is $250, and Third Prize is $100. The prizes will be presented at a special session of the Southern Festival of Books, in Nashville, in October 2001. Winning stories also may be included in a future Tennessee Writers Alliance anthology.

Eligibility
Only residents of Tennessee or members of the Tennessee Writers Alliance are eligible to enter the competition. Out-of state residents may qualify to enter by joining the Alliance. (Membership fees for the Alliance are $25.00 a year, or $15 a year for full-time students.)

Submission Guidelines
Submitted stories can be up to 3,500 words in length; and any form or subject matter. Stories must be original and previously unpublished. There is no limit on the number of stories that may be entered in the competition.

Each submitted entry must have two clear copies of the stories. All entries must be in typed form. The author's name MUST NOT appear on the story itself. A cover page containing the author's name, address, phone number, and the title of the story must accompany each entry. Include a separate cover page for each story submitted. Entries that do not meet these requirements will not be considered eligible for the competition. All entries must be postmarked no later than May 31, 2001.

Each submitted story must be accompanied by an entry fee of $10 for Alliance members, or $15 for non-members.

The Tennessee Writers Alliance reserves the right to disqualify any entry that does not adhere to the above rules. In the event that an entry must be disqualified, the entry fee will not be refunded. We regret that we cannot acknowledge receipt of manuscripts entered in the competition, nor can we provide reports on the status of entries before the winners are announced. Manuscripts will not be returned, but competition results will be sent to entrants who include a stamped, self-addressed envelope with their submission.

Each entry must be sent to the following address: TWA Literary Competition, Box 120396, Nashville, TN 37212.

Questions? Call (615) 385-5685 or e-mail Tnsal@aol.com.
Further information is also available on the TWA Home Page: www. Concerthall.com/t-w-a.html.

Deadline: May 31, 2001 postmark

THE H. JACKSON BROWN AWARDS FOR NON-FICTION
Twenty finalist will be chosen, from which the first, second, and third prize winners will be selected. First Prize is $500, Second Prize is $250, and Third Prize is $100. The awards and cash prizes, made possible through the generosity of H. Jackson Brown, will be presented at a special session of the Southern Festival of Books, in Nashville, in October 2001. Winning essays also may be included in a future Tennessee Writers Alliance anthology.

Eligibility
The contest is open to all writers.

Submission Guidelines
All submissions must be original and unpublished, typed and double spaced, and should not exceed 3,000 words in length. Entrants are strongly discouraged from submitting annotated work. Only one submission per individual, please.

Each entry should be submitted in two (2) copies, each with a separate cover sheet with the title of the piece submitted, the author's name, address, and phone number. The author's name MUST NOT appear anywhere on the manuscript. All entries must be post marked no later than May 31, 2001.

Each submission must be accompanied by an entry fee of $10 for members of the Tennessee Writers Alliance, and $15 for non-members.

The Tennessee Writers Alliance reserves the right to disqualify any entry that does not adhere to the above rules. In the event that an entry must be disqualified, the entry fee will not be refunded. We regret that we cannot acknowledge receipt of manuscripts entered in the competition, nor can we provide reports on the status of entries before the winners are announced. Manuscripts will not be returned, but competition results will be sent to entrants who include a stamped, self-addressed envelope with their submission.

Each entry must be sent to the following address: TWA Literary Competition, Box 120396, Nashville, TN 37212.

Questions? Call 615/385-5685 or e-mail Tnsal@aol.com.
Further information is also available on the TWA Home Page: www.Concerthall.com/t-w-a.html.

TENNIS WEEK

Eugene L. Scott, Publisher
341 Madison Avenue, 6th Floor
New York, NY 10017

Deadline: none

TENNIS WEEK WRITING AWARDS
Tennis Week presents its annual journalist competition open to tennis writers of all levels of experience. Each year prizes will be awarded to six winners. If you are a journalist or hope to someday be one, this is a unique opportunity to see your work in print.

The categories are:

1. Aspiring Journalists: For writers with no byline.

2. "Non-Tennis" Journalists: For writers who do not cover the tennis "beat" regularly (to expand the game's overall body of high quality journalism).

3. Tennis Journalists: For writers who specialize in tennis.

4,5,6. Tennis Journalism: Three categories for a tennis-related article, essay, or feature story that has appeared in any publication worldwide (English only). One award each to journalists who write to a daily deadline, and to the best book or manuscript.

Submission Guidelines
Submissions from authors in categories 1, 2, and 3 must be original works, 1,000-2,000 words in length, for publication in *Tennis Week*. All entries must be type written (word processor printer is acceptable). Each submission must be on 8-1/2 x 11 inch paper.

The rules are simple. The subject matter is tennis, and the format is limitless, narrative, essay, poem, fiction, and/or dialogue. The work must be in English.

All entries become property of *Tennis Week* and will not be returned.

All materials should be sent to: Eugene L. Scott, Publisher, *Tennis Week*, 341 Madison Ave., 6th Floor, New York, NY 10017.

THE TEXAS INSTITUTE OF LETTERS

Judy Alter
Box 298300
Fort Worth, Texas 76129

Deadline: January 3, 2001

The Texas Institute of letters annually awards almost $19,999 in competitions in fiction, nonfiction, poetry, translations, short story, journalism, design and children's books. Submissions must be made by the first working day of the new year.

For 2001 guidelines, inquire no earlier than 2001: Dr. Mark Busby, Center for Southwestern Studies, Southwest Texas State University, San Marcos TX 78666.

Contact Judy Alter at above address with any questions.

THEATRE CONSPIRACY INC.

Bill Taylor, Artistic Director
10091 McGregor Boulevard
Fort Myers, FL 33919
Phone (941) 936-3239; Fax (941) 936-0510

Deadline: January 31, 2001

FOURTH ANNUAL NEW PLAY CONTEST
Plays will be read and judged by qualified theatre teachers, directors and performers. The winning play will be part of the New Arts Festival, a nationally recognized festival of theatre, dance, music, and visual arts. Prize: $500 and full production in the New Arts Festival in early August of 2001.

Submission Guidelines
Plays must be full length with eight characters or less and have simple to moderate technical demands. The play must not have been previously produced. No musicals are accepted.

A non-refundable administrative fee of $10.00 payable to Theatre Conspiracy is required. Do not mail cash.

Send: complete script, self-addressed, stamped envelope with sufficient return postage if you would like script to be returned, playwright biography, and character breakdown to Bill Taylor at above contest and address.

TORONTO BOOK AWARDS

Toronto Book Awards Committee
c/o Toronto Protocol Office
City Clerk
10th Floor, West Tower, City Hall
Toronto, ON M5H 2N2 Canada
Phone (416) 392-8191
Website www.city.toronto.on.ca/ourcity/tba_index.htm

Deadline: February 28, 2001
The City of Toronto and the Toronto Book Awards Committee invites publishers and authors to submit books for consideration and review for the twenty-seventh annual Toronto Book Awards. To be eligible for the year 2001 awards, books must be published between January 1 and December 31, 2000. The deadline for the year 2001 submissions is February 28, 2001. These annual awards offering $15,000 in prize money are one of the richest book awards in Canada. Each short-listed author (usually four to six) receives $1,000 and the winning author is awarded the remainder (usually $9,000 to $11,000).

Guidelines
Fiction and non-fiction books for adults and/or children that are evocative of Toronto are eligible.

Reprints, textbooks and manuscripts are not eligible.

There are no separate categories: novels, short story collections, books of poetry, biographies, histories, social studies, children's books, books about sports, photographic collections, etc., are judged together.

There are no entry forms to complete. Simply submit five (5) copies of the book you consider eligible, along with your name, address and phone number to the above address.

The 2001 Toronto Book Awards short-list finalists will be announced in early September and the winner announced at The Word On The Street Festival which will be held in September 2001.

Judging will be done by the Toronto Book Awards Committee.

For more information on the Toronto Book Awards, visit the City of Toronto's website at www.city.toronto.on.ca/ourcity/tba_index.htm or call (416) 392-8191.

The Toronto Book Awards were first presented by Toronto City Council in 1974 to honour authors of books of literary or artistic merit that are evocative of Toronto.

To achieve its goal of elimination of illiteracy in the City of Toronto, the city continues to work with its community partners on numerous literacy projects and initiatives including the Toronto Book Awards. The announcement coincides with various International Literacy Month celebrations that take place in September.

TOWSON STATE UNIVERSITY

Dan L. Jones, Dean
College of Liberal Arts
Towson University
Towson, MD 21204-7097

Deadline: May 15, 2001

TOWSON STATE UNIVERSITY PRIZE FOR LITERATURE
Established with a grant from Alice and Franklin Cooley, the Towson State University Prize for Literature is awarded annually for a single book or book-length manuscript of fiction, poetry, drama, or imaginative non-fiction by a young Maryland writer. The $1,000 prize is granted on the basis of literary and aesthetic excellence as determined by a panel of distinguished judges appointed by the university.

Eligibility
Any individual, institution, group, or publisher may nominate one or more works for the prize. The prize shall be awarded for a single book or book-length manuscript of fiction, poetry, drama, or imaginative non-fiction published within the three years prior to the year of nomination (or be scheduled for publication within the year in which nominated).

The author must be no more than 40 years of age and must have resided within the State of Maryland at least three years at the time of nomination, and must be a resident of the State of Maryland at the time the prize is awarded. Verification of age and residence may be required.

The winning author must be willing to be present at the award ceremony and must grant to Towson State University the right to quote from the winning work in any publicity related to the prize.

Submission Guidelines
The applicant must submit by certified mail five (5) copies of each work, in bound form if it has been published; and in typewritten, double spaced manuscript form if it has not. If a typewritten manuscript is submitted, a copy of the contract or the letter of acceptance from the publisher indicating the proposed date of publication must be enclosed.

A completed nomination form must accompany each submission.

All submissions become the property of Towson State University and will not be returned.

The deadline for submission of all materials is May 15, each year.

For additional nomination forms and other details, write to Dan L. Jones, Dean, College of Liberal Arts, Towson University, Towson, MD 21204-7097.

Towson State University
Nomination Form

NAME OF AUTHOR ______________________

DATE OF BIRTH ______________________

ADDRESS ______________________

CITY/STATE/ZIP ______________________

PHONE (WORK) ______________ (HOME) ______________

NOMINATED BY ______________________

CATEGORY OF WORK ______________________

TITLE OF WORK ______________________

____

NUMBER OF PAGES ______________________

PUBLISHER ______________________

____

DATE OF PUBLICATION ______________________

ADDITIONAL INFORMATION ABOUT NOMINEE AND WORK ______________________

THE HARRY S. TRUMAN LIBRARY INSTITUTE FOR NATIONAL AND INTERNATIONAL AFFAIRS

500 West U.S. Highway 24
Independence, MO 64050-1798

Deadline: received before January 20, 2001

HARRY S. TRUMAN BOOK AWARD
Prize: $1,000
A biennial competition for the best book on Harry S. Truman or the period of his Presidency published between January 1, 1999 and December 31, 2000.

Award was established in 1963 for recognition of the best book written within a two-year period dealing primarily and substantially with some aspect of the history of the United States between April 12, 1945 and January 20, 1953 or with the public career of Harry S. Truman. The award is given in even numbered years.

Three copies of each book entered must be submitted to the Book Award Administrator, at the above address.

TWS CRITIQUE GROUP

P.O. Box 167
Forsyth, IL 62535

Deadline: July 15, 2001 postmark

TWS CRITIQUE GROUP SYNOPSIS CONTEST
Entry must be your own original work, a synopsis of no more that 100 words, excluding title, of an unpublished fiction novel written by you. Winner will be required to submit the entire manuscript. Do not submit non-fiction. One prize of $10 will be awarded. Winning synopsis and one runner-up will be published in winner's list by TWS (which retains one-time rights only). Contest is open to all writers except members of TWS Critique Group.

Submission Guidelines
Synopsis must be typed in proper manuscript format following Writer's Digest guidelines on one piece of 8-1/2 x 11 inch white paper. Put your name and address in the upper right-hand corner and word count in upper left-hand corner. Handwritten synopses and/or envelopes will be discarded.

Include a #10 typed, self-addressed, stamped envelope for winner's list. No entries returned.

Entry fee is six (6) loose first-class U.S. postage stamps. You may enter as often as you wish.

Annual postmark date is July 15th. Winner will be notified by October 15th.

Send entries to: TWS Critique Group, Synopsis Contest, P.O. Box 167, Forsyth, IL 62535.

UNICORN THEATRE

Herman Wilson
3828 Main Street
Kansas City, MO 64111
Phone (816) 531-PLAY, ext. 10; Fax (816) 531-0421

Deadline: September 1, 2001 – April 30, 2002

UNICORN THEATRE'S NATIONAL PLAYWRIGHTS' AWARD
Unicorn Theatre is looking for non-musical, issue-oriented, thought-provoking plays set in contemporary (post 1950s) times. We stipulate a cast limit of ten actors. You must note any double-casting in the character breakdown. All plays submitted must be original scripts which are unpublished and never received a professional production.

The winner of our National Playwrights' Award receives a royalty/prize fee of $1,000. In addition, the winning play is produced as a part of the Unicorn Theatre's next regular season of plays. All winners must agree to assign 2% subsidiary rights of future production of the scripts (in the United States and Canada) to the Unicorn Theatre for a period of five years from the close of the production, and all future productions must acknowledge the initial production by the Unicorn Theatre.

Submission Guidelines
Please send the manuscript with following information, even if you have already sent the same information with your inquiry:

1. A cover letter.
2. A brief biography of you.
3. A synopsis.
4. A complete character breakdown.
5. A self-addressed, stamped envelope for return of script and a self-addressed, stamped postcard if acknowledgment of receipt is desired.

Scripts must be typed and firmly bound.

All scripts will be handled with care but the Unicorn Theatre does not assume responsibility for lost or damaged manuscripts.

We accept scripts September through April. All scripts must be received no later than April 30 to be considered for the competition. Response time is generally four to six months.

Submit entries to: Herman Wilson, Unicorn Theatre, 3828 Main Street, Kansas City, MO 64111.

If you have any further questions, please contact us at the above address or phone (816) 531-7529, ext. 18.

UNITED STATES CIVIL WAR CENTER

Louisiana State University
Raphael Semmes Drive
Baton Rouge, LA 70803
Phone (225) 388-3151; Fax (225) 388-4876
E-mail lwood@cwc.lsu.edu

Deadline: December 31, 2002

THE PETER SEABORG AWARD FOR CIVIL WAR NON-FICTION
Award: $5,000 annually. Presented for the best non-fiction Civil War book that takes a unique approach, such as interdisciplinary study or examination of an unusual facet of the war. Children's books will be considered.

Nominations for the award should be made preferably by publishers and agents, but authors and critics may nominate as well.

Send six copies of the nominated work to above address at the United States Civil War Center by December 31, 2002.

Deadline: December 31, 2002

THE 2002 MICHAEL SHAARA AWARD FOR EXCELLENCE IN CIVIL WAR FICTION
Award: $1,000. Past winner: Madison Jones in 1998 was awarded the first annual Michael Shaara Award for Excellence in Civil War Fiction for his 1997 novel, *Nashville: 1864*.

Judges are novelists chosen by the USCWC Director and award sponsor Jeff Shaara. All Civil War fiction is eligible, including short story collections.

Nomination should be made, preferably, by the publisher, but authors and critics may also nominate.

To submit nominations send five copies of nominated work to: The United States Civil War Center, Attn: Leah Wood. These copies become the property of the Center. Deadline for the nomination is December 31, 2002

UNIVERSITIES WEST PRESS

P.O. Box 22310
Flagstaff, AZ 86002-2310

Deadline: August 31, 2001 postmark

EMILY DICKINSON AWARD IN POETRY
Award: $1,000 and publication.

Guidelines
For an unpublished poem in any form or style, and on any subject. All finalists will be considered for publication in an anthology of poems published by Universities West Press.

Submit up to three poems (total entry not to exceed six pages), a short biographical statement with return address, and a $10 check or money order reading fee made payable to Universities West Press. Simultaneous submissions are acceptable. Include a self-addressed, stamped envelope for the results of the award competition. Name may appear on manuscript, although names will be deleted from manuscripts submitted to final judge. Manuscripts will not be returned.

Final judge changes from year to year and is an award winning poet. Preliminary judging will be done by the editors of Universities West Press. This editorial board is comprised of creative writers and professors selected from Arizona Universities. Universities West Press reserves the right to change the final judge without notice. The decision of the judge is final and binding. The press will not enter into any correspondence thereon. Current students and employees of Northern Arizona University may not enter.

Winner and finalists will be notified by mail by April 15, 2002. The author of any poems selected for publication will receive a complimentary copy of the anthology. The copyright of each poem will remain with the author on the condition that the author agrees to grant Universities West Press the right to publish the poem in its anthology first.

Copies of the 1997 and/or the 1998 Award Anthology are available for $9 each.

Send submission to above contest name and address.

UNIVERSITY OF ALASKA ANCHORAGE

Alaska Native Plays Contest
University of Alaska Anchorage
Department of Theatre and Dance
3211 Providence Drive
Anchorage, AK 99508-8120
Phone (907) 786-1794
Website www.uaa.alaska.edu/theatre

Deadline: March 20, 2001

ALASKA NATIVE PLAYS CONTEST
A contest for plays about Native American characters, themes, or events. First Prize is $500, Second Prize is $200, and Third Prize is $100.

Cuttings from the winning scripts will receive a reading and adjudication at the Prince William Sound Community College Edward Albee Playwrights' Conference in August of each year. Playwrights are encouraged to attend and receive their prizes at that time.

Submission Guidelines

Plays may be serious or comic, but they MUST include North American Native themes, characters and/or issues. Plays may be any length. Plays based on other copyrighted material must include written permission form the original author.

Submitted scripts must not have been published or received full productions. (This does not preclude studio productions or readings.) Deadline for submission is March 20, 2001.

Winning playwrights agree to allow the University of Alaska Anchorage (UAA) to produce their winning scripts free of royalties. UAA Theatre retains exclusive Alaska production rights for five years from the date of the award. If UAA Theatre does not wish to produce any winning script, permission will be granted for other Alaska theatres within the five year period.

Winning playwrights agree that they will contact UAA Theatre should another Alaska theatre want to produce their winning script.

Submitting playwrights give UAA Theatre permission to copy scripts for judging purposes. Playwrights are encouraged to write and submit plays which would be producible in a university setting, i.e., 12 characters or less, simple sets, avoiding multiple set changes, and extravagant, special effects. These are recommendations only, but playwrights should be advised that "producibility" is a criterion for judging.

The original copy of the submitted script will only be returned upon receipt of a self-addressed, stamped envelope from the submitting playwright.

Plays should be typed in proper script format and sent to the following address: Alaska Native Plays Contest, Department of Theatre and Dance, University of Alaska Anchorage, 3211 Providence Drive, Anchorage, AK 99508.

For more information, please write or call: Alaska Native Plays Contest, University of Alaska Anchorage, Department of Theatre and Dance, 3211 Providence Drive, Anchorage, AK 99508-8120. Web site address: www.uaa.alaska.edu/theatre Telephone (907) 786-1794.

UNIVERSITY OF ARKANSAS

Department of Drama
Kimpel Hall, 619
University of Arkansas
Fayetteville, AR 72701
Phone (501) 575-2953

Deadline: January 1, 2001 – June 1, 2001 postmark

THE GEORGE R. KERNODLE PLAYWRITING COMPETITION
The University of Arkansas, Department of Drama announces the 16th annual George R. Kernodle Playwriting Competition. Three cash awards of $300, $200, and $100 are presented to the top three winners, plus the the possibility of a staged reading or a full production by the University of Arkansas, Department of Drama.

Eligibility
Competition is open to all playwrights residing in the United States and Canada.

Scripts must be original, previously unproduced, unpublished one-act plays written in English. Collaborations are permitted. Scripts given previous workshop productions may be entered. Children's plays, musicals, and adaptations are ineligible.

Guidelines
The Department of Drama makes the cash awards for the premiere productions. The decision of the judges is final and they reserve the right to withhold production, to modify cash awards if necessary, and to name no winner if an acceptable script is not found. The Department of Drama shall have the right to produce the winning entries for a period of one year without obligations to pay royalties. All additional rights remain with the playwright.

Scripts are to be typewritten in a legible manner and firmly bound. For confirmation of script arrival include a self-addressed, stamped postcard or envelope. Also, a self-addressed, stamped envelope must be enclosed if the scripts are to be returned. The Department of Drama cannot assume responsibility for lost, damaged, or unreturned scripts, but every reasonable care will be taken.

Once received, entries may not be withdrawn or rewritten. By entering the competition, the playwright accepts the published regulations governing the awards and agrees to the production of his or her script with full publicity.

Entries will be accepted beginning January 1, 2001 and must be postmarked no later than June 1, 2001. Notification will be November 1, 2001.

An application fee of $3 must accompany each script. Do not send cash. Make check or money order payable to U of A Dept. of Drama. NO MORE THAN THREE SCRIPTS MAY BE SUBMITTED.

Send scripts, eligibility statement, and application fee to: George R. Kernodle Playwriting Competition, Department of Drama, Kimpel Hall, 619, University of Arkansas, Fayetteville, AR 72701.

UNIVERSITY OF EVANSVILLE

Department of English
1800 Lincoln Avenue
Evansville, IN 47722
Phone (812) 479-2975

Deadline: December 1, 2001 postmark

THE RICHARD WILBUR AWARD
Prize: $1,000 and book publication

Guidelines
The competition welcomes submissions of unpublished, original poetry collections (public domain or permission-secured translations may comprise up to one-third of the manuscript). The competition is open to all American poets: those with or without previous book-length publication.

Manuscripts of between 50-100 typed pages may be submitted bound, unbound, or clipped. Manuscripts should be accompanied by two title pages: one with the title of the collection, the author's name, address, and telephone number, and one with only the title. Submitted manuscripts will not be returned.

The entry fee is $20 per manuscript made payable to the Richard Wilbur Award.

The winning manuscript will be published by the University of Evansville Press in 2002.

Send submissions to contest name at the above address. For notification of the contest results, include a self-addressed, stamped envelope.

UNIVERSITY OF IOWA PRESS

The Iowa Poetry Prize
100 Kuhl House
Iowa City, IA 52242

Iowa Short Fiction Award
Iowa Writers' Workshop
102 Dey House
Iowa City, IA 52242

UNIVERSITY OF IOWA PRESS PUBLICATION AWARDS

Deadline: August 1, 2001 – September 30, 2001

THE IOWA SHORT FICTION AWARD
THE JOHN SIMMONS SHORT FICTION AWARD

Any writer who has not previously published a volume of prose fiction is eligible to enter the competition for these awards. Revised manuscripts which have been previously entered may be resubmitted. Writers who have published a volume of poetry are eligible.

Award-winning manuscripts will be published by the University of Iowa Press under the Press's standard contract.

Submission Guidelines
The manuscript must be collection of short stories of at least 150 word-processed, double spaced pages. Stories previously published in periodicals are eligible for inclusion. Photocopied copies are acceptable. Stamped, self-addressed return packaging must accompany the manuscript. Please do not send cash, checks, or money orders. Reasonable care is taken, but we are not responsible for loss of manuscripts in the mails or for the return of those not accompanied by a stamped envelope. We assume the author retains a copy of the manuscript.

No application forms are necessary. Entries for the competition for the annual Iowa Short Fiction Award and the John Simmons Short Fiction Award should be submitted between August 1 and September 30, 2001. Announcement of the winners will be made early in the following year.

Manuscripts should be mailed to:
Iowa Short Fiction Award, Iowa Writers' Workshop, 102 Dey House, Iowa City, IA 52242.

Potential entrants wishing to read stories by previous winners may order *The Iowa Award: The Best Stories from Twenty Years* for $24.95

(cloth) and $15.95 (paper), plus $4.00 postage and handling, from the University of Iowa Order Department, 2222 Old Highway 218 South, Iowa City, IA 52242-1602. Phone (800) 235-2665. Individual titles may also be ordered.

Deadline: May 1, 2001 – May 31, 2001

THE IOWA POETRY PRIZE
The University of Iowa Press is pleased to announced the revitalization of its poetry series.

Two $1,000 prizes are awarded annually, and the winners are published by the University of Iowa Press under a standard royalty contract.

Manuscripts must be postmarked during the month of May; prize winners will be announced in July. The competition is open to writers of English who have published at least one book of poetry (a minimum of 50 pages in an edition of a least 500 copies). Poems included in the manuscripts may have been published in journals or anthologies; poems from previous books may be included only in manuscripts of selected or collected poems.

Manuscripts must be word-processed and should be no fewer than 50 and no more than 150 double spaced pages. We do not object to multiple submissions but ask that you notify us immediately if your manuscript has been accepted by another publisher.

Submissions must be accompanied by stamped, self-addressed packaging or they cannot be returned. We are not responsible for loss of manuscripts in the mail or for the return of those not accompanied by a stamped envelope. We assume that you retain a copy of the manuscript. Due to the anticipated number of submissions, manuscripts cannot be acknowledged, and only the winners will be notified.

Submissions should be mailed to:
The Iowa Poetry Prize, University of Iowa Press, 100 Kuhl House, Iowa City, IA 52242.

UNIVERSITY OF PITTSBURGH PRESS

3347 Forbes Avenue
Pittsburgh, PA 15261

UNIVERSITY OF PITTSBURGH PRESS AWARDS

Deadline: May 1, 2001 – June 30, 2001 postmark

THE DRUE HEINZ LITERATURE PRIZE
The University of Pittsburgh Press announces the Drue Heinz Literature Prize for a collection of short fiction. The prize carries a cash award of $10,000 and publication by the University of Pittsburgh Press under its standard contract. The winner will be announced in February of each year. No information about the winner will be released before the February announcement. The volume of manuscripts prevents the Press from offering critiques or entering into correspondence about manuscripts. Please do not call the Press.

Eligibility
The award is open to writers who have published a book-length collection of fiction or a minimum of three short stories or novellas in commercial magazines or literary journals of national distribution.

The award is open to writers in English, whether or not they are citizens of the United States.

Employees and students of the University of Pittsburgh are not eligible for the award.

Translations are not eligible if the translation was not done by the author.

Eligible submissions include a manuscript of short stories; one or more novellas (a novella may comprise a maximum of 150 double spaced typed pages); or a combination of one or more novellas and short stories. Manuscripts may be no fewer than 150 and no more than 300 typed pages.

Stories or novellas previously published in book form as part of an anthology are eligible.

Submissions Guidelines
Manuscripts also may be under consideration by other publishers, but if a manuscript is accepted for publication elsewhere, please notify the Press.

Authors may submit more than one manuscript to the competition as long as the manuscript or a portion thereof does not duplicate material submitted in another manuscript.

Manuscripts must be typed double spaced on quality white paper, and pages must be numbered consecutively. Clean, legible photocopies on high quality white paper are acceptable.

Each submission should include a list of the writer's published work, with full citations.

Manuscripts will be judged anonymously. Each manuscript should have two cover pages; one listing the title of the manuscript and the author's name, address, and telephone number; and a second listing only the manuscript title. The author's name must not appear after the first cover page.

Manuscripts must be mailed only during May and June 2001, and must be postmarked no later than June 30, 2001. Manuscripts received before May 1 or postmarked later than June 30 will be disqualified.

Manuscripts will NOT be returned.

Send submissions to: Drue Heinz Literature Prize, University of Pittsburgh Press, 3347 Forbes Avenue, Pittsburgh, PA 15261.

Deadline: March 1, 2001 – April 30, 2001

THE AGNES LYNCH STARRETT POETRY PRIZE
The University of Pittsburgh Press announces the Agnes Lynch Starrett Poetry Prize for a first full-length book of poems. Named after the first director of the Press, the prize carries a cash award of $3,000 and publication by the University of Pittsburgh Press in the Pitt Poetry Series under its standard royalty contract. The winner will be announced in the fall; no information about the winner will be released before the fall announcement. The Starrett Prize is our only venue for first-book poetry manuscripts.

The volume of manuscripts received prevents the Press from offering critiques or entering into correspondence about manuscripts other than the one chosen for publication. Manuscripts submitted to the contest will not be returned. Please keep a copy of the manuscript.

Eligibility
The award is open to any poet writing in English who has not had a full-length book published previously. We define a full-length book as a volume of 48 or more pages published in an edition of 750 or more copies. Books with publication costs borne by their authors are excluded from this definition. Employees and students of the University of Pittsburgh are not eligible for the award.

Submissions Guidelines
Manuscripts should be on good quality white paper, and no less than 48 and no more than 100 typescript pages. Clean, legible photocopies are acceptable. These are our only format requirements.

Results will be announced in major poetry and writing magazines once a winner had been chosen. Enclose a self-addressed, stamped post-card for manuscript acknowledgment and a self-addressed, stamped envelope for contest results.

Manuscripts being considered by other publishers are allowed, but if a manuscript is accepted for publication elsewhere, please notify the Press, in writing.

Manuscripts must be received and postmarked during March and April 2001.

Each manuscript must be accompanied by a check or money order in U.S. dollars for $15 payable to "University of Pittsburgh Press."

The address for submissions is: Agnes Lynch Starrett Poetry Prize, University of Pittsburgh Press, 3347 Forbes Avenue, Pittsburgh, PA 15261.

THE UNIVERSITY OF WISCONSIN PRESS

Ronald Wallace, Series Editor
The University of Wisconsin Press Poetry Series
114 North Murray Street
Madison, WI 53715

THE UNIVERSITY OF WISCONSIN PRESS POETRY SERIES

Deadline: September 1, 2001 – October 1, 2001

THE BRITTINGHAM PRIZE IN POETRY
THE FELIX POLLAK PRIZE IN POETRY
The University of Wisconsin Press announces the Brittingham Prize in Poetry and the Felix Pollak Prize in Poetry. These prizes, each consisting of $1,000 cash award and publication by the Press, are awarded annually to the two best book-length manuscripts of original poetry submitted in an open competition. There are no restrictions on the kind of poetry or subject matter, although translations are not acceptable. The winners will be announced and the prizes awarded in February of each calendar year, with publishing contracts to follow soon thereafter.

Submission Guidelines
To facilitate our careful handling of your manuscript, please adhere as closely as possible to the guidelines.

Manuscripts received September 1 through October 1 each calendar year will be considered. Manuscripts received before September 1 or after October 1 will be returned unread.

The manuscript must be previously unpublished in book form. Poems published in journals, chapbooks, and anthologies may be included but must be acknowledged. No changes in the manuscript will be considered between submission and acceptance.

Simultaneous submissions are permitted provided the poet agrees to inform the Press of the manuscript's acceptance for publication elsewhere.

Qualified readers appointed by the Press will screen all manuscripts. The final selections will be made by a distinguished poet who will remain anonymous until the winner is announced in mid-February.

All submissions must be typewritten on 8-1/2 x 11 inch paper, and should be 50-80 manuscript pages in length. Clean photocopies are acceptable.

Manuscripts must be unbound (no binders, clamps,etc. please). However, the use of a manila file folder with rubber bands and paper clips to keep your manuscript and enclosures intact is acceptable. Recycled paper is preferred.

The poet's name, address, and telephone number should appear on the title page. The Press should be informed of any address change.
A $20 non-refundable reading fee must accompany the manuscript. Please make checks or money orders payable to "The University of Wisconsin Press." Do not send cash or stamps. Foreign entries: remit reading fee in U.S. funds drawn on a U.S. bank.

Submit manuscripts via First Class or Priority Mail in an unpadded mailing envelope.

Manuscripts cannot be returned; unsuccessful submissions will be recycled. Please do not enclose return packaging.

For contest results, enclose a stamped, self-addressed business envelope (no postcards, please).

All manuscripts and correspondence should be sent to: Ronald Wallace, Series Editor, The University of Wisconsin Press Poetry Series, The University of Wisconsin Press, 114 North Murray Street, Madison, WI 53715.

URBAN STAGES

17 East 47th Street
New York, New York 10017-1920
Phone (212) 421-1380; Fax: (212) 421-1387

Deadline: Submissions are received throughout the year.

Urban Stages' mission is to develop new exciting multi-cultural works that speak to the whole of society. It is our belief that theatre should be inclusive. To that end ninety percent of our professional programming is free. Deadline: Submissions are received throughout the year. Finalists are first included as part of Urban Stages' fall or spring reading series. The award is usually announced in the spring.

Prize: $500 (in lieu of royalties) plus a staged production of the play in New York.

Guidelines
Open to all playwrights in the United States. Plays may have been developed elsewhere, but never produced in New York. Full-length plays are preferred. There is no limit to submission. Subject matter and character variations are open but cast size is limited to not more than nine. No translations or adaptations.

Plays that are finalists are presented as staged and workshop readings. These readings are a collaboration between playwright and director. Urban Stages reserves the right to withhold the prize and not declare a winner if no play of merit is found.

The play should be accompanied by a manuscript size self-addressed, stamped envelope to return the play. No loose cash, stamps, labels or metered postage.

Play will be returned. A self-addressed, stamped postcard should be included if you want acknowledgment of arrival. Include name, address and phone number of author on title page; biography and/or author's history of the play; cast of characters and brief description. All scripts must be firmly bound.

No changes or revisions accepted after submission. All scripts will be handled with care, but Urban Stages will not assume responsibility for lost or damaged scripts. Retain a copy of your script.

Before production of the award winning play, a contract will be signed between the playwright and the company. This contract is approved by the Dramatist Guild.

Please send manuscripts to “Emerging Playwright Award” at the above address. It usually takes from one to four months for us to read and process your script.

If you are in the New York City Area, call us about our Urban Stages On Tour schedule of presentations of new plays in New York Libraries and our productions.

UTAH STATE UNIVERSITY PRESS

Utah State University Press
7800 Old Main Hill
Logan, UT 84322-7800

Deadline: September 30, 2001

THE MARY SWENSON POETRY AWARD
Prize: $1,000 award, publication in the Spring of 2002, and royalties.

Guidelines
Submitted collections must be original poetry in English, 50 to 100 pages. No restriction on form or subject. Submit two copies of the manuscript with name and address on one copy only; $20 reading fee (includes copy of winning book); and self-addressed, stamped envelope for announcement of winner. Manuscripts will not be returned.

Judge reserves the right to declare no winner in any given year.

Send submissions to above address.

VAL-TECH PUBLISHING, INC.

P.O. Box 25376
St. Paul, MN 55125

Deadline: May 31, 2001

SHORT STORY CONTEST
First Prize is $50, Second Prize is $25, and Third Prize $15; plus honorable mentions. All winning entries will be published in the September/October 2001 issue and/or subsequent issues of *Writers' Journal.* (Write or call to verify dates.)

Submission Guidelines
Story length must not exceed 2,000 words. Limit four (4) entries per person maximum.

Only previously unpublished stories are accepted. Copyright to manuscripts remains with author. *Writers' Journal* requires only one-time rights to winning entries.

Manuscripts must be typed, double spaced on 8-1/2 x 11 inch paper.

Two (2) copies of each entry are required. On one copy write your name, address, and phone number on the top, left-hand corner of the first page; and your name and a key word from the title of the piece at the top of the second and succeeding pages. No name or address should appear on the second copy. Photocopies are accepted. Manuscripts will not be returned.

Enclose a #10 self-addressed, stamped envelope for winner's list.

A reading fee of $5 per entry must be included, U.S. funds only.

Send entries to: Short Story Contest, Val-Tech Publishing, Inc., P.O. Box 25376, St. Paul, MN 55125.

Deadline: April 30, 2001

POETRY CONTEST
Grand Prize is 2000 Poet's Market. First, Second, and Third prize winners will be published. All winning entries will be published in the July/August 2001 issue and or subsequent issues of *Writers' Journal.* (Write or call to verify dates.)

Submission Guidelines
Each poem may be no longer than 25 lines.

Each entrant may submit up to six poems (maximum).

Entries must be postmarked no later than deadline date. Submittals will not be returned.

Entries must by typed on 8-1/2 x 11 inch white paper, submitted in duplicate. Place your name and address in upper left corner of one sheet. No name or address on second sheet.

Winning entries relinquish one-time rights only.

A reading fee must accompany entries. Reading fee is $2 for first poem, $1 for each additional poem (U.S. funds). Enclose a #10 self-addressed, stamped envelope for winner's list.

Send entries to: Poetry Contest, Val-Tech Publishing, Inc, P.O. Box 25376, St. Paul, MN 55125.

VERVE

P.O. Box 3205
Simi Valley, CA 93093

Deadlines: April 1, 2001 postmark for Spring Vying
October 1, 2001 postmark for Fall Vying

VERVE POETRY CONTESTS
Verve magazine offers yearly awards for outstanding poetry. First Prize is The Valedictorian Award of $100, and publication in *Verve*. Second Prize is The VIP Award of $50 (and publication in *Verve* if space permits). Third Prize is The Velvet Award of $25 (and publication in *Verve* if space permits). There also will be up to three honorable mentions.

Winners will be notified by mail by May 15, 2001 for Spring Vying and November 15, 2001 for Fall Vying.

Guidelines
Any style; any subject; no limit on number of poems entered. Maximum 40 lines per poem.

Poems must be typewritten (one per page) on 8-1/2 x 11 inch paper. Send two (2) copies of each poem: one copy with poet's name and address on it, the second copy with poem and title only.

Poems must be in English, original, unpublished, and must not currently be submitted elsewhere.

Entry fee is $2 per poem. Please make checks payable to *Verve*.

Poems will not be returned.

Judges' decisions are final.

For contest results, enclose a self-addressed, stamped envelope marked "winners."

Send entries to: Verve Poetry Contest, P.O. Box 3205, Simi Valley, CA 93093.

VICE VERSA

David Bianco, Vice Versa Awards Administrator
P.O. Box 67780
Los Angeles, CA 90067
Toll Free (888) 383-7911
E-mail ViceVersas@aol.com.

Deadline: July 8, 2001

VICE VERSA AWARDS
The guidelines for the 5th annual Vice Versa Awards contest for excellence in the gay and lesbian press have been announced. The contest, which in its first year drew more than 450 submissions from 52 publications throughout the United States and Canada, has been expanded to reward more categories of excellence from more eligible publications than before.

Trophies will be awarded for Best Publication in each division and the number of cash prizes has been expanded from one to six.

In addition to gay and lesbian publications with a local or regional distribution, this year's awards also include a division for national publications. The number of categories has been expanded from 10 to 16, with new categories such as Best Photo, Best Front Page or Cover, and Best Publication Website. Other categories from last year's contest have been split into two or more categories, so dissimilar pieces are not judged together. For example, the category Best Interview or Personality Profile has been split into two categories, one each for news and one for entertainment-oriented pieces. Also, in a move that is intended to help the Vice Versa Awards continue to serve as a force for creating a stronger sense of community among the diverse publications that make up the gay press, the top awards will be given out at a special Fall awards ceremony. Gay press pioneer Lisa Ben was the guest of honor at the event.

Award recipients will be selected by an experienced, talented panel of judges familiar both with the standards of excellence in journalism and with the gay and lesbian community. The judges include several professors of journalism, communication, and writing; journalists working outside the gay press; and other distinguished gays and lesbians. All submissions are read by at least five judges.

Participating in the Vice Versa Awards contest is a great way for publications to honor the excellent work of their writers, editors, photographers, designers and artists.

Each winning entry receives at least one comment from the judges indicating why it was considered worthy of an award.

The contest is coordinated by Q Syndicate, the largest provider of syndicated material to the gay and lesbian press. The guidelines are listed below. If you have any questions, you may contact David Bianco, Vice Versa Awards administrator at (888) 383-7911 or ViceVersas@aol.com.

Eligibility

Eligibility. The following ARE eligible for Vice Versa Awards: content that appeared in newspapers, magazines, or newsletters of any size or frequency that primarily cater to gay and/or lesbian readers. Publications that primarily appeal to a subset of the gay and lesbian community (e.g., targeting bisexuals, or lesbians in California, or African-American gay men) are eligible, as are HIV or feminist publications for whom gays or lesbians are a primary but not exclusive audience. The following ARE NOT eligible for Vice Versa Awards: publications based outside North America, articles in any language other than English, or content distributed by the coordinator of the Awards (Q Syndicate).

Deadline. All submissions must be received no later than July 8, 2001. All submissions must have been published in issues dated July 1, 2000 through June 30, 2001.

Guidelines

Divisions. Each entry may be submitted in only one of the three divisions. Division A is for content that appeared in local or regional publications with more than 15 issues per year. Division B is for content that appeared in local or regional publications that put out 14 or fewer issues per year. Division C is for all national publications (U.S., Canada, or both).

Categories. Entries will be accepted in the following sixteen categories:

1. Best News Article
2. Best Comprehensive Coverage or Investigative Report
3. Best Editorial
4. Best Op-ed Piece or News Analysis
5. Best Health Article
6. Best News Interview or Personality Profile
7. Best Entertainment Interview or Personality Profile
8. Best First-person Column
9. Best Specialty Column
10. Best Review
11. Best Humor Piece
12. Best Illustration or Cartoon
13. Best Photo

14. Best Front page or Cover
15. Best Special Issue
16. Best Publication Website

A few explanations about the categories: Category 2 is for a series of articles on a single topic, or for longer articles that explore a topic in depth. Category 9 is for individual installments of any ongoing specialty column (gossip column, advice column, internet column, music column, horoscope, etc.). Category 12 is for hand-drawn or computer-assisted illustrations, editorial cartoons, and individual installments of cartoon strips. Category 15 is for both annual special issues (such as a Price or April Fool's edition), and themed special issues (such as a gays in the military or breast cancer edition). Category 16 is for web sites sponsored by a print publication. The Vice Versa Awards program reserves the right to re-assign an entry to a more appropriate category at its discretion.

Awards. Normally, the judges will award a first place, second place, and third place in each of the sixteen categories for each division, plus honorable mentions in some cases. Thus, publications that submit more than one entry in a given category can win two or even three awards in that category. However, the Vice Versa Awards contest and its judges reserve the right to give no award in a given category or combine categories or divisions at their discretion.

Certificates. Winning publications and contributors will receive award certificates and will be featured in a widely distributed press release in August 2001 announcing all the winners. The three publications receiving the highest number of awards in each division will receive special certificates of merit. In addition to the certificates, all winners will receive one or more comments from the judges explaining why the piece was considered worthy of an award.

Cash Prizes. After the winners in each category and division are announced in August, the second round will begin. All first place winners in categories 1 through 13 will be eligible for one of the cash awards: the Randy Shilts Award for Outstanding Achievement or the Sappho Award for Creative Expression. The Randy Shilts and the Sappho awards each come with a $250 cash prize and the opportunity to have the piece reprinted in dozens of publications nationwide. First and second runners-up for these awards will also receive cash prizes, for a total of six cash awards.

Trophies. All publications that win three or more Vice Versa Awards will be eligible to submit a portfolio to compete for the Best Publication trophy. In addition, all publications that began publishing in calendar year 2001 and win at least one Vice Versa Award will be eligible to submit a portfolio to compete for the Best New Publication trophy.

Entries. Entries will be accepted both from publications and from individual contributors. If a given piece is submitted by more than one source, only the first to be received will be entered into the contest and the rest will be returned. There is no maximum number of entries.

Decisions. Decisions of the Vice Versa Awards contest judges are final.

Cover Sheet. Each publication or contributor entering the contest must include an overall cover sheet with the following information: name of publication, address, phone number, e-mail address, name of contact person, and division you entered (Division A, B, or C); a list of all entries, listed by category (for example, 3. Best Editorial "Lesbian Center Needs Creative Solutions", or 10. Best Review "Object of My Affection Hits the Target"); and, if possible, names and e-mail addresses for all contributors so we may contact them directly if they win.

Release. To ensure the widest possible publicity for the "best of the best," the submissions that win the top cash awards will be provided to hundreds of publications to be reprinted at no cost. The Vice Versa Awards program also hopes to print a booklet containing many of the winning submissions. Therefore, to be eligible for cash awards, entrants are asked to fill out the Vice Versa Awards Permission to Reprint Release Form and have it signed by whoever has the right to grant permission to reprint the submission. This signed release is not mandatory to win a Vice Versa Award but only to compete for the cash awards.

Submissions. Each entry in Categories 1 through 11 should be photocopied from the original publication onto one or more 8-1/2 x 11 inch pieces of paper. Please, no newsprint clips or multiple submissions on one sheet of paper. Be sure that each sheet includes the name of the publication and the date of the issue in which the submission appeared. Please note that these entries will be reproduced so each judge can have her or his own copy; please leave reasonable margins. Entries in categories 12 through 15 can either be five (5) originals or five (5) photocopies (one for each judge). For Category 16, submit the website address and a password, if necessary.

Entry fee. Entry fees are $10 (U.S. funds) per submission. Include check, money order, or Visa/Mastercard authorization made payable to Vice Versa Awards. Entries must be received no later than July 8, 2001.

Send submissions to: Vice Versa Awards, P.O. Box 67780 Los Angeles, CA 90067.

If a street address is needed because submissions are sent via Federal Express or another such service, send it to: Vice Versa Awards, c/o Graphic Corp., 3348 Overland Ave., Los Angeles, CA 90034; local phone number (310) 201-9842.

For questions, and/or current informational updates call toll-free at 888-383-7911, or e-mail: ViceVersas@aol.com.

Vice Versa Awards
Permission to Reprint Release Form

"I hereby grant the Vice Versa Awards program the unlimited right to reprint my submission(s) in the event that they win an award, and the right to grant other publications the right to reprint them as well – provided that the original contributor and publication name are credited. I attest that I have the power to grant such rights."

Signed ______________________________

Date ______________________________

PLEASE PRINT

Name ______________________________

Publication/Company ______________________________

Address ______________________________

City/State/Zip ______________________________

Phone ______________________________

VICTORIA SCHOOL OF WRITING

The Community Arts Council Of Greater Victoria
Literary Info-Fair
First United Church Hall
Corner of Balmoral and Quadra Streets
Victoria, British Columbia CANADA
Phone 382-0986

Deadline: May 1, 2001 postmark

ILLUSTRATED POSTCARD STORY COMPETITION
First Prize is one full tuition to the Victoria School of Writing. In July this prize entitles you to four full days of workshops in your choice of poetry, fiction, non-fiction, mystery-writing, or editing a book-length work-in-progress. Second Prize is your choice of two tickets to Manulife Financial Literary Festival in May or a five hour manuscript evaluation with Tidewater Communications. Third Prize is two tickets to Shawnigan Lake Writer's Village in July or a three hour manuscript evaluation with Write Away!

Submission Guidelines
Postcard Stories must be unpublished, a maximum of 300 words.

Contest is limited to two entries per person.

All entries must be typed on a single sheet of plain 8-1/2 x 11 inch paper, single spaced.

Name, address, and phone number must not appear on the Postcard Story. Entrants must put the title of their piece (as well as the first ten words), their name, address, and phone number on a separate 8-1/2 x 11 inch sheet of paper. There is no entry form.

Entries must be postmarked before May 1, 2001 and include a $10 fee (checks payable to The Victoria School of Writing) OR hand-delivered (include $2) to the Literary Info-Fair, First United Church Hall, corner of Balmoral and Quadra Streets, Victoria, B.C. between 12 and 3 p.m. on May 9, 2001.

The postcard stories will be displayed on a wall at the Info-fair on May 9th so we are asking you to decorate or illustrate your postcard stories in any way you wish. Use cut-outs from magazines, computer graphics, felt pens, colored pencils, stencils, anything. Have fun!

Note: Judging will be blind and based on literacy merit alone.

Winners will be notified by phone.

VIRGINIA COMMONWEALTH UNIVERSITY DEPARTMENT OF ENGLISH

P.O. Box 842005
Richmond, VA 23284-2005
Phone (804) 828-1329

Deadline: January 15, 2001

LEVIS READING PRIZE
Prize: $1,000 and an expense paid trip for a public reading in September 2001.

Fourth Annual Levis Reading Prize for the best first or second book of poetry.

Entries may be submitted by author or publisher, and must include a copy of the book (48 pages or more), a cover letter, and a brief biography of the author. The book must have been published in the calendar year 2000. Include a self-addressed, stamped postcard if you wish acknowledgment of receipt. All entries after deadline will be returned unopened. Because we cannot guarantee their return, all entries will become the property of the VCU Department of English.

Send all entries to above address.

THE EDWARD LEWIS WALLANT BOOK AWARD

Irving and Fran Waltman
3 Brighton Road
West Hartford, CT 061117
Phone (860) 232-1421

The Edward Lewis Wallant Book Award is presented to an American writer for a published work. Novels and short stories are considered by a panel of judges who then make a selection.

For further details write or call using the above information.

WASHINGTON INDEPENDENT WRITERS LEGAL AND EDUCATIONAL FUND, INC.

220 Woodward Building
733 Fifteenth Street NW
Washington, DC 20005

Deadline: none

JOAN G. SUGARMAN CHILDREN'S BOOK AWARD
The Joan G. Sugarman Children's Book Award was established in 1987 to recognize excellence in children's literature. Published books geared for ages 15 and under that are written by authors residing in Washington, D.C. and the surrounding region are eligible. Entries may be submitted for consideration by publishing houses, agents, book-stores, libraries, and the authors themselves. The award is presented every two year, please write for dates.

Books must have been published during the time specified for each award. A team of judges reviews each book, fiction and non-fiction, focusing on the quality of the written language, originality, knowledge of the subject, its application and interest to a particular age group, and its universal appeal.

The award is administered under a grant to the Washington Independent Writers Legal and Educational Fund, Inc., a nonprofit organization founded in 1980 to defend First Amendment cases and address concerns of independent writers.

For complete information, please address correspondence to: Joan G. Sugarman Children's Book Award, Washington Independent Writers, Legal and Educational Fund, Inc., 220 Woodward Building, 733 Fifteenth Street NW, Washington, DC 20005.

WAYNE STATE UNIVERSITY

c/o English Department
Wayne State University
Detroit, MI 48202

Deadline: March 2, 2001

JUDITH SIEGEL PEARSON AWARD
Wayne State University is pleased to announce the Judith Siegel Pearson Award. The award is an annual prize for the best creative or scholarly work on a subject concerning women. At the discretion of the final judge, several awards may be given. The following yearly schedule of awards will be observed: 2001 Fiction, and 2002 Plays/Non-fictional Prose.

Submission Guidelines
Welcome (in their respective years) are unpublished fiction, drama, poetry, or essays in literary studies. Prose or drama entries should be limited to no more than 20 pages, double spaced (with standard documentation). Poetry entries should consist of four to ten poems (20 page limit). Subjects must concern women. Submissions are open to all interested writers and scholars.

Submissions should be anonymous with the author's name and address on a separate title page. There should be two (2) copies of each entry clearly typed on one side of 8-1/2 x 11 inch paper, double spaced, and proofread carefully.

Contestants retain copyright of all work submitted.

All manuscripts must be sent to the Judith Siegel Pearson Award, c/o English Department, Wayne State University, Detroit, MI 48202.

WELLSPRING MAGAZINE

Meg Miller, Chief Editor
4080 83rd Avenue North, Suite A
Brooklyn Park, MN 55443
Phone (612) 566-6663

Deadline: January 1, 2001 for Summer issue
July 1, 2001 for Winter issue

WELLSPRING MAGAZINE SHORT FICTION CONTEST

SHORT FICTION CONTEST FOR YOUNG ADULTS
Attention adults and high school students, *WellSpring* magazine announces its Short Fiction Contest for Young Adults!

Awards in the Adult Category are $100, $75, $25, and one to three honorable mentions. Awards in the Teenage Category are $50, $30, $20, and one to three honorable mentions. All winners will be published in *WellSpring,* a nationally distributed fiction magazine.

Entries are judged on intriguing, well-crafted work. Stories are evaluated using the following criteria.

The title is cohesive and draws the reader in. Story problems are stated clearly and are solved. The point of view is understandable at all times.

The story line is new, or a new twist of an old theme; the beginning pulls the reader into the story. The story is creatively written and major/minor characters are appropriately defined. Tone is expressed.

Appropriate grammar, spelling, and punctuation, etc., are followed.

The story is readable with smooth transition from beginning to end. Characters are consistent and believable; the story has good imagery and appropriate details.

The story has a powerful ending. The ending matches the story problem and is satisfactorily done.

Guidelines
Always follow our guidelines. Don't be disqualified after you've done the work!

Stories must be unpublished. *WellSpring* claims First and One Time Rights.

First page of manuscript should include the name, address, and phone number of the author and the story title, whether or not you include a cover letter.

Approximate word count should be a maximum of 2,000 words.

Consecutive pages should include (put in the upper left-hand corner): last name/story title/page number.

Always double space and indent your paragraphs. Don't quad space between paragraphs. Use one-inch margins on all sides. Typed entry should be single-sided, double spaced on 8-1/2 x 11 inch paper.

Use dark print and a 10 or 12 CPI, easy-to-read font.

Don't fold your submission – put it in a large 9 x 12 inch envelope to accommodate manuscript. Use a paper clip rather than staples or bindings.

When writing, whether for guidelines or with questions, always include a #10 self-addressed, stamped, business-size envelope. If you don't, your materials will be discarded. Also include a self-addressed, stamped envelope for a winner's list and written comments from the editor.

Deadlines are January 1 and July 1, yearly. Stories received before each deadline will be judged for inclusion in the subsequent issue. Manuscripts are not returned.

Include a $10 entry fee (Adults) or $5 entry fee (Teens) per story (no limit). Make checks payable to *WellSpring* Magazine. Ages 13 - 17 must have a parent/guardian signature on the cover page.

The magazine is available each summer and winter. Sample copies are available for $5.50 each.

Mail entry and fee to: *WellSpring* Magazine, Meg Miller, Chief Editor, 4080 83rd Avenue North, Suite A, Brooklyn Park, MN 55443.

WHITE EAGLE COFFEE STORE PRESS

P.O. Box 383
Fox River Grove, IL 60021-0383
Phone (847) 639-9200
Website http://members.aol.com/weespress

White Eagle Coffee Store Press is an established micropress with a long term plan to provide first, or early, publishing to writers whose works we admire. In fact, most of our publications have been first books. Alternately, we publish chapbooks by solicitation and by competition. Each writer published at our invitation agrees to judge a competition. Some contest winners have also agreed to be judges. Thus, the press represents many styles and methods, and presents a variety of visions. We expect to be quirky, to do the unexpected, to discover talent. Our readers tell us that's happening.

You should know that, unlike many small presses, White Eagle Coffee Store Press makes its selections on literary values alone. We do not promote or reject political, economic, social, sexual, religious, racial, or ethnic positions in a one-dimensional way. But, because we value literary writing, we discourage the strictly didactic or sentimental. WECSP favors work that is crafted and edgy. However, in a competition the judge's decision is final.

To readers who ask, the coffee store is more a state of mind than a material place. Under the publisher's home a carpenter once found a brass sign that reads: White Eagle Coffee Store. The sign is now on a kitchen cabinet. We do like fresh roasted and ground coffee, however but to make *Fresh Ground* a "new grind," the publisher's physician has ruled coffee off-limits for him!

Deadline: May 1, 2001 – June 30, 2001

FRESH GROUND – A POETRY ANNUAL
Edited by Paul Andrew E. Smith
In its 9th year, *Fresh Ground* is an eight-year-old poetry anthology published in chapbook format on high quality recycled paper by White Eagle Coffee Store Press. Poet and fiction writer P.A.E. Smith comes in during the summer, while the publisher is fishing, to edit this serial. This annual represents some of the best new writing by emerging and established poets.

Fresh Ground is open to beginning writers but is very selective. There are no restrictions on subject matter or form, but preachy or sentimental versification had best be sent elsewhere. The editor expects work that is crafted and loves poetry that takes risks.

During May through June, send two or three (only) unpublished poems with brief biography and a self-addressed, stamped envelope to: Editor, *Fresh Ground*, White Eagle Coffee Store Press, P.O. Box 383, Fox River Grove, IL 60021-0383.

Published each Fall, the anthology costs $5.95, including postage. ISSN1067-4543. To order *Fresh Ground* 2000, send $6.95 and your request to the address above.

Deadline: December 15, 2001 postmark

LONG FICTION CONTEST – A.E. COPPARD PRIZE FOR FICTION
Most fiction writers have learned, as did A.E. Coppard in his time, that it's nearly impossible to publish a short story much over 3,000 words. Given the costs of publishing and the size of most literary magazines, that limit seems unavoidable. But, we also know that not all fictions can be artificially limited. Other than short collections, there have been few opportunities for such publication. Since we're fond of long stories, we'd like to address that problem.

WECS Press offers a competition to select a long literary fiction for chapbook publication.

The winner is awarded $500, 25 copies, plus 40 copies sent free to book publishers/agents, and 10 press kits. All entrants will receive a copy of the book.

Manuscript length can be 8,000 to 14,000 words. Entries must be an unpublished single story, multiple part story, self-contained or novel.

Deadline is December 15, 2001 postmark. Entries must include a reading fee of $15 (U.S.). A second manuscript submitted in the same envelope is $5 (U.S.). Make all checks payable to "WECSP."

Submission Guidelines
Include a cover page with title, name, address, and phone. Also include a second title page with no name. Judging is blind.

Send a self-addressed, stamped envelope for announcement only. No stories are returned. All manuscripts are recycled.

Simultaneous submissions are OK. Previous publication of small parts of the manuscript OK, but include an acknowledgment.

There are no restrictions on style, method, or subject matter. We respect literary writing and enjoy everything, including experimental fiction.

Deadline: Spring Contest March 30, 2001 postmark
Fall Contest September 30, 2001 postmark

SPRING AND FALL POETRY CHAPBOOK CONTESTS
White Eagle Coffee Store Press invites poets to submit manuscripts to compete for chapbook publication. This is an open competition with no restrictions on style or subject matter.

First Prize Winner receives $200, and 25 copies, 40 copies sent free to major poets/poetry organizations, and 10 copies for press kits. All entrants receive a copy of the winning book.

To get a better sense of the press, and to support poetry publication, you might want to order a copy of the chapbook of your contest judge, other judges, and past winners.

Submission Guidelines
Manuscript entries should be 20 to 24 pages, typed or printed on a letter quality printer. No names should appear on the manuscript. Manuscript should include a paginated Table of Contents.

Include a cover title page with title, name, address, phone, and brief biography. Also include a second title page with no name. Judging is blind.

We ask you to provide a 125-word statement about your work to be included in the book, e.g., materials, methods, work habits, vision; whatever would introduce a new reader to your work.

Reading fee is $12. Make all checks payable to "WECSP." Winner is announced within 90 days of deadline. A self-addressed, stamped envelope should be submitted along with entry for contest results. All manuscripts are recycled.

Simultaneous submissions are OK, but please tell us if you are accepted for publication elsewhere. Provide a list of credits for previously published poems.

A catalog of chapbooks and list of competitions is available by writing to us at the address below. We do not mass produce chapbooks. Each book is carefully designed to be an aesthetic object. Printing is professionally done on high quality papers. Our signature design is a wrap-around cover that represents the literature but can stand alone as art.

To get a better sense of the Press, and to support poetry publication, you might want to order a copy of the chapbook of your contest judge, other judges, and/or past winners.

Submit entries to: White Eagle Coffee Store Press, P.O. Box 383, Fox River Grove, IL 60021-0383.

WICHITA STATE UNIVERSITY

Leroy Clark, Contest Director
University Theatre
Wichita State University
1845 Fairmount
Wichita, KS 67260-0153

Deadline: February 15, 2001 postmark

WICHITA STATE UNIVERSITY PLAYWRITING CONTEST AWARDS

Wichita State University (WSU) announces the 27th annual National Playwriting Contest Awards. The contest is open to all undergraduate and students enrolled at any college or university in the United States. (Please indicate school affiliation.) A production of the winning play by the WSU Theatre may be entered in the ACTF Playwriting Awards category. Transportation and housing for the playwright will be included. The judging will be done by a panel of three selected from the theatre faculty of WSU.

Submission Guidelines

Both full-length and one-act plays may be submitted. Full-length plays in one or more acts should be a minimum of 90 minutes playing time. Two or three short plays on related themes, by the same author, will be judged as one entry; the total playing time must be a minimum of 90 minutes.

Any subject or style is acceptable, with the exception of musicals or children's plays.

Plays must be original, unpublished, and unproduced.

Eligible playwrights may submit more than one entry.

One typewritten, bound copy should be submitted. Two title pages must be included: one bound, the other unbound. The unbound title page should contain the author's name, address, and telephone number. This information must appear nowhere else in the manuscript.

An appropriately sized self-addressed, stamped envelope must accompany each entry if manuscript return is requested. If the contestant desires acknowledgment of receipt, a self-addressed, stamped postcard or envelope must also be included.

Deadline for submission is (postmarked) February 15, 2001. Winners will be announced about April 15. No plays may be withdrawn from the contest after February 15, 2001.

Send manuscript to: Leroy Clark, Contest Director, University Theatre, Wichita State University, 1845 Fairmount, Wichita, KS 67260-0153.

WILLAMETTE WRITERS

9045 SW Barbur Boulevard, Suite 5A
Portland, OR 97219-4027
Phone (503) 452-1592; Fax (503) 452-0372
Martha Miller (503) 286-094
E-mail willwrite@teleport.com5

Deadline: May 15, 2001 postmark

KAY SNOW WRITING AWARDS
The purpose of this annual contest, named in honor of *Willamette Writers'* founder, Kay Snow, is to help writers reach professional goals in writing in a broad array of categories.

A first, second, and third place prize is awarded in each category. Prizes are $200, $100, and $50, respectively. One winner is chosen in each of the Student Writer grade divisions; each receives $50.

Finalists will be notified by mail in mid-July, and prizes will be awarded at the annual banquet. Excerpts from the winning entries may be published in the December 2001 issue of *Williamette Writers*. (Authors retain ownership of their work.)

Award categories include:

Adult Fiction. Any 2,500 words of fiction intended for an adult audience.

Adult Non-Fiction. Any 2,500 words of non-fiction intended for an adult market.

Poetry. May be any subject or form. Maximum length is five (5) pages for total entry. Entry should be single spaced; double spaced between stanzas.

Juvenile Fiction or Non-Fiction. Maximum length is 1,500 words, written by adults for juvenile readers. State target age group below the title.

Scriptwriting. Maximum length is ten (10) pages. Complete or partial script, any subject, in script format may be submitted.

Student Writer. There are three divisions: Grades 1-5; Grades 6-8; and Grades 9-12. Fiction only, with a maximum of 2,500 words.

Submissions will be judged anonymously and judges' decisions will be final. Judges reserve the right to withhold prizes in any category if entries do not meet their standards. Board members, staff, and conference speakers are not eligible to enter.

Submission Guidelines
Entries which do not follow all category guidelines and rules will be disqualified. All entries must be original and unpublished.

Entries must be typed, double spaced (except poetry), one side only, on 8-1/2 x 11 inch white paper using a 10 or 12 point font.

Type title and category at upper left on each page of entry. Type word count on upper right of first page. Number each page except the first.

To assure confidentiality, DO NOT PUT THE AUTHOR'S NAME ON MANUSCRIPT.

Submit three (3) copies of each entry Manuscripts will not be returned. Keep a copy of your entry.

Each entry must be accompanied by a 3x5 card with the author's name, address, phone number, title of entry, and category. Place the card in a plain white, sealed envelope, labeled with category and title.

Each entry must be accompanied by registration form and entry fee. Do not send cash. Send check, money order, or credit card information with entry. You may enter more than one category and submit more than one entry in each category, but each entry must be accompanied by the appropriate fee. Contest fees are not returnable.

Only one prize will be awarded to a winner in any given category.

If you need to correspond with Willamette Writers, use a self-addressed, stamped envelope.

Submit entries to: Williamette Writers Kay Snow Writing Awards, 9045 SW Barbur Boulevard, Suite 5A, Portland, OR 97219-4027.

Willamette Writers
2001 Kay Snow Writing Awards
Registration Form

Name ______________________________

Address ______________________________

State __________ Zip __________ Phone (   ) __________

Number of submissions entered ______________________________

Date of birth ______________________________ (if student entry)

Entry fee is $10 each for members; $15 each for non-members; none (free) for student writers.

Total amount enclosed $ ______________________________

Check (   ) Money Order (   ) ______________________________

MC/VISA Number ______________________________ Exp Date __________

DEADLINE IS MAY 15, 2001 POSTMARK
Return to: Willamette Writers, Kay Snow Writing Awards, 9045 SW Barbur Boulevard, Suite 5A, Portland, OR 97219-4027.

Questions??
Willamette Writers Office (503) 452-1592, fax (503) 452-0372
E-mail willwrite@teleport.com; Martha Miller (503) 286-0945

Finalists will be notified by mail in mid-July. Authors retain ownership of their work, but excerpts from the winning entries may be published in the December 2001 issue of *The Willamette Writer.*

Consent: If I am a winner of the WW 2001 Kay Snow Writing Awards, I hereby grant permission to *Willamette Writers* to print excerpts from my winning manuscript:

Signature ______________________________

Printed Name ______________________________

WIND PUBLICATIONS

Wind Publications
P.O. Box 24548
Lexington, KY 40524
Website http://lit-arts.com/wind

Deadline: June 30, 2001 postmark

THE ALLEN TATE MEMORIAL AWARD
Poem Competition: $500 and publication in the fall issue of *Wind Magazine* will be awarded for the poem judged best in *Wind's* annual single poem competition. Finalists receive a one-year subscription to the magazine.

Submit any number of unpublished poems of 100 lines or less and an entry/reading fee of $2 per poem (author's name and address must be on each page).

Include self-addressed, stamped envelope if notification of winners is desired. Poems will not be returned.

Deadline: April 30, 2001 postmark.

SHORT STORY COMPETITION
$500 and publication in the fall issue of *Wind Magazine* will be awarded for the short story judged best in *Wind's* annual fiction competition. Finalists receive a one-year subscription to the magazine.

Submit any number of unpublished stories, any subject matter, 5000 words or less, and an entry/reading fee of $10 per story. Author's name and address and the story title must appear on the first page of the story, the title and page number on each succeeding page.

Include self-addressed, stamped envelope if notification of winner is desired. Manuscripts will not be returned.

Deadline: October 31, 2001 postmark

THE QUENTIN R. HOWARD POETRY PRIZE
Poetry Chapbook Competition: Winners of the annual competition receive $100 and 25 copies of their published book. All entrants receive a copy of the winning book. Finalists also receive a one-year subscription to *Wind Magazine*.

Entry/reading fee $10.

Submit 24-28 pages, plus front matter and acknowledgments. Poet's name, address, and phone number must appear on one of two cover sheets only. Manuscripts must be typewritten or computer printed, no more than one poem per page. Any subject matter is acceptable.

Include self-addressed, stamped envelope for notification of winners. Manuscripts will not be returned. Simultaneous submissions are OK if Wind is notified immediately of acceptance elsewhere.

Entries must be postmarked no later than October 31 (if Sunday, next workday).

Author is responsible for copyright clearance on previously published poems. Submissions will be screened by the editors of *Wind Magazine*.

Final judge will be announced after the submission deadline. Announcement of the winning manuscript will be made on or before January 15. The winning poet and the finalists will be acknowledged in *Wind Magazine*.

Submit all entries to the above address.

WISCONSIN INSTITUTE FOR CREATIVE WRITING

Jesse Lee Kercheval
University of Wisconsin at Madison
English Department
Helen C. White Hall
600 N. Park Street
Madison, WI 53706
Website http:/polyglot.lss.wise.edu/english

WISCONSIN INSTITUTE FOR CREATIVE WRITING FELLOWSHIPS

Deadline: February 1, 2001 – February 28, 2001

THE CARL DJERASSI FELLOWSHIP
THE DIANE MIDDLEBROOK FELLOWSHIP
THE JAMES C. MCCREIGHT FELLOWSHIP
THE JAY C. AND RUTH HALLS FELLOWSHIP

The University of Wisconsin Institute for Creative Writing provides time, space, and an intellectual community for new writers working on a first book of poetry or fiction (novel, short stories). Poets and fiction writers who have completed an MFA or equivalent degree in creative writing are eligible to apply. Entrants must not yet have published, or had accepted for publication, a book by the application deadline.

Five writers will be invited to spend the academic year (August 15, 2001 – May 15, 2002) in Madison as Artists in Residence at the University of Wisconsin. Fellows will teach one creative writing workshop per semester and will give one public reading from work in progress. Fellows may also participate in the creative writing program, assisting with the Brittingham/Pollak Prizes in Poetry* (cosponsored by the English Department and the University of Wisconsin Press), the George B. Hill and Therese Muller Creative Writing Contests, and the *Madison Review.*

Fellowships will pay $22,000 for the academic year. Applications must be received in February. Fellows will be notified of their selection by May 1.

Applications must include a resumé or *vitae*, two letters of recommendation, and one story or novel excerpt of up to thirty pages in length (typed, double spaced, and stapled – no tearsheets or off-prints) OR ten (10) pages of poetry (typed, single spaced and stapled – no tearsheets or off-prints). Each entry should include a manuscript cover sheet with the applicant's name, address, telephone, social security number, and titles of work submitted. The applicant's name must not appear on any page of the manuscript except the cover sheet. Letters of recommendation may arrive under separate cover, but must also be received in February. Materials will not be returned. Please include a business-size, self-addressed, stamped envelope for results.

Send completed applications to: Jesse Lee Kercheval, Wisconsin Institute for Creative Writing, Department of English, 600 North Park Street, University of Wisconsin, Madison, WI 53706.

ALSO SEE the University of Wisconsin Press Poetry Series for details about the Brittingham/Pollack Prizes in Poetry; and the Madison Review.

WOMEN IN THE ARTS

P.O. Box 2907
Decatur, IL 62524-2907

Deadline: November 15, 2001 postmark

WOMEN IN THE ARTS SPRING FANTASY CONTESTS
Spring Fantasy is an annual anthology published by Women In The Arts (WITA). The booklet features art, poetry, fiction, personal essays, and photographs on any theme, as well as the winning entries from our *Spring Fantasy* contest. See Publication Guidelines on the next page for general submission information.

Contest categories are
Rhymed Poetry. Up to 32 lines.
Non-Rhymed Poetry. Up to 32 lines
Fiction. Up to 1,500 words.
Juvenile Fiction. Up to 1,500 words.

Winners will be notified by March 15, 2002. In addition to generous cash prizes awarded to in each category, Women in The Arts will publish the winning entries in the *Spring Fantasy.* Rights will revert to authors upon publication. Winners will receive one complimentary copy of *Spring Fantasy.*

Contests are open to all writers except members of Women In The Arts and their immediate families. Entries must be the original work of the author. Previously published works are acceptable.

Submission Guidelines
Poetry must be typed on 8-1/2 x 11 inch white paper with the title of poem in upper the left corner.

Fiction must be typed, doubled spaced with one-inch margins, on 8-1/2 x 11 inch white paper, with page numbers in the upper right corner and story title in the upper left corner of each page.

DO NOT put your name on any page of the manuscript. Do put your name, address, telephone number, title of your fiction or poems, submission categories, and word count for fiction on a cover sheet. Submit one cover sheet and one entry fee check, with all entries mailed in one envelope.

All entries will be subject to blind judging. Entries that do not comply with rules may be disqualified.

Entries must be postmarked by November 15, 2001. Include with your entry a #10 self-addressed, stamped envelope. No entries are returned. Entry fee is $2.00 per submission, limit five (5) submissions total per person.

Copies of *Spring Fantasy* may be purchased at $6 each; winners may purchase additional copies at $5 each.

Submit entries and entry fees (one check made payable to Women In the Arts) to: Women in The Arts, Spring Fantasy Contests, P.O. Box 2907, Decatur, IL 62524-2907.

Publication Guidelines for Women In The Arts *Spring Fantasy* Anthology

Spring Fantasy holds one-time publication rights to all material accepted for publication. Previously published work is acceptable. Rights revert to authors upon publication. Terms of payment: one (1) copy of issue in which submission appears, and authors receive a 20% discount on additional copies.

All written material submitted to *Spring Fantasy* must be on plain 8-1/2 x 11 inch paper, double spaced, typewritten or computer printed. Copy must include the author's name, address, and telephone number on the first page. Entries must be accompanied by a self-addressed, stamped envelope with enough postage for the return of materials.

Camera-ready, black-and-white art, and black-and-white photography submissions must be labeled on the back with the author's name, address, and telephone number. If you wish your art or photographs returned, a self-addressed, stamped envelope with enough postage for the return of materials must also be enclosed. Material submitted outside these guidelines or without an appropriate self-addressed, stamped envelope may not reviewed.

Poetry should be no more than 100 lines, including lines between stanzas. Fiction and Personal Essays should be 500 to 750 words.

Sample copy of *Spring Fantasy* may be purchased for $6 postage paid.

Submit entries to: Women In The Arts, *Spring Fantasy*, P.O. Box 2907, Decatur, IL 62524-2907.

WORD WORKS

Box 42164
Washington, DC 20015

Deadline: February 1, 2001 – March 1, 2001

2001 WASHINGTON PRIZE
Prize: $1,500 and publication by Words Works. For a volume of original poetry by a living American writer.

Send 48 to 64 page manuscript by deadline. Author's name, address, phone number, and signature should appear on the title page only. Include a table of contents containing the manuscript title, acknowledgments page, and brief biography. Use a binder clip to fasten the manuscript. No manuscripts will be returned.

Entry fee $20 US drawn on a US bank only, payable to Word Works. Winner will be selected by July 1, 2001. All entrants will receive a copy of the winning book when published.

Mail submissions to above address.

WRITERS UNLIMITED

Nina Mason
910 Grant Avenue
Pasagoula, MS 39567-7222

Deadline: September 1, 2001 postmark

WRITERS UNLIMITED INTERNATIONAL LITERARY COMPETITION
The Writers Unlimited 31st annual International Literary Competition offers the following awards:

1. WRITERS UNLIMITED AWARD.
A Narrative Poem of any subject (open). Line limit is a minimum of 40 to a maximum of 80 lines. Awards are First Place $50, Second Place $30, and Third Place $20; and three honorable mentions.
Sponsored by: Writers Unlimited.

2. THE CHEVRON AWARD.
Short Story, any subject (open), with a 2,500 word maximum. Awards are First Place $50, Second Place $30, and Third Place $20; and three honorable mentions.
Sponsored by: Chevron USA, Pasagoula, MS.

3. BERTIE MAE AVARA AWARD.
Poem, any form, (open). Subject: My Song. Line limit is 40 maximum. Awards are First Place $25, Second Place $15, and Third Place $10.
Sponsored by: Elva Avara.

4. MAGNOLIA AWARD.
Short Story with a Southern setting; word limit is 2,500. Awards are First Place $15, Second Place $10, and Third Place $5.

5. DESCRIPTIVE SENTENCE AWARD.
Use one grammatically correct sentence to paint a picture, without explanation or justification. Right example: The majestic mountains were clothed in a veil of morning mist. Wrong example: I saw majestic me. Awards are First Place $20, Second Place $15, and Third Place $10.

6. A SENTIMENTAL JOURNEY AWARD.
Prose. Subject: A journey through the past (school days, childhood memories, war-time, travels, etc.); 1,500 word limit. Awards are First Place $15, Second Place $10, and Third Place $5; and three honorable mentions.
Sponsored by: Valerie Lopez Richard of Escatawpa, MS.

7. TOUCH THE EARTH AWARD.
Poem. Subject: Simple, everyday things in life. Form: traditional rhymed poem, limit of 30 lines. Awards are First Place $15, Second Place $10,

and Third Place $5; and three or more honorable mentions.
Sponsored by: Eunice Barnes, in memory of George V. Barnes.

8. PATRIOTIC AWARD.
Prose or Poetry. Subject: My American Heritage. Prose, limit of 2,500 words. Poetry form: open, with a limit of 40 lines. Awards are First Place $12, Second Place $10, and Third Place $5; and three honorable mentions.
Sponsored by: Eunice Barnes, in memory of George V. Barnes.

9. PAST PRESIDENTS' AWARD
Essay as possible fiction. Limit of five (5) typed pages. Subject: "Where I was in Paris, or wherever I was that day long ago, it rained, what happened, and did it change your plans, your life? How? When?" Awards are First Place $15, Second Place $10, and Third Place $5; and three honorable mentions.
Sponsored by: H. C. Corben and Beverly B. Corben.

10. FANTASY AWARD.
A Fairy Tale beginning with "Once upon a time." A short story or narrative poem using your imagination and remembering when you believed in fairies, and stories like "Cinderella" and "Jack and the Beanstalk." Awards are First Place a Dragon, Second Place $15, and Third Place $5; and three honorable mentions.
Sponsored by: Judith Henderson Prestridge of Birmingham, AL. "Dedicated to my mother Mildred Rowan Henderson, who spurred my imagination from my earliest memories."

11. PASCAGOULA GARDEN CLUB AWARD.
Poem. Subject: State flower or your favorite flower. Form: open. Line limit: 42. Open to Residents of Mississippi. Awards are First Place $15 and Second Place $10; and three honorable mentions.

12. YOUTH AWARD: 6th through 8th grades.
Short Story or Poem. Short story any subject (open); word limit of 1,500. Poem any subject (open); 20 line limit. Awards are First Place $20, Second Place $10, and Third Place a book; and three honorable mentions.
Sponsored by: Nina Mason

13. YOUTH AWARD: High School Students.
Short Story or Poem. Short story, subject: My Career. Word limit: 1,500 words. Poem, subject (open). Line limit: 40. Awards are First Place $20, Second Place $10, and Third Place a book; and three honorable mentions.

YOUTH AWARD: open.
Essay. Subject: "Why I like My City or Town in Mississippi." Limit of 250-500 words. Awards are First Place $20, Second Place $10, and Third Place a book.
Sponsored by: Hazel Hall, President of Writers Limited.

Submission Guidelines

Entries must be on 8-1/2 x 11 inch white paper (no onionskin).

Entries must be original, unpublished, and not judged a Winner (1st place) in any other competition.

Only one entry per category is allowed.

On each manuscript, put the number and name of the category entered in the upper left-hand corner. DO NOT PUT YOUR NAME ON THE ENTRY.

On a 3x5 white index card (one for EACH entry), in the upper left-hand corner, put your name, address, the number and name of the category, title of work, and first line of work.

Do not use the subject of the category for the title of your entry.

Do stick to the subject and form where specified.

Do not send any work currently submitted elsewhere.

Enclose a self-addressed, stamped postcard with your phone number for Awards Banquet information. Enclose a self-addressed, stamped envelope for copy of winners list (optional).

An entry fee of $5 entitles the writer to one entry in EACH category except Category 1, which is a $2 fee. Only one entry per category is allowed.

Students pay NO entry fee for Youth Awards. Put entrant's name, address, age, grade, and school on left corner of a 3x5 card, with category number, the title and first line of the work. On entry, follow guideline above. Do NOT put your name on the entry.

Keep exact copies, as entries will be destroyed following the awards.

Entries should be postmarked no later than September 1, 2001.

Mail entries to: Nina Mason, 910 Grant Avenue, Pasagoula, MS 39567-7222.

YALE UNIVERSITY PRESS

302 Temple Street
New Haven, CT 06520

Mailing Address:
P.O. Box 209040
New Haven, CT 06520-9040
Phone (203) 432-0960; Fax (203) 432-0948
Marketing (203) 432-0961; Fax (203) 432-0948
Editorial (203) 432-0900; Fax (203) 432-2394
Production (203) 432-7484; Fax (203) 432-4061

Deadline: February 1, 2001 – February 28, 2001 postmark

THE YALE SERIES OF YOUNGER POETS
Each year Yale University Press seeks one new book of poetry to publish in the Yale Series of Younger Poets. Selection is made through a competition that is open to any American Citizen under forty years of age (at the time the manuscript is submitted) who has not previously published a volume of poetry. The author receives the standard royalties.

Eligibility
All poems must be original; translations are not acceptable. Writers who have had volumes of poetry printed privately or printed in limited editions of no more than 300 copies are eligible. A contestant may submit only one manuscript a year. Manuscripts submitted in previous years may be resubmitted.

Submission Guidelines
There is no official application form, but entries must meet these requirements:

1. The manuscript should be at least 48 pages and no more than 64 pages in length.
2. The manuscript should begin with a title page including the book's title, your name, address, and telephone number, and, if you have e-mail, your e-mail address. Submissions to the contest are not blind.
3. A Table of Contents and a list of acknowledgments should follow the title page.
4. The manuscript should be paginated, beginning with the first page of poetry.
5. There should be no more than one poem on each page. Poems may, however, run longer than one page.
6. A brief biography may be appended to the back the manuscript, but it is not obligatory and is not included in the page count.

Submissions must be postmarked during the month of February.

Please place your manuscript in a plain 8-1/2 x 11 inch envelope, without blinding of any sort. It should be accompanied by check in the amount of $15.00 made payable to "Yale University Press." If you wish receipt of your manuscript to be acknowledged, please include a stamped, self-addressed postcard. Do not send the only copy of your work. Manuscripts cannot be returned at the end of the competition, and individual comments on the manuscripts cannot be made. If you wish to be informed, during the summer, of the results of the competition, also send a stamped, self-addressed envelope.

Manuscripts and correspondence should be sent to: The Editor, Yale Series of Younger Poets, Box 209040, New Haven, CT 06520-9040.

Y.E.S. FESTIVAL

Sandra Forman, Project Director
Y.E.S Festival
Department of Theatre, FA 228
Northern Kentucky University
Nunn Drive
Highland Heights, KY 41099-1007
E-mail: conger@nku.edu

Deadline: May 1, 2001 – October 31, 2001
Attention playwrights and friends of playwrights! The Department of Theatre of Northern Kentucky University (NKU) is once again seeking scripts for its award-winning Y.E.S Festival of New Plays at Northern Kentucky University, To be staged in mid-April 2002.

Full-length plays and musicals are eligible for this 11th biennial year-end series. Three selected playwrights will each receive a cash prize of $400 and an expense-paid visit to NKU to see their winning plays. Plays will receive a full production; one additional play may be selected to receive a staged reading.

It is the Festival's intention to bring in a noted professional playwright to read the plays and see them in performance. He or she will meet with the festival winners to discuss their plays.

Submissions will be accepted from May 1 through October 31, 2001. Winners will be notified no later than December 31, 2001.

Guidelines
Scripts must be standard-sized, legibly typed, and bound. Standard Dramatist Guild form is preferred.

A play may not have had a previous professional or university production.

Scripts are not returnable (unless specifically requested and accompanied with a self-addressed envelope and postage).

Enclose a self-addressed, stamped postcard if you wish Y.E.S. to acknowledge receipt of your script.

All rights must be fully owned by the author.

No children's theatre, one-acts, or reader's theatre pieces will be considered. Adaptations will be considered only if the adapted work is in the public domain.

Musicals with small orchestra demands will be considered. Musicals should be submitted only if a vocal score and piano/conductor score is available.

In deciding which play to submit, a writer should know our actors will be students ranging in age from 17 to 25. Some faculty members or guest artists may be available for the Festival. However, a play with especially strong demands for mature character roles would not be as likely to be selected as one of equal quality with roles for young adults.

A Y.E.S. Entry Form should accompany each submitted script.

Scripts may be submitted from May 1 until October 31, 2001. Selections will be made and winners notified no later than December 31, 2001. Returnable scripts will be mailed back after the winners have been notified.

It is important that selected playwrights be available to visit the Festival in April 2002, so their visit can be arranged to include late rehearsals and the opening of their play. The visiting dates are at our discretion. Playwrights, and the directors of their plays, will participate in a post-show question-and-answer session with the audience.

In addition to the three plays selected for full productions, one script can be selected for a stage reading during the festival. The playwright of this script will also be brought in for late rehearsals and opening. Be sure and indicate on the Entry Form if you are willing to have your script considered for this reading.

To enter, fill out the Entry Form and send it with your manuscript to the Y.E.S Project Director. Mail all entries and correspondence to: Sandra Forman, Project Director, Y.E.S. Festival, Department of Theatre, Northern Kentucky University, Highland Heights, KY 41099-1007.

Y.E.S. Festival of New Plays
Northern Kentucky University
Entry Form

Playwright's Name ________________________________

Address ________________________________

City/State/Zip ________________________________

Telephone ________________________________

(Your signature indicates to us that you agree to abide by the "Guidelines" and will make yourself available for a short visit to NKU, at our expense, if your script is selected for production.)

Title of submitted play ________________________________

____

Signature ________________________ Date __________

If not selected for a full production, I (circle one):

would   would NOT

be interested in a staged reading for my script.

YOUNG PLAYWRIGHTS INC.

Sheri M. Goldhirsch, Artistic Director
Brett W. Reynolds, Managing Director
321 West 44th Street, Suite 906
New York, NY 10036
Phone (212) 307-1140; Fax: (212) 307-1454
E-mail writeaplay@aol.com
Website www.youngplaywrights.org

Deadline: April 15, 2001 postmark

2001 NEW YORK CITY HIGH SCHOOL PLAYWRITING CONTEST
Prizes: Cash awards for the 1st, 2nd, and 3rd place. Professionally staged readings of the winning plays at the annual Awards Ceremony in June. A Certificate of Merit, a written evaluation of the play, and an invitation to the Ceremony for every student who submits a play.

Guidelines
The contest is open to all NYC public high school students. Plays must be submitted by students, not teachers. There are no restrictions on length, style, or subject, but collaborations of more than two writers will not be accepted. Screenplays and musicals are not eligible, nor are adaptations of other authors' work. Scripts should be typed and stapled, and pages must be numbered. Scripts must have a cover page with all the following information: title of play, playwright's name, home address, (with apartment # and zip code), phone number, school, grade, and date of birth.

Submit a copy of your play and keep the original. Scripts will not be returned. Send scripts, by deadline, to above contest name and address.

Deadline: December 1, 2000 postmark

2001 NATIONAL PLAYWRITING COMPETITION
Prize: Each author receives an evaluation of their play and the winning writers attend the intense Young Playwrights Writers Conference in New York City.

Guidelines
You must be 18 years old or younger (as of deadline).
Style, subject, and length are up to you; you may submit more than one play. Scripts must be original. No screenplays, musicals or adaptations. Collaborations are permitted, but all writers must be 18 years old or younger. Scripts must be typed and stapled, with numbered pages.

Scripts must be submitted by the author, not by a teacher or parent. The title page must list your name, date of birth, complete home address, and telephone number. Please keep your original script and submit a copy. Scripts will not be returned. Send submissions to above contest and address by deadline.

ZOETROPE: ALL STORY

1350 Avenue of the Americas
New York, NY 10019

Deadline: April 15, 2001 postmark

SAM ADAMS/ZOETROPE SHORT STORY CONTEST
Award: all-expense paid trip to the Fifth Annual Zoetrope Short Story Writers' Workshop at Francis Ford Coppola's Blancaneaux Lodge in Belize.

Guidelines
5,000 words or under (no novel excerpts or short-shorts)

Clearly mark "Short Story Contest" on both the story and the outside of the envelope.

You must be 21 to enter.

One submission per entrant, please.

Short stories do not have to mention Sam Adams.

Copies of submitted stories will not be returned.

The contest is void in Texas, South Carolina, California, Utah and where otherwise prohibited by law.

Deadline: October 1, 2001 postmark

ZOETROPE: ALL-STORY SHORT FICTION CONTEST
Awards: First Prize, $1,000; Second Prize, $500; and Third Prize, $250

Guidelines
5,000 words or under (no novel excerpts or short-shorts)

Clearly mark "Short Story Contest" on both the story and the outside of the envelope.

$10 entry fee made payable to AZX Publications.

ZONE 3

Austin Peay State University
P.O. Box 4565
Clarksville, TN 37044

Deadline: January 1, 2002

FORTEENTH ANNUAL *ZONE 3* COMPETITION
The Rainmaker Awards in Poetry: First, $500; Second, $300; and Third, $100. *Zone 3* is a non-profit journal published in the Spring and Fall by the Center of Excellence for the creative arts at Austin Peay State University in Clarksville, Tennessee. Manuscript deadlines are January 1 (Fall/Winter) and July 1 (Spring/Summer issue).

Guidelines
A maximum of three poems should be submitted for the Fall/Winter, 2003 issue, postmarked no later than January 1, 2002. Mailed to the above address.

The entrance fee is a one year's subscription to *Zone 3*: one year (two issues); two years for $15.

Those who submit for the Fall/Winter issue without subscribing will be notified of the awards and invited to enter the competition by subscribing. Those submitting who prefer not to subscribe will be considered for publication but will not be included in the competition.

No simultaneous submissions.

Announcements of the winners will be made in the Fall/Winter 2003 issue of *Zone 3;* and their poems will be suitably featured.

The competition will be judged by the editors of *Zone 3* and by an independent finals judge, a poet of high reputation whose identity will be revealed when the awards are made.

Write for a subscription form!

APPENDIX
A

Circular 1

COPYRIGHT BASICS

Copyright Office, Library of Congress, Washington, D.C. 20559-6000

WHAT IS COPYRIGHT?

Copyright is a form of protection provided by the laws of the United States (title 17, U.S. Code) to the authors of "original works of authorship" including literary, dramatic, musical, artistic, and certain other intellectual works. This protection is available to both published and unpublished works. Section 106 of the 1976 Copyright Act generally gives the owner of copyright the exclusive right to do and to authorize others to do the following:

- ***To reproduce*** the work in copies or phonorecords;
- To prepare ***derivative works*** based upon the work;
- ***To distribute copies or phonorecords*** of the work to the public by sale or other transfer of ownership, or by rental, lease, or lending;
- ***To perform the work publicly,*** in the case of literary, musical, dramatic, and choreographic works, pantomimes, and pictorial, graphic, or sculptural works, including the individual images of a motion picture or other audiovisual work; and
- ***To display the work publicly,*** in the case of literary, musical, dramatic, and choreographic works, pantomimes, and pictorial, graphic, or sculptural works, including the individual images of a motion picture or other audiovisual work; and
- In the case of ***sound recordings, to perform the work publicly*** by means of a ***digital audio transmission.***

In addition, certain authors of works of visual art have the right of attribution and integrity as described in section 106A of the 1976 Copyright Act. For further information, request Circular 40.

It is illegal for anyone to violate any of the rights provided by the copyright code to the owner of copyright. These rights, however, are not unlimited in scope. Sections 107 through 120 of the 1976 Copyright Act establish limitations on these rights. In some cases, these limitations are specified exemptions from copyright liability. One major limitation is the doctrine of "fair use," which is given a statutory basis in section 107 of the 1976 Copyright Act. In other instances the limitation takes the form of a "compulsory license" under which certain limited uses of copyrighted works are permitted upon payment of specified royalties and compliance with statutory conditions. For further information about the limitations of any of these rights, consult the copyright code or write to the Copyright Office.

WHO CAN CLAIM COPYRIGHT?

Copyright protection subsists from the time the work is created in fixed form. The copyright in the work of authorship ***immediately*** becomes the property of the author who created the work. Only the author of those deriving their rights through the author can rightfully claim copyright.

In the case of works made for hire, the employer and not the employee is considered to be the author. Section 101 of the copyright statute defines a "work made for hire" as;

(1) a work prepared by an employee within the scope of his or her employment; or

(2) a work specially ordered or commissioned for use as a contribution to a collective work, as a part of a motion picture or other audiovisual work, as a translation, as a supplementary work, as a compilation, as an instructional text, as a test, as answer material for a test, or as an atlas, if the parties expressly agree in a written instrument signed by them that the work shall be considered a work made for hire.

The authors of a joint work are co-owners of the copyright in the work, unless there is an agreement to the contrary.

Copyright in each separate contribution to a periodical or other collective work is distinct from copyright in the collective work as a whole and vests initially with the author of the contribution.

Two General Principles

- Mere ownership of a book, manuscript, painting, or any other copy or phonorecord does not give the possessor the copyright. The law provides that transfer of ownership of any material object that embodies a protected work does not of itself convey any rights in the copyright.

- Minors may claim copyright, but state laws may regulate the business dealings involving copyrights owned by minors. For information on relevant state laws, consult an attorney.

COPYRIGHT AND NATIONAL ORIGIN OF THE WORK

Copyright protection is available for all unpublished works, regardless of the nationality or domicile of the author.

Published works are eligible for copyright protection in the United States if ***any*** one of the following conditions is met:

- On the date of first publication, one or more of the authors is a national or domiciliary of the United States or is a national, domiciliary, or sovereign authority of a foreign nation that is party to a copyright treaty to which the United States is also a party, or is a stateless person wherever that person may be domiciled; or

- The work is first published in the United States or in a foreign nation that, on the date of first publication, is a party to the Universal Copyright Convention; or the work comes within the scope of a Presidential proclamation; or

- The work is first published on or after March 1, 1989, in a foreign nation that on the date of first publication is a party to the Berne Convention; or, if the work is not first published in a country party to the Berne Convention, it is published (on or after March 1, 1989) within 30 days of first publication in a country that is party to the Berne Convention; or the work first published on or after March 1, 1989, is a pictorial, graphic, or sculptural work that is incorporated in a permanent structure located in the United States; or, if the work, first published on or after March 1, 1989 is a published audiovisual work, all the authors are legal entities with headquarters in the United States.

- The work is a foreign work that was in the public domain in the United States prior to 1996 and its copyright was restored under the Uruguay Round Agreements Act (URAA). Request Circular 38b for further information.

WHAT WORKS ARE PROTECTED?

Copyright protects "original works of authorship" that are fixed in a tangible form of expression. The fixation need not be directly perceptible so long as it may be communicated with the aid of a machine or device. Copyrightable works include the following categories:
(1) literary works;
(2) musical works, including any accompanying words;
(3) dramatic works, including any accompanying works;
(4) pantomimes and choreographic works;
(5) pictorial, graphic, and sculptural works;
(6) motion pictures and other audiovisual works;

(7) sound recordings; and
(8) architectural works.

These categories should be viewed broadly. For example, computer programs and most "compilations" may be registered as "literary works"; maps and architectural plans may be registered as "pictorial, graphic, and sculptural works."

WHAT IS NOT PROTECTED BY COPYRIGHT?

Several categories of material are generally not eligible for Federal copyright protection. These include among others:

- Works that have ***not*** been fixed in a tangible form of expression. For example: choreographic works that have not been notated or recorded, or improvisational speeches or performances that have not been written or recorded.

- Titles, names, short phrases, and slogans; familiar symbols or designs; mere variations of typographic ornamentation, lettering, or coloring; mere listings of ingredients or contents.

- Ideas, procedures, methods, systems, processes, concepts, principles, discoveries, or devices, as distinguished from a description, explanation, or illustration.

- Works consisting ***entirely*** of information that is common property and containing no original authorship. For example; standard calendars, height and weight charts, tape measures and rulers, and lists or tables taken from public documents or to the common sources.

HOW TO SECURE A COPYRIGHT

Copyright Secured Automatically Upon Creation

The way in which copyright protection is secured is frequently misunderstood. No publication or registration or other action in the Copyright Office is required to secure copyright. (See following NOTE.) There are, however, certain definite advantages to registration. See "Copyright Registration" below.

Copyright is secured ***automatically*** when the work is created, and a work is "created" when it is fixed in a copy or phonorecord for the first time. "Copies" are material objects from which a work can be read or visually perceived either directly or with the aid of a machine or device, such as books, manuscripts, sheet music, film, videotape, or microfilm. "Phonorecords" are material objects embodying fixations of sounds (excluding, by statutory definition, motion picture soundtracks), such as cassette tapes, CDs, or LPs. Thus, for example, a song (the "work") can be fixed in sheet music ("copies") or in phonograph discs ("phonorecords"), or both.

If a work is prepared over a period of time, the part of the work that is fixed on a particular date constitutes the created work as of that date.

PUBLICATION

Publication is no longer the key to obtaining Federal copyright as it was under the Copyright Act of 1909. However, publication remains important to copyright owners.

The Copyright Act defines publication as follows:

> "Publication" is the distribution of copies or phonorecords of a work to the public by sale or other transfer of ownership, or by rental, lease, or lending. The offering to distribute copies or phonorecords to a group of persons for purposes of further distribution, public performance, or public display constitutes publication. A public performance or display of a work does not of itself constitute publication.

NOTE: Before 1978, Federal copyright was generally secured by the act of publication with notice of copyright, assuming compliance with all other relevant statutory conditions. U.S. works in the public domain on January 1, 1978, (for example, works published without satisfying all conditions for securing Federal copyright under the Copyright Act of 1909) remain in the public domain under the 1976 Copyright Act.

Certain foreign works originally published without notice had their copyrights restored under the Uruguay Round Agreements Act (URAA). Request Circular 38b and see the "Notice of Copyright" section below for further information.

Federal copyright could also be secured before 1978 by the act of registration in the case of certain unpublished works and works eligible for ad interim copyright. The 1976 Copyright Act automatically extends to full term (section 304 sets the term) copyright for all works including those subject to ad interim copyright if ad interim registration has been made on or before June 30, 1978.

A further discussion of the definition of "publication" can be found in the legislative history of the 1976 Copyright Act.

The legislative reports define "to the public" as distribution to persons under no explicit or implicit restrictions with respect to disclosure of the contents. The reports state that the definition makes it clear that the sale of phonorecords constitutes publication of the underlying work, for example, the musical, dramatic, or literary work embodied in a phonorecord. The reports also state that it is clear that any form of dissemination in which the material object does not change hands, for example, performances or displays on television, is not a publication no matter how many people are exposed to the work. However, when copies or phonorecords are offered for sale or lease to a group of wholesalers, broadcasters, or motion picture theaters, publication does take place if the purpose is further distribution, public performance, or public display.

Publication is an important concept in the copyright law for several reasons:

- Works that are published in the United States are subject to mandatory deposit with the Library of Congress. See discussion on "Mandatory Deposit for Works Published in the United States" below.

- Publication of a work can affect the limitations on the exclusive rights of the copyright owner that are set forth in sections 107 through 120 of the law.

- The year of publication may determine the duration of copyright protection for anonymous and pseudonymous works (when the author's identity is not revealed in the records of the Copyright Office) and for works made for hire.

- Deposit requirements for registration of published works differ from those for registration of unpublished works. See discussion on "Registration Procedures" below.

- When a work is published, it may bear a notice of copyright to identify the year of publication and the name of the copyright owner and to inform the public that the work is protected by copyright. Copies of works published before March 1, 1989 must bear the notice or risk loss of copyright protection. See discussion on "Notice of Copyright" below.

NOTICE OF COPYRIGHT

The use of a copyright notice is no longer required under U.S. law, although it is often beneficial. Because prior law did contain such a requirement, however, the use of notice is still relevant to the copyright status of older works.

Notice was required under the 1976 Copyright Act. This requirement was eliminated when the United States adhered to the Berne Convention, effective March 1, 1989. Although works published without notice before that date could have entered the public domain in the United States, the Uruguay Round Agreements Act (URAA0 restores copyright in certain foreign works originally published without notice. For further information about copyright amendments in the URAA, request Circular 38b.

The Copyright Office does not take a position on whether copies of works first published with notice before March 1, 1989, which are distributed on or after March 1, 1989, must bear the copyright notice.

Use of the notice may be important because it informs the public that the work is protected by copyright, identifies the copyright owner, and shows the year of first publication. Furthermore, in the event that a work is infringed, if a proper notice of copyright appears on the published copy or copies to which a defendant in a copyright infringement suit had access, then no weight shall be given to such a defendant's interposition of a defense based on innocent infringement in mitigation of actual or statutory damages, except as provided in section 504(c)(2) of the copyright code. Innocent infringement occurs when the infringer did not realize that the work was protected.

The use of the copyright notice is the responsibility of the copyright owner and does not require advance permission from, or registration with, the Copyright Office.

Form of Notice For Visually Perceptible Copies

The notice for visually perceptible copies should contain all of the following three elements:

1. ***The symbol*** © (the letter C in a circle), or the word "Copyright," or

the abbreviation "Copr."; and

2. ***The year of first publication*** of the work. In the case of compilations or derivative works incorporating previously published material, the year date of first publication of the compilation or derivative work is sufficient. The year date may be omitted where a pictorial, graphic, or sculptural work, with accompanying textual matter, if any, is reproduced in or on greeting cards, postcards, stationery, jewelry, dolls, toys, or any useful article; and

3. ***The name of the owner of copyright*** in the work, or an abbreviation by which the name can be recognized, or a generally known alternative designation of the owner.

Example: © 1996 Joe Doe

The "C in a circle" notice is used only on "visually perceptible copies." Certain kinds of works – for example, musical, dramatic, and literary works – may be fixed not in "copies" but by means of sound in an audio recording. Since audio recordings such as audio tapes and phonograph disks are "phonorecords", and not "copies," the "C in a circle" notice is not used to indicate protection of the underlying musical, dramatic, or literary work that is recorded.

Form of Notice for Phonorecords of Sound Recordings*

The notice for phonorecords embodying a sound recording should contain all of the following three elements:

1 ***The symbol*** Ⓟ (the letter P in a circle); and

2. ***The year of first publication*** of the sound recording; and

3. ***The name of the owner of copyright*** in the soundrecording, or an abbreviation by which the name can be recognized, or a generally known alternative designation of the owner. If the producer of the

---

** Sound recordings are defined in the law as "works that result from the fixation of a series of musical, spoken, or other sounds, but not including the sounds accompanying a motion picture or other audiovisual work." Common examples include recordings of music, drama, or lectures. A sound recording is not the same as a phonorecord. A phonorecord is the physical object in which works of authorship are embodied. The word "phonorecord" includes cassette tapes, CDs, LPs, 45 r.p.m. disks, as well as other formats.*

sound recording is named on the phonorecord label or container and if no other name appears in conjunction with the notice, the producer's name shall be considered a part of the notice.

Example: Ⓟ 1996 A.B.C. Records Inc.

NOTE: Since questions may arise from the use of variant forms of the notice, you may wish to seek legal advice before using any form of the notice other than those given here.

Position of Notice

The copyright notice should be affixed to copies or phonorecords in such a way as to "give reasonable notice of the claim of copyright." The three elements of the notice should ordinarily appear together on the copies or phonorecords or on the phonorecord label or container. The Copyright Office has issued regulations concerning the form and position of the copyright notice in the Code of Federal Regulations (37 CFR Part 201). For more information, request Circular 3.

Publications Incorporating U.S. Government Works

Works by the U.S. Government are not eligible for U.S. copyright protection. For works published on and after March 1, 1989, the previous notice requirement for works consisting primarily of one or more U.S. Government works has been eliminated. However, use of a notice on such a work will defeat a claim of innocent infringement as previously described ***provided*** the notice also includes a statement that identifies either those portions of the work in which copyright is claimed or those portions that constitute U.S. Government material.

Example: © 1996 James Brown. Copyright claimed in Chapters 7-10, exclusive of U.S. Government maps

Copies of works published before March 1, 1989, that consist primarily of one or more works of the U.S. Government should have a notice and the identifying statement.

Unpublished Works

The author or copyright owner may wish to place a copyright notice on any unpublished copies or phonorecords that leave his or her control.

Example: Unpublished work © 1996 Jane Doe

Omission of Notice and Errors in Notice

The 1976 Copyright Act attempted to ameliorate the strict consequences of failure to include notice under prior law. It contained provisions that set out specific corrective steps to cure omissions or certain errors in notice. Under these provisions, an applicant had 5 years after publication to cure omission of notice or certain errors. Although these provisions are technically still in the law, their impact has been limited by the amendment making notice optional for all works published on and after March 1, 1989. For further information, request Circular 3.

HOW LONG COPYRIGHT PROTECTION ENDURES

Works Originally Created On or After January 1, 1978

A work that is created (fixed in tangible form for the first time) on or after January 1, 1978, is automatically protected from the moment of its creation and is ordinarily given a term enduring for the author's life plus an additional 50 years after the author's death. In the case of a "joint work prepared by two or more authors who did not work for hire," the term lasts for 50 years after the last surviving author's death. For works made for hire, and for anonymous and pseudonymous works (unless the author's identity is revealed in Copyright Office records), the duration of copyright will be 75 years from publication or 100 years from creation, whichever is shorter.

Works Originally Created Before January 1, 1978, But Not Published or Registered by That Date

These works have been automatically brought under the statute and are now given Federal copyright protection. The duration of copyright in these works will generally be computed in the same way as for works created on or after January 1, 1978: the life-plus-50 or 75/100-year terms will apply to them as well. The law provides that in no case will the term of copyright for works in this category expire before December 31, 2002, and for works published on or before December 31, 2002, the term of copyright will not expire before December 31, 2027.

Works Originally Created and Published or Registered Before January 1, 1978

Under the law in effect before 1978, copyright was secured either on that date a work was published or on the date of registration if the work was registered in unpublished form. In either case, the copyright endured for a first term of 28 years from the date it was secured. During the last (28th) year of the first term, the copyright was eligible for renewal. The current copyright law has extended the renewal term from 28 to 47 years for copyrights that were subsisting on January 1, 1978, making these works eligible for a total term of protection 75 years.

Public Law 102-307, enacted on June 26, 1992, amended the 1976 Copyright Act to extend automatically the term of copyrights secured between January 1, 1964, and December 31, 1977, to the further term of 47 years although the renewal term is automatically provided, the Copyright Office does not issue a renewal certificate for these works unless a renewal application and fee are received and registered in the Copyright Office.

P.L. 102-307 makes renewal registration optional. There is no need to make the renewal filing in order to extend the original 28-year copyright term to the full 75 years. **However, some benefits accrue from making a renewal registration during the 28th year of the original term.**

For more detailed information on the renewal of copyright and the copyright term, request Circulars 15, 15a and 15t.

TRANSFER OF COPYRIGHT

Any or all of the copyright owner's exclusive rights or any subdivision of those rights may be transferred, but the transfer of exclusive rights is not valid unless that transfer is in writing and signed by the owner of the rights conveyed or such owner's duly authorized agent. Transfer of a right on a nonexclusive basis does not require a written agreement.

A copyright may also be conveyed by operation of law and may be bequeathed by will or pass as personal property by the applicable laws of intestate succession.

Copyright is a personal property right, and it is subject to the various state laws and regulations that govern the ownership, inheritance, or transfer of personal property as well as terms of contracts or conduct of business. For information about relevant state laws, consult an attorney.

Transfers of copyright are normally made by contract. The Copyright Office does not have any forms for such transfers. The law does provide for the recordation in the Copyright Office of transfers of copyright ownership. Although recordation is not required to make a valid transfer between the parties, it does provide certain legal advantages and may be required to validate the transfer as against third parties. For information on recordation of transfers and other documents related to copyright, request Circular 12.

Termination of Transfers

Under the previous law, the copyright in a work reverted to the author, if living, or if the author was not living, to other specified beneficiaries, provided a renewal claim was registered in the 28th year of the original term.* The present law drops the renewal feature except for works already in the first term of statutory protection when the present law took effect. Instead, the present law permits termination of a grant of rights after 35 years under certain conditions by serving written notice on the transferee within specified time limits.

For works already under statutory copyright protection before 1978, the present law provides a similar right of termination covering the newly added years that extended the former maximum term of the copyright from 56 to 75 years. For further information, request Circulars 15a and 15t.

INTERNATIONAL COPYRIGHT PROTECTION

There is no such thing as an "international copyright" that will automatically protect an author's writings throughout the entire world. Protection against unauthorized use in a particular country depends, basically, on the national laws of that country. However, most countries do offer protection to foreign works under certain conditions, and these conditions have been greatly simplified by international copyright treaties and conventions. For further information and a list of countries which maintain copyright relations with the United States request Circular 38a.

** The copyright in works eligible for renewal on or after June 26, 1992, will vest in the name of the renewal claimant on the effective date of any renewal, registration made during the 28th year of the original term. Otherwise, the renewal copyright will vest in the party entitled to claim renewal as of December 31, of the 28th year.*

COPYRIGHT REGISTRATION

In general, copyright registration is a legal formality intended to make a public record of the basic facts of a particular copyright. However, registration is not a condition of copyright protection. Even though registration is not a requirement for protection, the copyright law provides several inducements or advantages to encourage copyright owners to make registration. Among these advantages are the following:

- Registration establishes a public record of the copyright claim;
- Before an infringement suit may be filed in court, registration is necessary for works of U.S. original and for foreign works not originating in a Berne Union country;
- If made before or within 5 years of publication, registration will establish prima facie evidence in court of the validity of the copyright and of the facts stated in the certificate;
- If registration is made within 3 months after publication of the work or prior to an infringement of the work, statutory damages and attorney's fees will be available to the copyright owner in court actions. Otherwise, only an award of actual damages and profits is available to the copyright owner;
- Registration allows the owner of the copyright to record the registration with the U.S. Customs Service for protection against the importation of infringing copies. For additional information, request Publication No. 563 from: Commissioner of Customs, ATTN: IPR Branch, Franklin Court, Suite 4000, U.S. Customs Service, 1301 Constitution Avenue, N.W., Washington, D.C. 20229.

Registration may be made at any time within the life of the copyright. Unlike the law before 1978,when a work has been registered in unpublished form, it is not necessary to make another registration when the work becomes published, although the copyright owner may register the published edition, if desired.

REGISTRATION PROCEDURES

Original Registration

To register a work, send the following three elements ***in the same envelope or package*** to:

Register of Copyrights
Copyright Office
Library of Congress
Washington, D.C. 20559-6000

1. A properly completed application form;
2. A nonrefundable filing fee of $20* for each application;
3. A nonrefundable deposit of the work being registered. The deposit requirements vary in particular situations. The ***general*** requirements follow. Also note the information under "Special Deposit Requirements" below.

- If the work is unpublished, one complete copy of phonorecord.
- If the work was first published in the United States on or after January 1, 1978, two complete copies or phonorecords of the best edition.
- If the work was first published in the United States before January 1, 1978, two complete copies or phonorecords of the work as first published.
- If the work was first published outside the United States, one complete copy or phonorecord or the work as first published.

What Happens If the Three Elements Are Not Received Together

Applications and fees received without appropriate copies, phonorecords, or identifying material will not be processed and ordinarily will be returned. Unpublished deposits without applications or fees ordinarily will be returned, also. In most cases, published deposits received without applications and fees can be immediately transferred to the collections of the Library of Congress. This practice is in accor-

---

* *For the fee structure for application Form SE/GROUP, Form GATT, Form GATT/GRP, and Form G/DN, see the instructions on these forms.*

dance with section 408 of the law, which provides that the published deposit required for the collections of the Library of Congress may be used for registration only if the deposit is "accompanied by the prescribed application and fee..."

After the deposit is received and transferred to another service unit of the Library for its collections or other disposition, it is no longer available to the Copyright Office. If you wish to register the work, you must deposit additional copies or phonorecords with your application and fee.

Renewal Registration

To register a renewal, send:
1. A properly completed application Form RE; and
2. A nonrefundable filing fee of $20 for each work.

> **NOTE:** Complete the application form using black ink pen or typewriter. You may photocopy blank application forms. However, photocopied forms, submitted to the Copyright Office must be clear, legible, on a good grade of 8 1/2- inch by 11-inch white paper suitable for automatic feeding through a photocopier. The forms should be printed, preferably in black ink, head-to-head so that when you turn the sheet over, the top of page 2 is directly behind the top of page 1. Forms not meeting these requirements will be returned and registration will be delayed.

Special Deposit Requirements

Special deposit requirements exist for many types of works. The following are prominent examples of exceptions to the general deposit requirements:

- If the work is a motion picture, the deposit requirement is one complete copy of the unpublished or published motion picture ***and*** a separate written description of its contents, such as a continuity, press book, or synopsis.

- If the work is a literary, dramatic, or musical work ***published only on phonorecord,*** the deposit requirement is one complete phonorecord.

- If the work is an unpublished or published computer program, the deposit requirement is one visually perceptible copy in source code of the ***first 25 and last 25 pages*** of the program. For a program of fewer than 50 pages, the deposit is a copy of the entire program. For more information on computer program registration, including deposits for revised programs and provisions for trade secrets, request Circular 61.

- If the work is in a CD-ROM format, the deposit requirement is one complete copy of the material, that is, the CD-ROM, the operating software, and any manual(s) accompanying it. If registration is sought for the computer program on the CD-ROM, the deposit should also include a printout of the first 25 and last 25 pages of source code for the program.

In the case of works reproduced in three-dimensional copies, identifying material such as photographs or drawings is ordinarily required. Other examples of special deposit requirements (but by no means an exhaustive list) include many works of the visual arts such as greeting cards, toys, fabrics, oversized materials (request Circular 40A); video games and other machine-readable audiovisual works (request Circular 61); automated databases (request Circular 65); and contributions to collective works. For information about deposit requirements for group registration of serials, request Circular 62.

If you are unsure of the deposit requirement for your work, write or call the Copyright Office and describe the work you wish to register.

Unpublished Collections

Under the following conditions, a work may be registered in unpublished form as a "collection," with one application form and one fee:

- The elements of the collection are assembled in an orderly form;

- The combined elements bear a single title identifying the collection as a whole;

- The copyright claimant in all the elements and in the collection as a whole is the same; and

- All of the elements are by the same author; or, if they are by different authors, at least one of the authors has contributed copyrightable authorship to each element.

An unpublished collection is not indexed under the individual titles of the contents but under the title of the collection.

> **NOTE: A Library of Congress Catalog Card Number** is different from a copyright registration number. The Cataloging in Publication (CIP) Division of the Library of Congress is responsible for assigning LC Catalog Numbers and is operationally separate from the Copyright Office. A book may be registered in or deposited with the Copyright Office but necessarily cataloged and added to the Library's collections. For information about obtaining an LC Catalog Card Number, contact the CIP Division, Library of Congress, Washington, D.C. 20540-4320. For information on International Standard Book Numbering (ISBN), write to: ISBN, R.R. Bowker, 121 Chanlon Road, New Providence, N.J. 07974. Call (908) 665-6770. For information on International Standard Serial Numbering (ISSN), write to: Library of Congress, National Serials Data Program, Serial Record Division, Washington, D.C. 20540-4160. Call (202) 707-6453. Or obtain information via the World Wide Web at *http://www.loc.gov/issn/.*

EFFECTIVE DATE OF REGISTRATION

A copyright registration is effective on the date the Copyright Office receives all of the required elements in acceptable form, regardless of how long it then takes to process the application and mail the certificate of registration. The time the Copyright Office requires to process an application varies, depending on the amount of material the Office is receiving and the personnel available. Keep in mind that it may take a number of days for mailed material to reach the Copyright Office and for the certificate of registration to reach the recipient after being mailed by the Copyright Office.

If you are filing an application for copyright registration in the Copyright Office, you ***will not*** receive an acknowledgement that your application has been received, but you can expect:

- A letter or telephone call from a Copyright Office staff member if further information is needed;

- A certificate of registration to indicate the work has been registered; or
- If registration cannot be made, a letter explaining why it has been refused.

Please allow 120 days to receive a letter or certificate of registration. Requests to have certificates available for pickup in the Public Information Office or to have certificates sent by Federal Express or another express mail service cannot be honored.

If you want to know when the Copyright Office receives your material, you should send it by registered or certified mail and request a return receipt from the post office. Allow at least 3 weeks for the return of your receipt. For further information, request Circular 4.

CORRECTIONS AND APPLICATIONS OF EXISTING REGISTRATIONS

To correct an error in a copyright registration or to amplify the information given in a registration, file a supplementary registration form – Form CA – with the Copyright Office. The information in a supplementary registration augments but does not supersede that contained in the earlier registration. Note also that a supplementary registration is not a substitute for an original registration, for a renewal registration, or for recording a transfer of ownership. For further information about supplementary registration, request Circular 8.

MANDATORY DEPOSIT FOR WORKS PUBLISHED IN THE UNITED STATES

Although a copyright registration is not required, the Copyright Act establishes a mandatory deposit requirement for works published in the United States. See the definition of "publication" on page 4. In general, the owner of copyright or the owner of the exclusive right of publication in the work has a legal obligation to deposit in the Copyright Office within 3 months of publication in the United States, two copies (or in the case of sound recordings, two phonorecords) for the use of the Library of Congress. Failure to make the deposit can result in fines and other penalties but does not affect copyright protection.

Certain categories of works are ***exempt entirely*** from the mandatory deposit requirements, and the obligation is reduced for certain other categories. For further information about mandatory deposit, request Circular 7d.

USE OF MANDATORY DEPOSIT TO SATISFY REGISTRATION REQUIREMENTS

For works published in the United States, the copyright code contains a provision under which a single deposit can be made to satisfy both the deposit requirements for the Library and the registration requirements. In order to have this dual effect, the copies or phonorecords must be accompanied by the prescribed application form and filing fee.

WHO MAY FILE AN APPLICATION FORM?

The following persons are legally entitled to submit an application form:

- **The author.** This is either the person who actually created the work, or, if the work was made for hire, the employer or other person for whom the work was prepared.
- **The copyright claimant.** The copyright claimant is defined in Copyright Office regulations as either the author of the work or a person or organization that has obtained ownership of all the rights under the copyright initially belonging to the author. This category includes a person or organization who has obtained by contract the right to claim legal title to the copyright in an application for copyright registration.
- **The owner of exclusive right(s).** Under the law, any of the exclusive rights that go to make up a copyright and any subdivision of them can be transferred and owned separately, even though the transfer may be limited in time or place of effect. The term "copyright owner" with respect to any one of the exclusive rights contained in a copyright refers to the owner of that particular right. Any owner of an exclusive right may apply for registration of a claim in the work.
- **The duly authorized agent** of such author, other copyright claimant, or owner of exclusive right(s). Any person authorized to act on behalf of the author, other copyright claimant, or owner of exclusive rights may apply for registration.

There is no requirement that applications be prepared or filed by an attorney.

APPLICATION FORMS

For Original Registration

Form PA: for published and unpublished works of the performing arts (musical and dramatic works, pantomimes and choreographic works, motion pictures and other audiovisual works)

Form SE: for serials, works issued or intended to be issued in successive parts bearing numerical or chronological designations and intended to be continued indefinitely (periodicals, newspapers, magazines, newsletters, annuals, journals, etc.)

Form SR: for published and unpublished soundrecordings

Form TX: for published and unpublished non-dramatic literary works

Form VA: for published and unpublished works of the visual arts (pictorial, graphic, and sculptural works, including architectural works)

FORM G/DN: a specialized form to register a complete month's issues of a daily newspaper when certain conditions are met

Short Form/SE and Form SE/GROUP: specialized SE forms for use when certain requirements are met

Short Forms TX, PA, and VA: short versions of applications for original registration. For further information about using the short forms, request publication SL-7.

Form GATT and Form GATT/GRP: specialized forms to register a claim in a work or group of related works in which U.S.copyright was restored under the 1994 Uruguay Round Agreements Act (URAA). For further information, request Circular 38b.

For Renewal Registration

Form RE: for claims to renewal copyright in works copyrighted under the law in effect through December 31, 1977 (1909 Copyright Act)

For Corrections and Amplifications

Form CA: for supplementary registration to correct or amplify information given in the Copyright Office record of an earlier registration

For a Group of Contributions to Periodicals

Form GR/CP: an adjunct application to be used for registration of a group of contributions to periodicals in addition to an application. Form TX, PA, or Va

Free application forms are supplied by the Copyright Office.

How to Obtain Application Forms

You may order copyright application forms as well as circulars 24 hours a day from the Copyright Office Forms Hotline (202)707-9100, or write:

Publications Section, LM-455
Copyright Office
Library of Congress
Washington, D.C. 20559-6000

Or you may obtain application forms via the Internet. All copyright application forms may be downloaded from the Internet and printed for use in registering a claim to copyright. The forms may be accessed and downloaded by connecting to the Library of Congress home page on the World Wide Web and selecting the copyright link. The address is: *http:/www.loc.gov.*

You may also connect through the Copyright Office home page. The address is: *http:/www.loc.gov/copyright.*

You must have Adobe Acrobat Reader installed on your computer to view and print the forms. Adobe Acrobat Reader may be downloaded free from Adobe Systems Incorporated through links from the same internet site from which the forms are available.

Print forms head to head (top of page 2 is directly behind the top of page 1) on a single piece of good quality, 8 1/2-inch by 11-inch white paper. To achieve the best quality copies of the application forms, use a laser printer.

FEES

All remittances should be in the form of drafts, that is, checks, money orders, or bank drafts, payable to: **Register of Copyrights**. Do not send cash. Drafts must be redeemable without service or exchange fee through a U. S. institution, must be payable in U.S. dollars, and must be imprinted with American Banking Association routing numbers. International Money orders and Postal Money Orders that are negotiable only at a post office are not acceptable.

If a check received in payment of the filing fee is returned to the Copyright Office as uncollectible, the Copyright office will cancel the registration and will notify the remitter.

The fee for processing an original, supplementary, or renewal claim is nonrefundable, whether or not copyright registration is ultimately made.

Do not send cash. The Copyright Office cannot assume any responsibility for the loss of currency sent in payment of copyright fees. For further information, request Circular 4.

SEARCH OF COPYRIGHT RECORDS

The records of the Copyright Office are open for inspection and searching by the public. Moreover, on request, the Copyright Office will search its records for you at the statutory rate of $20 for each hour or fraction of an hour. For information on searching the Office records concerning the copyright status of ownership of a work, request Circulars 22 and 23.

Copyright Office records in machine-readable form cataloged from January 1, 1978, to the present including registration information and recorded documents are now available for searching on the Internet. You may connect via the World Wide Web: *http://www.loc.gov/copyright* or gopher: *marvel.loc.gov* (port 70).

FOR FURTHER INFORMATION

To request Copyright Office publications including application forms and circular write to:

Publications Section, LM-455
Copyright Office
Library of Congress
Washington, D.C. 20559-6000

There is no charge for circulars and application forms supplied by the Copyright Office.

To speak with an information specialist, call (202) 707-3000 or TTY: (202) 707-6737, 8:30 a.m. to 5:00 p.m. Monday to Friday, eastern time, except Federal holidays. Recorded information is available 24 hours a day.

Selected circulars and announcements are available via fax. Call (202) 707-2600 from any touchtone telephone. Key in your fax number at the prompt and the document number of the item(s) you want. The item(s) will be transmitted to your fax machine. If you do not know the document number of the item(s) you want, you may request that a menu be faxed to you. You may order up to three items at a time. Note that copyright application forms are not available by fax.

Frequently requested Copyright Office circulars, announcements, regulations, and all copyright application forms are available at the internet address cited above.

For a list of other material published by the Copyright Office, request Circular 2, "Publications on Copyright."

The Copyright Public Information Office is open to the public 8:30 a.m. to 5:00 p.m. Monday to Friday, eastern time, except Federal holidays. The office is located in the Library of Congress, James Madison Memorial Building. Room 401, at 101 Independence Avenue, S.E. Washington, D.C., near the Capitol South Metro stop. Information specialists are available to answer questions, provide circulars, and accept applications for registration. Access for disabled individuals is at the front door on Independence Avenue, S.E.

The Copyright Office is not permitted to give legal advice. If information or guidance is needed on matters such as disputes over the ownership of a copyright, suits against possible infringers, the procedure for getting a work published, or the method of obtaining royalty payments, it may be necessary to consult an attorney.

Copyright Office, Library of Congress, Washington, D.C. 20559-6000

FILLING OUT APPLICATION FORM TX

Detach and read these instructions before completing this form. Make sure all applicable spaces have been filled in before you return this form.

Basic Information

When to Use This Form: Use TX for registration of published or unpublished nondramatic literary works, excluding periodicals or serial issues. This class includes a wide variety of works: fiction, nonfiction, poetry, textbooks, reference works, directories, catalogs, advertising copy, compilations of information, and computer programs. For periodicals and serials, use form SE.

Deposit to accompany Application: An application for copyright registration must be accompanied by a deposit consisting of copies or phonorecords representing the entire work for which registration is to be made. The following are the general deposit requirements as set forth in the statue:

> **Unpublished Work:** Deposit one complete copy (or phonorecord).
> **Published Work:** Deposit two complete copies (or one phonorecord) of the best edition.
> **Work First Published Outside the United States:** Deposit one complete copy (or phonorecord) of the first foreign edition.
> **Contribution to a Collective Work:** Deposit one complete copy (or phonorecord) of the best edition of the collective work.

The Copyright Notice: For works first published on or after March 1, 1989, the law provides that a copyright notice in a specified form "may be placed on all publicly distributed copies from which the work can be visually perceived." Use of the copyright notice is the responsibility of the copyright owner and does not require advance permission from the Copyright Office. The required form of the notice for copies generally consists of three elements: (1) the symbol "©" or the word "Copyright," or the abbreviation "Copr."; (2) the year of first publication; and (3) the name of the owner of copyright. For example: "© 1995 Jane Cole." The notice is to be affixed to the copies "in such manner and location as to give reasonable notice of the claim of copyright." Works first published prior to March 1, 1989 **must** carry the notice or risk loss of copyright protection.

For information about notice requirements for works published before March 1, 1989, or other copyright information, write: Information Section, LM-401, Copyright Office, Library of Congress, Washington, D.C. 20559-6000.

PRIVACY ACT ADVISORY STATEMENT
Required by the Privacy Act of 1974
(Public Law 93-579)

AUTHORITY FOR REQUESTING THIS INFORMATION:
- Title 17, U.S.C., Secs. 409 and 410

FURNISHING THE REQUESTED INFORMATION IS:
- Voluntary

BUT IF THE INFORMATION IS NOT FURNISHED:
- It may be necessary to delay or refuse registration
- You may not be entitled to certain relief, remedies, and benefits provided in chapters 4 and 5 of title 17, U.S.C.

PRINCIPAL USES OF REQUESTED INFORMATION:
- Establishment and maintenance of a public record
- Examination of the application for compliance with legal requirements

OTHER ROUTINE USES:
- Public inspection and copying
- Preparation of public indexes
- Preparation of public catalogs of copyright registrations
- Preparation of search reports upon request

NOTE:
- No other advisory statement will be given you in connection with this application
- Please keep this statement and refer to it if we communicate with you regarding this application

Line-By-Line Instructions

Please type or print using black ink.

1 SPACE 1: **Title**

Title of This Work: Every work submitted for copyright registration must be given a title to identify that particular work. If the copies or phonorecords of the work bear a title or an identifying phrase that could serve as a title, transcribe that wording *completely* and *exactly* on the application. Indexing of the registration and future identification of the work will depend on the information you give here.

Previous or Alternative Titles: Complete this space if there are any additional titles for the work under which someone searching for the registration might be likely to look or under which a document pertaining to the work might be recorded.

Publication as a Contribution: If the work being registered is a contribution to a periodical, serial, or collection, give the title of the contribution in the "Title of this Work" space. Then, in the line headed "Publication as a Contribution," give information about the collective work in which the contribution appeared.

2 SPACE 2: **Author(s)**

General Instructions: After reading these instructions, decide who are the "authors" of this work for copyright purposes. Then, unless the work is a "collective work", give the requested information about every "author" who contributed any appreciable amount of copyrightable matter to this version of the work. If you need further space, request Continuation sheets. In the case of a collective work such as an anthology, collection of essays, or encyclopedia, give information about the author of the collective work as a whole.

Name of Author: The fullest form of the author's name should be given. Unless the work was "made for hire", the individual who actually created work is its "author." In the case of a work made for hire, the statute provides that "the employer or other person for whom the work was prepared is considered the author."

What is a "Work Made For Hire"? A "work made for hire" is defined as (1) "a work prepared by an employee within the scope of his or her employment"; or (2) "a work specially ordered or commissioned for use as a contribution to a collective work, as a part of a motion picture or other audiovisual work, as a translation, as a supplementary work, as a compilation, as an instructional text, as a test, as answer material for a test, or as an atlas, if the parties expressly agree in a written instrument signed by them that the works shall be considered a work made for hire." If you have checked "yes" to indicate that the work was "made for hire," you must give the full legal name of the employer (or the person for whom the work was prepared). You may also include the name of the employee along with the name of the employer (for example: Elster Publishing Co., employer for hire of John Ferguson").

"Anonymous" or "Pseudonymous" Work: An author's contribution to a work is "anonymous" if that author is not identified on the copies or phonorecords of the work. An author's contribution to a work is "pseudonymous" if that author is identified on the copies or phonorecords under a fictitious name. If the work is "anonymous" you may: (1) leave the line blank; or (2) state "anonymous" on the line; or (3) reveal the author's identity. If the work is "pseudonymous" you must: (1) leave the line blank; or (2) give the pseudonym and identify it as such (for example: "Huntley Haverstock, pseudonym"); or (3) reveal the author's name, making clear which is the real name and which is the pseudonym (for example, "Judith Barton, whose pseudonym is Madeline Elster"). However, the citizenship or domicile of the author **must** be given in all cases.

Dates of Birth and Death: If the author is dead, the statute requires that the year of death be included in the application unless the work is anonymous or pseudonymous. The author's birth date is optional but is useful as a form of identification. Leave this space blank if the author's contribution was a "work made for hire."

Author's Nationality or Domicile: Give the country of which the author is a citizen or the country in which the author is domiciled. Nationality or domicile **must** be given in all cases.

Nature of Authorship: After the words "Nature of Authorship," give a brief general statement of the nature of this particular author's contribution to the work. Examples: "Entire text"; "Coauthor of entire text"; "Computer program"; "Editorial revisions"; "Compilation and English translation"; "New text."

3 SPACE 3: **Creation and Publication**

General Instructions: Do not confuse "creation" with "publication." Every application for copyright registration must state "the year in which creation of the work was completed." Give the date and nation of first publication only if the work has been published.

Creation: Under the statute, a work is "created" when it is fixed in a copy or phonorecord for the first time. Where a work has been prepared over a period of time, the part of the work existing in fixed form on a particular date constitutes the created work on that date. The date you give here should be the year in which the author completed the particular version for which registration is now being sought, even if other versions exist or if further changes or additions are planned.

Publication: The statute defines "publication" as "the distribution of copies of phonorecords of a work to the public by sale or other transfer of ownership, or by rental, lease, or lending"; a work is also "published" if there has been an "offering to distribute copies or phonorecords to a group of persons for purposes of further distribution, public performance, or public display." Give the full date (month, day, year) when, and the country where, publication first occurred. If first publication took place simultaneously in the United States and other countries, it is sufficient to state "U.S.A."

4 SPACE 4: **Claimant(s)**

Name(s) and address(es) of Copyright Claimant(s): Give the name(s) and address(es) of the copyright claimant(s) in this work even if the claimant is the same as the author. Copyright in a work belongs initially to the author of the work (including, in the case of a work made for hire, the employer or other person for whom the work was prepared). The copyright claimant is either the author of the work or a person or organization to whom the copyright initially belonging to the author has been transferred.

Transfer: The statute provides that, if the copyright claimant is not the author, the application for registration must contain " a brief statement of how the claimant obtained ownership of the copyright." If any copyright claimant named in space 4 is not an author named in space 2, give a brief statement explaining how the claimant(s) obtained ownership of the copyright. Examples: "By written contract"; "Transfer of all right by author"; "Assignment"; "By will." Do not attach transfer documents or other attachments or riders.

5 SPACE 5: **Previous Registration**

General Instructions: The questions in space 5 are intended to show whether an earlier registration has been made for this work and, if so, whether there is any basis for a new registration. As a general rule, only one basic copyright registration can be made for the same version of a particular work.

Same Version: If this version is substantially the same as the work covered by a previous registration, a second registration is not generally possible unless: (1) the work has been registered in unpublished form and a second registration is now being sought to cover this first published edition; or (2) someone other than the author is identified as a copyright claimant in the earlier registration, and the author is now seeking registration in his or her own name. If either of these two exceptions apply, check the appropriate box and give the earlier registration number and date. Otherwise, do not submit Form TX; instead, write the Copyright Office for information about supplementary registration or recordation of transfers of copyright ownership.

Changed Version: If the work has been changed and you are now seeking registration to cover the additions or revisions, check the last box in space 5, give the earlier registration number and date, and complete both parts of space 6 in accordance with the instructions below.

Previous Registration Number and Date: If more than one previous registration has been made for the work, give the number and date of the latest registration.

6 SPACE 6: **Derivative Work or Compilation**

General Instructions: Complete space 6 if this work is a "changed version," "compilation," or "derivative work" and if it incorporates one or more earlier works that have already been published or registered for copyright or that have fallen into the public domain. A "compilation" is defined as "a work formed by the collection and assembling of preexisting materials or of data that are selected, coordinated, or arranged in such a way that the resulting work as a whole constitutes an original work of authorship." A "derivative work" is a "work based on one or more preexisting works." Examples of derivative works include translations, fictionalizations, abridgments, condensations, or "any other form in which a work may be recast, transformed, or adapted." Derivative works also include works "consisting of editorial revisions, annotations, or other modifications" if these changes, as a whole, represent an original work of authorship.

Preexisting Material (space 6a): For derivative works, complete this space **and** space 6b. In space 6a identify the preexisting work that has been recast, transformed, or adapted. An example of preexisting material might be "Russian version of Goncharov's 'Oblomov'." Do not complete space 6a for compilations.

Material Added to This Work (space 6b): Give a brief, general statement of the new material covered by the copyright claim for which registration is sought. **Derivative work** examples include: "Foreword, editing, critical annotations"; "Translation"; "Chapters 11-17." If the work is a **compilation**, describe both the compilation itself and the material that has been compiled. Example: "Compilation of certain 1917 Speeches by Woodrow Wilson." A work may be both a derivative work and compilation, in which case a sample statement might be: "Compilation and additional new material."

7 SPACE 7: **Manufacturing Provisions**
Due to the expiration of the Manufacturing Clause of the copyright law on June 30,1986, this space has been deleted.

8 SPACE 8: **Reproduction for use of Blind or Physically Handicapped Individuals**
General Instructions: One of the major programs of the Library of Congress is to provide Braille editions and special recordings of works for the exclusive use of the blind and physically handicapped. In an effort to simplify and speed up the copyright licensing procedures that are a necessary part of this program, section 710 of the copyright statute provides for the establishment of a voluntary licensing system to be tied in with copyright registration. Copyright Office regulations provide that you may grant a license for such reproduction and distribution solely for the use of persons who are certified by competent authority as unable to read normal printed material as a result of physical limitations. The license is entirely voluntary, nonexclusive, and may be terminated upon 90 days notice.

How to Grant the License: If you wish to grant it, check one of the three boxes in space 8. Your check in one of those boxes together with your signature in space 10 will mean that the Library of Congress can proceed to reproduce and distribute under the license without further paperwork. For further information, write for Circular 63.

9, 10, 11 SPACE 9,10,11: **Fee, Correspondence, Certification, Return Address**
Deposit Account: If you maintain a Deposit Account in the Copyright Office, identify it in space 9. Otherwise leave the space blank and send the fee of $20 with your application and deposit.

Correspondence (space 9): This space should contain the name, address, area code, and telephone number of the person to be consulted if correspondence about this application becomes necessary.

Certification (space 10): The application can not be accepted unless it bears the date and the **handwritten signature** of the author or other copyright claimant, or of the owner of the exclusive right(s), or of the duly authorized agent of the author, claimant, or owner of exclusive right(s).

Address for Return of Certificate (space 11): The address box must be completed legibly since the certificate will be returned in a window envelope.

APPENDIX
B

ASSOCIATION OF AUTHORS' REPRESENTATIVES, INC.

CANON OF ETHICS

10 Astor Place, 3rd Floor, New York, N.Y. 10003
(212) 353-3709

September 3, 1997

1. The members of the Association of Authors' Representatives, Inc. are committed to the highest standard of conduct in the performance of their professional activities. While affirming the necessity and desirability of maintaining their full individuality and freedom of action, the members pledge themselves to loyal service to their clients' business and artistic needs, and will allow no conflicts of interest that would interfere with such service. They pledge their support to the Association itself and to the principles of honorable coexistence, directness, and honesty in their relationships with their co-members. They undertake never to mislead, deceive, dupe, defraud, or victimize their clients, other members of the Association, the general public, or any person with whom they do business as a member of the Association.

2. Members shall take responsible measures to protect the security and integrity of clients' funds. Members must maintain separate bank accounts for money due their clients so there is no commingling of clients' and members' funds. Members shall deposit funds received on behalf of clients promptly upon receipt. and shall make payments of domestic earnings due clients promptly, but in no event later than ten business days after clearance. Revenues from foreign rights over $50 shall be paid to clients within ten business days after clearance. Sums under $50 shall be paid within a reasonable time of clearance. However, on stock and similar rights, statements of royalties and payments shall be made not later than the month following the member's receipt, each statement and payment to cover all royalties received to the 25th day of the previous calendar month. Payments for amateur rights shall be made not less frequently than every six months. A member's books of account must be open to the client at all times with respect to transactions concerning the client.

3. In addition to the compensation for agency services that is agreed upon between a member and a client, a member may, subject to the approval of the client, pass along charges incurred by the member on the client's behalf, such as copyright fees, manuscript retyping, photocopies, copies of books for use in the sale of other rights, long distance calls, special messenger fees, etc. Such charges shall be made only if the client has agreed to reimburse such expenses.

4. A member shall keep each client apprised of matters entrusted to the member and shall promptly furnish such information as the client may reasonably request.

5. Members shall not represent both buyer and seller in the same transaction. Except as provided in the next sentence, a member who represents a client in the grant of rights in any property owned or controlled by the client may not accept any compensation or other payment from the acquirer of such rights, including but not limited to so-called "packaging fees," it being understood that the member's compensation, if any, shall be derived solely from the client. Notwithstanding the foregoing, a member may accept (or participate) in a so-called "packaging fee" paid by an acquirer of television rights to a property owned or controlled by a client if the member: a) fully discloses to the client at the earliest practical time the possibility that the member may be offered such a "packaging fee" which the member may choose to accept; b) delivers to the client at such time a copy of the Association's statement regarding packaging and packaging fees; and c) offers the client at such time the opportunity to arrange for other representation in the transaction. In no event shall the member accept (or participate in) both a packaging fee and compensation from the client with respect to the transaction. For transactions subject to Writers Guild of America (WGA) jurisdiction, the regulations of the WGA shall take precedence over the requirements of this paragraph.

6. Members may not receive a secret profit in connection with any transaction involving a client. If such profit is received, the member must promptly pay over the entire amount to the client.

7. Members shall treat their clients' financial affairs as private and confidential, except for information customarily disclosed to interested parties as part of the process of placing rights, as required by law, or, if agreed with the client, for other purposes.

8. The AAR believes that the practice of literary agents charging clients or potential clients for reading and evaluating literary works (including outlines, proposals, and partial or complete manuscripts) is subject to serious abuse that reflects adversely on our profession. For that reason, members may not charge clients or potential clients for reading and evaluating literary works and may not benefit, directly or indirectly from the charging for such services by other person or entity. The term "charge" in the previous sentence includes any request for payment other than to cover the actual cost of returning materials.

ONCE YOU'VE FOUND AN AGENT

The following is a suggested list of topics for authors to discuss with literary agents who have offered to represent them:

1. Are you a member of the Association of Authors' Representatives?

2. Is your agency a sole proprietorship? A partnership? A corporation?

3. How long have you been in business as an agent?

4. How many people does your agency employ?

5. Of the total number of employees, how many are agents, as opposed to clerical workers?

6. Do you have specialists at your agency who handle movie and television rights? Foreign rights? Do you have sub-agents or corresponding agents overseas and in Hollywood?

7. Do you represent other authors in my area of interest?

8. Who in your agency will actually be handling my work? Will the other staff members be familiar with my work and the status of my business at your agency? Will you oversee or at least keep me apprised of the work that your agency is doing on my behalf?

9. Do you issue an agent-author contract? May I review a specimen copy? And may I review the language of the agency clause that appears in contracts you negotiate for your clients?

10. What is your approach to providing editorial input and career guidance for your clients or for me specifically?

11. How do you keep your clients informed of your activities on their behalf? Do you regularly send them copies of publishers' rejection letters? Do you provide them with submission lists and rejection letters on request? Do you regularly, or upon request, send out updated activity reports?

12. Do you consult with your clients on any and all offers?

13. Some agencies sign subsidiary contracts on behalf of their clients to expedite processing. Do you?
14. What are your commissions for: 1) basic sales to U.S. publishers; 2) sales of movie and television rights; 3) audio and multimedia rights; 4) British and foreign translation rights?

15. What are your procedures and time-frames for processing and disbursing client funds? Do you keep different bank accounts separating author funds from agency revenue?

16. What are your policies about charging clients for expenses incurred by your agency? Will you list such expenses for me? Do you advance money for such expenses? Do you consult with your clients before advancing certain expenditures? Is there a ceiling on such expenses above which you feel you must consult with your clients?

17. How do you handle legal, accounting, public relations, or similar professional services that fall outside the normal range of a literary agency's functions?

18. Do you issue 1099 tax forms at the end of each year? Do you also furnish clients upon request with a detailed account of their financial activity, such as gross income, commissions and other deductions, and net income, for the past year?

19. In the event of your death or disability, or the death or disability of the principal person running the agency, what provisions exist for continuing operation of my account, for the processing of money due to me, and for the handling of my books and editorial needs?

20. If we should part company, what is your policy about handling any unsold subsidiary rights to my work that were reserved to me under the original publishing contracts?

21. What are your expectations of me as your client?

22. Do you have a list of Do's and Don'ts for your clients that will enable me to help you do your job better?

(Please bear in mind that most agents are NOT going to be willing to spend the time answering these questions unless they have already read your material and wish to represent you.)

APPENDIX C

ARTS COUNCILS OF THE UNITED STATES AND CANADA

STATE AND PROVINCIAL GRANTS

Arts councils in the United States and Canada provide assistance to artists by awarding annual fellowships or grants. These grants will be substantial; however, **only state or province residents are eligible.** Inquire to the addresses with a SASE for more information.

UNITED STATES ART AGENCIES

Alabama State Council on the Arts
Becky Mullens, Literature Programs Manager
201 Monroe St., Suite 110
Montgomery, AL 36130
(334) 242-4076

Alaska State Council on the Arts
Timothy Wilson, Executive Director
411 W. Fourth Ave., Suite 1-E
Anchorage, AK 99501-2343
(907) 269-6610

Arizona Commission on the Arts
Tonda Gorton, Public Information Office
417 W. Roosevelt
Phoenix, AZ 85003
(602) 255-5882

Arkansas Arts Council
Sally Williams, Artists Program Coordinator
1500 Tower Bldg.
323 Center St.
Little Rock, AR 72201
(501) 324-9150

California Arts Council
Carol Schiffman, Individual Fellowships
1300 I St., Suite 930
Sacramento, CA 95814
(916) 322-6555

Colorado Council on the Arts and Humanities
Daniel Salazar, Individual Artists Program Director
750 Pennsylvania St.
Denver, CO 80203-3699
(303) 894-2619

Connecticut Commission on the Arts
Linda Dente, Grants Information
One Financial Plaza Lobby
755 Main St.
Hartford, CT 06103
(860) 566-7076

Delaware State Arts Council
Barbara King, Coordinator
Individual Artist Fellowships
Carvel State Office Building
820 N. French St.
Wilmington, DE 19801
(302) 577-8278

District of Columbia Commission on the Arts and Humanities
Carlos Aryan, Program Coordinator
Stables Art Center, 5th Floor
410 Eighth St., NW
Washington, DC 20004
(202) 724-5613

Florida Arts Council
Valerie Ohlsson, Arts Consultant
Division of Cultural Affairs
Florida Dept. of State
The Capitol
Tallahassee, FL 32399-0250
(904) 487-2980

Georgia Council for the Arts
Ann Davis, Program Manager
Community Arts Development
530 Means St. NW, Suite 115
Atlanta, GA 30318-5793
(404) 651-7920

Hawaii State Foundation on Culture & Arts
Hinano Campton, Artist Grant Coordinator
44 Merchant St.
Honolulu, MI 96813
(808) 586-0300

Idaho Commission on the Arts
Diane Josephy Peavey, Literature Director
P.O. Box 83720
Boise, ID 83720-0008
(208) 334-2119

Illinois Arts Council
Richard Gage, Communication Art Director
100 W. Randolph, Suite 10-500
Chicago, IL 60601
(312) 814-6750

Indiana Arts Commission
Joyce Ribble, Assistant Director for Programs
402 W. Washington St., Room W072
Indianapolis, IN 46204-2741
(317) 232-1268

Iowa Arts Council
Julie Bailey, Grants Coordinator
Capitol Complex
600 E. Locust
Des Moines, IA 50319-0290
(515) 281-4451

Kansas Arts Commission
Tom Klocke, Program Coordinator
Jay Hawk Tower
700 Jackson, Suite 1004
Topeka, KS 66603
(913) 296-3335

Kentucky Arts Council
Irwin Pickett, Program Branch Manager
31 Fountain Place
Frankfort, KY 40601-1942
(502) 564-3757

Louisiana State Arts Council
James Border, Program Director
P.O. Box 44247
Baton Rouge, LA 70804
(504) 342-8180

Maine State Arts Commission
Kathy Ann Jones, Associate for Contemporary Arts
State House, Station 25
55 Capital St.
Augusta, ME 04333-0025
(207) 287-2750

Maryland State Arts Council
Charles Camp, Grants Officer
601 N. Howard St.
Baltimore, MD 21201
(410) 333-8232

Massachusetts Cultural Council
Lisa Sasier, Public Information
120 Boylston St., 2nd Floor
Boston, MA 02118
(617) 727-3668

Arts Foundation of Michigan
Kim Adams, Executive Director
645 Griswold, Suite 2164
Detroit, MI 48266
(313) 964-2244

Minnesota State Arts Board
Karen Mueller, Program Associate
Park Square Court
400 Sibley St., Suite 200
St. Paul, MN 55101
(612) 215-1600

Mississippi Arts Council
Kathleen Stept, Program Administrator
239 N. Lamar St., Suite 207
Jackson, MS 39201
(601) 359-6030

Montana Arts Council
Fran Morrow, Director of Art Services/Programs
316 N. Park Ave., Suite 252
Helena, MT 59620
(406) 444-6430

Nebraska Arts Council
Suzanne Wise, Manager of Programs
3838 Davenport St.
Omaha, NE 68131-2329
(402) 595-2122

Nevada State Council on the Arts
Susan Bofkoff, Executive Director
602 N. Curry
Carson City, NV 89703
(702) 687-6680

New Hampshire State Council on the Arts
Audrey Sylvester, Artists Services Coordinator
Phoenix Hall
40 N. Main St.
Concord, NH 03301
(603) 271-2789

New Jersey State Council on the Arts
Steve Runk, Grants Coordinator
CN 306, 3rd Floor, Roebling Bldg.
20 W. State St.
Trenton, NJ 08625
(609) 292-6130

New Mexico Arts Division
Virginia Castellano, Operations Coordinator
228 E. Palace Ave.
Santa Fe, NM 87501
(505) 827-6490

New York State Council on the Arts
Kathleen Masterson, Director, Literature Program
915 Broadway
New York, NY 10010
(212) 387-7022

North Carolina Arts Council
Deborah McGill, Literature Director
Dept. of Cultural Resources
221 E. Lane St.
Raleigh, NC 27601-2807
(919) 733-2111

North Dakota Council on the Arts
Patsy Thompson, Executive Director
418 E. Broadway, Suite 70
Bismark, ND 58501-4086
(701) 328-3954

Ohio Arts Council
Bob Fox, Literature Coordinator
727 E. Main St.
Columbus, OH 43205
(614) 466-2613

State Arts Council of Oklahoma
Betty Price, Executive Director
P.O. Box 52001-2001
Oklahoma City, OK 73152-2001
(405) 521-2931

Oregon Arts Commission
Vincent Dunn, Assistant Director
775 Summer St. NE
Salem, OR 97310
(503) 986-0086

Pennsylvania Council on the Arts
Jim Woland, Literature Program Director
Finance Bldg., Room 216
Harrisburg, PA 17120
(717) 787-6883

Institute of Puerto Rican Culture
P.O. Box 4184
San Juan, PR 00902-4184
(787) 724-0700

Rhode Island State Council on the Arts
Randall Rosenbaum, Executive Director
95 Cedar St., Suite 103
Providence, RI 02903
(401) 277-3880

South Carolina Arts Commission
Sara June Goldstein, Literary Arts Director
1800 Gervais St.
Columbia, SC 29201
(803) 734-8696

South Dakota Arts Council
Dennis Holub, Director
800 Governors Dr.
Pierre, SD 57501
(605) 773-3131

Tennessee Arts Commission
Alice Swanson, Director of Literary Arts
401 Charlotte Ave.
Nashville, TN 37243-0780
(615) 741-1701

Texas Commission on the Arts
Laura Weigand, Program Director
Visual and Communication Arts
P.O. Box 13406
Austin, TX 78711-3406
(512) 463-5535

Utah Arts Council
Guy Lebeda, Literary Coordinator
617 E. South Temple
Salt Lake City, UT 84102-1177
(801) 533-5895

Vermont Council on the Arts
Alexander Aldrich, Executive Director
136 State St., Drawer 33
Montpelier, VT 05633-6001
(802) 828-3291

Virgin Islands Council on the Arts
Marie Daniel, Grants Officer
41-42 Norre Gada
St. Thomas VI 00802
(340) 774-5984

Virginia Commission for the Arts
Susan Fitzpatrick, Program Coordinator
223 Governor St.
Richmond, VA 23219
(804) 225-3132

Washington State Arts Commission
Artists Fellowship
Karen Gose, Executive Director
234 E. Eighth Avenue
Olympia, WA 98504-2675
(360) 753-3860

West Virginia Arts and Humanities Division
Jill Ellis, Grants Coordinator
Cultural Center
1900 Kanawha Blvd. E.
Charleston, WV 23505-0300
(304) 558-0220

Wisconsin Arts Board
Mark Fraire, Individual Artists Program Director
101 S. Wilson St., 1st Floor
Madison, WI 53702
(608) 264-8191

Wyoming Council on the Arts
Michael Shay, Literature Arts Coordinator
2320 Capitol Ave.
Cheyenne, WY 82002
(307) 777-7742

CANADIAN PROVINCES ART AGENCIES

Alberta Arts and Cultural Industries Branch
Clive Padfield, Director
10405 Jasper Ave., 9th Floor
Edmonton, Alberta T5J 4R7
(403) 427-6315

British Columbia Arts Council
Cultural Services Branch
Walter Quan, Coordinator of Individual Awards Program
800 Johnson St., 5th Floor
Victoria, British Columbia V8V 1X4
(250) 356-1728

Manitoba Arts Council
Pat Sanders, Writing/Publishing Officer
525 - 93 Lombard Ave.
Winnipeg, Manitoba R3B 3B1
(204) 945-0422

New Brunswick Department of Tourism, Recreation, and Heritage
Arts Branch
c/o Desmond Maillet
P.O. Box 6000
Fredericton, New Brunswick E3B 5H1
(506) 453-2555

Newfoundland & Labrador Arts Council
Randy Follett, Executive Director
P.O. Box 98
St. John's, Newfoundland A1C 5H5
(709) 726-2212

Nova Scotia Arts Council
Peter Kirby, Program Officer for Individual Artists
P.O. Box 666, Halifax Central
Halifax, Nova Scotia B3J 2T3
(902) 422-1123

The Canada Council
Lorraine Filyer, Literature Officer
151 Bloor St. W., 6th Floor
Toronto, Ontario M5S 1T6
(416) 961-1660

Prince Edward Island Council of the Arts
Judy McDonald, Executive Director
115 Richmond
Charlottetown, Prince Edward Island CIA 1H7
(902) 368-4410

Saskatchewan Arts Board
Gail Paul Armstrong
Literary & Multidisciplinary Arts Consultant
3475 Albert St.
Regina, Saskatchewan S45 6X6
(306) 787-4056

Government of Yukon Arts Branch
Laurel Parry, Arts Consultant
P.O. Box 2703
Whitehorse, Yukon YIA 2C6
(403) 667-5264

APPENDIX D

CONTACTS FOR WRITERS

Poets and Writers
(212) 226-3586

Academy of American Poets
(212) 274-0343

Poetry Society of America
(212) 254-9628

Mystery Writers of America
(212) 888-8171

Science Fiction & Fantasy Writers of America
(207) 861-8078

Pen American Center
(212) 334-1660

Pen Center USA West
(213) 365-8500

Volunteer Lawyers for the Arts
(212) 319-2787

Publishing Triangle
(212) 366-4470

National Writers Union
(212) 254-0279

Associated Writing Programs
(703) 993-4301

Author's Guild
(212) 563- 5904

Western Writers of America
(615) 791-1444

Publishers Weekly
(800) 278- 2991

Teachers and Writers
(212) 691-6590

The Writer
(617) 423-3157

APPENDIX E

EXAMPLE OF AN ON-LINE SUBMISSION

On-line submissions are becoming more popular. In case you have yet to see one and how it works we are displaying an example here for your viewing. This is a poetry submission 21 lines or less.

Type your name address and poem below . . . then click on submit.

Poet's Name:

First [ ]

Middle [ ]

Last [ ]

E-mail Address:

E-mail [ ]

Complete Address:

Address [ ]

City [ ]

State [ ]

Postal Code [ ]

Country [ ]

Title of your poem [ ]

Your poem: (21 lines or less)

[ ]

Note: if your poem does not fit in this box, it exceeds 21 lines and does not qualify.

Submit your poem ❑ Erase and start over ❑

It is not only poetry and limited line count on poetry that are taking electronic submissions. Magazines and journals are beginning to take submissions via e-mail from a floppy disk. We hope this encourages you to submit more work at an easier and faster rate.

www.ingramcontent.com/pod-product-compliance
Lightning Source LLC
LaVergne TN
LVHW020726100926
847443LV00010B/40